Churchill and the Admirals

"TACHY METRIC" A-A control
SYSTEM P. 181 (FN)

Churchill (1874-1965) and the Admirals

STEPHEN ROSKILL , RN
[1903 — 1982]

PEN & SWORD MILITARY CLASSICS

First published in Great Britain in 1977 by William Collins
Published in 2004 in this format by
PEN & SWORD MILITARY CLASSICS
an imprint of
Pen & Sword Books Limited
47 Church Street
Barnsley
S. Yorkshire
S70 2AS

ISBN 1 84415 104 2

A CIP record for this book
is available from the British Library.

Printed and bound in Great Britain by
CPI UK

Pen & Sword Books Limited incorporates the imprints of
Pen & Sword Aviation, Pen & Sword Maritime, Pen & Sword Military,
Wharncliffe Local History, Pen & Sword Select,
Pen & Sword Military Classics and Leo Cooper

For a complete list of Pen & Sword titles please contact:
PEN & SWORD BOOKS LIMITED
47 Church Street, Barnsley, South Yorkshire, S70 2AS, England.
E-mail: enquiries@pen-and-sword.co.uk
Website: www.pen-and-sword.co.uk

This book is dedicated to the
staff of the military section
of the War Cabinet Secretariat
1939-1945 whose contribution to
victory was unobtrusive but vital

Contents

Ilustrations

[BETWEEN PP. 160-161]

Churchill as First Lord in 1913 (*Chartwell Archive*)
On board the *Prince of Wales* in 1941 (*Chartwell Archive*)
With Keyes in 1941 (*Imperial War Museum*)
Keyes at Gallipoli in 1915 (*Imperial War Museum*)
King George VI and Admiral Forbes (*Commander Sir Godfrey Style*)
The *Gneisenau* in action off Norway (*Imperial War Museum*)
The Norwegian campaign: a sloop hit by bombers and a cruiser towing a burning tanker out of harbour (*Imperial War Museum*)
Alexandria harbour 21 May 1940, showing British and French warships (*Imperial War Museum*)
The attack on the French fleet at Mers el Kébir, 3 July 1940 (*Musée de la Marine*)
The escape of the *Strasbourg* (*Musée de la Marine*)
HMS *Barham* off Dakar, September 1940 (*Imperial War Museum*)
Grand Harbour, Malta, under air attack, January 1941 (*Imperial War Museum*)
Admiral Tovey on board *Prince of Wales*, 1941 (*Chartwell Archive*)
Suda Bay, Crete, after an air raid, May 1941 (*Imperial War Museum*)
Convoy PQ17 assembling July 1942 (*US Navy Department, Washington*)
British prisoners marching through Dieppe after the raid of 19 August 1942 (*Imperial War Museum*)
Max Horton and Tovey aboard *King George V* (*Imperial War Museum*)
The sinking of *Prince of Wales* and *Repulse* off Malaya (*Imperial War Museum*)
The aircraft carrier *Hermes* sinking off Ceylon, 9 April 1942 (*Imperial War Museum*)
The Casablanca conference, January 1943 (*Broadlands Archive*)
Eisenhower and Cunningham at Algiers, 1943 (*Imperial War Museum*)
A U-boat sinking after attack by an aircraft of Coastal Command (*Imperial War Museum*)

Maps

Foreword

In 1949 I was appointed to the Cabinet Office Historical Section to write the volumes of the United Kingdom Military History Series published as *The War at Sea 1939–1945* (HMSO 1954–61) under the editorship of the late Professor Sir James Butler. Though often referred to colloquially as the 'official histories' of World War II that description is in fact incorrect, as anyone who troubles to read the Editor's Preface to my first volume can easily ascertain, since the organization and conditions under which the Military History Series was written are there clearly described.

After some months devoted to 'reading myself into' the subject I was required to handle, and to studying the archival material available, I asked the Admiralty for access to the First Lord's and First Sea Lord's papers of my period. I did this as a test case regarding the guarantee of full and free access to all relevant documents promised to the authors of the Military Histories, since, largely thanks to Admiral Sir Herbert Richmond, I was fully apprised of the serious troubles Sir Julian Corbett had experienced with the Admiralty over his volumes of the Official Naval History of World War I. Although, perhaps too imaginatively, I visualized the flurry of embarrassment which my request for such closely guarded records caused among the civil servants across the Horseguards Parade, the papers were made available to me – after some delay. I have here used them – or the survivors from among them – again, though more extensively and with greater freedom than was prudent a quarter of a century ago.

In 1949 I also got into touch with all the leading naval men of my period. Their response was without exception extremely helpful and cordial, they all agreed to read and criticize the drafts of chapters describing events in which they had taken part, or of which they had special knowledge, and they sent me a large number of valuable letters in amplification of the official records of those events. Later on some of those officers either appointed me as their literary executor, or reserved their papers and diaries for my sole use, or made Churchill College, Cambridge, of which I became a Fellow in 1961, the repository for their own collections of documents and letters. Not surprisingly a good deal of my correspondence with them dealt with the ever-fascinating subject of their relations with Winston Churchill both as First Lord of the Admiralty and as Prime Minister; and many of those officers continued to correspond with me on that subject to the day of their deaths. One end product of this correspondence, and of the prolonged thought I gave to the subject, was a series of articles published in the *Sunday Telegraph* in February 1962 entitled 'Churchill and his Admirals'. (The use of the possessive pronoun was of course incorrect, as correspondents hastened to point out, since all officers held their commissions from the Monarch and not the Prime Minister, and Flag Rank was conferred by the Lords Commissioners of the Admiralty. In my typescript I had used the definite article 'Churchill and *the* Admirals', but for some reason best known to himself the Editor altered it before printing). Despite this gaffe the reception accorded by naval men to those articles was very warm, and some of them sent me supplementary material on the subject. I thus came to accumulate a considerable archive, to which I have continuously added the fruits of further correspondence and interviews.

It was actually my Publisher's Editor for many years Mr Richard Ollard, to whom I owe an immense debt for historical and literary guidance, who suggested that I should expand the *Sunday Telegraph* articles into a book; and the work now presented to the public, not without a good deal of diffidence on my part, is the result.

It is I think essential to make clear that one of the chief sources I have used, namely the minutes, memoranda and letters which Churchill addressed to the Admiralty (generally to the First Lord and First Sea Lord), and the replies sent to him were produced in totally different ways. As to the former, though Churchill sometimes acted on advice or suggestions made to him by the members of his 'Secret Circle' or Inner Cabinet, they nearly all bear the unmistakable and inimitable mark of his own style, and were probably dictated directly from the ever-active volcano of his mind. The replies on the other hand, though generally signed by A. V. Alexander the First Lord or, less commonly by the First Sea Lord, were in essence the considered view of the naval staff. When one of Churchill's minutes, often referred to colloquially as 'prayers' because of his custom of beginning them with a request such as 'Pray consider' something or other, arrived in the Admiralty it would first go to the staff division or supply department chiefly concerned, and a reply would be drafted there. If it bore one of his 'Action This Day' labels it would next be taken by hand to any other staff division concerned, where additions or amendments might be made, and then to the member of the Board of Admiralty or 'Super-intending Lord' responsible for that particular aspect of the navy's administration or operations. Again amendments might be made before it was taken, again by hand, to the offices of the VCNS and First Sea Lord, from which, if they approved the draft, it would be cleared with the branch of the Secretariat concerned and then taken to the First Lord's Private Office. Although in cases of extreme urgency some of the above steps might be cut out such was the practice generally followed; and it is noteworthy that the First Sea Lord and First Lord usually accepted the drafts which reached them – perhaps making some minor amendments. I have found few cases where they disagreed so fundamentally that the proposed reply was sent back down the line for review and reconsideration. Thus the Admiralty's answers, though usually well expressed and clearly worded, strike quite a different note to that sounded by the Churchillian minutes they were answering, and one does not find in them the picturesque metaphor and graphic phraseology, let alone the occasional hortatory or minatory note, which characterized the latter. The difference lay of course in the fact that whereas the minutes were the product of a brilliant, if sometimes erratic, mind the answers had to represent the less distinctive but carefully considered departmental view. A similar difference will be found between the many signals and letters Churchill addressed direct to Commanders-in-Chief of the major fleets or, less frequently, to commanders of squadrons, and for the same reasons but with the Flag Officers' staff acting in place of the naval staff in Whitehall.

In the case of Churchill's more formal letters and telegrams, and especially those of political or diplomatic significance, though he often prepared a first draft himself for circulation to the Ministers and Officials concerned, he sought, and often accepted amendments which they suggested. Where the first draft was prepared in one of the departments he commonly made amendments in his own hand; but the proposal or answer as finally despatched nearly always bore the highly individual flavour of his own style.

Copies of most of Churchill's dictated and typewritten minutes, as well as his holograph notes on signals and letters submitted to him, will now be found in the Public Record Office under references 'Prem. 3 and 4', which are described as the 'Prime Minister's Office Operational Papers' and 'Confidential Papers' respectively. The former, which overlap with the Ministry of Defence's secretarial files now in the Public Record Office Cab. 120 series, were formerly kept in the War Cabinet Office close to the underground War Room, and I had access to them and used some of them in my war history. The latter were formerly kept at 10 Downing Street, and although I could and sometimes did obtain information contained in them from the secretariat I had no general access to them. For this book I have, in general, found it simpler and less confusing to take what I needed from the Admiralty's First Lord's and First Sea Lord's papers (Adm. 199 and 250 series), supplemented by the Adm. 1 and 116 series (Secretary's Department Correspondence and Cases respectively) and other Admiralty records, because it is in them that the minutes by the naval staff and by members of the Board of Admiralty written in reply to Churchill are to be found; but I have supplemented those records from the Prem. 3 and 4 files where further light is thrown on facts or on Churchill's relations with admirals, or where he made marginal comments which do not always appear in the copies in the Admiralty's records.

For permission to quote copyright material I am indebted to the following: The Lady Beatrix Evison for the papers and letters of her father the Earl Alexander of Hillsborough; The 2nd Earl Beatty for the papers and correspondence of his father Admiral of the Fleet Earl Beatty; General The Viscount Bridgeman for the diary of the 1st Viscount Bridgeman and for his own memoir of his father's political career; Lady Buzzard for the papers and letters of her husband Admiral Sir Anthony Buzzard Bart; C & T Publications for permission to quote unpublished papers of Sir Winston Churchill; The Baron Chatfield for the papers and letters of his father Admiral of the Fleet Baron Chatfield; Mr J. K. H. Cunningham for the letters of his father Admiral of the Fleet Sir John Cunningham; Viscountess Cunningham of Hyndhope for the correspondence and diary of Admiral of the Fleet Viscount Cunningham; Lady Edwards for the diaries of Admiral Sir Ralph Edwards; Lady Forbes and the Executors of the Will of Admiral of the Fleet Sir Charles Forbes, Miss Elizabeth Forbes and Mr Henry Forbes, for the letters of the Admiral of the Fleet; Viscount Hood for the papers and correspondence of his father Admiral The Hon. Sir Horace Hood; The Baron Keyes for the papers and correspondence of Admiral of the Fleet Baron Keyes; Lady Lambe for the correspondence of Admiral of the Fleet Sir Charles Lambe; Lady North for the papers and correspondence of Admiral Sir Dudley North; Admiral of the Fleet the Earl Mountbatten for his correspondence and papers, now the property of the Broadlands Archives Trust; Baroness Portal for the letters of Marshal of the RAF Viscount Portal of Hungerford; Admiral Sir Manley Power for his own memoirs; the late Admiral Sir Francis Pridham for his own memoirs; Commander John Somerville for the papers, correspondence and diaries of Admiral of the Fleet Sir James Somerville; Lieutenant-Colonel A. H. Tovey for the letters of Admiral of the Fleet Baron Tovey of Langton Matravers; Lady Willis for the papers and correspondence of Admiral of the Fleet Sir Algernon Willis.

The recent enormous rise in the cost of books (which I hold to be the foundation stone of civilization), and the consequential inability of would-be readers to buy them, have made me consider what steps I could take to keep down the price of this one. As a result I have abandoned my long-held practice of having notes and source references printed on the page to which they refer, which my publisher tells me is very expensive. Though I regret the change I have here placed almost all notes at the end of the book, and I trust the reader will not find this excessively inconvenient. I have also omitted a Glossary of Abbreviations and a Bibliography. The abbreviations here used are in most cases now well known or are self-evident, and appropriate Glossaries exist in my earlier works. Bibliographies dealing with most, though not the whole of the period covered by this book will also be found there; so I hope that this omission will be found acceptable.

Because a great many naval signals appear in my narrative and notes it is I think desirable to say a little about the 'Times of Origin' by which they were always identified. For such purposes the world was divided into 24 equal zones each of 15 degrees of longitude (1 hour of time) measured from the Greenwich Meridian. Greenwich Mean Time (GMT) was always indicated by the suffix Z, and Z time therefore extended from 7½ degrees West to 7½ degrees East. From the latter point each zone was given an alphabetical letter such as A to signify GMT plus one hour (7½ to 22½ degrees East), B (22½ to 37½ degrees East) and so on around the world east-about. To avoid confusion with numbers the letters I and O were omitted. Except for local signals, which were sent in local time, wireless messages were given GMT Times of Origin, and special clocks were kept in wireless offices showing that time. British Summer Time was of course Zone A, and Double Summer Time Zone B. Where no suffix is here given it may be assumed that the Time of Origin shows GMT.

I am once again deeply indebted to Mr J. R. Ede, the Keeper of Records, and to the staff of the Public Record Office at Chancery Lane and Portugal Street for their unstinting help with my research in the departmental records of the period. All quotations from official records are Crown Copyright and are reproduced by kind permission of The Controller, HM Stationery Office. I owe a similar debt to Dr D. P. Waley, Keeper of the Department of Manuscripts at the British Library, for access to the papers of Admirals of the Fleet Viscount Cunningham of Hyndhope and Sir Charles Forbes, and to Mr David Proctor, Head of Education and Research Facilities at the National Maritime Museum, Greenwich for access to the papers of Admiral of the Fleet Lord Chatfield. Commander R. C. Burton and Group-Captain E. B. Haslam, respectively Heads of the Naval and Air Historical Branches have been equally helpful in answering my many importunities; while Commander Geoffrey Hare has once more given me unstinted and invaluable help with research in the naval and War Cabinet records in the Public Record Office.

I am grateful to Professor Arthur J. Marder of the University of California for copies of some interesting papers written for him by participants in the events here discussed, and for permission to reproduce the letter sent to him by Sir Eric Seal on 8 September 1971 and printed in Marder's book *From the Dardanelles to Oran* (Oxford UP, 1974, pages 169–70). Also to The Controller, HM Stationery Office for permission to reproduce a passage printed in my own history *The War at Sea 1939–1945*, vol. I (HMSO, 1954, sixth impression 1976, page 202). Commander Harry Pursey has once again placed me in his debt by allowing me to exploit his unrivalled knowledge of the history of promotions from the lower deck of the navy to commissioned rank. I have made every endeavour to trace the owner of copyright in all quotations here printed; but if I have failed in any case to obtain the necessary permission I trust that my apologies will be accepted.

The following persons, all of whom had special knowledge of some aspect of my subject, have helped by answering my inquiries, and in many cases have granted me interviews as well: Mrs Joan Astley; the late Commander R. T. Bower; Captain A. W. Clarke; Sir John Colville; Admiral Sir Victor Crutchley VC; Admiral Sir William Davis; the late Admiral The Hon. Sir Reginald Plunkett-Ernle-Erle-Drax; Vice-Admiral Sir Kaye Edden; Captain Godfrey French; the late Rear-Admiral John H. Godfrey; Admiral Sir Angus Cunninghame Graham of Gartmore; the late Wing-Commander Sir John Hodsoll; The Hon. Alexander and Mrs Hood and The Viscount Hood; General Sir Ian Jacob; Wing-Commander Sir Archibald James; Commander Peter Kemp; Sir John Lang; the late Rear-Admiral Alan Laybourne; Admiral of the Fleet The Earl Mountbatten of Burma; the late Rear-Admiral A. D. Nicholl; Lady Packer; the late General Sir Henry Pownall; Commander H. Pursey; Captain G. H. Roberts; Rear-

Admiral M. W. St L. Searle and Commander Sir Godfrey Style.

Miss E. V. Eales has once again typed the whole of my manuscript with exemplary care and accuracy, and has re-typed much of it many times. In addition to Miss Eales I owe much to Mrs Rosemary Gooch and Mrs Patsy Devoy who have helped me to cope with the large correspondence in which this work has involved me, and to Douglas Matthews for compiling the index with his usual skill. Finally I owe an inestimable debt to my wife for the cheerful patience with which she has borne my idiosyncratic hours and habits.

It has long been my practice to carry out a final check of the quotations and source references used in my books before they are actually sent to be printed. But in the present case the move of the Public Record Office from Chancery Lane and Portugal Street in central London to its new accommodation at Kew, and the consequential dispersal of various categories of papers which I have used, has made it impossible for me to adhere to that practice with regard to the official records. Though I must obviously accept responsibility for any mistakes which may be found in this book the reader may perhaps be prepared to accept that extenuating circumstances have contributed to their appearance.

Stephen W. Roskill
Churchill College
Cambridge
September 1977

Frostlake Cottage
Malting Lane
Cambridge

First Contacts

1911-1914

Though this book is planned chiefly to discuss, and perhaps illuminate a little, Churchill's relation with the British Admirals of World War II, and the characters of those officers, it is essential first to outline his dealings with those of an earlier generation, since the personalities, plans and prejudices of the latter influenced his later actions and outlook profoundly.

On the last day of May 1904 Churchill, the Conservative member for Oldham, crossed the floor of the House of Commons to take a seat on the Liberal benches. The primary cause of this first change of political sides was the Free Trade issue, and Churchill had in fact made up his mind to withdraw his allegiance from Balfour's government seven months earlier when he wrote 'I am an English Liberal. I hate the Tory party, their men, their words and their methods.'[1]

The General Election of January-February 1906 brought the Liberals decisively back into power under Sir Henry Campbell-Bannerman; but after a heart attack he resigned on 3 April 1908 and died on the 22nd. He was succeeded by H. H. Asquith, and in the reconstruction of the government which followed three Cabinet offices – the Colonial Office, the Admiralty and the Local Government Board were considered for Churchill, whose abilities had already gained wide, though by no means unanimous recognition. He himself strongly disliked the prospect of the Local Government Board, and would have preferred the Colonial Office, where he had served as Under-Secretary for the previous two years; but on 8 April Asquith offered him the Board of Trade. He thus achieved Cabinet rank at the early age of thirty-three; but in doing so he aroused the venomous hostility of his former party, which opposed him in the by-election which in those days had to follow promotion of an MP to the Cabinet. Churchill was adopted by the North-West Manchester constituency, but was beaten by 429 votes in a poll of 10,681 – a severe blow to the Free Trade party. However, he soon found a home in the safe Liberal seat of Dundee, which returned him with a majority of 2709 in a poll of 16,118 – despite the 'progressive' vote being split. We are not here concerned with Churchill's work at the Board of Trade, but the offer to him by Asquith in February 1910 of the Home Office, then as now the premier

Secretaryship-of-State, shows how rapidly his star was rising and provides important background to the events of the following year.

By the autumn of 1911 Asquith had become convinced of the need to replace Reginald McKenna as First Lord of the Admiralty in order to damp down public and parliamentary criticism of the state of the navy, its readiness to meet the increasing threat from Germany, and in particular the refusal of the naval members of the Board to set up a properly organized staff analogous to that created in the War Office by Lord Esher and R. B. (later Viscount) Haldane some five years earlier. In October 1911, when Churchill was staying with Asquith in Scotland, the Prime Minister asked him whether he would like to go to the Admiralty. Churchill has recorded that he 'accepted with alacrity', and the exchange of offices between him and McKenna passed off smoothly – though it had a somewhat mixed reception in the Press.[2] Thus began what Churchill, writing in the early 1920s, described as 'the four most memorable years of my life'.[3]

Churchill came to the Admiralty, like most previous First Lords, with little knowledge of naval affairs. His training at Sandhurst and the whole of the experience of war which he had gained as a young man had indoctrinated him with a basically military outlook.[4] Indeed he always remained in many respects a Hussar officer, and it is noteworthy that in his later speeches and writings he often used military expressions and metaphors but hardly ever used naval ones. But whereas earlier First Lords, notable H. C. Eardley Childers, who held the office 1868–71 and accomplished some much needed reforms, had regarded it as their 'personal prerogative personally to interfere in naval matters' whilst never acquiring 'the knowledge which would have enabled them to intervene successfully',[5] right from the beginning Churchill made every endeavour to become well informed on the strategic, technical and personnel aspects of naval policy and administration. This purpose he accomplished chiefly by long discussions with his naval advisers and visits to ships and naval establishments.

The chief opponent to the creation of a naval staff, and so the chief cause of dissension between Churchill and his naval colleagues, was Admiral Sir Arthur Wilson, First Sea Lord 1910–12 in succession to Admiral Sir John ('Jacky') Fisher. Though no outstanding holder of that office, Wilson remained loyal to his former chief, and later refused to serve under any other master.[6] Sir Francis Bridgeman, whom Churchill chose as Wilson's successor, certainly possessed greater intellectual ability; but he soon became irritated by his political chief's habit of circulating 'peremptory orders to the Sea Lords' and sending signals to the fleet without the authority of the Board as a whole.[7] His virtual dismissal by Churchill, after only a year in office, produced an acrimonious correspondence, the full publication of which demonstrated for the first time the ruthlessness which Churchill could show when opposed – notably by his reading extracts from Bridgeman's private letters in Parliament in order to justify his claim that the admiral's health was indifferent.[8]

In November 1913 a cataclysmic row, for which Churchill was at any rate partly responsible, broke over the Admiralty's Board Room. It derived from a visit by the Admiralty yacht to Sheerness with Churchill on board, and from a junior officer very improperly telling him that the decision of his Captain (G. W. Vivian) regarding the use by the naval air service of some land on the bank of the Medway was wrong. Churchill sent for the Captain and told him that the young officer's view was to be accepted. Then the officer unwisely told the Captain that if his recommendation was disregarded he would write to the First Lord, and that Churchill had told him to do so. Such a breach of discipline was in Vivian's eyes intolerable and he complained to the C-in-C, The Nore, Admiral Sir Richard Poore, who passed it on to the Second Sea Lord, Sir John Jellicoe, who was responsible both for discipline and for the naval air service. Churchill, however, got wind of what was happening, and told Jellicoe he was to pass on to him any reports received on the matter. When Jellicoe read Poore's strongly worded protest he returned it to him for amendment, and enclosed a private letter with his own comments. Churchill was furious and ordered the GPO to return the letter *to him.* That was done, and although he claimed not to have read Jellicoe's private letter he announced that he intended to order Poore to haul down his flag. Jellicoe said he would resign if that intention was carried out, and the Third and Fourth Sea Lords (Admirals Sir Archibald Moore and Sir William Pakenham) were prepared to follow suit. Prince Louis of Battenberg, who had replaced Bridgeman as First Sea Lord in December 1912, was dissuaded from joining them by Churchill, and in the end Poore was induced to withdraw his critical letter and apologize. The young officer who had caused the fracas also apologized to his Captain and to Churchill for his gross indiscretion; but knowledge of what Professor Marder calls Churchill's 'flagrant interference with the discipline of the fleet' leaked out, and, coming so soon after the row over Bridgeman's dismissal, did him great harm in political as well as naval circles.[9] If the explosion of November 1913 was something of a storm in a teacup it did show up Churchill's tactlessness as well as his ruthlessness. Though harsh, there is something in the description of his conduct by Battenberg's biographer as resembling that of 'a thwarted spoilt schoolboy'.[10] Nor, as will be told later, was it the last occasion when he infuriated the Captain of a ship by seeking the opinion on service matters of officers much junior to him.

The selection of Prince Louis of Battenberg as the successor to Bridgeman was in the prevailing circumstances perfectly understandable. He had proved a successful Director of Intelligence 1902–5, and was a very able ship handler and tactician. In 1904 Fisher described him as 'out and away the best man inside the Admiralty building',[11] and Battenberg's influence on Fisher at the time when he was driving through his far-reaching reforms was wholly beneficial. Though Battenberg's German ancestry and royal blood produced serious difficulties for him within the navy, and aroused the vicious antagonism of Admiral Lord Charles Beresford, the fact that he and Churchill both came of ancient and aristocratic lineage made it far more likely that they would work amicably together than had been the case with Wilson or Bridgeman. On the day Churchill took over the Admiralty Fisher, who was at the time in retirement, had urged him to make Battenberg First Sea Lord,[12] but political opposition was so strong that in the end he was only made Second Sea Lord – though he had in fact to deputize for the ailing Bridgeman during a great deal of the following year.[13]

The initiative in improving the pay, conditions of service and promotion prospects of naval ratings and marines came from Fisher who, as First Sea Lord and afterwards constantly corresponded with Lionel Yexley, the influential editor of the lower deck organ *The Fleet* and author of the book *Our Fighting Sea Men* which caused a furore when it appeared in 1911 and led to the Admiralty setting up a committee to consider the very grave charges he made. Soon after Churchill became First Lord he met Fisher, who produced a five-point plan for the amelioration of lower deck hardships and disabilities and for opening the road to commissioned rank. This plan, which may reasonably be described as the Fisher-Yexley Reforms, received strong support from Churchill, but in most respects it was coolly received by the Sea Lords. However in March 1912 Battenberg produced a paper proposing that '100 very carefully selected Gunners and Boatswains' should be 'promoted very early in their career'; and it was they who became the first 'Mates' under the new scheme to be referred to he did not envisage officers so promoted reaching a higher rank than Commander; and, secondly, that he wanted totally to exclude engineers and other technicians.[14] In 1914, when Jellicoe was Second Sea Lord, the scheme was extended to include engineers who became known as 'Mates (E)'.

About a week after Battenberg's paper was written Churchill introduced his first Naval Estimates in the House of Commons, and in his speech he followed closely the line taken by his adviser on personnel problems – ending with the remark 'It is probable that the great bulk of them [the Mates] will retire content with a career which will have carried them from bluejacket to Commander.'[15] Lord Charles Beresford, then an MP despite his still being on the active list, assured the House that the newly promoted officers 'will be received with open arms in the Fleet'.[16] In fact the Mate Scheme was a failure, partly because it stigmatized officers so promoted as being different from those who had entered as cadets, and partly because they proved, as Battenberg and Churchill had anticipated and accepted, too old to stand a chance of reaching the higher ranks. Those disabilities were not eliminated until 1931.

In his speech on the 1912 estimates Churchill also announced that an inquiry was to take place 'into the system of summary punishments' inflicted by Captains of ships and establishments 'including the consequential effects as regards pay, position, [good conduct] badges and pension'[17] – which had been one of the grievances aired by Yexley. This was the origin of the Committee set up under Admiral F. E. Brock which reported, somewhat cautiously, in the following July and resulted in the abolition of the most humiliating and purposeless summary punishments.[17A] Churchill also took up the matter of improving the pay of both officers and men, admitting that statements made in the House that there had been no increase during the preceding sixty years was 'true in form' but 'not altogether just in fact' – because they took account only of substantive pay, and many specialist allowances had recently been introduced.[18] His proposals for improvements were published as a Command Paper before the end of the year, but were severely emasculated by the Treasury.[19]

If Battenberg's share in the introduction of the Mate Scheme was flawed his support for the idea of a naval staff, to which Fisher and Wilson had been opposed, was whole-hearted. But it was Battenberg's action as First Sea Lord in cancelling the demobilization of the fleet on 26 July 1914, when Churchill was absent from the Admiralty, justly described by Professor Marder as his 'master stroke', that should

chiefly have earned him the nation's gratitude.[20] Fisher, however, had
meanwhile started to intrigue for return to office and now described
Battenberg as 'only a superior sort of *commis voyageur* [commercial
traveller]';[21] while that *eminence grise* Lord Esher regarded him as
'NOT a first class intellect. He may be the best of an indifferent lot.'[22]
Professor Marder also exhibits some ambivalence regarding Battenberg,
describing him and Bridgeman, as 'not especially forceful characters' in
one place and Battenberg as 'brilliant' in another.[23] What is certain is
that Battenberg never exhibited the *furor navalis* to which some early
twentieth-century admirals were so prone, and that he worked far
more amicably with Churchill than either of his two predecessors. His
son Admiral of the Fleet Earl Mountbatten, who also became First
Sea Lord, has expressed the view that Battenberg was 'almost the last
Admiral Churchill loved in World War I';[24] and it is certainly the
case that he fell out violently with most of those who followed in
Prince Louis's footsteps. It will be told later how, after the outbreak of
war, nothing went right for Battenberg.

Fisher's long-standing friendship with Churchill, and the admiration
felt by the latter for the man who had shaken the navy out of its
nineteenth-century torpor, produced a great harvest between 1911
and 1913 – especially in the field of ship and weapon design. The
creation of a War Staff was announced on 8 January 1912 and was well
received; but unfortunately there were no trained staff officers to
man it, and it was not until 1918 that, largely thanks to the stimulus
applied by Captain (later Admiral Sir) Herbert Richmond, a staff in
the modern sense of the word was created. None the less the achievements of Churchill's first period as First Lord were substantial – in
offering opportunities for ratings to achieve commissioned rank,[25] in
the development of the fast and heavily armed battleships of the
Queen Elizabeth class, and in the change from coal to oil firing. But if
much was done that needed doing certain serious weaknesses were
overlooked until the harsh experience of war drove them home.
Such were the inadequate protection of the magazines of Fisher's fast
battle-cruisers, the inefficiency of the British heavy shell and mines and
the lack of night fighting equipment.[26]

Although it is true that in August 1914 'The Fleet was ready' it was a
fleet which suffered from serious defects. Some of them are attributable
to the sheer pace of Fisher's reforms before Churchill came to the
Admiralty; but others derived from the tremendous pressure applied
by Churchill to get new or improved ships and weapons into service –
often without carrying out proper tests of their efficiency.

Nor were Churchill's relations with his political colleagues always tactful. For example in September 1912 he wrote to Harcourt, the Colonial Secretary, that 'where questions of policy lie in the sphere of what I may call Colonial diplomacy . . . it is essential that the Colonial Office *should be our ambassador and act for the Admiralty*' (italics supplied). Though Harcourt accepted this interpretation of his department's functions the Admiralty's custom of communicating direct with the Australian Naval Board instead of using the normal channel of Colonial Secretary to Governor-General became a source of serious friction. Sir Ronald Munro-Ferguson (later Viscount Novar), the Governor-General of Australia throughout the war, resented the practice strongly, as did W. M. Hughes as Federal Prime Minister.[27]

Churchill's support of the new air arm merits special mention. The naval air service of the period constituted the naval wing of the Royal Flying Corps, and it remained so from April 1912 until the Admiralty unilaterally declared it to be a branch of the navy under its own jurisdiction at the end of July 1915.[28] From the beginning of his time as First Lord Churchill took a great interest in all aspects of what was then rather quaintly called 'aerial navigation' and its application to sea warfare; and, typically, he learnt to fly himself. Fisher, though out of office, 'pressed him [Churchill] to push on with Navy air machines of all types',[29] and a small band of enthusiasts from both services soon made their influence felt. Among the Sea Lords there existed what may be described as conditional acceptance of aeronautical developments – the chief condition being that its personnel conformed to normal naval customs and discipline – which the pioneers soon found irksome.

In his memoirs Churchill wrote 'I rated the Zeppelin much lower as a weapon of war than almost anyone else . . . I was sure the fighting aeroplane . . . would harry, rout and burn these gaseous monsters . . . *I therefore did everything in my power in the years before the war to restrict expenditure upon airships and to concentrate our narrow and stinted resources upon aeroplanes*' (italics supplied).[30] But the records of the period tell a different story. For example at CID meetings in December 1912 and February 1913 we find Churchill arguing strongly in favour of airships which, he declared, 'we could not afford any longer to neglect', and Admiral Wilson, who though no longer First Sea Lord was a member of the CID, stating emphatically the case against them.[31] At the meeting on 6 February 1913 Colonel J. E. B. Seely, the Secretary of State for War, said that airship development 'was being left to the Navy' and 'the army was concentrating its attention on aeroplanes:[32] and the Admiralty's report of the same date, which Churchill must have approved, came down strongly in favour of the airship, though they did ask for thirty-five more aeroplanes and hydro-aeroplanes (i.e. seaplanes).[33] Not until April 1915, the month before Churchill left the Admiralty, do we find him admitting, correctly, that the superiority of aeroplanes over airships had not been fully appreciated before the war, and asking for '1000 efficient aeroplanes and 300 efficient seaplanes'.[34] It is true that in 1916, after Churchill had been dismissed, the Admiralty, impressed by the apparent but in fact delusive potentiality of the Zeppelin, became convinced of the merits of the rigid airship, and that a big effort and a great deal of money were thereafter expended on producing them to the German model;[35] but Churchill's statement of his pre-war attitude on the airship versus aeroplane dispute plainly requires considerable qualification.

In March 1913 Churchill vetoed a proposal to separate the naval from the military wings of the RFC, and as long as he remained in office the new corps continued to be united. A stream of minutes emanated from him on all aspects of the naval wing's work – from the pay and rank of pilots and the Admiralty's administration of the wing to the costing of the production programmes.[36] If Churchill was too optimistic about the capabilities of airships his interest in and support of all aerial developments were certainly beneficial, and the bitter strife between the Admiralty and War Office over the control and operations of the RN Air Service did not begin until after he had left the Admiralty.[37]

Churchill's admiration for the elder Pitt, so strongly evidenced by his only novel *Savrola*, and his study of his ancestor Marlborough's campaigns and strategy probably contributed to his lively and enduring interest in amphibious operations and in 'peripheral strategy'. But it should be mentioned that Dutch scholars have been highly critical of Churchill's biography of his ancestor, especially with regard to his prejudice against the Dutch 'Field Deputy' Sicco van Goslinga.[38] It is interesting to find that Churchill describes him as 'a military minded civilian fascinated (without any professional knowledge) by the art of war . . . He combined the valour of ignorance with a mind fertile in plans of action. His military judgement was almost childishly defective; his energy was overflowing'.[39] Much of that passage was, in the eyes of the top British service men of both World Wars applicable to Churchill himself.

Early in 1913 Churchill instigated an investigation by the Admiralty into seizing and holding a base on the 'Dutch, Danish or Scandinavian coasts' for use by light warships in the event of war with Germany.[40] He paid scant attention, then or later, to whether any of those countries might be neutral, or to what the effects of violating their neutrality might be. In the middle of that year he produced plans for seizing the Dutch Friesian island of Borkum and the German island of Sylt off western Schleswig, including the landing of large numbers of soldiers on them. The seizure of Heligoland and an even more hazardous raid up the River Elbe were also considered, and on the eve of war Churchill sent Asquith copies of the reports produced by his planners. He rightly insisted on close co-operation between the Admiralty and War Office, which had been sadly lacking in recent years, in any such undertakings; but in all other respects the eight alternatives considered (which included objectives in Norway, Sweden and Denmark as well as in Holland) presented enormous difficulties. Ameland (Dutch) was his favourite target, but Richmond, then Assistant Director of Operations, denounced the 'strategical and tactical futility' of such an undertaking, and Churchill was forced to drop what Professor Marder aptly calls 'this harum-scarum project'.[41] Then Admiral Wilson, who had been brought back to the Admiralty to join the War Staff group, put up a plan to attack Heligoland – which in 1913 Churchill had described as 'an almost impregnable fortress'. Though Churchill had not advocated this plan he was willing, with Battenberg's concurrence, to put it to Jellicoe and flag officers of the Grand Fleet when he met them at Loch Ewe shortly after the outbreak of war. Jellicoe, like Richmond, doubted the sanity of those who could put forward ideas which were bound to incur heavy losses for dubious gains.

Though it is a truism to say that wars can only be won by offensive blows those early plans and proposals, and the impetus which Churchill applied to them, do emphasize that he did not come near to under-standing the dangers and complexities of amphibious operations, the most hazardous undertakings of war, nor the need for large quantities of specialized equipment and a high degree of training on the part of the men of all services committed to their execution. Nor did Churchill or some of the admirals, adequately appreciate the handicap from which low trajectory high-velocity naval guns suffered when engaging well-sited shore batteries, or the vulnerability of ships to return fire by the latter. These blind spots, which can reasonably be attributed chiefly to misinterpreting history, were to influence Churchill's outlook and actions almost to the end of his career, and will recur again and again in our story. We will return later to the form taken by his search for a naval offensive in 1914-15.

As regards the intellectual ability of senior naval officers of the early twentieth century Churchill has written that when he went to the Admiralty he found that 'there was no moment in the career and training of a naval officer when he is obliged to read a single book about naval war, or pass even the most rudimentary examination in naval history. The Royal Navy had made no important contribution to Naval literature'.[42] The first sentence of that indictment ignores the fact that naval history was taught as part of the curriculum at Osborne and Dartmouth colleges, and that prizes were awarded for proficiency in that subject which were open to cadets during their course at Dartmouth and as part of their final examinations. An example of the former is the Graham Naval History Prize for cadets which was instituted in 1909 in memory of Admiral Sir William Graham by his widow. The validity of the remainder of Churchill's attack depends of course on the word 'obliged'; but the implication that no officers did any reading in the field of their profession is a considerable exaggeration. Finally Churchill's last sentence ignores the works of the brothers Captain Sir John Colomb RMA and Admiral Philip Colomb, who have been described by a close student of their writings as 'a remarkable couple of men',[43] and who moreover entered the field well before the American Captain A. T. Mahan whose histories Churchill singled out for praise. Though the Colomb brothers never achieved the popularity of Mahan they blazed the trail for a number of distinguished British successors. They were in truth 'pioneers in the application of serious but non-technical thinking to British military problems'[44] – especially by Philip Colomb's use of historical study to provide a guide to the development of strategic thought. Furthermore the Royal United Services Institution provided a forum for the discussion of such issues, and its annual prize essay competition, won by Philip Colomb in 1878, attracted entries from a number of thoughtful officers.[45] Nor were essay competitions confined to the RUSI, since 'Jacky' Fisher, though he dismissed Philip Colomb as 'a theoretical Admiral', himself instituted a similar scheme as C-in-C, Mediterranean 1897–1902; and those competitions attracted entries from, among others, the future Lord Hankey, who was to achieve great renown as Secretary of the Committee of Imperial Defence 1912–38 and of the Cabinet 1916–38, and who may justly be described as an early example of the 'military intellectual'.[46]

Another indication that by the time Churchill first entered the Admiralty officers of middle rank were giving serious thought to the non-technical side of their profession, and the strategic aspects of naval warfare, as well as to the need to study and apply the lessons of history, was the formation in October 1912 of The Naval Society by a group of intellectually-minded officers. It began publication of a quarterly journal called *The Naval Review* for circulation among the Society's members; and the fact that the original sixty members of 1913 had grown to 1260 two years later is surely a convincing rebuttal of Churchill's sweeping indictment.[47]

When Churchill became First Lord he undoubtedly considered bringing 'Jacky' Fisher, then seventy-one years old, back to the office of First Sea Lord, which he had held from 1904–10;[48] for Churchill had developed a strong admiration for the ebullient, energetic, and strongly reformist but incurably combative admiral. Perhaps he would have been wiser to have adhered to his first impulse, rather than bring Fisher back in October 1914 when Battenberg was forced to resign because of his German antecedents; for, although Professor Marder has declared that the old admiral 'was quite fit for the job' in his seventy-fourth year he was not the man he had been three years earlier.[49]

As regards Churchill's relations with senior naval officers one has to remember that, when he became First Lord, there still existed a number who can reasonably be classified as the 'Fabulous Admirals' of the book of that title;[50] and such exotic characters did not disappear from the naval service until World War II. The outstanding characteristics of such men were arrogance and combativeness. Though few if any of them can justly be described as vicious, and their arrogance was sometimes mitigated by a peculiar and highly individualistic brand of humour,[51] they were not easy men to serve under. Although in the sea-going fleet and squadrons they were generally regarded with tolerant amusement their inclusion in a Board of Admiralty of which Churchill was the head would certainly have produced even worse explosions than actually took place; for Churchill's own make-up was certainly not devoid of the characteristics which he found so distasteful in admirals.

Taken as a whole the senior officers of this period suffered from a serious handicap in dealing with so loquacious and argumentative a person as Churchill – namely that they lacked the ability to state a case concisely and clearly and then to sustain it against hostile dialectic – an art at which Churchill excelled, provided that he had been given time to prepare his case. Admiral Wilson was a classic example of this disability, as was demonstrated very clearly at the famous CID meeting of 23 August 1911 when the strategy to be adopted in the event of war with Germany was discussed.[52] This disability probably derived, at any rate in part, from the fact that after leaving the naval colleges officers received little further education – except of a strictly professional nature. It is small wonder that a person equipped with as lively a mind as Churchill's should have regarded such men as inadequate. 'They,' he wrote of the senior officers in the Admiralty in 1911, 'are so cocksure, *insouciant* and apathetic';[53] but the first of Churchill's critical adjectives was surely not wholly inapplicable to himself.

Though Fisher, A. K. Wilson, Bridgeman and a good many lesser naval luminaries of the period 1900–15 were wholly opposed to Churchill's concept of and pressure for a naval staff, one admiral – Lord Charles Beresford – had seen the need well before Churchill went to the Admiralty. Not only did he succeed, after a long battle, in getting a Naval Intelligence Department instituted as early as 1887 but he thereafter kept up pressure to accomplish what Churchill also saw to be essential to operational efficiency.[54] Unfortunately Beresford certainly merits a place among the 'Fabulous Admirals' already referred to, and his conduct was often so outrageous that his merits became obscured. What Fisher reasonably called his 'overweening vanity' made enemies everywhere. His intemperate attack on Churchill in April 1914 made the breach between them so wide that the First Lord refused to have anything more to do with the man whom he contemptuously dismissed as 'this old clown' in April 1915.[55]

Two of the appointments made by Churchill at this time merit special consideration. The first was the selection of a very young Rear-Admiral called David Beatty as his Naval Secretary, and the second was his choice, instigated by Fisher, of John Jellicoe to command the Grand Fleet if war came. Though Beatty was certainly not free from arrogance he was to prove himself the finest fighting admiral on the British side in World War I, and a very successful First Sea Lord for the unusually long period of seven and a half difficult years (November 1919 to July 1927). As to Jellicoe, Fisher's description of him as 'a second Nelson' was an absurd exaggeration, and his tendency to pessimism, which finally became chronic, seems to have been overlooked. It is of course true that Jellicoe's responsibilities in war were immense; but neither his time in command of the Grand Fleet nor his period as First Sea Lord (December 1916 to December 1917) justifies claiming for him a place among the greatest naval leaders. Reviewing the senior officers of 1911–14 as a whole it is clear that Churchill's complaint regarding their intellectual capacity was not without some foundation; but, as was to become plainer with the passage of time, it is also the case that Churchill's judgement of character was sometimes very faulty.

In conclusion of this brief survey of pre-war naval policies and personalities it is fair to mention that, no matter how great was the debt owed to Churchill's vision and energy, his order to the navy, issued just after the outbreak of war, to plan for a conflict lasting one year, with the greatest effort concentrated in the first six months, suggests that his perception was sometimes little if at all less faulty than that of the admirals whom he later criticized so harshly – a view which is hardly substantiated by his own memoirs.[56]

CHAPTER 2

Blunders and Disasters
1914-1915

Despite the success with which the mobilization and movement of the fleet to its war stations were carried out before the actual outbreak of hostilities on 4 August 1914 there soon took place a whole series of blunders which greatly vitiated the confidence of the public in the Royal Navy and also, in the longer view, the authority and standing of the First Lord. In part, but only in part, these errors stemmed from the lack of a properly organized staff, already mentioned; for the Naval War Council instituted in 1909 under the First Sea Lord to consider strategic problems and war plans and the so-called War Staff which replaced it in January 1912 with the object of studying the operational aspects of maritime war, were both of them wholly inadequate substitutes, and the latter was merely an advisory body. As Professor Marder has remarked the 'major flaw' was that the First Sea Lord was not also the Chief of Staff;[1] and with a man of Churchill's ebullient energy and insatiable interest in even the minutiae of operations and administration it was inevitable that he should take on himself much of the functions which should have been handled by the Chief of Staff.

The first series of incidents which glaringly exposed the deficiencies of the prevailing system, and which was in the long term to produce very serious repercussions, began with the arrival of the powerful German battle-cruiser *Goeben* and the light cruiser *Breslau* at Messina on 2 August. Admiral Sir Berkeley Milne, the C-in-C, Mediterranean, who was certainly not one of the brightest stars in the naval firmament, had been told on 30 July that his first task was to help cover the transport of the French North African troops to metropolitan ports, but that his objects should also 'if possible [include] bringing to action individual fast German ships, particularly *Goeben*'. The latter task was, however, qualified by the instruction that he should not 'at this stage be brought to action against superior forces, except in combination with the French . . .' This was an ambiguous, and fatal, qualification since the meaning of 'superior forces' was not defined; and although Milne had under his command three battle-cruisers with he : armaments than the *Goeben* he was plainly required to give the saf of the French transports priority. That Churchill himself had a big hand in the despatch of this and subsequent signals by which the initial confusion was compounded is proved beyond doubt by the draft of the message quoted above, which has been preserved, being in his hand[2] – a fact which Professor Marder has overlooked when he states that he is 'disposed to accept' that this message was 'the principal factor in this almost incredible train of errors emanating from White-hall'.[3] This is not the place to recapitulate the story of the escape of the two ships to Constantinople; but the resultant entry of Turkey into the war on the side of the Central Powers on 5 November must be attributed at any rate in part to the intrusion of Churchill into the operational sphere, as well as to the inadequacies of Milne and the unfortunate decision of his subordinate Admiral Thomas Troubridge not to engage the allegedly 'superior forces' of the enemy when his four armoured cruisers supported by lighter forces could have done so early on 7 August. Though it is futile to speculate on what the result of such a battle might have been it is difficult not to share the fury felt by Fisher, Beatty and others over what was, in Marder's words 'a blow to British naval prestige and naval morale'. Where one may disagree with that authority, is in his placing the blame equally on the Admiralty and Troubridge, with Milne as the third delinquent, and ignoring Churchill's personal share in the Admiralty's contribution to the disaster. It may also be remarked that in the authorized biography of Churchill the author entirely glosses over the latter aspect of the muddle.[4]

Nor did events in home waters in August–September 1914 in any way compensate for the bungling of the opening moves in the Mediter-ranean. The establishment of a 'distant blockade' of the German North Sea bases instead of the 'close blockade' envisaged until 1912, by which time the peril from mines and submarines had plainly rendered it impracticable, greatly reduced the likelihood of the German High Seas Fleet offering battle in the manner hoped for in the Grand Fleet, and indeed throughout the British navy. Though Churchill, who always belonged to the 'seek out and destroy school', and sought unremittingly for a 'naval offensive' was very reluctant to accept the change to a defensive strategy it was in truth inevitable.[5]

The transport of the British Expeditionary Force to France without loss within three weeks of the declaration of war was a striking demon-stration of the navy's control of the narrow seas; while the Battle of Heligoland Bight of 28 August, though a confused action marred by indifferent planning and lack of co-ordination between the three

squadrons involved, ended in a heartening success for the British, who
sank three light cruisers and a destroyer without loss to themselves.
But the action was certainly not the glorious victory which Churchill
among others claimed it to be at the time.[6] Its most important result
probably was to discourage the Kaiser still further from risking the
main units of his fleet. Less than a month later its beneficial effects
were offset by the sinking of three old armoured cruisers, which were
patrolling unescorted at slow speed and on a steady course off the
Dutch coast, by a single U-boat with the loss of 1459 lives.[7] In fact the
danger of their exposed position was appreciated by Churchill just
before the disaster occurred – though his proposal to transfer these
vulnerable ships to the western Channel did not specifically refer to
the submarine menace.[8] The brunt of the criticism of the Admiralty
fell, unfairly, on the First Lord; but once again the true cause was
indifferent staff work, and the chief blame should have been placed on
the First Sea Lord and the Chief of the War Staff (Battenberg and
Sturdee). Nor was the sinking of the three old cruisers by any means
the only loss inflicted by mines and by submarine torpedoes during
the first months of the war. The battleship *Audacious* was sunk by a
mine off northern Ireland on 27 October 1914, and many lesser vessels
fell victims to the same weapons; while two cruisers (*Hawke* and
Hermes) were sunk by submarine torpedoes before the end of the
year, and the old battleship *Formidable* suffered a like fate on 1 January
1915 in the Channel.

The foregoing losses to weapons whose deadliness had not been
recognized before the war, except by Fisher who had foreseen the far-
reaching influence of the submarine as early as 1904,[9] combined with the
proven vulnerability of the Grand Fleet's principal base at Scapa
Flow, now began to influence all naval strategy and tactics. Though
the responsibility for neglect of the study of the influence of underwater weapons must surely be placed chiefly on the Sea Lords of the
pre-war period and the lack of a proper staff, as Churchill insisted on
having a finger in every naval pie it is difficult to acquit him wholly
for this expensive failure – as his own account would have us believe.[10]
When the vulnerability of Scapa became apparent Churchill considered
Jellicoe's apprehensions exaggerated, holding that the anchorage was
'protected by its currents'. Presumably he was thinking of the approach
to the main entrance from the Pentland Firth, with its fierce tidal
streams, for there are no currents in Scapa itself and there are several
entrances to the Flow. Not until 1915 was the anchorage reasonably
secure against submarines; and it may here be remarked that exactly

the same state of affairs arose again in 1939 – but with more serious results on that occasion. Although when money for the services is tight, as it always is in peace time, base defences will never be given the priority they deserve Churchill's Board of Admiralty can hardly be acquitted of responsibility for the defenceless state of Scapa in 1914; and the same applies to the inefficient mines and torpedoes supplied to the fleet – the failure of which can be traced back to Fisher's time as First Sea Lord. By contrast the German mines were very efficient, and soon became a serious menace which called for an immense minesweeping effort. Not until we had copied the German mine in 1917 did we possess an efficient weapon of that type. The comparative neglect of underwater warfare before 1914, despite the well-known fact that it is the submerged parts of a ship that are the most vulnerable, is attributable to the excessive dominance of the gunnery specialist branch in the counsels of the Admiralty; and that state of affairs was to be repeated between the wars.

While these preliminary moves and engagements were taking place in the North Sea the German armies were sweeping across Belgium and into France, and were not seriously checked until the First Battle of the Marne early in September. The continued resistance of the fortress of Antwerp far to the rear of the main German armies, and the fact that their rapid advance to the south-west left a flank dangerously open on the Belgian coast was appreciated by no one more clearly than Churchill. Towards the end of September he was allowed to send a hastily collected brigade of Marines and two recently formed and ill-trained brigades of naval volunteers to reinforce the defenders of Antwerp; while one regular and one cavalry division were sent to Ostend and Zeebrugge with the object of moving overland to raise the siege of the beleagured fortress. Churchill's view of the strategic opportunity offered by a landing on the exposed German flank is fully confirmed by our later knowledge of the German High Command's nervousness about the possible consequences of such a move. Unfortunately it was made in such meagre strength that it could do no more than delay the surrender of Antwerp until 10 October and cover the withdrawal of the Belgian field army down the coast. Yet the opportunity to use our sea power in that traditional manner was there, and if Kitchener had been prepared to send some of the eleven Territorial divisions available in England the potential threat might well have been turned into reality.[11]

On 3 October, after a false start on the previous day, Churchill set out for Antwerp, and it is well known how his offer to take command of the forces in the field, resigning his office in the government, was received by the Cabinet 'with roars of incredulous laughter' – except by Kitchener, who was prepared to give him high military rank if Asquith would release him. But the Prime Minister sent a blunt refusal and peremptorily ordered his return to London.[12] Professor Marder writes that 'Churchill, I am certain, would have been superb as a field commander', but he does not specify how high a command he had in mind; and such a statement is of course purely speculative.[13] The elevation of a Lieutenant of Hussars without experience of any kind of command to Lieutenant-General (as Kitchener had offered) might surely have proved somewhat rash. In high naval circles, including, surprisingly, Beatty and Richmond, Churchill's flamboyant activities aroused anger, and even contempt; while his Cabinet colleagues considered his judgement defective and viewed him with increasing mistrust. Yet in retrospect there is much to admire in his energy, courage and initiative at this time. R. W. Thompson, who has studied Churchill closely over a long period, sums it all up well when he writes 'Winston's behaviour at the Admiralty in 1914 is the real Winston, the best Winston in many ways. Brilliant, foolish, brash – actually likeable. He wants to be First Lord and man of action combined, wielding the Navy . . . while defending Antwerp in person.'[14] Yet the scapegoat for the Antwerp fiasco and the other naval set-backs mentioned above was not Churchill but Battenberg who, after a malicious Press campaign, was asked by the Cabinet to resign, and did so on 28 October. It must, however, be admitted that some senior naval men, including Fisher, held that Battenberg was not only 'played out' physically and mentally but was too much Churchill's 'fac le dupe'. But Fisher, anxious as he was to be recalled to office, can hardly be regarded as an impartial witness regarding Battenberg's condition and ability.[15]

Despite the King's misgivings Churchill got his way, and Fisher was recalled on 30 October. Among other changes in the Admiralty Sturdee, who had not been a success as Chief of the War Staff and whom Fisher strongly disliked, was replaced by the far more able Admiral H. F. Oliver. The return of Fisher was on the whole well received by the Press and in the navy. With him and Churchill working in tandem the Admiralty's creaking machinery moved into top gear. Vast numbers of new warships were soon ordered; but they included more of the fast but lightly-protected battle-cruisers which had always been Fisher's particular pets. In their latest guise, the *Renown* and *Repulse* and the *Courageous* class (which ultimately became aircraft carriers) they never really justified their progenitor's enthusiasm for them.

At the time when Churchill was making every effort to attack the open right flank of the German army on the Belgian coast the key British naval command was that of Dover, where Rear-Admiral The Hon. H. L. A. Hood flew his flag. Hood was one of the ablest of the younger admirals and had gained very early promotion. From 1910–13 he had been Captain of Osborne College, the cadet training establishment in the Isle of Wight, and his work there earned him a warm commendation from Churchill. In 1914 he was appointed to the key post of Naval Secretary to the First Lord.[16] He was clearly marked out for high rank; but in October 1914 he was subjected to a bombardment of signals and instructions unquestionably originated by Churchill, which suggest less than complete confidence in his capacity to do what was needed without prodding. The first such message which has been preserved told him '. . . Recognize importance of navy dominating Belgian coast. Make the most of your opportunity.'[17] Next day he was told 'Have everything ready at Dunkerque for Ostend bombardment. Congratulate you on success of vigorous conduct of so much hazard.'[18] On the 27th Churchill told him in a personal message 'You have done very well . . . Keep it up. Certainly go on; but husband ammunition till good targets show, but risks must be run and allies' left [wing] must be supported without fail by navy.'[19] Though Hood received many compliments on his efforts from the Belgians and French and from the C-in-C, British Expeditionary Force[20] Churchill cannot have been satisfied because on 9 April 1915 he wrote to Hood that he was to be relieved by Rear-Admiral R. H. S. Bacon who had retired as long ago as 1909, after two years as Director of Naval Ordnance, to become General Manager of the Coventry Ordnance Works. Hood was given command of a force of elderly cruisers working out of Queenstown. Though Churchill told him that his supersession had nothing to do with dissatisfaction over his work off the Belgian coast, which, he wrote, 'has been greatly appreciated' the admiral plainly thought otherwise.[21] He evidently protested to Fisher, but all he got by way of reply was an almost illegible scrawl saying 'as you well know Flag Officers' appointments are the prerogative (?) of the First Lord and I endeavour to avoid meddling in his business'[22] – a statement which Professor Marder's volumes of Fisher's correspondence show to have been patently untrue. Moreover Bacon had long been a protégé of Fisher's. Both Jellicoe and Beatty wrote to Hood expressing their astonishment at the treatment meted out to him, the former declaring that 'such strange things have happened in the matter of changes since last August that I have ceased to be surprised at anything'; while the latter strongly disapproved of bringing Bacon back from retirement.[23] That the change was made with Fisher's approval is strongly suggested by the fact that on 22 May, only a week after he had walked out of the Admiralty, Hood was given the far more important command of the 3rd Battle Cruiser Squadron, which formed part of Beatty's force in the Grand Fleet. There he did very well, fully confirming Jellicoe's and Beatty's confidence in him, until he lost his life when the *Invincible* was blown up during the battle of Jutland on 31 May 1916. As to Bacon, he did not prove a complete success at Dover, and was replaced by Keyes at the end of 1917.[24] The story of the relief of Hood has been told in some detail because it illustrates very clearly the way appointments were juggled during the Churchill-Fisher régime of 1914-15. Moreover Professor Marder appears to have overlooked it.[25]

To return to the autumn of 1914, on 1 November, only three days after Fisher's return to the Admiralty as First Sea Lord, Admiral Christopher Cradock's weak and ill-assorted squadron on the South American station was, except for one light cruiser, destroyed by Admiral Graf von Spee's powerful and highly efficient East Asiatic Squadron in the Battle of Coronel off the Chilean coast. In part the responsibility for the successful concentration of the initially scattered German squadron must be placed on Churchill, since it was on his initiative that the plans of Admiral Sir Martyn Jerram, commander of the China Station, were radically altered by an order to concentrate at Hong Kong instead of in a position 900 miles to the south-east where he would have been far better placed to counter a southward move by von Spee. The British commander of the ships in Australian and New Zealand waters, which had been placed under the Admiralty's operational control, suffered similarly from instructions to carry out operations which 'they had not previously conceived or which ran counter to their own plans'.[26] Such was the diversion of the Australian Navy's strength to cover expeditionary forces sent to capture the German colonies of Samoa and New Guinea at the Admiralty's insistence, instead of being employed on catching von Spee's force – which, as the senior officers on the Australian Naval Board and in command of the RAN squadron clearly realized, should be their primary objective. Once that had been accomplished the colonies could of course have been taken at leisure; and the tragedy of Coronel might also have been avoided. There was some truth in the remark by an officer in one of the marauding German cruisers that 'we had in the

First Lord of the Admiralty, an involuntary ally'.[27]

The outcome of the muddles and confusion arising from the attempt to control operations many thousands of miles from Whitehall was that in late October Cradock only had with him two elderly armoured cruisers (*Good Hope* and *Monmouth*), one light cruiser (*Glasgow*) and an armed merchant cruiser. The slow, old and ill-manned battleship *Canopus* (1897-9 vintage), whose four 12-inch guns Churchill believed would keep the German ships at bay, Cradock left behind as more of a handicap than a reinforcement when he moved north up the Chilean coast to seek von Spee. In his memoirs Churchill wrote that 'I cannot accept for the Admiralty any share for the responsibility for what followed';[28] but the implication that the whole responsibility should be placed on Cradock is surely unacceptable. Though the admiral certainly cannot be wholly acquitted of error, what Geoffrey Bennett has called 'The Admiralty's confused, unrealistic and, consequently, misleading instructions' were a very important factor; and so 'to Churchill belongs a considerable measure of personal responsibility for the disaster' of 1 November 1914.[29] The shock to British morale of the defeat off Coronel was as great as the jubilation produced by von Spee's success in Germany. However, Fisher and Churchill at once put in hand energetic measures to forestall a dangerous situation if von Spee moved to the South Atlantic.

On 4 November Fisher, with Churchill's full support, ordered Jellicoe to detach the battle-cruisers *Invincible* and *Inflexible* and send them to Devonport to prepare with all haste for overseas service. A third battle-cruiser (*Princess Royal*) was sent to the West Indies to guard against the contingency of von Spee's squadron coming north, passing through the Panama Canal (as it was entitled to do) and wreaking havoc to the Caribbean trade. Taking account of the fact that the margin of superiority of the Grand Fleet was at the time very narrow it took great courage to weaken it in such a manner. Thanks to the Admiralty's ruthless pressure on Devonport dockyard the two south-bound ships sailed on 11 November under Admiral Sturdee, and reached the Falkland Islands early on 7 December.[30] At 7.50 a.m. next day the German ships' mastheads were sighted from Port Stanley, where the battle-cruisers were coaling. Though the preparation of the two battle-cruisers for distant service was far from being a well-kept secret the German Admiralty had failed to get a warning through to von Spee, who was taken completely by surprise. What followed is well known – a chase to the south-east, followed by three separate but linked gun actions. The *Nürnberg* and *Leipzig* were overhauled and sunk by British light and armoured cruisers, while the two battle-cruisers dealt with the *Scharnhorst* and *Gneisenau*. Only the *Dresden* escaped, to play hide and seek with searching British warships in the tortuous fiords of Patagonia, until she was located and destroyed in the Juan Fernandez islands in March 1915.

The only jarring note in the aftermath of jubilation was Fisher's treatment of Sturdee – chiefly for having allowed the *Dresden* to escape; but the old admiral's vindictiveness and malevolence never diminished. If it was Fisher who initiated the series of critical messages to Sturdee surely Churchill, who so often preached magnanimity even towards foes, should have stepped in and stopped exchanges which illustrated the pettiness by which his chief naval adviser's character was so grievously flawed.

If the cleansing of the seas of German warship raiders, and for a loss of no more than 215,000 tons of merchant shipping, marked an important milestone on the road to victory, a less satisfactory feature of the Falkland Islands battle was the huge expenditure of 12-inch ammunition (1174 rounds) by the two battle-cruisers. It suggested that all was not well with British fire control systems or with the performance of our heavy armour-piercing shell; but many months were to elapse, and a heavy price was to be exacted before those deficiencies were confirmed, let alone made good. The 8 December 1914 also marked the spring tide of the association between Fisher and Churchill, who may justly share the credit for what was done.

CHAPTER 3

Dismissal
1915

If the first six months of the war had produced, both for Churchill and the admirals, many disappointments and setbacks the following year was to be worse. Though the origins of the Dardanelles expedition have already been thoroughly explored its consequences were so momentous, and are so germane to our story, that it is essential to give them in outline here;[1] but it must be remarked that, although Churchill was not the first to press for an attack on Turkey, and always regarded the North Sea and Baltic as his favourite theatres for an offensive, he did initiate the steps which resulted in the purely naval attack. The failure of both that attack and of the later military assault on the Gallipoli peninsula not only affected Churchill's political career profoundly, but embittered his relations with the senior army and navy officers involved. Indeed it probably does not go too far to say that Gallipoli, coming on top of the naval disasters already recounted, the terrible slaughter of the Somme battle and the misuse of the first 'caterpillars' or tanks on that same battlefield soured his outlook towards the great majority of high-ranking soldiers and sailors, most of whom he lumped together in his mind as obstinate and unimaginative obstructors of the new ideas constantly produced by his fertile brain.

The story of the Dardanelles campaign begins with the Russian appeal of 2 January 1915 for action to relieve Turkish pressure in the Caucasus, which produced a promise of help in the form of 'a demonstration' which Kitchener, the Secretary of State for War, insisted should take place against the defences of the Dardanelles, and would have to be a purely naval undertaking. On 3 January Churchill received Fisher's typically hyperbolic letter urging action against Turkey – but '*only* if it's *immediate*', and enclosing a plan to land large forces – which actually could not be made available for a long time – on the Asiatic coast south of the entrance to the Dardanelles, while a large number of the older battleships forced a passage through the Straits. Churchill seized on the latter feature and ignored the former. That same day he telegraphed to Admiral S. H. Carden, who commanded a small force already in the Aegean, asking whether he considered the Dardanelles

could be forced 'by the use of ships alone'. Carden, who was actually a
second-rate officer who found himself unexpectedly in a sea command
instead of in charge of Malta dockyard, replied that while he did not
think the Dardanelles 'can be rushed' they might be 'forced by extended
operations with a large number of ships'. This was encouraging enough
for Churchill to put on pressure by claiming, not entirely correctly,
that 'high authorities' in the Admiralty agreed with Carden, who was
told to signal his detailed proposals. Churchill claimed later that the
resultant plan 'made a great impression on everyone who saw it';[2] and
it is a fact that Admirals Oliver and Jackson of the War Staff Group, as
well as Fisher the First Sea Lord, supported the naval attack. The pity
of it is that such an idea was in flat contradiction to the conclusions
drawn from a study of the problem made by the General Staff in 1906
and considered by the CID in January 1907, when the great risks involved in an assault on the Gallipoli peninsula were heavily stressed.[3]
Although Hankey recirculated those papers early in 1915 the warning
was disregarded, and from that time Churchill became the chief
advocate of the undertaking. Fisher lent his support by proposing that
the brand new and very powerful battleship *Queen Elizabeth* should
pit her 15-inch guns against the much lighter weapons defending the
Straits – a proposal which further stimulated Churchill's euphoria. On
13 January he brought the plan before the War Council, and argued his
case with great eloquence and forensic skill. The outcome was the
extraordinary decision, drafted by Asquith, that 'The Admiralty
should prepare for a naval expedition in February to bombard and
take the Gallipoli peninsula, with Constantinople as its objective.'[4]
Yet it should have been obvious that the navy could not by itself seize
the Gallipoli peninsula or capture Constantinople, and in fact at the
end of January Fisher threatened resignation if the operation was not
made a joint naval and military one.[5] A fortnight later Hankey warned
Asquith of the need for troops, and he agreed; while Jackson as well
as Fisher now took the same line.[6] But what really mattered was that
the War Council's decision of 13 January gave Churchill all the
authority he needed, and he went ahead with all his customary vigour –
and impatience. Fisher opened his heart to Jellicoe soon after the
decision had been taken, writing that 'I just abominate the Dardanelles
operation unless . . . it is settled to be a military operation, with 200,000
men in conjunction with the fleet.'[7] In the early hours of the 15th
Churchill telegraphed to Carden that he had authority to go ahead
with 'methodical piecemeal reductions of the forts *as the Germans did at
Antwerp*' (italics supplied); but the analogy was a false one as it was

chiefly the heavy German howitzers, with very steep trajectories quite unlike those of high-velocity naval guns, which did the execution on the Belgian forts.

On 25 January Fisher warned Asquith strongly about the unsoundness of the navy trying to do the job alone, and about the inevitable weakening of the Grand Fleet which would result; but the Prime Minister left the paper uncirculated, as he was inclined to do with disruptive memoranda.[8] Churchill assured Fisher that he fully agreed about keeping the Grand Fleet up to strength, but argued that there was a surplus of ships which could be 'used for the general cause'. Even if there was a surplus in some important classes such as destroyers and submarines, which is doubtful, Churchill certainly went too far in telling Fisher that there was 'no difference in principle between us'.[9] These written and verbal exchanges show how extraordinarily difficult it was, even for as gifted and eloquent an admiral as Fisher, to deflect Churchill from a line of action on which he had made up his mind. The truth is that neither Fisher nor any other admiral was, as Asquith's daughter Violet Bonham-Carter has remarked, 'a match for Winston as a dialectician'.[10] If in the case of the Dardanelles operation Churchill was right in seeing it as a possible means of breaking the costly deadlock in the west, it was Fisher and the admirals of the War Staff Group, A. K. Wilson, H. F. Oliver and Henry Jackson, who saw more clearly the need for a properly mounted combined operation.

At the War Council on 28 January Churchill announced that preparations were in hand to start the naval attack in mid-February; and when Asquith overruled Fisher's objections he got up and started to leave the room. Pursued and pleaded with by Kitchener he resumed his seat; but his opposition to the naval attack had been made abundantly clear. Yet later that day, after the Council had adjourned, Churchill persuaded the old admiral to go along with him. A semblance of unity having been restored Fisher devoted all his energy to the attempt to achieve success – for a time. Though a formidable body of service opinion, including the influential Hankey, supported Fisher in the belief that a combined operation was greatly to be preferred to a naval attack, Kitchener's initial refusal to find the 150,000 men needed resulted in the inferior plan being adopted. In Professor Marder's words Churchill's 'impetuosity, eloquence, and doggedness carried the day'; and Lloyd George has made very much the same judgement.[11] Moreover Churchill's belief that the heavy guns of the battleships could not only outrange the shore batteries but would be able to knock them out was, as history had repeatedly shown, a highly optimistic

assumption. Though the admirals of the War Staff Group must share
with Churchill the responsibility on that score one has to remember
how very difficult it was for service men to convince him on a matter
which went against his own inclination or conviction; and for someone
of lower rank to attempt to do so could be dangerous, and even fatal
to his career. Whether a properly organized naval staff would have
been more successful in bringing the need for a combined operation
and the limitations of naval gunfire into proper perspective is of
course speculative; but this writer's view of the events of 1940–1, to be
discussed later, makes him doubt whether even a carefully argued case
by such a staff would have deflected Churchill.

Just as serious as the exaggerated belief in the effect of naval gunfire
on shore emplacements was the failure to appreciate that concealed
mobile guns could be used to reinforce the fixed defences; while
minefields could seriously obstruct and endanger the bombarding
ships. Finally little or no consideration was given to what would
happen if the warships succeeded in forcing The Narrows and entering
the Sea of Marmora while both shores were still in enemy hands. In
fact the fleet's communications would have been hazardous in the
extreme, and the initial success might well have led to a disaster. Apart
from the Sea Lords' support for the naval attack being a good deal less
than enthusiastic, there was no consultation at all between the Admiralty and War Office on the battleships versus forts question.
Churchill drove ahead with all the dynamić energy of which he was
capable, ignoring and brushing aside warnings such as Fisher's on the
need for troops and Jellicoe's apprehensions with regard to the weakening of the Grand Fleet.

As to Fisher's attitude, his dislike of the Dardanelles project was in all
probability influenced by his support for the Baltic operation put
forward early in the war; and, secondly, no record exists of his having
stated his objections verbally or in writing *at the time the Dardanelles
plan was gestating*. His silence at the War Council meetings on 13 and
28 January can be explained by the fact that he and the top soldiers
regarded themselves as 'expert advisers' and were not full members
of the Council. Furthermore he certainly felt a strong sense of loyalty
towards the First Lord who had recalled him to office, and that may
have made him reluctant to publicize their differences. Churchill on
the other hand certainly should have asked Fisher and Wilson to speak
up at the War Council meetings, or should at least have represented
their views himself. Instead he undoubtedly left the impression that
he was speaking on behalf of a united Board of Admiralty – which was

far from the truth; and even Hankey, who knew all those involved intimately, gained the strong impression that the admirals' silence meant concurrence with Churchill's ideas. Not until Fisher's attempt to walk out of the meeting on the 28th was the strength of his feelings made plain; and even then the Council as a whole and Asquith in particular failed to probe the reasons for his very unusual action. In sum much of the blame for the decision to go ahead with the naval attack undoubtedly rests with Asquith and Churchill; and although the First Lord's naval advisers were in fact far less sanguine than he they went along with him because of the confident assurance that, if the naval attack failed, the operation could be broken off at any time and was therefore unlikely to produce a serious disaster. The junior Sea Lords, and authoritative outsiders, were never consulted at all; and not a single meeting of the full Board of Admiralty was held to review and discuss all aspects of the operation. As to Churchill's political colleagues, they were in effect dazzled by the prospect of the tremendous strategic benefits which he held before their eyes.

Carden's plan was to proceed up the Straits in three stages, first destroying the forts at the southern entrance, then the intermediate defences leading to The Narrows, which started about fourteen miles from the entrance, and finally tackling the very powerful complex of inner defences which covered the principal minefields. The latter could not be swept while the forts, many of which could enfilade The Narrows, remained in action; the naval guns were bound to find it difficult if not impossible to silence the forts; and the searchlights which the German military advisers to the Turkish army had installed to make night minesweeping extremely hazardous made clearance of the minefields, and so close engagement of the shore defences, very difficult to accomplish. Finally Carden was far from being a good choice, either physically or psychologically, to lead and press ahead with a difficult and dangerous undertaking.

It should not be thought that no voice was raised against the concept of the naval attack on the Dardanelles. In mid-January that highly original but often difficult character Captain H. W. Richmond, who had been Assistant Director of Operations since February 1913, described it as being 'in violation of all experience of war';[12] and when his worst fears were realized by the total loss of the element of surprise and he suggested instead a landing at Haifa athwart the main Turkish line of communications to Arabia he was dismissed on the grounds that 'it was not my business to interfere in proposals that had been approved'.[13] It was a great misfortune that such a brilliant thinker as Richmond should have been so intolerant and tactless when the need was to convince his superiors of the correctness of his views.

Churchill, having convinced the War Council that the navy could and would force the Straits alone not only refused to call on the army for help but even declined to send out the whole Royal Naval Division, which was at his disposal and which Oliver and Richmond had proposed to use as an amphibious assault force in February. Only two of its Marine battalions were sent – to complete the demolition of the forts after the guns of the fleet had put them out of action. Yet as the days passed the need for troops became ever clearer, and Richmond's strongly-argued paper entitled 'Remarks on Present Strategy' of 14 February was warmly praised by Fisher and Hankey.[14] Next day Jackson wrote that the naval attack could not be recommended 'unless a strong military force is ready to assist in the operation'; and these warnings raised doubts in Churchill's mind regarding whether Carden's original assessment had been right, and to look around again for troops.

Meanwhile Kitchener had promised that if the navy asked for the help of land forces 'at a later stage that assistance would be forthcoming', and the 29th Division, which had previously been earmarked for Salonika, became available shortly afterwards. At an emergency meeting of the War Council on 16 February, when Churchill and Fisher were both present, the decision was taken to send that Division to the Aegean island of Lemnos, though its function was left undefined until the result of the naval attack was known. The Australian and New Zealand troops then in Egypt were to be transported to the same island. Though the soldiers were only to be used after the warships had forced a passage through The Narrows the whole nature of the enterprise had now obviously changed.

In fact the first bombardment of the outer forts on 19 February accomplished little, and bad weather prevented it being renewed until the 25th, when the guns on both sides of the entrance were silenced. The Marines' demolition parties landed next day to finish the job and met no opposition. This success was sufficient for Carden to consider Phase I completed and to start Phase II on 1 March, when the sweepers would clear the main minefields preparatory to the battleships' attack on the defences of The Narrows. Meanwhile the view that large-scale military help would be needed was spreading among the top Generals; but on 19 February Kitchener cancelled the despatch of the 29th Division; and Churchill's strong pleas for it to be made available went unheeded. Not until 10 March did Kitchener agree to release the troops – a three-week delay which was to have momentous consequences, as

Churchill was later to argue in contradiction of his earlier view that the navy could do the job alone.

On 12 March General Sir Ian Hamilton was appointed to command the troops, which now numbered about 81,000 men including a French division, the Anzacs, the whole of the RN Division and the 29th; but the orders given to Hamilton were far from clear and unambiguous. Furthermore when he reached Mudros on the island of Lemnos, where headquarters had been set up, he found that the loading of the transports and supply ships was so chaotic that he had no choice but to send them all to Alexandria to sort out the confusion. Churchill himself cannot be wholly acquitted of responsibility for the loading muddle, since he had appointed a civilian as Director of Transports in the Admiralty in December 1914 against the advice of Admiral Oliver and of Sir Graham Greene, the Permanent Secretary of the Admiralty.

Despite all the troubles, muddles and difficulties which now seem so inexcusable, as the fateful day approached optimism prevailed in London, and on 9 March Churchill wrote to Jellicoe that 'Our affairs in the Dardanelles are prospering, though we have not yet cracked the nut'. He was even looking ahead to what should be done after the capture of Constantinople. On 5 March Carden, who shared the prevailing optimism, opened the bombardment of the forts at The Narrows. Three days later it was obvious that the naval attack had not succeeded and was not going to succeed. On the 10th Carden was forced to admit that 'our experience shows that gunfire alone will not render forts innocuous' – a conclusion which, one may feel, proper study and planning should have anticipated three months earlier. Moreover experience had shown that the available sweepers could not clear the path for the heavy ships because they had to work in the full glare of the searchlights and under heavy fire. Yet on the 11th a message drafted by Churchill and approved by Fisher and Oliver showed that in Whitehall there was impatience over the apparent lack of drive and determination behind Carden's efforts. This was one of those Churchillian messages telling the man on the spot not only what to do but how to do it which a later generation of Flag Officers was to find particularly objectionable. Carden, however, replied expressing his agreement with the Admiralty's purposes. Next night (13–14 March) the sweepers made a new attempt to clear a channel up to The Narrows – and failed. Only one possibility now remained – namely to silence the forts and so allow the sweepers to get on with clearance of the minefields in daylight. Orders were accordingly issued on the 15th; but on that same day Carden resigned his command on grounds of ill health.

Two days later Churchill appointed Admiral J. M. de Robeck, whom he has described as 'a good seaman and a fine disciplinarian', as his successor – which certainly was an improvement. On the 18th de Robeck put the new daylight plan of attack into action, and by the early afternoon the forts defending The Narrows were nearly silenced. Unfortunately ten days earlier a small Turkish steamer had laid a line of twenty mines parallel to the Asiatic shore unobserved, and that small effort turned the scale by causing the loss of three old battle-ships (two British and one French), and three other big ships (including a battle-cruiser) were put out of action. Yet evidence received after the war from German and Turkish sources does suggest that a deter-mined effort, mounted quickly after this check might well have brought success; and Churchill has accepted such statements at face value.[15]

Meanwhile in London Hankey, who had all along pressed for the despatch of troops and for thorough preparations to be made for a combined operation, had sent Asquith a comprehensive statement regarding the measures and equipment needed;[16] but the War Council took no action on it, and when Hankey warned Churchill that, at the best, landings in face of powerful defences would be 'of extraordinary difficulty' the latter optimistically riposted 'that he could not see that there was any difficulty at all'[17] a remark which reveals with dis-concerting clarity one of his blind spots. On the 19th, the day after the check below The Narrows, Hankey recorded in this diary how, from the very beginning he had warned Ministers and soldiers that the 'Fleet could not effect [the] passage without troops', and had also 'urged Churchill to have troops to co-operate, but he wouldn't listen, insisting that [the] Navy could do it alone'. He believed that 'Churchill wanted to bring off [the] coup by Navy alone to rehabilitate his reputation, which was damaged (unjustly) by [the] Antwerp affair' of October 1914[18] – a piece of conjecture to which Churchill's vigorous support of the naval attack lends weight.

The reader will recall that one of the arguments originally used in favour of the purely naval attack was that it could always be broken off if it ran into trouble. It is therefore difficult to understand why it was not called off after the repulse of 18 March. The only explanation surely is that no commander likes to admit failure – especially in the face of the involvement of a First Lord of Churchill's energy and ruthlessness. At any rate de Robeck at first expressed the intention of trying again – a view which Churchill supported whole-heartedly, and which even Fisher favoured. Only the Generals, who had witnessed the bombardment of the 18th, were sceptical; but as they were not yet ready to launch an amphibious assault their views carried less weight than they should have done. Then on the 22nd came a complete volte-face by de Robeck, who announced at a conference on board his flagship that 'he was now quite clear [that] he could not get through without the help of all my [i.e. General Hamilton's] troops';[19] and the earliest date the army could be ready was 14 April. Churchill tells us that he read de Robeck's resultant telegram 'with consternation', which is probably no exaggeration; but he complains that at the ensuing War Council none of the admirals present (Fisher, Wilson and Jackson) supported his desire to press the C-in-C to renew the attempt.[20] On the 24th Churchill himself sent de Robeck a long and fervent appeal; but it had no effect beyond producing a clear and forceful appreciation of the situation – which the First Lord reluctantly accepted. But for him to write that the admiral's views were actuated by 'a sentimental' regard for his 'sacred' battleships is both unfair to de Robeck and disregards all the experience recently gained. In truth de Robeck's decision must have demanded considerable moral courage, and for Churchill to write that 'The "No" principle had become established in men's minds, and nothing could ever eradicate it' is wholly unjustified.[21] It also ignores the flimsy arguments on which the whole concept of the naval attack had been based – and pressed by Churchill himself.

We are not here concerned with the details of later events at the Dardanelles. Moreover the story of the terribly costly assaults at Cape Helles and Anzac Cove on 25 April, and the subsequent stalemate with the heights commanding The Narrows still in enemy hands, has often been told.[22] But mention must be made of the final tragedy of the lost opportunity which followed the successful surprise landing behind the western flank of the enemy at Suvla Bay on 6 August – because the incompetence of the elderly commanding General Sir Frederick Stopford (who had retired in 1909), and General Hamilton's reluctance to step in and *order* him to press ahead and seize the advantage won by the initial surprise, must have influenced Churchill profoundly – though with regard to the military rather than the naval leadership of combined operations.

On 12 May the elderly battleship *Goliath* was sunk by a Turkish torpedo-boat, and Fisher now tried to deprive de Robeck of any initiative.* Though Churchill at first refused to 'paralyse' the admiral

---

* It is interesting to note Fisher's reference on 12 May to Churchill's *'ceaseless prodding'*

he finally gave way entirely to Fisher.[28] None the less on the 14th the old admiral wrote to Hankey in terms which stressed his view that the First Lord 'had been unreasonable'.[24] Plainly a crisis of the first magnitude was imminent, and publication by *The Times* of reports on the alleged shell shortage in France on that same day certainly stoked it.

Early on 15 May Fisher received proposals from Churchill for many more ships to be sent to the Dardanelles than had been agreed between them the previous evening. It was the last straw, and convinced the admiral that there would never be any finality to Churchill's demands, and that agreements reached between them became invalid almost before the ink on them was dry. That same morning he carried out his frequently made threat to resign, and resisted all appeals and pressure to reconsider his decision. Worse still he absented himself from the Admiralty on the 17th when a sortie by the High Seas Fleet appeared imminent; and, finally, by his preposterous letter to Asquith of the 19th stating the terms on which he would return he utterly destroyed his own prospects. The Prime Minister was justified in telling the King that it 'indicated signs of mental aberration'; and Churchill's final judgement that 'hysteria rather than conspiracy' explained the admiral's extraordinary conduct – in other words that he suffered a nervous breakdown – is probably near to the truth and is certainly not lacking in generosity.[25]

On Churchill's side by 17 May it was plain that his position was shaky, and three days later Asquith decided that he could not stay at the Admiralty – despite the earnest pleadings to which he had been subjected by the incumbent. The only disagreeable note is that sounded by the appeals Churchill sent to Asquith pleading that some office in the government, even the lowest, should be given to him – which suggest that personal ambition played a big part in his conduct and purposes, and that love of power was a very strong feature in his character. He was in truth 'desperate to be retained in the government', and his wife later recorded that she 'thought he would die of grief' at his exclusion from a major office.[26] He had first refused Asquith's offer of the Colonial Office and then repented of it – which caused the Prime Minister to remark that 'the situation for Churchill has no other meaning than his own prospects'.[27] In the end he accepted what

---

(his italics) in a memorandum to Asquith. (Quoted Gilbert, *Churchill*, III, p. 427). This was exactly the description which Admiral Sir Andrew Cunningham was to apply to Churchill's many messages to him as C-in-C, Mediterranean in World War II. (See *A Sailor's Odyssey*, pp. 231-2) One wonders whether Cunningham had read or heard of Fisher's aphorism.

Anthony Trollope has described as 'the fainéant office of Chancellor of the Duchy of Lancaster',[28] without a seat in the Cabinet. But a sinecure post in which all real power and authority was lacking was most unlikely to provide an adequate outlet for his phenomenal energy, or scope for furthering, let alone fulfilling his burning ambition.

We can now see that the basic causes of the May crisis were, firstly, the clash between two men of powerful personality and active minds, both of whom were accustomed to getting their own way and were intolerant of opposition. Secondly there was the difference between their habits and hours of work – Churchill staying late in bed, resting each afternoon, and reaching a climax of activity in the small hours of the morning, while Fisher woke very early and probably did his best work before breakfast, but was tired out by the afternoon and took to his bed at about 9 p.m. – just when Churchill's mental machinery was getting into high gear. The late hours kept by Churchill, and his complete inconsiderateness about them, were to be a source of strain and irritation to his advisers and staff in both wars. Thirdly there was Churchill's interpretation of the Orders in Council establishing that the First Lord was solely responsible to the government and Parliament for all the Admiralty's business. Some First Lords never found it difficult to reconcile that responsibility with leaving professional matters in the hands of the Sea Lords; but to Churchill such a derogation of his power and his rights was unthinkable, and his stream of proposals, suggestions and criticisms understandably irritated Fisher. A more serious source of friction was Churchill's habit of initiating signals to the fleet, and only consulting the First Sea Lord *after* they had been sent. We saw earlier the unhappy consequences which such action had in the case of the escape of the *Goeben* and *Breslau*. Though even in this matter it can hardly be said that Churchill exceeded his lawful powers his methods did go dead against the accepted, and on the whole wise convention that initiative in such matters rested with the First Sea Lord.

It was the Dardanelles operation which brought all these powder trains together and then set a match to them. Yet, although it is undeniable that Churchill was the chief instigator of the campaign and that it was his pressure that prevented the naval attack being broken off, the contemporary obloquy heaped on his head now seems to have been very harsh and excessive. Even though it is pure speculation to argue that, if the Fleet had arrived off Constantinople Turkey would have thrown in the sponge, the strategic concept was at any rate greatly to be preferred to the 'carnage incomparable, and human squander'[29] of the frontal attacks in the west. Yet once again Churchill cannot be totally acquitted of responsibility for the failure of the attempt, since although it was inefficient minesweeping rather than ineffective gunfire which kept The Narrows closed to the fleet, he did exaggerate the effects of naval gunfire against fixed or mobile shore batteries. Then there was the really colossal blunder of starting the naval operations before adequate and properly trained military forces were available, so sacrificing the inestimable advantage of initial surprise. The final criticism which may be levelled against him in this context concerns his relations with his professional advisers. Churchill neither consulted the War Staff group adequately – notably by asking regularly for considered Staff Appreciations as the situation, which was always very complex, changed;* nor did he represent the top sailors' views adequately to the War Council. Taken together these faults and failings add up to a formidable indictment – though none of them are admitted in Churchill's historical defence of his actions.

As to Churchill's relations with the admirals, the combined effect of de Robeck's refusal to renew the attack after 18 March and Fisher's resignation undoubtedly left a very bitter taste in his mouth, and produced an ineradicable mistrust of senior naval officers whom he could not dominate. On the other hand the gallant, fire-eating Roger Keyes, de Robeck's Chief of Staff, who fought hard to improve the minesweeping organization and technique and pressed for renewal of the naval attack, rose correspondingly in Churchill's estimation. This accounts for his later blindness to Keyes's failing as C-in-C, Mediterranean in the 1920s, and to his recalling him for service in Hitler's war.

Professor Marder in his latest recapitulation of the Dardanelles campaign concludes that if the fleet had appeared off Constantinople there was a 50:50 chance that Turkey would have surrendered.[30] Despite the fact that the Turks were short of ammunition and stores, and had suffered heavy losses, it seems to this historian more likely that the Germans, who enjoyed the great advantage of interior lines of communication, would have got men and weapons to the shores of the Bosphorus far more quickly than the British could have done. Furthermore the fleet simply did not have the resources to occupy and control a city of about a million inhabitants – let alone set up adequate defence lines in the approaches to it from the west. Thus as long as troops were lacking, which was the case until late in April, it seems probable that a naval advance through The Narrows and across the

---

* Jackson was asked for appreciations early in January, but none were requested later.

Sea of Marmora would have resulted in as ignominious and costly a retreat from Constantinople as Admiral John Thomas Duckworth was forced to undertake in 1807. Though such speculations are in truth profitless, to the British the failure of 1915 will always seem fraught with tragedy; for it not only threw serious doubts on our competence to plan and conduct war operations efficiently but it revealed for the first time that, despite the splendid qualities of its fighting men, the greatest empire of the day might prove to be built on a foundation of sand.

Churchill sent Asquith two letters of resignation, on 30 October and 11 November, and in the latter he placed himself 'unreservedly at the disposal of the military authorities', hinting that he wished to join his regiment in France. He had, however, set his sights much higher when, a few days earlier, he asked Asquith to make him Governor and C-in-C in British East Africa.[31] That Churchill would have proved fully capable of carrying a high military command after he had gained adequate experience is very probable; but for him to leap at once far up in the army hierarchy, over other men's shoulders, could not possibly have been justified, and might well have been damaging to himself. In the event even the intention of Sir John French, who was soon to be dismissed as C-in-C in France, that Churchill should have a Brigade aroused hostility in London and was finally vetoed by Asquith – to Churchill's disappointment and anger.[32] He finally went to the Grenadier Guards for training as a Battalion Commander, and on 1 January 1916 he was appointed to command the 6th Royal Scots Fusiliers.

In the light of Churchill's later criticism of the British military leaders it is interesting to find that, during his early days in France he evidently got on as well with Sir Douglas Haig, who took over as C-in-C, BEF on 19 December 1915, as with his predecessor and other high-ranking soldiers; and he quickly won the confidence of the regimental officers who had initially viewed his appointment with alarm.[33] He also established himself as a brave and resourceful battalion commander, and won the admiration of his juniors; but he was all the time still hoping for a higher command and greater responsibilities.[34]

CHAPTER 4

Excluded
1915-1917

We here are not concerned with the details of Churchill's active service in France, which have been admirably described by his authorized biographer;[1] but his bloodstream was so inoculated with politics that neither the German shells and bullets in the Ypres salient nor the responsibility for caring for nearly 1000 officers and men, which he took very seriously, could keep his mind off events in and around the House of Commons and Downing Street. He was moreover greatly concerned to defend his part in the Dardanelles campaign by pressing the government to publish the relevant papers – a desire for vindication which, though understandable, can hardly be described as selfless or timely in the circumstances of 1916. Nor did his hopes for a return to office ever abate one whit. In January reports that the RN Air Service, in which Churchill had taken such a lively interest as First Lord, and the Royal Flying Corps were to be combined and placed under a new Minister caused him to tell his wife that he would certainly accept such a post, though he was sure that Asquith would not offer it to him.[2] He also kept in touch either through his ever-solicitous and clear-sighted wife or by direct correspondence with the principal political figures who might prove influential in the event of the First Coalition collapsing – such as Lloyd George, Bonar Law, F. E. Smith (later Lord Birkenhead), Carson and Curzon. It will be noted that all the foregoing except Lloyd George were Conservatives, while Churchill was of course still ostensibly a Liberal; but his rancour against Asquith, 'the fatal drag on our success' as he described him, remained unabated.[3] Thereby he linked his fortunes, most injudiciously and to Mrs Churchill's alarm, with 'Jacky' Fisher, who was also a strong critic of the Prime Minister and was working behind the scenes to return to the Admiralty. That Asquith might replace the ineffective First Sea Lord Admiral Sir Henry Jackson by Fisher aroused Churchill's grave misgivings. 'Fisher without me to manage him', he wrote to his wife on 2 February, 'wd be disastrous.' But the old admiral continued to intrigue, sometimes trying to involve Hankey in his interest,[4] and often enlisting the support of influential journalists such as J. L. Garvin of the *Observer* and C. P. Scott of the *Manchester Guardian*. Though

Hankey was too discreet and far-sighted to give any overt support to Fisher, Garvin gave publicity to the idea that Churchill should become Air Minister and Fisher return to the Admiralty. Nor was Lloyd George averse to the latter proposal, telling Lord Riddell, the owner of the *News of the World*, that 'Fisher has a genius for war'.[5] Churchill at this stage had no part in Fisher's intrigues, describing him as 'the old rogue' and probably realizing that, no matter what the newspapers might say, the admiral had no political support whatever. It was attacks in the *Morning Post* on the Admiralty's alleged neglect of the air defence of London under Churchill which first stimulated him to consider making a speech in his own defence while on leave in February 1916; and as the Admiralty had only taken on the air defence responsibility at Kitchener's request in order to release as much of the army as possible for France in September 1914 Churchill certainly could have answered such criticisms effectively – had he confined himself to that point.[6]

Ignoring his wife's misgivings and warnings Churchill met Fisher on 5 March, and he then read to the admiral the speech he intended to make during the forthcoming debate on the Navy Estimates. It comprised not only a strong attack on the conduct of naval affairs by the Balfour-Jackson régime but an appeal for Fisher's immediate return to the office of First Sea Lord – whereby he hoped to show that for the country's sake he had buried the hatchet of May 1915.[7] The admiral was not slow to seize his chance, and next day he sent Churchill the first of a series of typically hortatory, passionate and adjectival letters – ending *'To win the War . . . do we two coalesce! We can do it! Come on!'* Asquith, on hearing of Churchill's intentions, considered them most unwise; but Churchill, probably stimulated and excited by Fisher's forecast that *'You can be Prime Minister if you like'* was not to be deterred, and proceeded to furnish all his critics and enemies with evidence that 'he lacked the mature judgement of statesmanship'.[8] That Fisher was largely responsible for this fatal mistake is undeniable.

Churchill spoke from the Opposition front bench late in the afternoon of Tuesday 7 March 1916. After recapitulating what he, with Battenberg and Fisher, had accomplished at the Admiralty, he turned to the attack on the failure to complete the building programmes which he had initiated; and his indictment of the failure to deal with the submarine menace and the Zeppelin raids, as well as the non-completion of naval building programmes, was extremely severe and effective, though in some respects it now seems exaggerated. The

House, however, listened with rapt attention – until Churchill came to his peroration – urging Balfour 'without delay to fortify himself, to vitalize and animate his Board of Admiralty by recalling Lord Fisher to his post as First Sea Lord'. Hankey, who attended the debate, described in a letter to his wife how 'Jacky was sitting just in front of me with a face like an Indian god', and how Balfour's speech in defence of the Admiralty was received in 'profound and ominous silence', but there 'were unmistakable and loud murmurs of assent' when Churchill 'said the Board lacked driving power'. But, he continued, 'his suggestion to bring Fisher back was received only moderately enthusiastically' – which was a considerable understatement.[9] According to Churchill's biographer it was received 'in stunned silence', and his friends and supporters were anguished; while the government seized the weapon he had placed in their hands and reacted swiftly and savagely. Balfour's speech of 8 March was, coming from a Minister who was usually so suave and courteous, a deadly riposte – to which Churchill could make no effective answer.

Though Fisher had intended to continue his campaign in the House of Lords Hankey gave him a strong hint to keep quiet. But the admiral still entertained hopes that Churchill, who asked to give up his military command and stay in England in order 'to give undivided attention to Parliamentary and public business', would continue the fight on his behalf. If Churchill was extraordinarily naïve in believing that his appeal to recall Fisher would be taken as an act of magnanimity put forward in the national interest, and Fisher blind to the fact that his day had passed for good, Asquith realized that he now had nothing to fear from the former and that the latter was a spent force. On 11 and 12 March Fisher tried, in letters to Hankey and Churchill, to convince the former that the government was about to fall and to persuade the latter to stay in England and continue the fight; but Mrs Churchill saw the situation clearly, and bravely persuaded her husband that he should return, even if only temporarily, to his battalion and so miss taking part in the debate on the Army Estimates. Yet his experience had convinced him that his 'true war station' was the House of Commons';[10] and it was of course quite absurd that a leader of his quality should continue to risk his life in France for a day longer than was essential. Yet there was real danger that if he returned to politics too soon his position would be further, and perhaps fatally weakened; and all the time there hung over the scene the severity of the depression which struck him, and of which his wife was so deeply conscious, when things went wrong for him. Fisher of course did not suffer from any such psychosis.

That Fisher did great harm to Churchill in May 1915 and again in March of the following year, in the long as well as the short view, is surely indisputable. His main purpose was on both occasions to gain power for himself; and on the second of them he used Churchill's own ambition and love of power to further his ends. It now seems surprising that Churchill should have ignored the warnings and pleadings of his wife and intimate friends when in 1916 Fisher saw, or thought he saw, an opportunity to rectify the fatal error of his letter to Asquith of 19 May 1915 demanding supreme power in naval affairs; and to this historian the defence proffered by Churchill's biographer, namely that the explanation for his extraordinary proposal of 7 March 1916 lies in the fact that he had during the previous months been 'cut off from the inner working of politics, rejected, as he believed, by his former colleagues, and denied any place in a Government in which he believed he could play a decisive part' does not seem convincing;[11] since even while in France he had sufficient correspondence and encounters with politicians and journalists of many shades of opinion to keep him adequately informed about what was going on at home. If that be accepted the only explanation for his blunder must surely lie in the defective judgement of which so many contemporary politicians accused him.

On Fisher's side it is difficult to find any excuses for his conduct. Though it is true that he had always pursued his aims by means of reiteration, exaggerated emphasis and the production of short easily remembered aphorisms to support his arguments and theories, it is difficult not to feel that by early 1916 these habits, bred of long years of controversy, had become so ingrained that his mental condition was at the best unbalanced and at the worst verged on lunacy. We will return later to the long-term, slowly developed effects of Fisher's conduct on Churchill's outlook towards admirals in general; but here it may be remarked that in my opinion Professor Marder exaggerates Fisher's qualities and plays down his faults by describing him in his final *summa* as 'A man truly great despite his idiosyncracies and truly good despite his faults'.[12] For his actions in 1915–16 were surely worse than idiosyncratic; while the harm he did to Churchill, taken with the motives which inspired his conduct, makes the Professor's attribution of goodness to him read rather oddly. Not until the clash of arms was over does Fisher appear to have realized the consequences of what he had done, writing 'Everyone is running Winston down, nevertheless he has the fighting necessities in him: COURAGE, AUDACITY, CELERITY,

IMAGINATION': and again 'He had courage and imagination. He was a war man!'[13] But by then it was too late to repair the damage he had done.

The months of March and April 1916 were a difficult period for Churchill; for while his wife was warning him of the danger of too precipitate a return he could not but be aware that public dissatisfaction with the conduct of the war was rising, and that the First Coalition might fall to pieces at any time. As to strategy, the experiences of the offensives at Loos, Arras and in Champagne, and the prodigious slaughter on both sides at Verdun had convinced him of the futility of frontal attacks in France; and he still wanted to concentrate on the destruction of Turkey, though he produced no clear plan regarding how this was to be accomplished. As regards the war at sea he accepted the need to strengthen the battle squadrons of the Grand Fleet and to remedy the deficiencies from which it suffered; but he also saw that the submarine menace had by no means been mastered, and that the naval air service had not developed the potential which he had foreseen before the war. For the Balfour-Jackson régime at the Admiralty his contempt was little if at all less than Fisher's.

Early in May 1916 the break-up of Churchill's battalion provided the opportunity, now favoured by his wife, for his permanent return to politics, his request was approved, and the warmth of the farewell given to him by the officers and men with whom he had shared the hardship of trench warfare speaks volumes for his qualities of leadership.[14]

In Churchill's first speech in the House of Commons after his return home he vigorously defended the Admiralty when it had been under his control, both as regards the defence of London against bombing by Zeppelins and the alleged priority given before the war to the production of aeroplanes instead of airships, mentioned earlier. He was moreover absolutely right in the strictures he directed against the Air Board, recently set up by Asquith under Lord Curzon, which proved totally unfitted to cope with the problems produced by the advent of the new arm, and with the prevailing superiority of German aircraft – of which Churchill had recent first-hand experience in France.[15] His recommendation was for the creation of an Air Ministry with powers equivalent to those of the older departments; and, as we saw earlier, he was willing, even anxious, to be appointed its first head. But this, and subsequent defence of his own actions and policies, and his attacks on the government, had little impact because of his lack of Parliamentary support. Churchill's isolation was so complete, and the government spokesmen's rejection of his criticisms so contemptuous, that it is perhaps not altogether surprising that at the end of May he should have written to Fisher suggesting another meeting;[16] but nothing came of it, nor could do so as long as the First Coalition clung to office. To us it is only of interest in showing how oblivious Churchill was to the damage Fisher had done him.

On 31 May 1916 there took place in the North Sea the only major encounter of the war between the two sides' battle fleets. The tactical success achieved by the Germans, and the far heavier losses they inflicted, together with the inept first communiqué issued by the Admiralty, shrouded and concealed the fact that the Germans had suffered a strategic defeat, and that they were no nearer achieving command of the *surface* waters of the North Sea than before. But the outcome of the encounter was a severe shock to the British public, which had confidently expected a second Trafalgar. Furthermore it is a striking commentary on the incapacity and unimaginativeness of the Balfour-Jackson régime that Churchill should have been called in to help draft the more balanced communiqué on the battle by which the government hoped to remedy the damage done by the first one.

Though another ten years were to elapse before Churchill publicly involved himself in the 'Jutland Controversy' by giving the battle a large amount of space in the third volume of his memoirs he can hardly have been unaware that the controversy between the pro-Jellicoe and pro-Beatty factions had begun to simmer while the war was still in progress. Moreover it was stoked by the publication of a censored version of Jellicoe's despatch on the battle, together with Beatty's report on 24 June. Thus it is reasonable to summarize here the views and conclusions which Churchill finally put forward. He begins his account by outlining Jellicoe's qualities and experience, and admits that he 'was the only man on either side who could lose the war in an afternoon'[17] – by the Grand Fleet suffering a decisive defeat. But thereafter the general tone of his account is strongly pro-Beatty. It is plain that Churchill had access to, among other documents relating to the battle, the secret 'Naval Staff Appreciation' written by the brothers A. C. and K. G. B. Dewar at the behest of Beatty after he had become First Sea Lord in 1919. Indeed some of Churchill's criticisms of Jellicoe's tactics follow very closely, and at times are almost verbatim reproductions of the arguments put forward by the Dewar brothers.* Such is his case for

* By an odd series of coincidences Jellicoe's copy of this book came into the possession of the author shortly before the death of Sir Frank Spickernell, the Admiral's one-time secretary, who had preserved it when in 1928 Admiral Sir Charles Madden, Jellicoe's

deployment of the Grand Fleet from its cruising formation of six columns disposed abeam into single line ahead. The Dewars suggested . that deployment on the centre column was preferable to deployment on either of the wing columns, and Churchill followed them closely. Indeed his diagram of the alternative deployments is clearly based on the one in the Staff Appreciation.[18]

The Dewar brothers were early examples of officers who have been described as 'military intellectuals',[19] and because they both had a strongly developed critical sense they aroused a good deal of mistrust, and even dislike among more conventional officers. Yet when in 1928 K. G. B. Dewar was in deep trouble over the so-called 'Royal Oak Incident', and was to be tried by Court Martial,[20] Churchill wrote to W. C. Bridgeman the First Lord, protesting that 'If officers of that distinction are to be punished with such severity for making a complaint absolutely justified in fact [about Rear-Admiral B. St G. Collard's conduct], though irregular in form what chance has an ordinary rating of having his grievances considered? The moral of these Courts Martial seems most threatening to all ranks and ratings who have cause to complain of harsh or unjust treatment . . . The Navy cannot afford to lose men like Dewar.'[21] It is therefore obvious, firstly, that Churchill had earlier associations with Dewar – notably over Jutland and also the introduction of convoy in 1917 – and, secondly, that he was much in sympathy with his thought and outlook. Richmond also went into action with Bridgeman on behalf of Dewar, quoting the first Lord Hood's definition of a good staff officer that 'he should always be an honest and candid counsellor and adviser' equipped with 'that fearlessness of responsibility, both in his opinions and his acts, that [Lord] St Vincent called the first test of a man's courage'. Obviously Richmond considered that Dewar met those requirements fully; and he urged that he should not be placed on the retired list.[22]

To return to the 'Naval Staff Appreciation' Jellicoe's complaint that it was 'a purely Battle Cruiser Fleet account, looked at with BCF eyes' had substance in it. Churchill's admiration for courage and *élan*, and his dislike for cautious prudence in war made him temperamentally far more sympathetic towards Beatty than Jellicoe; and that probably explains why his account of Jutland plays down, or totally ignores what may reasonably be described as tactical mistakes by Beatty. Such

Chief of Staff at Jutland, ordered all copies to be destroyed shortly after he succeeded Beatty as First Sea Lord. This copy has marked in it the deletions which presumably Jellicoe would have asked for had Beatty's intention to circulate it confidentially been carried out.

were, firstly, his failure to keep the very powerful and fast 5th Battle Squadron (four *Queen Elizabeths* mounting thirty-two 15-inch guns) in close support of his six more lightly armed and much less well protected battle-cruisers; secondly the error in fire distribution which resulted in one of Admiral Hipper's five battle-cruisers being left unmolested at a critical stage of the first clash; and, thirdly, the muddle over Beatty's order to the 5th Battle Squadron to turn 180 degrees to the north when he himself executed such a turn in order to continue the fight on a parallel instead of an opposite course to Hipper's.[23] Furthermore Churchill is highly critical of Jellicoe turning the Grand Fleet away from instead of towards the enemy when, later in the day, Admiral Scheer sent his destroyers in to make torpedo attacks on the Grand Fleet in order to cover the 180 degree 'Battle Turn Away' needed to extract himself from the extreme danger produced by the cordon of battleships which Jellicoe had placed right across his line of retreat.[24] In sum Churchill's account of Jutland lacks balance and cannot be said to have stood the test of time. His concluding remark that the navy's accomplishments and reputation owed most 'to Beatty and the battle-cruisers, to Keyes at Zeebrugge [of which more will be said later], to Tyrwhitt and his Harwich striking force . . .' shows very clearly where his sympathies lay.[25]

For the purpose of this study Churchill's attitude towards the admirals named above helps to explain a good deal of his conduct towards top naval men in later years, and especially as a Minister in Lloyd George's post-war Coalition government and as Chancellor of the Exchequer 1924–9 under Baldwin; for he then showed greater respect for the views and purposes of Beatty as First Sea Lord than for any other admiral of the period with the possible exception of Keyes. In Churchill's eyes those two possessed the qualities he most admired – physical courage, a high degree of stamina and determination, and an unflagging resolve to strike offensive blows at the enemy. Keyes had of course won Churchill's heart by his strenuous efforts to persuade de Robeck to renew the naval attack at the Dardanelles, and by his attempts to persuade Asquith and his colleagues to persevere with that undertaking; while it was the dashing spirit and willingness to accept risks shown by Beatty in the North Sea battles, from Heligoland Bight to Jutland, that caused Churchill mentally to place him in the Valhalla reserved for Britain's greatest naval leaders, and to disqualify Jellicoe from inclusion in such company. There may also have been social aspects which favoured Beatty, since the vast wealth of his American-born wife enabled him to move in the aristocratic circle which Churchill enjoyed as a side product of his lineage.

By the time the battle of Jutland was fought Churchill realized that his return to power depended very largely on public and Parliamentary criticism of his part in the Dardanelles campaign being answered by the publication of at least the most important papers – such as those which proved that in late February he had pressed for the despatch of substantial military forces. Fisher was of like mind, though it was his attempted resignation on 28 January 1915 on which he laid chief emphasis. And so it came to pass that these two once more found themselves in alliance, though their object was not now the more effective prosecution of the war but the less commendable one of self-justification.[26] As regards Churchill this purpose was, at any rate in his eyes, justified by his confidence that he, and only he, could bring greater drive and energy to the conduct of the war as a whole, and the naval and air aspects in particular, and could also find a more effective and less costly strategy than the frontal attacks on the western front. But Fisher can only have been aiming at the more limited purpose of achieving his own return to the office of First Sea Lord – which almost all people of influence regarded as quite out of the question. General Hamilton, now back in London, had a similar self-justificatory purpose, and joined the other two in pressing for publication of papers. But whereas the above mentioned trio were in the main looking at the past the government was more concerned with the future than with analysing water which had long since flowed under the bridge of time. However, Kitchener's death when the cruiser *Hampshire* was sunk on her way to Russia on 5 June knocked the stuffing out of Hamilton's indictment of the War Minister's neglect of his many requests for more men and ammunition.[27]

Though Churchill probably did hope that if Lloyd George moved to the War Office he himself would be given the Ministry of Munitions Asquith had no such intentions, and temporarily took on the vacant post himself. Furthermore the Prime Minister had become increasingly reluctant to publish the Dardanelles documents, partly because of the discredit which might thereby be brought on his government, and partly, one may guess, from unwillingness to stir up heated controversy in the middle of a great war. Hankey was brought into the argument, and his opposition to publishing the government's secret deliberations so soon after the event was surely justified. The Foreign Office insisted that all diplomatic telegrams should be withheld, while the Admiralty and War Office were equally reluctant to release their sides of the story.[28] Plainly by July the fulfilment of Churchill's purpose, let alone that of Fisher and Hamilton, had become remote.

On 18 July Asquith withdrew the offer he had made to Churchill six weeks earlier to publish the principal documents, and told the House of Commons that none would be published – to Churchill's great indignation.[29] However, after a long debate Asquith agreed, to Hamilton's fury, to set up Select Committees to inquire into both the Dardanelles and the Mesopotamian campaigns.[30] We here are not concerned with the latter inquiry, but a Select Committee was of course not at all what Churchill had hoped for in order to vindicate himself and make his return to office possible.

It is unnecessary to follow the story of the great effort Churchill and Fisher put into preparing their evidence for the Dardanelles Commission. Hankey was the person on whom the greatest share of the work fell, because he was to be the chief government witness – and even chief counsel for the defence of the government. In addition to preparing his own monumental brief he went to great trouble to help both Churchill and Fisher prepare their evidence – probably because he had always admired and got on well with both of them – except with Fisher at the time of his resignation and disappearance from the Admiralty.[31] Churchill and Fisher also collaborated together closely, and one result of this was that neither they nor Hankey said a word about the admiral's extraordinary conduct in May 1915.[32] Yet after studying the vast mountain of paper produced by the Commission, and the two comprehensive reports produced by it, one is left with a feeling of astonishment that the government could have agreed to a protracted post-mortem at such a time of crisis. And, though Fisher came well out of his presentation of evidence, it did not further his hopes one whit; while for Churchill the grotesquely biased conclusions of the Commission were a severe blow, and as his own voluminous evidence was not published, the inquiry did not bring him an inch nearer to the vindication he was seeking.[33]

During the summer of 1916 Churchill continued his attacks on the government on many counts, but especially the futility of the Somme offensive – which had been launched during Asquith's temporary tenure at the War Office. Nor did the Admiralty escape the lash of his tongue, chiefly on the score of failure to get the building programmes initiated by himself and Fisher completed; but his rhetoric made little impact except that his criticisms were received in friendly manner by Lloyd George.[34]

The political crisis which resulted in the fall of Asquith and the

First Coalition in December 1916 has often been described, and will not be repeated here. To Churchill the chief danger was that Bonar Law might come to power as head of a Conservative government; since he would certainly have excluded Churchill from office. But if Lloyd George became the new Prime Minister his prospects would be greatly enhanced, since he was well aware of Churchill's abilities, and had often lent a friendly ear to his criticisms of Asquith's administration. After many manoeuvres and changes of mind Lloyd George finally resigned, and on 5 December the leading Conservatives in the Coalition did likewise. With his government in dissolution Asquith tendered his own resignation that evening, and the King then sent for Bonar Law and invited him to form an administration. Lloyd George was willing to serve under Law, and Churchill's future hung in the balance. Asquith, however, refused to serve in such a government, and after a meeting of the leaders of all three parties at Buckingham Palace on the 6th, Law gave up the attempt. That evening the King sent for Lloyd George who thereupon became Prime Minister of the Second Coalition, from which Asquith was excluded; nor was Churchill considered for any place except possibly that of Air Minister – had an Air Ministry been created. His exclusion undoubtedly derived from Conservative hostility, which overcame Lloyd George's readiness to give him office. The Admiralty was given to Carson, a greatly inferior man to Churchill in every way, while Balfour moved to the Foreign Office. Public and Press criticisms of Churchill's part in Antwerp and the Dardanelles, together with Asquith's refusal to publish papers about the latter, and the widespread mistrust which he had aroused by his 'strident self-confidence', had damaged his prospects irreparably – as it then seemed. Only Mrs Churchill both fully understood the cause of the mistrust and told him what had produced it.[35] Although the view expressed by Churchill in 1916 that history would vindicate his policies and achievements has in the main proved true, we are today able to understand more clearly than was possible at the time the faults of character and method which brought him to the sorry pass.

Perhaps the most puzzling feature of the period covered by this chapter is the seemingly irresistible attraction which Fisher had for Churchill. Despite all that had happened in May 1915 he was drawn to the old admiral again and again as surely as steel filings are drawn to a magnet. Fisher's personality was of course magnetic, but by 1915 his violence of temperament and expression had become obsessive. That Churchill, unlike his wife, did not appreciate what a dangerous ally he was suggests, as later experience was to confirm, that judgement of character was not Churchill's strong suit. Yet, as will be told in due course, there are good grounds for believing that, perhaps as a result of his wife's clearer understanding of Fisher's faults, the association between them did in the end greatly influence Churchill's attitude towards the admirals of a later generation.

CHAPTER 5

Recall
1917-1918

Despite Lloyd George being favourably disposed towards Churchill it took the three-fold crisis of 1917, namely the total and costly failure of General Nivelle's offensive on the Chemin des Dames in April leading to widespread mutinies in the French army, the collapse of Russia which released huge German forces to the western front, and perhaps above all the increasing success of the German unrestricted submarine campaign to enable Lloyd George to overcome Conservative mistrust and recall him to office as Minister of Munitions on 17 July 1917. We here are not concerned with the military disasters of 1917; but the naval problems of the period affected Churchill's attitude towards the Admiralty and its senior officers profoundly.

The indecisive outcome of the battle of Jutland and the effects on Jellicoe's health of over two years in command of the Grand Fleet brought about a crisis of confidence in his leadership. Moreover there was a rising star in the fleet in the colourful personality of Admiral Sir David Beatty, who had commanded the Grand Fleet's battle-cruiser force since the beginning of the war, and had shown great verve if less than complete tactical success in all the actions in which he had been engaged, such as Heligoland Bight on 28 August 1914, the Dogger Bank fight of 24 January 1915 and at Jutland. Moreover his personality was far more arresting, not to say flamboyant than Jellicoe's, which made him very much the type of leader admired by Churchill. Although early in the war Beatty had been highly critical of Churchill as First Lord, notably over his involvement in the Antwerp fiasco of October 1914, and had been dubious of his wisdom in recalling Fisher as First Sea Lord,[1] he was widely held to be more 'offensively minded', in both the tactical and strategical sense, than Jellicoe; and that was bound to appeal to Churchill who as First Lord was, as already mentioned, always searching for a 'naval offensive'.

Jellicoe was accordingly called to take Jackson's place as First Sea Lord at the end of November 1916; but he was allowed hardly any rest before taking up an appointment which, in some respects, was more taxing and arduous than that which he had vacated.[2] Moreover the streak of pessimism in his character, to which many first-hand

observers have borne witness, had become more marked – perhaps
as a result of his physical ailments. Though Churchill had of course no
hand in Jellicoe's appointment, and had regarded Jackson as a poor
substitute for Fisher, his mistrust of the judgement, imagination and
general capacity of the former did not come to a head until early in
1918; nor did he and Beatty get on more intimate terms until after the
latter had taken command of the Grand Fleet. However, once Churchill
had returned to office and was seeing all State papers and important
Admiralty signals his earlier conviction that the submarine threat was
not being handled with enough drive, energy and imagination must
surely have been strengthened; and he cannot have remained unaware
of Jellicoe's defeatism about finding an effective antidote, and of his
chronic pessimism – which contributed to the terribly costly decision
to continue the Third Battle of Ypres into the autumn of 1917 with
the object of capturing the Belgian ports of Ostend and Zeebrugge.
In fact, as the larger U-boats were all operating from Germany's
North Sea naval bases, the capture of the Belgian ports would have
made little difference to the defeat of the threat.

The issue came to a head when Commander (later Admiral Sir
Reginald) Henderson, who was serving on the Admiralty's War
Staff, discovered that the monthly statistics recording the safe arrivals
and losses of merchant ships prepared by the Admiralty contained a
highly misleading element. Because they included coastal shipping,
which might call at several ports within a short period and so come to
be counted several times among the 'safe arrivals', the total of the
latter became greatly inflated by comparison with losses – most of
which were of ocean-going steamers. Henderson passed this information to Hankey in strict confidence, because to act behind the
backs of his superiors might well have proved fatal to his career; but
Norman (later Sir Norman) Leslie, the liaison officer between the
Admiralty and the Ministry of Shipping, was almost certainly let
into the secret by Henderson, while Hankey probably gave the information to General Smuts, who was a member of the Imperial War
Cabinet and with whom he was on intimate terms, in order to gain his
support if the matter came before the Cabinet.[3] Henderson, Leslie
and Hankey all believed that only the adoption of the traditional
strategy of convoy could save the situation; but Jellicoe and Admiral
Duff, the Director of the Anti-Submarine Division of the naval staff,
and the Board of Admiralty as a whole, were totally opposed to such a
step, on the grounds that sufficient escorts could not be provided, that
convoy would delay the turn-round of ships and cause unacceptable

congestion in the ports of departure and arrival, and would provide larger and easier targets for the U-boats. Lloyd George himself was at first lukewarm about adopting convoy,[4] but when in February 1917 shipping losses rose to 540,000 tons and in April to the enormous total of 881,000 tons it was obvious that drastic measures had to be adopted. On the last day of that month Hankey circulated a paper which was in sum a strong indictment of the Admiralty's policy and attitude. On that same day Lloyd George, supported by Hankey, went to the Admiralty to discuss the matter with Carson and Jellicoe.[5] He did not, as Beaverbrook wrote, 'seat himself in the First Lord's chair' and dictate what should be done,[6] for the simple reason that the Admiralty had recently changed its mind. Four days earlier Duff had proposed that convoy should be adopted, and Jellicoe had approved that an experimental convoy should be organized and escorted home from Gibraltar on 10 May – which voyage it completed without loss. Thereafter the new strategy was gradually put into practice, and shipping losses steadily fell.

Hankey always regarded his part in getting convoy adopted as his greatest contribution to winning the war, and Lloyd George recalled two years later that he thereby performed 'a great service'; but to Churchill, sitting on the side lines and receiving confidences from many sources, the long delay in introducing convoy must have lent support to his increasingly low opinion of the Admiralty in general and of Jellicoe in particular. Nor had Carson proved a great improvement on Balfour as First Lord; not least because in Hankey's view he was as bad a pessimist as Jellicoe.[7] Not only was Carson anxious to leave the Admiralty, where he found the top admirals difficult to work with, but Lloyd George had, probably because of the long delay over the adoption of convoy, lost confidence in him and wanted to replace him by 'a thoroughly capable business man'[8] – a type of person to whom he was fond of delegating particular aspects of running governing departments. In the event his choice fell on Sir Eric Geddes, whose experience lay chiefly in railway management, and who was already Controller of the Navy (then a civilian appointment) with responsibility for shipbuilding.

The new First Lord, who was not remarkable for his tact, soon got on bad terms with Jellicoe, and after consulting Lloyd George he dismissed him somewhat ungraciously on 24 December 1917, having previously ensured that the First Sea Lord's deputy Admiral Sir Rosslyn Wemyss was prepared to take his place.[9] Though this action provoked a threat of resignation by the other Sea Lords Geddes unquestionably acted within his rights and had no difficulty in quelling the revolt in the Board of Admiralty.[10] To Churchill the whole story of the delay in introducing convoy and the dismissal of Jellicoe plainly strengthened his mistrust of senior naval men – as his memoirs plainly show.[11] If the naval events and errors of 1916 and 1917 produced in Churchill's mind the feeling, amounting to conviction, that he was a far better Captain of War than the top admirals, the army's mistakes, such as the misuse of the first tanks in the Somme battle and the obsession with frontal attacks in the west, had exactly the same effect with regard to the top soldiers, and especially Generals Robertson (CIGS December 1915–February 1918) and Haig (C-in-C, BEF from December 1915). Though the army story has no place in this study these personal prejudices are important to us because without knowledge of them much of Churchill's conduct in World War II cannot be understood. As to Fisher, he of course tried to reap advantage and further his hopes by drawing attention to the fact that the prophecies he had made before the war had nearly all come true, using Hankey as the medium through whom he still hoped that his claims would be recognized by the Cabinet; but although Hankey always answered the old admiral's letters courteously he was far too astute and clear sighted not to realize that Fisher's sun had in fact set for ever in May 1915.[12]

Second only to finding the solution to the submarine menace in 1917 came the improvement in the use of the new weapon of air power, of which, as told earlier, Churchill had been a strong protagonist ever since he went to the Admiralty in 1911, but towards which not a few admirals were a good deal less than enthusiastic. Churchill had from the beginning held that a unified air service was the right principle and that the navy's aircraft and flying personnel should remain a wing of the Royal Flying Corps. In June 1914 he recorded that 'he had always looked on the Naval and Military Wings as branches of one great service';[13] and as long as he remained First Lord that organization continued. It has already been told how in July 1915, little more than two months after Churchill's dismissal, the Admiralty brought the RNAS under their own wing as 'an integral part of the Royal Navy'.[14] Thereby they sowed the seeds of an acrimonious inter-service controversy which lasted for more than twenty years.

Churchill himself had, while serving in France, witnessed the effects of the prevailing German superiority in the air, and in speeches in Parliament he had proposed the formation of an Air Ministry. Under the Admiralty, however, the RNAS did, despite prejudice on the part of certain senior officers, make good progress in some directions – though not those concerned exclusively with the use of aircraft in the naval war. For example bomber squadrons were formed and sent deep into France with the object of carrying out under Admiralty orders what later came to be called Strategic Bombing. This action so infuriated Haig, the C-in-C, BEF, that the squadrons had to be withdrawn or placed under the army commander. But the main source of friction was that the Admiralty, being unlike the War Office a supply department which placed all the contracts required to meet its own needs, ordered aircraft, engines and other aeronautical equipment in direct competition with the needs of the RFC.[15] This state of affairs, and the Admiralty's attempt to boycott Curzon's Air Board aroused the fury of its head, who sent the Cabinet long papers describing the department's methods in vitriolic language. Though Balfour as First Lord showed his usual dialectical skill in defending the Admiralty, the feeling that the prevailing state of affairs could not be allowed to continue became increasingly strong. Accordingly in 1916 a new Air Board was established under Lord Cowdray with far wider powers than the Curzon Board. It was in effect though not in name an Air Ministry.

The next step was the creation of a committee under General Smuts in July 1917 to examine the whole programme and recommend what organization should govern and administer the air services.[16] Those who wanted an Air Ministry and an independent air service gained an unexpected ally in Beatty, who told the Admiralty that he saw no reason why the new service should not meet naval needs, though he insisted that training should 'be exclusively naval'.[17] Perhaps this rather muddled thinking arose, at any rate in part, from the failure to make any effective use of air reconnaissance on the day of the battle of Jutland; but Beatty's views obviously embarrassed the Admiralty when it came to presenting their case to the Smuts Committee. Recent changes in the department had left the Board in some disarray, which made it difficult to get a well-argued case for retention of the RNAS prepared – though Geddes himself was dubious about accepting the Smuts Committee's recommendations.[18] Churchill and Curzon supported the Smuts report, the former probably because he was well aware of the confusion and duplication on the supply side, and had always favoured a unified air service; while the latter had so recently experienced the Admiralty's obstructive attitude towards the Air Board that he would obviously prefer any alternative to continuation of the prevailing state of affairs. The Cabinet approved the recommendations of the Smuts Committee in their entirety, and it therefore only remained to create the new Ministry and the Royal Air Force. The only important concession achieved by the Admiralty during these negotiations was that they successfully resisted the attempted take-over of the aircraft and seaplane carriers themselves. The actual birth of the RAF can be dated to 5 February 1918 when the King signed an Order in Council; but the 2500 naval aircraft and 55,000 officers and men were not transferred until 1 April. The most serious result of the change from the navy's point of view was that it lost almost all its experienced aviators; and neither Churchill, Beatty nor Wemyss foresaw the unhappy results this would bring about when in World War II the aircraft carrier displaced the big gun battleship as the dominant instrument in maritime war. It is of course impossible to say what the result of the Royal Navy continuing to control its own air service would have been, and it is quite likely that the battleship-minded Boards of Admiralty would have starved it of funds in between the wars; but the fact that the United States and Japanese navies did retain control of their own air services must surely be judged an important factor in their very marked superiority over the RN in that respect in 1941–2.

In summary of Churchill's development and achievement in the years 1911–18 I cannot do better than quote Ronald Lewin, who wrote that 'As a member of Asquith's administration he acquired the rudiments [of war management], particularly during his fertile period as First Lord. But it was those last six years of Lloyd George's premiership [1917–22] which were, for Churchill, a finishing school in the art and craft of handling the business of State.' But that author rightly adds the qualification that 'After 1918 it was not only the politicians who doubted; for most of the country, also, the sound that Churchill's trumpet uttered was tinny, and even cracked.'[19] We have seen how Antwerp 1914 and the Dardanelles 1915 combined to give that impression. The next chapter will tell how Churchill himself reinforced such misgivings.

CHAPTER 6

The Transition to Peace
1919–1929

Although Churchill as Minister of Munitions from July 1917 to January 1919 only had marginal dealings with the Admiralty his attendance at War Cabinet meetings ensured that he was fully informed on important issues affecting that department – notably the tardy introduction of convoy and the transfer of the RNAS to the newly-formed RAF. Early in 1919, almost simultaneously with the opening of the Paris Peace Conference, at which Churchill was not a British delegate, Lloyd George appointed him Secretary of State for War and Air – with a seat in the Cabinet. This was a curious fusion of offices which even Churchill's great capacity for work was unlikely to make successful; and it was less than fair to the infant RAF to place it under a Minister who was also head of one of the older departments. In fact Churchill would have much preferred to be the first incumbent of a Ministry of Defence; but Lloyd George evidently felt no enthusiasm for such a proposal – or was perhaps reluctant to place so much power in Churchill's hands.[1] Furthermore ever since the Russian revolution of October 1917 Churchill had been one of the most vocal advocates of military intervention against the Bolsheviks – which Lloyd George and most of his Ministers viewed with increased misgivings once Germany had been defeated, and which ran wholly counter to a large and influential body of British opinion.[2] In February 1919 Churchill on his own initiative attended a few Council of Ten (i.e. Foreign Ministers) sessions in Paris, and pressed for full intervention by the Allies on the White Russian side. Hankey, who was present in Paris, later described this action as 'Churchill at his worst', and it may well have revived the earlier misgivings among political leaders of both parties regarding the soundness of his judgement. Far from accepting the Churchill line the Cabinet decided to disentangle itself from the Russian imbroglio as quickly as possible, and in the autumn of 1919 withdrew all British forces from the Archangel front. A year later the War of Intervention ended in complete success for the Bolsheviks – except for the fact that the Baltic states (Latvia, Estonia and Lithuania) gained their independence – largely thanks to British naval support.[3]

Perhaps Churchill's greatest contribution while holding the double offices of War and Air was that he had a big hand in the drafting and presentation to Parliament of the document often referred to as 'the Charter of the RAF'.[4] From the naval point of view the most important statement in it was that the 'small parts of the RAF' trained for work with the Navy and Army would 'probably become, in the future, an arm of the older services'. This was a marked change from Churchill's pre-war attitude, and may have been inserted at Beatty's request. At any rate it was chiefly on this statement that the Admiralty based its frequent attempts to recover full control of the RNAS in later years. In fact, however, the control of that service remained governed by the complicated compromise of 1924 known as the 'Trenchard-Keyes Agreement' until the eve of World War II.[5]

While the Paris Conference was laboriously progressing with the settlement of the peace terms which were to be presented to the Central Powers, and with the immensely difficult task of delineating the frontiers of the newly created 'Succession States' to the Austro-Hungarian empire in accordance with President Wilson's ideas on 'self-determination' the future of the Defence Services, which were still very large indeed, was under constant discussion in London. It was actually Hankey, who was deeply conscious of the immense burden of debt incurred by the country and of the economic weakness brought about through the loss of so much of her export trade, who first proposed that the Service Estimates should in future be based on the assumption that there would be no major war for ten years.[6] This 'Ten Year Rule' was at the time a perfectly reasonable prognostication, and in fact proved fairly accurate; but it played a very large part in Churchill's relations with the Defence departments, and the Admiralty in particular, in the 1920s.

Beatty took over from Wemyss as First Sea Lord on 1 November 1919, at a time when the Admiralty was greatly concerned about the prospect of the Americans completing their huge 1916 naval building programme, which would have placed the Royal Navy in a position of marked inferiority. As the government had declared quite recently that the British navy should not be inferior to that of any other power the Admiralty accordingly prepared to restart building capital ships – which would be extremely costly.[7] Strong protests were soon being expressed in Parliament and the Press, and in consequence a special sub-committee of the CID was set up under Bonar Law (Lord Privy Seal). Both Churchill (still Minister for War and Air) and Beatty were members, and it was before this body that the first round of the long Battleship versus Bomber dispute took place. Lengthy and usually highly subjective evidence was given by the protagonists on both sides; but Churchill came down heavily on the Admiralty's side, declaring that he considered there was 'an overwhelming case for the capital ship'. He wanted to initiate building programmes of four such ships a year for four or five years – just as he had done with Germany in view as the probable enemy in 1912. This was surely a case where his previous experience and his sense of history misled him badly, since in 1920 the circumstances were quite different. No possible enemy except the USA was in view, and all Ministers and service chiefs regarded war with that country as 'unthinkable'. Be that as it may this powerful support delighted Beatty and his colleagues on the Board of Admiralty; but in retrospect Churchill's proposals seem to have been little short of fiscal lunacy. The report rendered to the Cabinet by the Bonar Law Committee was in the end a divided one. Law, Geddes (First Lord 1917–19) and Sir Robert Horne (Board of Trade) expressed doubts about the battleship's continued dominance; but Churchill sided with Walter Long (First Lord) and Beatty, who not only refused to accept such a heresy but wanted to start building new battleships at once.[8] The contrast between Churchill's attitude in 1920 and that which he adopted four years later when he was holding the nation's purse strings as Chancellor of the Exchequer will become apparent later.

In February 1921 Churchill moved from War and Air to the Colonial Office, and in his new capacity became Chairman of the Cabinet Committee on Irish Affairs. He thus came to play a prominent part in the 'troubles' of 1919–21. At first he lent strong support to those who favoured repression and 'legalized reprisals' for the murder of police or of British soldiers;[9] but he finally backed Lloyd George fully and skilfully in achieving the treaty signed on 6 December.[10] Our interest in that story only arises through the fact that Churchill and Beatty were again closely involved, and again reached a solution satisfactory to them both – this time over the retention by Britain of her right to the use of naval bases in the newly-constituted Irish Free State. Churchill, however, went too far when in the debate on the Treaty he assured the House of Commons that 'all naval needs were safeguarded', and that 'in times of war we have an absolute right to the freest possible use of all harbours and inlets on the Irish coast'.[11]

Before the Irish Treaty had been signed the whole question of the cost of the Fighting Services had come to a head, and when in August 1921 the Admiralty had to ask Parliament to approve a large Supplementary Estimate the Cabinet appointed a Committee on National

Expenditure under Sir Eric Geddes – Lloyd George's 'thoroughly capable business man' of 1917 – to review the whole issue. The outcome was the notorious 'Geddes Axe' by which hundreds of long-service officers were got rid of – with only a miserable pittance by way of compensation – and slashing cuts in all the Estimates were proposed. In January 1922 Churchill described the Geddes Report as 'a fine, massive, comprehensive piece of work', which scarcely accorded with the line he had taken at the time of the Bonar Law Inquiry – though he admitted that he did not agree with all of it.[12] The Geddes Committee's support for the creation of a Ministry of Defence aroused predictable opposition from the Admiralty, and the Board reacted very vigorously against the proposed cut in the Naval Estimates from £81 to £60 millions; while the other Service Departments took a similar line. In face of this opposition the Cabinet appointed another committee, with Churchill as chairman, to review the Geddes proposals; and as it was again chiefly Beatty who fought the navy's case the close association between the two of them continued. Although at the outset Churchill showed signs of taking a very tough line, and of delving into every nook and cranny of the Admiralty's organization in order to achieve economies, Beatty was soon able to tell his wife that the clouds were lifting as he and Churchill had met for face to face negotiations. By March 1922 he was able to report agreement between them. The Churchill Committee did not accept the Ministry of Defence proposal, though they admitted that such a reorganization might well prove 'the ultimate solution'. Instead they proposed that the CID should meet in constant session all the year round – which was what Hankey, who enjoyed very close and friendly relations with Churchill at this time – had always wanted.[13] In his report Churchill even paid a warm tribute to the Admiralty as a whole and to Beatty in particular for the 'immense financial savings' which he was able to recommend; and as the other two departments were not awarded any comparable eulogy it is a fair assumption that Churchill had found Beatty a more able and agreeable negotiator than the War Office and Air Ministry representatives. Churchill did, however, admit that his task had been made much easier by the signature in Feburary 1922 of the Washington Naval Treaty, and it is therefore to the conference which led to that agreement that we must now turn.

The principal British Empire delegates were Balfour (Lord President of Council), Lord Lee (First Lord) and Admiral Ernle (later Lord) Chatfield who had been Beatty's Flag Captain during the war and became Assistant Chief of Naval Staff in 1920. Though he possessed none of Beatty's panache his character was not flawed by flamboyance, extravagant living and snobbery – as was Beatty's. His strength of will was enormous, and his quiet spoken words and well written papers came to carry great weight in Whitehall. Without doubt he was, after Beatty, the most outstanding naval officer of the period between the wars. The preparations for the Washington Conference, which was called on President Warren Harding's initiative, fell on Chatfield, and he took with him detailed proposals stating how far Britain was prepared to go in naval limitation – which was then measured chiefly in capital ship numbers and tonnage. We will not here attempt to follow the prolonged and intricate negotiations between the delegates from the British Empire, America, Japan and France, which this author has described elsewhere;[14] but the records make it plain that Churchill, who had remained in England, was among those who were determined to reach agreement with the USA and so forestall a capital ship building race.[15] In the end agreement was reached that the principal naval powers' capital ship tonnage should be regulated by ratios of 5:5:3 for Britain, the USA and Japan respectively; while France and Italy were given a ratio of 1.75. Upper limits of displacement and gun calibre were also agreed. To bring these ratios into effect the USA and Japan were allowed to complete certain ships, construction of which was already far advanced, while Britain was allowed to build two new 35,000-ton, 16-inch ships in order to preserve the desired 'parity' with USA. Those ships (*Nelson* and *Rodney*, included in the 1922 programme and completed in 1927) constituted the only concession ever made to the ambitious plans put forward by the Admiralty at the Bonar Law Inquiry of 1921. The total of aircraft carrier tonnage allowed to the principal powers was also agreed, but no limitations on cruisers were included in the treaty except for 10,000 tons displacement and 8-inch guns; and the use of submarines against merchant shipping (which the British had wished to make totally illegal) was only covered by an amorphous and vaguely worded Resolution adopted by the conference. None of the powers were satisfied with what was done at Washington, but the conference is none the less historically important as the first attempt at arms limitation by negotiation, and by the fact that it marked the end of British naval dominance. Despite his friendship with Beatty Churchill supported ratification of the agreement when it came before Parliament. Limitation of land and air armaments found no place in the series of Treaties and Resolutions (totalling nine and twelve respectively) adopted; and the naval treaty, though it curbed competitive building of capital ships, left the road open for competition in cruiser building – of which all the powers soon took advantage. On the British side the first serious clash between the Admiralty and Treasury took place on that issue.

In 1922 the events generally known as the Chanak Crisis, brought about by the decisive defeat of the Greeks in Asia Minor by the revived Turkish Nationalist army under Kemal Pasha, whose military prowess had contributed so much to the British failure at Gallipoli in 1915, brought Britain to the verge of war with Turkey. Though the local military and naval commanders (General Sir Charles Harington and Admiral Sir Osmond Brock) handled a very delicate situation with great tact and patience, a telegram to the Dominion Prime Ministers drafted by Churchill and approved by the Cabinet on 15 September had not reached the addressees by the time a Press communiqué agreed between Churchill and Lloyd George appeared in the London papers next day. This mishap or misjudgement gave the Dominions, and also large sections of the British Press and public, the impression that the country was being hustled into a new war – principally by Churchill. Only New Zealand and Newfoundland responded favourably to Lloyd George's appeal for support. On the 29th Harington was sent the terms of an ultimatum to be delivered to the Turks to withdraw their forces from the neutral zone at Chanak; but fortunately the General ignored it, and instead worked successfully to open negotiations.[16] Though all ended happily at the Mudania Conference in October, Churchill's bellicosity certainly did him no good in the public's estimation. Moreover the handling of the Chanak crisis was the chief cause of the fall of the Second Coalition after the famous Carlton Club meeting of 19 October, and to Churchill being rejected by the voters of Dundee at the following General Election – leaving him without a seat in Parliament for the first time for twenty-two years. He was however now moving gradually towards the Conservative Party, and after being very narrowly rejected as Independent Anti-Socialist candidate for the Abbey Division of Westminster in March 1924 he won the Epping seat as a Constitutionalist by a large majority in the General Election of the following October.[17]

One of the most outstanding traits in Churchill's character was the way in which he threw himself whole-heartedly on to the side of any department of which he became head, and deployed all his formidable dialectical skill in the department's interest. Thus when in November 1924 Baldwin returned to power and offered him the office of Chancellor of the Exchequer – to Churchill's great surprise and delight – the poacher in the naval interest of earlier times became the Treasury's gamekeeper.

The first serious clash between him and the Admiralty took place over the proposal to build larger numbers of 'Washington Treaty' cruisers put forward late in 1923.[18] When the first slice of this programme was included in the 1925-6 Estimates a fierce battle took place between W. C. Bridgeman (First Lord) and Beatty on the Admiralty's side and Churchill on the Treasury's. The latter tried at first to get practically all new construction deleted from the estimates; and his attack is extraordinarily reminiscent of Lloyd George's assault on Churchill's own naval estimates for 1913-14 – though with Japan substituted for Germany as the most likely adversary. As was the case in 1921 Beatty took a far more prominent part in the high-level negotiations than was usual for a First Sea Lord; but this time he had a valuable ally in Bridgeman. Beatty told his wife 'I have had some bitter struggles in the past, but never so bitter as this – although there is no bad feeling about it. Winston and I are very good friends . . .';[19] and so it was to continue right up to Beatty's retirement in July 1927. In the end, and only after Bridgeman and Beatty had made it plain that they were prepared to resign on this issue, Baldwin himself proposed a compromise whereby the Admiralty would get four new cruisers in 1925-6 and three more in the following year.[20] When the proposal was debated in Parliament Churchill described the programme as 'no more than any reasonable man would regard as necessary for a sober yet solid defence of our naval position'; but in truth the compromise was a substantial victory over the formidable Chancellor – as Lloyd George and Ramsay MacDonald, the Labour leader, pointed out from the Opposition benches.[21]

The other big issues of this period were the building of a new naval base at Singapore, which was first put forward officially in 1921, and which Churchill had viewed sympathetically in his report on the Geddes Committee's proposals. But when he became Chancellor he fought very hard against the appropriation of any funds for the purpose, and in fact the base became a political shuttlecock throughout the 1920s and early 1930s. Second to the Singapore base came the Admiralty's persistent attempts to get the 1918 decision regarding transfer of the RNAS to the Air Ministry reversed. In 1923 the government set up a committee under Lord Salisbury to review the whole question of inter-service 'co-operation and co-ordination', and that body threw off a sub-committee under Balfour to investigate 'the relations of the Navy and Air Force as regards the control of Fleet air work'. The deliberations of both bodies were very protracted, and although we here are not concerned with the Salisbury Committee's report mention must be made of the fact that it instituted the Chiefs of Staffs' sub-committee of the CID, which started badly because of the intense rivalry between the Air Ministry and the older departments but proved invaluable in World War II. As Churchill was not a member of the Salisbury or Balfour committees, when Beatty gave his evidence to the latter there was no repetition of the clash between them over the cruiser programme. Thanks very largely to Lord Weir's influence, the committee finally came down strongly against the Admiralty's claim; and the Salisbury Committee accepted its recommendations.[22] Beatty and the other Sea Lords were greatly disappointed by this decision, and resolved to continue the fight whenever a chance presented itself.

Throughout Churchill's battles with the Admiralty over the 1924–5 and 1925–6 Naval Estimates, the cruiser building programme, the proposal to increase the submarine strength based on Hong Kong and the construction of the Singapore base his constantly reiterated refrain was that the navy was preparing for a war with Japan which he considered a highly improbable contingency. 'A war with Japan!' he scornfully told Baldwin. 'But why should there be a war with Japan? I do not believe there is the slightest chance of it in our lifetime'; and he concluded with the affirmation 'I am therefore convinced that war with Japan is not a possibility any reasonable government need to take into account.'[23] On submarine strength in the Far East and the request for funds to start the Singapore base he adopted an equally intransigent line, to which he adhered when these issues came before the CID, the Naval Programme Committee set up under Lord Birkenhead's chairmanship and the Cabinet. Churchill seems never to have realized how deeply the inferior ratio forced on Japan at the Washington Conference was resented in that country, and that such sentiments were producing an increasing trend towards a dangerous form of militarism. Nor were his references to Japan as being still an ally of Britain's soundly based, because the Anglo-Japanese Treaty had, in deference to American and Canadian pressure, been replaced by the Four Power Pact signed at Washington. One may find in these strenuous denials of any serious danger to the vast British interests in the Far East the origins of Churchill's later blindness to the extent of Japanese naval building, and to the compulsive expansionism which it both gave birth to and encouraged. However his desire that the defence of Singapore, if the base was built, should be provided by aircraft rather than by fixed heavy guns, which was almost certainly inspired by Trenchard the CAS, was to prove well founded.

We can pass briefly over the second half of Churchill's tenure of the office of Chancellor of the Exchequer, because the pattern of the earlier battles over the estimates was repeated every year. But mention must be made of how in June 1928 he proposed to the CID that the Ten Year Rule of 1919 should be made self-perpetuating – that is to say that the likelihood of a major war receded by twenty-four hours every day. In the atmosphere of the time, with the Locarno Treaty of Mutual Guarantee of 1925 having reduced the likelihood of the renewal of a Franco-German war over the frontier question, and the signatories of the Kellogg-Briand (or Paris) Pact of August 1928 having agreed to the renunciation of war as an instrument of policy except in self-defence, the alteration to the Ten Year Rule was not wholly unreasonable. Yet it did make it more difficult for the services to maintain even a modest degree of strength and provide themselves with up-to-date equipment, because whenever a proposal of such a nature was put forward the Treasury was able to claim that it conflicted with the Ten Year Rule.

One other naval issue which arose in the period covered by this chapter over which Churchill came into conflict with the Admiralty, concerned the long-standing British claim to exercise what were known as 'Belligerent Rights' at sea in time of war – namely the right to intercept and detain neutral merchant ships, and to confiscate their cargoes if it could be shown before a Prize Court that they were destined for an enemy country. The exercise of this claim, which was never recognized under International Law, had given great offence to neutral nations, and especially the USA, during World War I; and the whole issue was reinvestigated by the CID in 1928. Churchill then suggested that because in his view Britain would be unable to defend her merchant shipping in a new war, it might prove advantageous to her to abandon the claim to Belligerent Rights in order to exempt merchant ships from capture at sea. In the event, and largely because of Hankey's strong opposition to any change, progress was very slow, and Baldwin's government had fallen before any decision was reached.[24] But this is surely another case where Churchill showed surprising lack of foresight. Though MacDonald's Labour government of 1929–31 was more sympathetic than Baldwin's to a change of policy regarding Belligerent Rights Hankey managed to keep the whole issue off the agenda for the discussions held between MacDonald and President Hoover as a preliminary step towards the 1930 London Naval Conference;[25] and in fact no change had been made by the time war broke out in 1939.

With the retirement of Beatty in 1927, the succession of Admiral Sir Charles Madden, a rather colourless officer, to the post of First Sea Lord, and the departure of Churchill from the Treasury with the defeat of the Conservatives in the 1929 General Election, relations between the top naval men and their political masters moved into a very different, though no less difficult period. Though Churchill continued to take a great interest in naval affairs and defence problems, especially after Hitler had come to power in 1933, his long exclusion from office deprived him, as it had done from 1915–17, of any appreciable influence. His gradual reinvolvement in such matters as the international scene darkened in the 1930s will be reviewed in the next chapter.

CHAPTER 7

Out of Office but Active
1929-1939

Unless the Churchill papers, when released to historians, should produce evidence to the contrary it seems true to say that after the fall of Baldwin's government in May 1929 Churchill took no very active interest in naval affairs, including the Invergordon Mutiny of September 1931, until well after the formation of the National Government under Ramsay MacDonald in August of that year. His exclusion from office on the return of what was in fact though not in name a Conservative administration at least left him more time to devote to his literary and historical work; and the 1930s were a very prolific period in that field.* Because his historical works throw light on Churchill's character it is permissible to draw the reader's attention to the suppression of evidence regarding his famous ancestor which was in his hands, remarked on by Professor J. H. Plumb,[1] and to the bias shown in the biography of Marlborough already remarked on which has been severely criticized by Dutch historians of the highest calibre. Taken together these criticisms do lend substance to the view that, although Churchill developed an extremely readable, even gripping style his historical works cannot be regarded as reliable sources. There probably also was some truth in the remark he made many years later to his Research Assistant 'Give me the facts and I will twist them the way I want to suit my argument.'[2] Nor is this feeling mitigated by the fact that neither his son Randolph, who began the 'authorized biography' nor Martin Gilbert, who has continued it, can be regarded as uncommitted men – the former for reasons of filial piety and the latter because he has been a leader of what may be called the 'Guilty Men Syndrome' whereby all the errors and tragedies of the 1930s are heaped on to Neville Chamberlain and his colleagues.[3] It is, however, noteworthy that in recent years such a view has come under increasingly critical scrutiny as more records and correspondence are released for study, and the passage of time has enabled a more balanced perspective to be achieved.[4]

---

* The principal books were *My Early Life* (1930), *Thoughts and Adventures* (1932), *Marlborough*, Vol. I (1933), Vol. II (1934), Vol. III (1936) and Vol. IV (1938), and *Great Contemporaries* (1939).

In the early 1930s Churchill's political energies were deployed chiefly against the government's policy of guiding India towards self-government within the Commonwealth, and defence problems played a comparatively small part in his activities. As Professor Norman Gibbs has put it, Churchill at that time 'seemed more anxious about new policies in India than about the emergence of a new threat from Japan';[5] and, as we shall see later, he continued to the end to show a blind spot about the nature and strength of that threat. What is beyond doubt is that the violence of Churchill's attack on the government over the India Bill, which finally became law on 4 August 1935, did him great harm in the public eye and made it unnecessarily difficult for Baldwin to recall him to office – as he probably would have liked to do by 1936.[6]

While in the political wilderness Churchill naturally saw a good deal of the friends with whom he had, in earlier times, become intimate. Such were F. E. Smith (1st Earl of Birkenhead), who died in 1930, Lord Beaverbrook, Brendan Bracken, Frederick Lindemann ('The Prof') and Desmond Morton; and as one surveys that band it is difficult not to accept both Anthony Storr's view that he was attracted by 'energetic adventurers' and Liddell Hart's that he was 'only comfortable with men of lesser calibre than himself'.[7] Among naval men his closest intimate in the 1930s was Admiral Sir Roger Keyes, who went into Parliament as a National Conservative in 1934. Keyes was a very brave man, with something of the sixteenth-century buccaneer in his character – a type which always appealed to Churchill; but in retrospect it seems that his intelligence and mental capacity hardly justified his promotion to the highest rank in the naval hierarchy. His attraction for Churchill arose largely from his efforts to renew the naval attack on the Dardanelles in March-April 1915, and from his leadership of the famous – though in fact unsuccessful – Zeebrugge raid of April 1918. Of Churchill's other intimates Lindemann and Morton had most to do with advising him on matters concerning the Fighting Services. Lindemann first met Churchill at Eaton Hall, the Duke of Westminster's vast house near Chester in the early 1920s; and he immediately cultivated Churchill's friendship – initially by showing interest in and kindness towards his children. By such means he soon obtained the invitation to Chartwell for which he was obviously working;[8] and that led to his becoming Churchill's principal adviser on scientific and technological matters – from which he extended his activities later into the field of strategy. Churchill's readiness to accept his advice and opinions derived, at any rate in part, from his knowledge

of the fallacious arguments put up by the Admiralty against the
introduction of convoy in 1917, and of the irregular activities of
certain officers which exposed the fallacy and enabled its effects to be
overcome – just in time.[9] Desmond Morton appealed to Churchill
for much the same reason as Keyes. He had a very gallant record in
World War I, including survival from a bullet in his heart. After the
war he joined the Secret Intelligence Service, in which capacity he
was able to give Churchill information of the type he relished. From
1927 onwards Morton made the study of foreign industrial capacity,
especially for war purposes, his special field; and with Hankey's
strong support he was instrumental in forming the Industrial Intelligence
Centre, of which he became Director two years later.[10] The information
which thereby came into Churchill's hands, particularly with regard
to German preparations for rearmament, made Morton a very valuable
member of Churchill's intimate circle.* As one surveys the small
group of intimates whom Churchill assembled round himself while
in the political wilderness Anthony Storr's view that judgement
of character was *not* his strong suit appears well founded.[11] We will
return later to Lindemann's activities and influence during World
War II.

As Mussolini began to show increasingly aggressive designs, and
Hitler increasing determination to cast off the 'shackles' of the Versailles
Treaty and rearm his country Churchill's interest in defence problems,
which had always occupied a large place in his thought and writings,
quickened; and neither MacDonald nor Baldwin raised any objection
to his being accorded special treatment over the receipt of classified
information – notably from Morton, who was particularly well
placed to meet Churchill's needs. The two Prime Ministers may of
course have adopted this generous line towards one of their most
vociferous critics with the object of mitigating his attacks; but
Churchill's contacts, outside Parliament as well as inside it, were so
numerous and generally well-informed that he was in any case likely

* R. W. Thomson, *Churchill and Morton* (Hodder and Stoughton, 1976). The suggestion made by some reviewers of this book that Morton became a disappointed man after the war, because Churchill had more or less dropped him, gains no support from my own post-war association with Morton. His old age was actually very happy and contented; and he enjoyed a wide range of interests – notably the hospital of which he was Chairman and the Roman Catholic Church of which he had become a member after World War I. His retrospective and candid views, which he did not express lightly, have caused the more hagiographic writers on Churchill to represent an unfair and distorted picture of Morton. In fact the contributors to *Four Faces* attribute much the same faults to Churchill as Morton.

to find out a great deal about what was happening behind the closed corridors of Whitehall.

A sub-committee of the CID 'to investigate scientific aspects of A-A defence' had actually been formed in April 1925, and Lindemann was invited to serve on it – almost certainly on Churchill's initiative. But this first attempt to apply scientific principles to an important defence problem languished, and in November 1928 Baldwin 'suspended' the committee.[12] It was not revived until 1933, and then led to perhaps the most notorious scientific feud of modern times – between Henry Tizard, the chairman of the new committee and Lindemann. The Tizard Committee comprised some of the ablest scientists of the period (A. V. Hill, P. M. S. Blackett and H. E. Wimperis with A. P. Rowe as its secretary); but from February 1935, when the Air Ministry invited Lindemann to join it – probably at Baldwin's instigation the committee did not, in C. P. Snow's words, 'know half an hour's harmony or work undisturbed'.[13] The basic issue was that the Tizard Committee had decided to put the maximum possible effort into the development of what came to be known as Radar for air defence purposes, while Lindemann argued in favour of infra-red detection and the use of 'aerial mines', which were bombs attached to wires dropped by parachute in the anticipated paths of enemy bombers. The crisis came with the Tizard Committee's Progress Report of July 1936, which Lindemann refused to accept. Blackett and Hill, soon followed by Tizard himself, thereupon resigned; and when in October the committee was reconstituted Edward Appleton replaced Lindemann.[14] The most curious part about this story is that, although as the 1930s advanced it became increasingly apparent that the Tizard Committee's decision in favour of Radar was absolutely right, Churchill's confidence in Lindemann's scientific judgement was in no way vitiated.

Early in 1935 Lindemann protested to Hankey about the alleged sluggishness of the Air Ministry over developing counter-measures to bombing. He wanted a sub-committee of the CID to be formed to stimulate research in that field on a higher level than the Tizard Committee. Churchill certainly knew all about this proposal, and in March Baldwin announced that Sir Philip Cunliffe-Lister (soon to become Lord Swinton), who was about to replace Lord Londonderry as Air Minister, had agreed to become chairman of the new body, generally known as the Swinton Committee. In June Churchill, who had been showing increasing interest in air defence, and great concern over the rise of the new Luftwaffe, was invited to join it.[15] Thus did he re-enter the inner circle of Ministers and officials who received all reports on defence problems. At the same time he was receiving unofficially from Lindemann and Morton, and surreptitiously from certain members of the Air Staff, figures comparing the present and prospective air strengths of Britain and Germany.* In the debate of 29 November 1934 Baldwin rebutted Churchill's estimate of the comparative air strengths for 1935; and we now know that his figures were nearer the truth than Churchill's. But the trouble was that Baldwin gave the impression that we would not fall behind Germany in 1936 or 1937; and the possible, even probable expansion of German productivity was in fact so rapid that this conjecture proved to be far from true.[16]

On his re-entry into the government's inner councils on defence Churchill naturally did not confine himself to the air side. Indeed his interest ranged over every aspect of the field, and top naval men seem to have been as glad to discuss their problems with him as were those of the other services. Probably this was because they all knew what a valuable ally he could be inside and outside the House of Commons; and possibly they realized that he was likely to return to office some day. As regards the navy although one of his last acts as Chancellor of the Exchequer had been to make a strong attack on the very modest proposals for the expansion of the Fleet Air Arm,[17] in 1936 he told Admiral Chatfield, the First Sea Lord, that he intended 'to press continually in the House of Commons' for the transfer of control of the Fleet Air Arm to the Admiralty'[18] – a measure which he had resisted, not without good reason, when he had been Air Minister in 1919–20 and the infant RAF was struggling against extinction at the hands of the older services. Also in 1936 Churchill wrote to Admiral Keyes, who was campaigning on behalf of the Admiralty, 'It seems to me we ought to make an effort to settle this dispute', and proposed a meeting with the Admiral.[19] In the following year Lord Louis Mountbatten, then a commander serving in the Air Division of the naval staff, briefed Churchill on the case for placing *all* aircraft and aircrews, whether seaborne or shore-based, 'under the control of a single service' – by which of course he meant the navy.[20] Though it anticipates later

* Gilbert, *Churchill*, *V*, deals fully with Churchill's informants on defence matters, and especially German air rearmament and the deficiencies from which the RAF suffered. Wing-Commanders C. T. Anderson and M. G. Christie, and Desmond Morton were probably the most valuable sources. Anderson was a serving officer but Christie, though retired had many business contacts in Germany. See op. cit., pp. 742 and 756, *notes* regarding their careers. Those of Christie's papers which have survived are in Churchill College, Cambridge.

events it is relevant to mention here that early in 1940 Churchill, now First Lord again, wrote to Admiral Pound the First Sea Lord 'I have always been a strong advocate of the FAA, in fact I drafted for Sir T. Inskip [Minister for Co-ordination of Defence] the compromise decision to which he eventually came in 1938.'[21] Though Churchill was at the time referred to still out of office it is quite likely that Inskip consulted him; but I have found no mention of Churchill's part in reaching the compromise in the Cabinet, Swinton, Weir or Inskip (Lord Caldecote) papers, all of which deal with the negotiations in question. In fact a note from Hankey to Inskip dated 3 May 1937 shows that it was he who suggested the compromise finally adopted;[22] but it is of course possible that Hankey, who was then in close touch with Churchill, got the idea from him and passed it on to Inskip. There is, however, in the Keyes papers a copy of an unsigned and undated, though obviously 1937, paper on the subject by Churchill which, with the permission of the latter, Keyes sent on to Chatfield on 22 April. In it Churchill wrote 'It is impossible to resist an Admiral's claim that he must have complete control of and confidence in the aircraft of the battle fleet . . . These are his very eyes. Therefore the Admiralty view must prevail in all that is required to secure this result . . . The Admiralty should have plenary control and provide the entire personnel of the Fleet Air Arm . . . [and] will decide upon the types of aircraft which their approved functions demand.' As, however, there is nothing in this paper about the shore-based aircraft of Coastal Command remaining an integral part of the RAF, an omission which Keyes and Chatfield at once spotted, Churchill's 1940 claim to have initiated the compromise finally accepted requires qualification. Keyes did, however, tell Chatfield that Chamberlain, the Prime Minister, had made it 'quite clear that operational control [of the shore-based aircraft] would be given to the Navy' – though that intention did not appear in Chamberlain's speech on the compromise in the House of Commons, and did not actually come to pass until April 1941.

It must surely have been Churchill's memory of the crisis of 1917 which caused him to interest himself in the defence of merchant shipping against air as well as submarine attack as the international scene darkened in the mid-1930s. On this aspect of naval policy the Admiralty misled Churchill by exaggerating the effectiveness both of A-A gunfire and of the Asdic submarine detection device. Having demonstrated the latter to Churchill he accepted that what he called 'the faithful effort' had 'relieved us of our great danger'. But war experience quickly proved that the Admiralty's optimism was in both cases excessive.[23]

As regards the design of new warships, in 1933 the Admiralty decided to build a class of smaller cruiser (the *Arethusas* of about 5200 tons) in order to get as many ships of that type as possible within the total tonnage permitted by the 1930 London Treaty. Churchill attacked this policy strongly, and repeated his attack when in 1936 the Admiralty produced a totally new design of cruiser with dual purpose (i.e. HA/LA) armaments – the *Dido* class.[24] Churchill also attacked Chatfield's Board later for building the 14-inch gunned *King George V* class battleships; but here again he seems to have ignored the extraordinarily difficult problems imposed by the naval limitation treaties signed at Washington in 1922 and at London in 1930 and 1935. The truth of the matter was that it was impossible to obtain all the *desiderata* – good protection, high speed, heavy A-A armaments and catapult aircraft for reconnaissance and spotting, as well as 16-inch guns – within the treaty limitation of 35,000 tons.[25] The two *Nelson* class battleships, completed in 1927, did have 16-inch guns; but they could steam at no more than twenty-three knots – which by 1936 was totally inadequate. Not until a Protocol to the 1935 London Treaty was signed in June 1938 was the Admiralty able to place orders for 16-inch ships capable of thirty knots; and the displacement of the *Lion* class, which were actually never completed, went up to 42,500 tons – comparable to the German *Bismarcks*, which were to cause us so much trouble and anxiety because of their superiority over all British capital ships.

Throughout the uneasy but critical period of the 1930s the Chiefs of Staff were haunted by the prospect of a war with all three dictatorships simultaneously, and so worked to restore friendly relations with Italy after the fiasco of sanctions over her Abyssinian aggression. The Admiralty also pressed for acceptance of the German offer to limit their naval strength to 35% of Britain's (100% in submarines). This was in fact the first agreement on armaments achieved by any country with Nazi Germany; but its value did of course depend wholly on that country's good faith. Chatfield, the First Sea Lord, strongly favoured the agreement; but Churchill opposed it in the House of Commons on the curious ground that it would give the Germans control of the Baltic, which we were in any case unable to dispute except with submarines, and that if we had to retain 35% of our strength at home it would make the situation in the Far East, to which we were committed to send a sufficient fleet to contain Japan's strength, much more dangerous.[26] Yet in March 1939, little more than three years later, in a letter to Chamberlain he discounted completely the likelihood of a serious Japanese attack on Singapore;[27] and his blindness regarding the realities of the Japanese threat and our own weakness in that vast theatre continued, as Liddell Hart has pointed out, almost to the time of the Japanese attack in December 1941.[28] Nor was that the only example of Churchill's judgement playing him false, since as late as the autumn of 1937 he no longer took the German threat as seriously as earlier, declaring his belief 'that a major war is not imminent'.[29] In the same speech he reproduced his old hostility to Soviet Russia, declaring that 'I will not pretend that, if I had to choose between Communism and Nazism, I would choose Communism';[30] and in 1937 he republished an article on Hitler produced two years earlier, in which he wrote that 'one may dislike Hitler's system and yet admire his patriotic achievement' – a remark which took little account of the price exacted for the patriotic achievement.[31]

In that same year Churchill formed a group, designated 'Focus', of which Liddell Hart was a member, to review strategic issues. Liddell Hart later recalled how, although during the group's meetings, Churchill 'listened, in a sense, he did not really take in a point except in so far as it fitted with his own thought'.[32] It is true that Churchill's pressure for more rapid rearmament in the 1930s suffered from the misfortune that his movement for 'Arms and the Covenant' coincided exactly with, and was swamped by the crisis over the abdication of King Edward VIII; but his misjudgement of the perils in the Far East cannot be attributed to that cause, since as late as March 1939 he wrote to Chamberlain 'consider how vain is the menace that Japan will send a fleet and army to conquer Singapore'.[33] Another major misjudgement of Churchill's was his description of the French army, only a year before the war, as 'the most perfectly trained and faithful mobile force in Europe'.[34] On the other hand Churchill cannot be blamed for accepting the Naval Staff's view that the Asdic had conquered the submarine, and that ships could defend themselves successfully against air attacks. The responsibility for the propagation of such fallacies rests firmly with the Admiralty, and their exposure probably aggravated Churchill's mistrust of service 'experts', and contributed to his determination to equip himself with independent scientific advice in the shape of Professor Lindemann and his associates. The truth is of course that neither Churchill himself nor the service staffs enjoyed a monopoly of correct prophecy; and if the staffs were wrong on some important issues Churchill himself had contributed to the difficulties of the mid-

1930s by his policy as Chancellor of the Exchequer 1924–9.[35] The change of public attitude towards Churchill, which he himself had inflamed by his belligerence, came suddenly – and at the eleventh hour – in the summer of 1939.

As regards Churchill's views on the purposes and limitations of sea power and the application of a maritime strategy, one may doubt whether he ever really grasped the principles involved. From the beginning of his premiership he pressed unremittingly for operations which in his eyes were 'offensive', whilst deprecating the strategy of convoy and escort combined with blockade, because he regarded them as basically defensive. Therein lay the fundamental cause of so many of his disagreements with the admirals of World War II.

In the parliamentary debates of this period Churchill lent his full authority to all measures of rearmament; and he seems to have won the confidence of the top naval men, especially Chatfield the First Sea Lord, about whom he wrote to Keyes that he 'strikes me as a very fine fellow'.[36] Doubtless Churchill's support for the transfer of the Fleet Air Arm to full Admiralty control, for which Chatfield was assiduously working and which he finally accomplished after the Inskip Inquiry of 1937,[37] contributed to the warm feelings being reciprocated by the admiral. On the other hand Churchill's desire to see a fully-fledged Ministry of Defence eliminate the long-standing rivalry between the service departments certainly aroused no enthusiasm in naval breasts. Nor did his readiness, even anxiety to become the head of the new department attract much support among service men.[38] The chief reason for this attitude of mind was of course that he had so often proved his own worst enemy during the previous two decades. There does in fact seem to be some substance in the view expressed by the German ambassador in London in 1936 and by Liddell Hart some five years later, that such an appointment would have precipitated war – long before our rearmament programme had begun to produce the means of waging it successfully.[39]

Here it is relevant to mention the fundamental reason for the extra-ordinary and complete about-turn which Churchill performed towards Chatfield between March 1938, when he had praised him most warmly in the House of Commons,[40] and 1940 when he sacked him from the War Cabinet and thereafter denied him any significant role in the prosecution of the war.[41] During World War I, when Chatfield was Flag Captain to Beatty in the *Lion*, Churchill visited the ship and questioned junior officers about their seniors – which annoyed Chatfield so much that he protested to the First Lord. The incident is reminiscent of Churchill's conduct in the case of Admiral Poore in 1913, mentioned earlier. His Flag Lieutenant of later years recalls Chatfield telling him that, at the time he made this protest he had remarked that, if Churchill ever returned to the Admiralty he would find himself out of a job[42] – a prophecy which was to prove only too true, and which deprived the navy of by far the ablest and best qualified officer for the post of First Sea Lord during the first years of World War II.

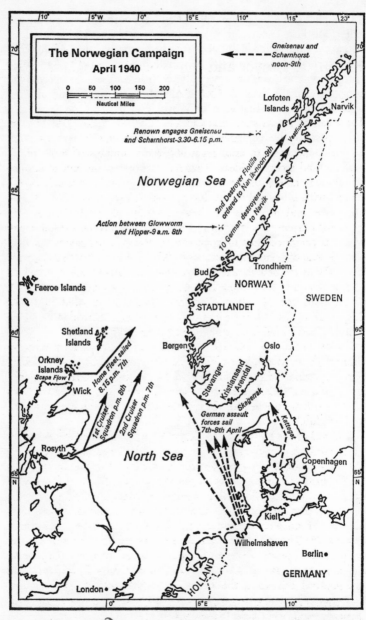

The Norwegian Campaign
April 1940

0   50   100   150   200
Nautical Miles

Gneisenau and Scharnhorst-noon-9th

Lofoten Islands

Narvik

Renown engages Gneisenau and Scharnhorst-3.30-6.15 p.m.

2nd Destroyer Flotilla ordered to Narvik-noon-9th

Vestfiord

Norwegian Sea

Action between Glowworm and Hipper-9 a.m. 8th

10 German destroyers to Narvik

Bud

Trondhiem

NORWAY

SWEDEN

STADTLANDET

Faeroe Islands

Shetland Islands

Bergen

Oslo

Orkney Islands
Scapa Flow

Stavanger
Kristiansand
Arendal

Wick

Home Fleet sailed 8.15 p.m. 7th

1st Cruiser Squadron p.m. 8th

2nd Cruiser Squadron p.m. 7th

Skagerak

Rosyth

North Sea

German assault forces sail 7th-8th April

Kattegat

Copenhagen

55° N

Kiel

Wilhelmshaven

Berlin

London

HOLLAND

GERMANY

MAP (1)

CHAPTER 8

Return to Power and the Norwegian Campaign
1939-1940

There can be no question that Churchill's return to the Admiralty in September 1939 was warmly welcomed throughout the navy, though doubts soon began to arise regarding the soundness of some of his strategic and technical ideas. That he invigorated the whole administrative machinery of the department and made his personality felt far and wide is beyond doubt; but he also diverted to fruitless schemes manpower and materials which were sorely needed for more conventional purposes – sometimes on the advice of Professor Lindemann who was convinced that his rocket weapons could provide better A-A defence than conventional guns. As in World War I Churchill regarded the Baltic as the best theatre for launching the 'naval offensive' which he was always seeking. Since he himself has given a full account of the preparations for operation 'Catherine' there is no need to repeat them here in detail;[1] but some of the exchanges it produced, which have not been published before, are relevant to this study.

On 18 September the first of a series of meetings took place in Churchill's room to discuss War Plans in general and a paper which two very senior admirals, Sir Reginald Drax and Sir Gerald Dickens, had produced.* Their conclusion was that we could not be ready to take the offensive at sea for six months – which was highly distasteful to Churchill.[2]

Admiral of the Fleet Lord Cork and Orrery, who had last served at sea in command of the Home Fleet 1933-5 and was sixty-seven years old, was brought in to prepare for 'Catherine', the object of which was defined as being 'to force a passage into the Baltic and maintain there a naval force'. Churchill proceeded cautiously, and on 20 September stated that 'At present the decision is only for exploration and no question of *action* arises. But the search for a naval offensive must be incessant.'[3] Though Cork repeatedly pressed for a decision on whether the operation was to be launched, and was obviously ready and anxious to lead it, at the end of the year Churchill told him that 'the political situation in the theatre has considerably changed', doubt-

* Sir Reginald Plunkett-Ernle-Erle-Drax was C-in-C, The Nore 1939-41. Sir Gerald Dickens, a grandson of Charles Dickens, had retired in 1938.

less due to the Russo–Finnish war, and he should therefore review his plan. Neither the Admiralty nor the Government was, he stated, committed to action. The position was that 'the gun is to be loaded ready for firing. This and no more'.[4]

Meanwhile Admiral Sir Dudley Pound, the First Sea Lord, and the naval staff had developed and expressed strong doubts about the feasibility of the undertaking; and Cork himself described it as 'very hazardous'.[5] On 10 January 1940 Pound told Churchill that he and Cork had discussed the plan thoroughly, and he was 'of the opinion that a strong force of submarines could achieve the object we desire while a surface force could not'. He was anxious that 'we should if possible end the war with our sea supremacy unchallenged' – a somewhat long-term hope. If we lost all the submarines sent to the Baltic 'it would not really matter' he wrote; but 'if we lost a considerable part of our surface fleet the story would be a very different one';[6] which shows how wedded Pound was to the 'battle fleet concept' and how little aware of the growing influence of air and underwater weapons. The outcome was that on 23 January 1940 the order was given that preparations to carry out the operation that year were to cease.[7] In retrospect the decision was a wise one, since no surface force could possibly have survived for long against the air, submarine and mine counter measures which the Germans would certainly have brought to bear against it. It does therefore seem very unfair that the able Director of Plans, Captain V. H. Danckwerts, should have been sacked for criticizing the plan too vigorously; but his departure was an ominous warning to staff officers of the fate which awaited them if they opposed Churchill's ideas.[8]

Another Director of a Staff Division who brought about his dismissal by 'arguing the toss' with Churchill was Captain A. G. Talbot, the Director of Anti-Submarine Warfare. The staff had assessed that by 10 March 1940 only nineteen U-boats had been sunk and forty-three were fit for service. The actual figure was we now know fifteen sunk; but Churchill had publicly made far more optimistic claims and, doubtless advised by Lindemann, strongly challenged the staff's figures. His estimate that only a dozen U-boats remained effective (Pound admitted it might be twenty-two) was in fact fantastic; and the minute whereby he demanded, and obtained Talbot's dismissal was an act of cruel injustice.[9] One does feel that, if Pound was caught in the unhappy dilemma of finding his loyalty to Churchill in conflict with the loyalty he owed to his senior staff officers, the latter had a right to look to the head of their service to defend them. Pound did at least see that Talbot got a good command – namely the aircraft carrier *Furious*.

We saw earlier how Churchill considered the lack of a proper naval staff one of the Admiralty's worst failures in the pre-1914 era, and that he also held that the naval officers of that generation were lacking in general education. What is puzzling about his frequent strictures on the World War II naval administration is that he does not seem to have appreciated that a properly organized and trained body of staff officers had gradually come into being since 1918; and many of its ablest men were serving in the Admiralty when he was First Lord. Furthermore officers of that generation who had reached the rank of Commander or Captain were far better educated than their World War I counterparts. Thus the frequent and often strident criticisms which he hurled at the staff of 1939–40 suggest that he viewed its members in the light of the knowledge and experience of the deficiencies he had gained during the first war. Therein must surely lie the true explanation of his bringing to the Admiralty his own team of advisers, headed by Professor Lindemann, which, apart from the duplication and confusion it caused, was hardly a fair assessment of the ability of the staff and the scientists already available.

As regards naval strategy, as in World War I, Churchill never relaxed his search for 'a naval offensive'. Towards the end of 1939 he protested to Pound that 'we are being driven day by day into an absolute defensive by far weaker forces . . . I cd never be responsible for a naval strategy wh excluded the offensive principle, and relegated us to keeping open lines of communication and maintaining the blockade'; and he reiterated the same theme a week later, urging that 'The entry of the Baltic, for instance would soon bring the [German warship] raiders home and give us measureless relief.'[10] Obviously he had in mind a possible subsidiary benefit which might be gained from operation 'Catherine'.

Early in 1940 Churchill's mind reverted to the problem of control over naval aviation. He reminded Pound of the part he had played in resolving the Navy-RAF quarrel of the 1930s, and distinguished between the attitude of the Air Ministry in its early days, when they were 'very jealous of their sphere', and their attitude 'now that prime importance has come to them', which had made them 'much more tolerant'. He therefore asked for plans to be drawn up to form six to nine shore-based naval squadrons with a view to making an approach to the Air Ministry 'to relieve them of the whole coastal work in home waters'.[11] No reply appears to have been sent to Churchill regarding this take-over bid; at any rate it was not followed up. In November 1940, however, Beaverbrook (Minister for Aircraft Production and an intimate friend of Churchill's) proposed that Coastal Command should be taken over by the Admiralty;[12] but as the only change made was to transfer operational control to that department one may presume that Churchill, now Prime Minister, no longer held the opinion he had expressed in the previous January.

For the rest, the period of the 'phoney war' brought many problems, such as the magnetic mine threat and the losses caused by the far-ranging German warship raiders; and Churchill applied his vast energy to every one of them that arose.

Although the forces engaged in the Norwegian campaign of 1940 were, with the exception of the navy's, very small in comparison with those engaged in later operations in all theatres it is of particular interest to us because of the predominant part played in its initiation and execution by Churchill. It is also revealing with regard to his relations with the COS Committee, the Cabinet, and the C-in-C, Home Fleet, who was responsible for the maritime side of the campaign.[13] It also ruthlessly exposed for the first time what the German dive-bombers could do to warships operating close inshore with inadequate or no fighter cover, and confirmed our early experience of what the RAF's heavy bombers, which were designed to meet Trenchard's addiction to the concept of strategic bombing, could *not* do to similarly placed enemy warships.[14]

To understand the background to the campaign the importance attached to the stoppage of the very large imports of high grade iron ore from Sweden to Germany must be emphasized. In 1938 total German imports of that vital commodity were estimated at 22 million tons, of which 9 million came from Sweden. But between about December and April each year the Baltic was usually frozen, and the only outlet for the traffic in iron ore then became the port of Narvik in north Norway, to which a railway ran from the Swedish ore fields. Furthermore the geography of the Norwegian coast was such that ships could travel between Norway and Germany using the 'Inner Leads', a route which lay almost wholly inside Norwegian territorial waters. Very early in the war Churchill pressed the War Cabinet for permission to lay mines in the Leads to the north of Bergen, with the object of forcing German ships out into more open waters where they could legally be intercepted. He was apparently as little concerned with the infringement of neutral rights by mining the Leads as he had been in the case of his offensive plans of 1914, referred to earlier. In

December 1939 Churchill put his proposal to the Supreme War Council; but that body was as apprehensive as the War Cabinet regarding the likely consequences of such action in the eyes of other neutral nations, and especially the United States. Early in 1940 a diplomatic approach was made to Norway and Sweden in the hope that they would agree to the minelaying operation, on the grounds that German submarines were notoriously attacking Allied shipping in those waters; but permission to go ahead with Churchill's plan was bluntly refused.

Meanwhile the Russian attack on Finland on 30 November 1939, leading to 'the winter war' had complicated the issue. The French and British governments wanted to help the Finns, difficult though it was with the Germans in control of the Baltic. Moreover at that time Germany was friendly to the USSR as a result of the Moscow pact signed in August 1939; while the Scandinavian countries were determined to do nothing which might provoke the Germans to treating them as they had recently treated Poland. However, a plan was prepared to land a force at Narvik to go to the aid of the Finns, and incidentally reach the Swedish iron mines by April. Other forces were to land at the key Norwegian ports of Stavanger, Bergen and Trondheim. The officer selected to command the naval side of this operation was Admiral Sir Edward Evans (later Lord Mountevans), who had been second-in-command of Scott's last expedition to the Antarctic and had gained a reputation for gallantry as a destroyer captain in World War I.[15] Though Evans's knowledge of Norway (his second wife was Norwegian) and his earlier record of service certainly had advantages he had retired from the navy shortly before the war. His recall to active service in 1940 shows yet again how addicted Churchill and Pound were to seeking leaders from those who had given distinguished service in the first conflict.

On 16 February 1940, before any active steps had been taken to carry out the foregoing plan, the so-called 'Altmark incident' took place. A British destroyer entered Norwegian waters near Bergen and boarded the German tanker *Altmark*, which had been acting as a supply vessel for the pocket-battleship *Graf Spee* during her commerce raiding operations. She had 299 British merchant navy prisoners on board, and was proceeding home by way of the Leads. The rescue operation was completely successful; but it provoked a strong protest from the Norwegian government.[16] Yet in British eyes it provided further proof of the use by the Germans of neutral waters for military purposes. Then the surrender of the Finns to the overwhelmingly superior forces of Soviet Russia eliminated what little likelihood there had ever been of Norway and Sweden putting their neutral status at hazard by conniving at British and French aid to Finland being allowed to pass through their countries.

On 21 March Churchill resurrected his plan to mine the Leads, and an associated operation (known as 'Plan R4') was produced to prepare to occupy the Norwegian ports already named on the assumption that there would be no opposition. The minelaying operation, originally scheduled for 5 April, actually took place in the early hours of the 8th with the Home Fleet providing cover.[17] But indications had already been received that a strong German reaction was imminent; and we now know that ever since October 1939 Admiral Erich Raeder, the C-in-C of the German Navy, had in fact been pressing Hitler for action against Denmark and Norway in order to eliminate the geographical and strategic handicaps from which his service suffered. Because of the German navy's inferiority his plan had to depend for its success on 'secrecy, speed and deception'.[18] It was finally put in train on 7 April – the day before our minelaying operation. Six groups were organized to seize the principal Norwegian ports, while the German battle-cruisers *Scharnhorst* and *Gneisenau* carried out a diversionary operation in the far north. From the German point of view the risks were heavy, especially in the case of the forces sent to occupy Narvik; but they took elaborate steps to minimize them by, for example, loading the merchant ships which were to carry men, stores and equipment to the key ports in the utmost secrecy.

Virtually the whole of the German navy was committed, and when it became plain that exceptional movements were afoot Admiral Sir Charles Forbes, the C-in-C, Home Fleet, took his main force to sea from Scapa Flow in the Orkneys on the evening of 7 April and steered to the north-east. His appreciation was that another break-out to attack our vital trade in the Atlantic was in train. Churchill, however, evidently recalled the sorties by the High Seas Fleet in World War I, and believed that another battle on the Jutland model might be imminent.

As part of 'Plan R4' troops had been embarked in four cruisers under Rear-Admiral J. H. D. Cunningham at Rosyth to prepare to occupy Stavanger and Bergen, and on 8 April the Cabinet met to discuss, among other subjects, whether they should sail to carry out that purpose. General Sir Ian Jacob who was Military Assistant Secretary to the War Cabinet 1939–46, writes 'I have the clearest possible memory of the Cabinet meeting at which Chamberlain asked Churchill whether the cruisers had sailed or could sail to put the troops ashore, and Churchill replying that they had been disembarked so that the cruisers could join the fleet. He looked decidedly sheepish. The PM said "Oh" and there was a distinct silence.'[19] Though it is in fact improbable that, had Churchill not intervened, the troops could have established themselves in the Norwegian ports before the Germans arrived, the incident is of importance because it shows that, in Jacob's words, he 'did not insist on a reference to the COSs or Cabinet' before ordering the troops to be put ashore.[20] Though the order to disembark them was actually telephoned to Rosyth by Pound and, as Jacob has written, 'it is always difficult to disentangle Winston and Pound when the former was 1st Lord', there is no doubt that the decision was taken by Churchill. 'In naval matters', the same witness has recorded, 'his mind moved around the idea of the fleet action', which he finds 'the more surprising' when one takes account of German naval inferiority in 1940.[21]

Such was Churchill's first intervention in the naval side of the Norwegian campaign; and it provides an interesting example of his highly selective interpretation of history. But there is more to it than that. Admiral Forbes told the author that the order to disembark the troops was given 'entirely on their [the Admiralty's] own responsibility and much to my surprise'.[22] Furthermore the statement in Churchill's memoirs that 'all these decisive steps were concerted with the C-in-C' is manifestly incorrect,[23] since Forbes was at sea at the time and keeping wireless silence.

The bold German plan for the invasion of Denmark and Norway achieved complete success, though at a heavy cost to their navy. On the afternoon of the 8th the Admiralty told Rear-Admiral W. J. Whitworth, whose flag was flying in the battle-cruiser *Renown*, 'to concentrate on preventing any German force proceeding to Narvik'. But the destroyers sent to lay the minefield in the approaches to Vestfiord and their escort had been withdrawn on Admiralty orders and sent to join Whitworth, with the result that the ten big German destroyers allocated to the seizure of Narvik reached their destination unmolested, and quickly gained control of the town early on the 9th.

Before dealing with the naval operations off Norway something must be said about the exceptional difficulties they produced for the Flag Officers and Captains involved. Not only are those northern waters very stormy – and a violent gale was blowing at the time the operations began – but fog was common in April. This and the natural hazards of the rock-bound Norwegian coast made navigation and pilotage, and the operation of carrier-borne aircraft both dangerous and difficult – as we were to learn to our cost.

During the night of 8–9 April a number of signals reached Admiral Forbes from the Admiralty; but they did little to dispel the fog of war which had enveloped Norway. Early on the 9th the C-in-C asked for information about the enemy's strength in Bergen, which he proposed to attack. The Admiralty had a similar idea at about the same time, but wanted Forbes to prepare to attack Trondheim and keep an eye on Narvik as well – which was asking a lot of the forces available. However, shortly before noon Forbes detached a squadron of four modern cruisers and seven destroyers to attack Bergen. Early in the afternoon an air report came in that two modern German light cruisers and a smaller ship (the *Bremse*) were in the harbour; but it was believed, actually incorrectly, that the coastal batteries might be in enemy hands, which would make the passage of our ships up the fiord hazardous. Accordingly the Admiralty cancelled the attack. Though it was Pound who initiated the change of plan Churchill undoubtedly approved it – a decision which in retrospect he regretted.[24] As we now know that most of the enemy force which had been detailed to occupy Bergen was in fact still in harbour the chance of achieving an important success was thus sacrificed.

To return to Narvik, on the afternoon of 9 April Admiral Whit-worth detached some destroyers of the 2nd Flotilla, commanded by Captain B. A. W. Warburton-Lee, to patrol the entrance to Vestfiord. There the captain learnt from the Norwegian pilot station the truth about the strength of the German force which had gone up to Narvik. He signalled this information to the Admiralty, the C-in-C and Whit-worth, and added the words 'Intend attacking at dawn high water' on the 10th. Now every British naval officer of those days was familiar with the convention whereby the originator of a signal using the word 'Intend' neither demanded nor expected an answer *unless the addressee disapproved of the intention expressed*. Yet at 10 p.m. the Admiralty signalled giving Warburton-Lee discretion regarding what he should do, and in the early hours of the 10th they added 'You alone can judge whether in these circumstances [presumably a reference to the enemy's strength being greater than expected] attack should be made. We shall support whatever decision you take' – which has a Churchillian ring about it though Pound is shown as the originator. Whatever may be the truth about its composition this was an extraordinary message, since it took out of the hands of Forbes and Whitworth the decision whether Warburton–Lee's meagre strength of five destroyers should be reinforced – even at the price of delaying the attack. In fact Whitworth, with the battle cruisers *Renown* and *Repulse*, a light cruiser and four destroyers was not far off at the time; but he decided, partly to avoid the loss of surprise, not to tell Warburton–Lee to await the arrival of more ships. In retrospect Whitworth reproached himself bitterly on this account, writing that his decision arose from 'the Admiralty's intolerable action in communicating direct to ships under my command and entirely ignoring my presence'.[25] Though one may feel that a Nelson would have ignored the Admiralty's intervention and told Warburton–Lee to wait until reinforcements reached him, the outcome was unfortunate, since it resulted in the loss of two of his flotilla and its commander's death; and only two German destroyers were sunk and three others damaged.

Here we may quote some of the entries which Captain R. A. B. (later Admiral Sir Ralph) Edwards made in the two diaries he kept covering this period. One was an 'instant' or rough diary, here marked 'A', while the other was written up a short time later and is marked 'B'.[26] Though Edwards had been appointed Deputy Director of Operations (Home) he took over the duty of Director of that staff division on the afternoon of 5 April, and in that capacity was present in the Operational Intelligence Centre [OIC] or the War Room when policy and fleet movements were being discussed by the top naval hierarchy.

4 April 'A' I am sure we ought to cancel Operation Wilfred [the mine-laying operation]. Winston however is obsessed with the idea of forcing the enemy ships out of the fiords into the open waters . . .

5 April 'A' The more I think about the latter operation [Wilfred] the more convinced I am that it is a political blunder . . . We deliberately infringe international waters and therefore the law – I thought we were fighting for international law and order.

7 April 'B' I recommended that Operation Wilfred be postponed, but the 1st Lord and DCNS [Phillips] would not agree.

 'A' The First Sea Lord was away down at Broadlands [the Mountbattens' estate near Romsey] fishing for salmon and arrived back rather late in the evening.

 'B' The old man had been fishing all day and was dead beat, DCNS was tired and the 1st Lord well dined. The result was they all failed to come to any useful decision.

'A'   Winston Churchill is taking a great personal interest and tends
       to interfere with the sailor's business. He is an extraordinary
       man and has an astonishing grasp on the situation, but I wish
       he would keep to his own sphere . . . I am pretty sure that
       Sir Charles [Forbes] at Scapa was just as obsessed with the
       'break out into the Atlantic' theory as the First Sea Lord.

8 April 'A'   and 'B' Operation Wilfred was carried out in Vestfiord at
                0400 . . .

'A'   Senior Officers are exceedingly tired and DCNS who
       normally has a masterly grip appeared himself to be carried
       with the crowd. The fleet is still steaming madly to the north.

9 April 'B'   News was received in the very early morning that Norway
                was being invaded at many points up and down the coast . . .
                in fact from Oslo to Narvik.

'A'   There was a long discussion as to whether or not we ought to
       go into Bergen. It was approved and then called off.

11 April 'B' There was a very long meeting with WSC in the evening. He
                was half cocked as usual . . . but they came to the conclusion
                about 2315 that they ought to attack Trondheim. It was
                decided therefore to go and see CIGS. The meeting was
                going well when Winston lost his temper and spoilt the
                whole show.*

12 April 'A' Everyone is very indignant about the conduct of affairs and
                Winston appears to be the chief target. He will try and be a
                naval strategist if not an actual tactician.

Though one must obviously not take all the diarist's entries *au pied de
la lettre* the foregoing extracts do illustrate the muddle and confusion
which reigned in Whitehall, and the very intimate part played by
Churchill in the field of strategy as well as in the conduct of operations.
  On 12 April a carrier air attack on the German ships in Narvik
produced no results, so the Admiralty told Forbes to use surface ships
to finish them off. Next day Whitworth, having transferred his flag to
the battleship *Warspite*, took her and nine destroyers up to Narvik,
where they annihilated the German ships which had survived the first
attack. Whitworth considered that this success had so demoralized the

* This must surely have been the meeting described in *The Ironside Diaries*, ed. R.
MacLeod and D. Kelly (Constable, 1962) p. 257 but there retrospectively dated 14
April.

German garrison that a quick landing would have gained control of the town. But no troops were available, and the expedition for the capture of the place was in fact being sent initially to the Norwegian military centre of Harstad on the north side of Vestfiord some thirty-five miles west of Narvik as the crow flies.

Meanwhile the Germans had by a combination of boldness and ruthlessness gained control of Oslo and of the defended ports of Bergen and Trondheim in west Norway, as well as the vital airfields in Denmark (Aalborg), near Stavanger (Sola) and Trondheim (Vaernes), from all of which bombers and fighters were soon operating. The handicap which this imposed on all naval operations off south Norway soon became apparent, since RAF aircraft working from home bases could not provide adequate cover and our carrier-borne aircraft were completely outclassed by the enemy's fighters.

The military forces initially available for a counter-offensive in Norway were those which had been allocated to 'Plan R4', but its cancellation left the eight British battalions involved seriously disorganized by the confusion of the first days of the campaign; and in any case they had only been equipped for an unopposed landing and so had no artillery or tanks. Nor were the six French battalions earmarked for Narvik in much better state. On 10 April Admiral of the Fleet Lord Cork and Orrery, whom we encountered earlier as commander designate for the Baltic operation 'Catherine', was appointed Flag Officer, Narvik, and next day the first troop convoy sailed from the Clyde for that destination. Lord Cork was of course senior to Admiral Forbes the C-in-C, Home Fleet, but although his last sea-going command had ended five years earlier his personality had proved attractive to Churchill as an 'offensive-minded' officer. But he received only the most perfunctory briefing from the First Lord and First Sea Lord before he left London, was given no written instructions, and had not met the military Commander Major-General P. J. Mackesy until both arrived – in different cruisers – at Harstad. Thus were sown plentiful seeds for muddle and confusion. We will return later to events in the Narvik area because before any active operations were undertaken the focus of interest shifted to Trondheim in central Norway – which occupied a key strategic position.

The first plan was for a direct attack on the port (operation 'Hammer') involving the heavy ships of the Home Fleet, ten battalions of infantry and bombing attacks on enemy-held airfields by the RAF. Forbes first learnt of the plan on 14 April while still at sea off north Norway, and pointed out that if troop transports were employed very heavy losses to the German bombers were certain to be incurred, and that his ships had on board no high explosive shell suitable for bombardment. Churchill, however, strongly favoured the idea and on the 15th pressed Forbes to 'consider this important project further'. Details of the plan were sent to the C-in-C on his return to Scapa, and he declared himself ready to carry it out – provided that the troops were embarked in warships, not in merchant vessels.

We saw earlier how Admiral Keyes's strong support for the Dardanelles campaign of 1915, and the dominant part he played in the planning and execution of the Zeebrugge raid of April 1918, resulted in Churchill developing a strong admiration for and confidence in him. As soon as the Germans attacked Norway Keyes began to press on Churchill the need for a vigorous counter-blow against the occupied ports, and especially Trondheim. While operation 'Hammer' was being discussed he told his wife how he had 'suggested that he should get the old Rs [R. Class battleships] and any other obsolescent ships and prepare to smash up the Norwegian ports'. He also pressed his readiness to lead such an attack himself; but Churchill's reaction had been cool. He told the Admiral that he had 'worked himself into a state of excitement', that he 'had to take the advice of his professional advisers', and that he 'was not fit for command [because] he had been unemployed so long'.[27] As Keyes's last sea-going appointment had in fact been the Mediterranean command in 1925–8 he had been ashore even longer than Lord Cork, and was moreover a year older than him. However Keyes kept up the pressure until Churchill apparently lost patience, and told him he was 'astonished that you should think all this [the counter-measures in Norway] has not been examined by people who know exactly what resources are available, and what the dangers would be'.[28] Keyes also attacked Pound for his alleged opposition to giving him a sea-going command – which provoked an angry denial from the First Sea Lord.[29] In fact by the time these interchanges took place the direct attack on Trondheim had been cancelled, and the decision taken to substitute landings to the north and south of the port in the endeavour to close in on it by a pincer movement.[30] Accordingly on 14 April, on the initiative of Churchill, two of the five ships in the first troop convoy bound for Narvik were diverted to the more northerly of the two landings – an example of the sudden changes of plan and the switching of forces from one objective to another which were such a marked feature of this campaign, and which were bound to cause confusion.

The actual landings north and south of Trondheim were successfully carried out, and the soldiers attempted to press inland to accomplish their purpose; but German mastery of the air was so complete and the training and equipment of their forces so superior that all prospect of success quickly vanished, and the British and French navies were finally faced by the hazardous task of evacuating about 10,500 soldiers. That was successfully accomplished between 30 April and 3 May. Although in retrospect Churchill regretted that we had not persevered with 'Hammer',[31] the geographic and strategic conditions at Trondheim were such that it would probably have ended in a costly failure. One benefit which accrued from the strategy actually adopted was the rescue of the King of Norway and his government, which thereafter gave valuable help to the Allied cause.

To return to Narvik, difficulties soon arose between Lord Cork and General Mackesy. The former wished to press ahead with an early assault on the town, while the latter considered it unduly hazardous, if not impossible in the deep snow which still covered the country. The General also stressed the fact that because only a small number of the new and specially designed landing craft were available most of the troops would have to be ferried to the assault points, probably in face of machine-gun fire, in open naval boats.

Meanwhile Churchill was taking the liveliest interest in the progress of the undertaking, and was instrumental in placing Lord Cork in supreme command on 20 April and in having Mackesy replaced by General Auchinleck on 13 May. It is interesting to see how this clash appeared in the Admiralty, as recorded in Captain Edwards's diary.

20 April 'A'   I gather the General and the Admiral up in the northern area are fighting cat and dog. But if you will send two men from Whitehall with a completely and utterly different conception of what they are to do, and not meet until a battle is imminent what are you to expect?

'B'   Lord Cork has been placed in Supreme Command of northern operations.

21 April 'A'   It appears there is a first class row brewing between Cork and Mackesy and the First Lord is taking a hand in the game. I have just discovered that Cork and First Lord have their own private line of communication and they may exchange all sorts of messages without the Admiralty having the slightest idea of what is going on. [Note. This was correct. See Appendix.] I have reported it to the First Sea Lord.

29 April 'A'   C-in-C Home Fleet and Lord Cork appear to be having
their usual bickering match ... Winston entered the fray and
decided against the recommendation of the Naval Staff. This
interference is appalling and we don't appear strong enough
to stand up to it.

General Mackesy certainly cannot be numbered among the thrusting,
offensively-minded officers who appealed to Churchill; and he had
been unenthusiastic about the Narvik expedition from the start. But
close investigation of the events after he arrived at Harstad, from
German as well as British sources, lends support to the view that
Narvik could not have been captured by a *coup de main* soon after the
destruction of the naval forces there, and that an assault with the
forces available on his arrival would almost certainly have ended in a
costly failure. Mackesy's son, a distinguished Oxford historian, has
brought all the evidence together in an admirably objective study, in
which he concludes that, although the General's expression of his views
and his ability to work amicably with the naval commander could have
been improved on, his tactical purposes were sound.[32] Certainly he
did not deserve the account of the expedition 'cast in a framework of
factual inaccuracy, of careful innuendo, and of inconsistencies' which
Churchill published in his memoirs eight years later.[33] It should also
be remarked that the operations ultimately launched to capture the
town corresponded almost exactly to those which Mackesy had put
forward early in the campaign.[34]

Although we will examine Churchill's part in the Narvik operations
more closely at the end of this work* it is appropriate to mention here
that he may well have seen in General Mackesy a replica of General Sir
Frederick Stopford, the elderly and dilatory commander of the forces
which achieved surprise in the Suvla Bay landing of 6 August 1915
but totally failed to exploit the opportunity to gain the commanding
heights of the Gallipoli peninsula. Moreover Churchill can hardly
have forgotten how General Sir Ian Hamilton, the army C-in-C, was
both reluctant to *order* Stopford to advance and slow to have him
replaced.[35] The conclusion surely is that in Churchill's mind the
clouds of Gallipoli 1915 hung over the snows of Narvik 1940.

The German assault on the Low Countries and France began on
10 May, and it was obviously impossible for us to maintain a large
expeditionary force in north Norway and also meet the heavy commitments in the west. Accordingly on the 24th the Cabinet approved

* See Appendix, pp. 283-99

evacuation after the town had been captured. That took place on the 28th, after which all efforts had to be concentrated on bringing home some 24,000 troops and as much of their equipment as possible. Also the RAF fighters which had, at a great expense of effort, recently been working from newly constructed but primitive airfields near Narvik, had to be saved if possible, since they would plainly soon be needed for the defence of Britain. The only way this could be accomplished was by flying them on to the Home Fleet's aircraft carriers, on board which preparations were accordingly made.

The evacuation began on 4 June when the first of a series of homeward bound convoys of troopships and supply vessels sailed, and continued until the 8th when the last soldiers were embarked. But neither the Admiralty nor Lord Cork had kept Admiral Forbes fully informed of these important movements, with the result that a sortie by the German battle-cruisers *Scharnhorst* and *Gneisenau* and the heavy cruiser *Hipper* on 4 June caught the British defenders by surprise. The German ships' first victims were not of great importance; but on the afternoon of the 8th they sighted the aircraft carrier *Glorious*, which had just completed flying on a squadron of RAF Hurricanes. After accomplishing that her Captain requested permission to return to Scapa independently, which the Admiral, Aircraft Carriers in the *Ark Royal* approved. For a long time it was believed that the *Glorious*'s request was based on shortage of fuel; and her endurance was certainly less than the *Ark Royal*'s. In his memoirs Churchill described this explanation as 'unconvincing', and argued that 'All [the warships] should have been kept together.'[36] Though I shall be publishing elsewhere a full account of the circumstances attending the loss of the *Glorious* it is relevant to mention here that the story of fuel shortage is false. Not only had she replenished at Scapa before sailing for the last time, but the captain of the destroyer *Diana* took in a long visual signal made by the *Glorious* to the *Ark Royal* asking permission to proceed to Scapa 'in order to expedite Courts Martial' – by which the captain of the *Glorious* undoubtedly meant the trial of his own Commander (Flying) with whom he had recently had a serious clash over the use of the ships' aircraft for a bombing attack on certain vaguely defined targets in Norway. The *Diana*'s captain has recently added a note to that effect to the official Admiralty records of the disaster.[37]

For some inexplicable reason the *Glorious* was not maintaining a patrol with the reconnaissance aircraft which the Admiralty had ordered her to keep on board for her own protection, and was thus caught completely unawares. Though her two escorting destroyers did their utmost to shield the carrier they were soon sunk; but one of them obtained a lucky torpedo hit on the *Scharnhorst* when in her death throes, and the German admiral thereupon broke off the operation and returned to Trondheim. Thus the sinking of the *Glorious* and her escort, though it cost 1470 lives, probably saved the lightly escorted troop convoys further north.

So ended a campaign in which, as Professor Marder has remarked, 'there can be no dispute about Churchill's strong influence on the inept overall strategy . . . including the constant changes of plan, as well as upon the combined operations'; and again 'That the Admiralty intervened seriously in naval operations, particularly in the early stages of the campaign is an indisputable fact, as is the fact that this caused much resentment in the fleet at the time.'[38] With those conclusions I am in complete accord, though I cannot understand how, taking account of Churchill's own view of his responsibilities already quoted, the Professor can apparently regard the First Lord as having had little or no share in what he calls the interventions by '*the Admiralty*'.

Shortly after the Germans began their great offensive in the west the question of giving the Americans most or all of our technical knowledge and experience was raised by Alexander proposing to Churchill that we should make 'an unrestricted offer to pool technical information', and also reconsider the request of the US Navy to appoint 'observers' to our principal warships – which Churchill had turned down as First Lord.[39] In fact a good deal of interchange of technical information, in which this author had a part, was already in progress with the US Naval Attaché's staff; but it was plainly desirable to regularize the position. Churchill was however surprisingly cool about extending it, apparently because his earlier offer to exchange our Asdic for the Norden bombsight had been rejected. Though Lindemann favoured a full and free exchange Churchill minuted 'I am still disinclined to do this at the moment', and that he was 'waiting for a further development of the American attitude'.[40] Next Beaverbrook came out in favour of 'giving the Americans all our secrets in exchange for money or money's worth' – a somewhat commercial concept of the purpose;[41] but Churchill told General Ismay that he did not see 'what we are going to get out of this arrangement . . . Generally speaking I am not in a hurry until the United States is much nearer to the war than she is now'. He also expected that anything we gave the Americans would be passed to the Germans.[42]

Meanwhile Professor A. V. Hill, the renowned physiologist and biochemist of Cambridge University, whose friendship with Royal

Navy men, especially of the Gunnery branch, dated back to World War I, had gone to the USA on a mission. He reported that 'great facilities [were] potentially available' to us in that country, and the President, whom Hill had met, let it be known that he would be glad if 'a special mission could come as soon as possible'.[43] Such were the origins of the famous Tizard mission of September 1940, which took to America what Roosevelt called 'the most valuable cargo ever to reach our shores'.[44] The Admiralty was represented on the mission, and on its conclusion a special committee under Admiral Sir Thomas Binney was appointed to deal with all the problems of arranging a virtually unrestricted exchange of scientific and technical knowledge and of our war experience. By the time the strong American naval mission under Admiral R. C. Ghormley arrived in London in the autumn arrangements for the transmission of nearly all our developments and experience had been fully worked out.*

It will be convenient to bring in here some account of Churchill's dealings with the Admiralty in the months shortly after he had become Prime Minister. In August 1940 he set out his ideas on future naval building; and that gave him an opening to attack the Admiralty for their 'disastrous neglect' to convert the old *R. Class* battleships 'into properly armoured and bulged bombarding vessels' – for which he had pressed when his Baltic plan 'Catherine' was being seriously considered. He demanded a list of the occasions when he had put up this proposal as First Lord. But he never seems to have come near to understanding the enormous amount of work involved in such reconstructions, and the huge quantities of scarce materials, such as armour plate, needed. Furthermore to give those old ships what he called 'cocked up' main armament guns (i.e. 30 degrees elevation instead of 20) in fact involved great technical difficulties and the manufacture of many new parts for the gun mountings. His strictures describing the failure to carry out all this work during the first year of the war as ranking with 'the most melancholy pages of the Admiralty annals' produced a vigorous protest from Alexander and Pound.[45]

Churchill's next attack concerned the alleged delay in getting reserve ships into commission, especially the 15-inch gun monitor *Erebus*, which had been in use as a cadet training ship before the war but which he now wanted for bombardment purposes. In September Pound told him that because of the shortage of trained men and the

---

* This author was the Naval Staff officer deputed to give the able gunnery expert on the Ghormley mission Commander (later Rear-Admiral) E. M. Eller all that he needed – especially about our progress in radar control of weapons.

widespread dilution of all crews with 'Hostilities Only' ratings, working
ships up to full efficiency was bound to take far longer. This statement
produced an explosion from Churchill, who declared that according to
the policy he had laid down (presumably as First Lord) the 'best ships
should be given matured crews, taken from older ships'; and he claimed
that if the old battleship *Revenge*'s crew had been 'turned over' to the
new *King George V* the latter could have 'come into service several
weeks earlier'. He accused the department of the Second Sea Lord
(Admiral Sir Charles Little) of having 'sagged back into their old way
of putting the rawest crews on the finest ships' – which he described
as 'nothing less than a scandal'. Little told Pound the obvious fact that
'block transfer [of crews] is just not practicable'; and as the two ships
named by Churchill had totally different armaments prolonged re-
training would in any case have been necessary. But Churchill was not
satisfied by that explanation, telling Alexander that it 'would require
continuous pressure from yourself to make any headway against them
[presumably the Second Sea Lord's department]'.[46] This rumpus
probably explains why Churchill formed an unjustifiably poor opinion
of Admiral Little, with consequences to which we will revert later.

The foregoing exchanges have been recounted in some detail
because they show how, even after Churchill became Prime Minister,
he continued to act as though he were still First Lord. The strategic
issues, such as counter-measures to invasion, came of course within his
province as Minister of Defence; but on details of manning and
training he virtually usurped the functions of the Board of Admiralty –
and without the technical knowledge on which criticisms of their
policy and actions might perhaps have been justified.

We may conclude this chapter by describing Churchill's dealings
with certain other admirals in shore appointments. The clash between
him and Sir Roger Keyes about attacking the enemy-occupied Norwegian ports in April 1940 has already been mentioned. But that disagreement did not cause Churchill to lose confidence in the bellicose,
fire-eating admiral. On 27 April, when the Norwegian campaign was
at its height, he asked Keyes to produce 'at your earliest convenience . . .
three or four proposals for medium-sized action (i.e. between 5000
and 10,000 men) in raids against enemy-held objectives'[47] – a request
which Keyes was very ready to meet even though the number of men
trained for such enterprises did not come anywhere near the total
envisaged by Churchill. In the following July, by which time he was
Prime Minister, Churchill appointed Keyes Director of Combined
Operations (DCO) in place of General A. G. Bourne, the Royal Marine

officer who had been holding the post known as Commander of Raiding Operations but was required for appointment as Adjutant-General of his Corps.* As soon as he took over the job which he had so ardently wanted and worked for Keyes flung himself whole-heartedly into the recruitment of volunteers for the Commandos, obtaining and fitting out the necessary assault ships and landing craft, and creating establishments where the necessary training would be carried out.

Though Lord Mountbatten told me that, when he took over as DCO from Keyes he inherited 'absolutely nothing' of value the records suggest that this was less than fair to his predecessor,[48] since by the autumn of 1940 Keyes told Churchill he had 5000 men organized in ten Commandos ready for action. He was also planning a large number of small, and some not so small raiding operations, a few of which will be recounted later. But unfortunately the admiral's methods were so single-minded and tactless that he antagonized the conventional staffs and the COSs, who of course had to take a wider view of the war as a whole than came within the compass, and indeed the experience, of the DCO. Though Churchill gave Keyes his support for nearly a year the final outcome was inevitable. We will return to the débâcle of the autumn of 1941 later.

One admiral whose dealings with Churchill are of considerable interest despite the fact that he never flew his flag afloat is Admiral A. F. (later Sir Francis) Pridham. He would almost certainly have been given a sea-going command early in the war had he not got athwart Pound's hawse when captain of the battle-cruiser *Hood*, of which he took command early in 1936 after two years as Captain of the gunnery school *Excellent* at Portsmouth. The fact that Pridham was given two such plum jobs in succession indicates that he was marked for high promotion; but it was not to be. In 1938 all captains of ships received an Admiralty memorandum entitled 'Disaffection' – doubtless an end product of the Invergordon mutiny of 1931. Pridham has written that he 'took a violent dislike to the title', which should in his view have been 'boldly called "Mutiny"';[49] and he had in fact anticipated its purpose by producing a 'Captain's Memorandum' on the subject,

* The date of Keyes's official appointment as DCO was 17 July 1940. According to him the First Lord, A. V. Alexander, had a big hand in getting him given the appointment, and in a letter dated 5 December 1941 Keyes thanked him for his services in that respect. Alexander may well have played a part in his selection, but it seems far more likely that Churchill initiated it and the First Lord merely gave his support. Keyes papers KEYS 13/1.

which all his officers were required to study on joining the *Hood*. As he greatly preferred this approach to the Admiralty's alternative he put pen to paper and told his C-in-C exactly why he had not carried out the Admiralty's order to read their memorandum to his officers. Unfortunately it was Admiral Pound who as Second Sea Lord had produced it; and in 1938 Pound took over as C-in-C, Mediterranean – the station on which the *Hood* was serving. He never spoke to Pridham again, and even refused him an appointment to pay a farewell call on leaving the station.⁵⁰ It thus came to pass that when war broke out shortly after Pound had replaced the dying Sir Roger Backhouse as First Sea Lord in June 1939 Pridham was given the very inferior appointment of Flag Officer, Humber, instead of command of the cruiser squadron he had been promised.

In November 1940 Pridham became Vice-President of the Ordnance Board, an inter-service body responsible for research and development in weaponry and for design of new armaments. On taking up the appointment A. V. Alexander gave him a brief emanating from Churchill. It instructed him 'to go down to Woolwich [Arsenal], find out what those silly old men are doing, and make them do their job or sack the lot'.*⁵¹ After a year as Vice-President during which Pridham became very much aware of the deficiencies of the organization he was serving, he was appointed President of the Board; and that brought him into direct touch with Lord Hankey, who was chairman of the Scientific Advisory Committee and, later, of its Engineering counterpart.⁵² Moreover the President of the Ordnance Board was solely responsible to the COSs, which brought Pridham into contact with Lord Cherwell and so with Churchill.† Pridham established excellent relations with Cherwell, who was at the time engaged on creating the organization which was ironically dubbed 'Winston Churchill's Toyshop.' It produced and tested a vast variety of new weapons and gadgets – some of which were successful though others bordered on the fantastic.⁵³

Two years later Pridham's term of appointment was about to expire, and his relief (a Gunner Major-General) had been nominated. Then, on Cherwell's initiative, Churchill intervened with one of his famous 'Prayers'. 'I am informed,' it read, 'that the President of the Ordnance

---

* The Ordnance Board had in fact been widely dispersed from Woolwich at that time. The Research Department was at Shrewsbury and the Design Deaprtment near Chislehurst in Kent – a separation which produced great inefficiency.

† Professor Lindemann was elevated to the Peerage in 1941 and took the title of Lord Cherwell after the river on which Oxford University stands.

Board is about to be relieved. Pray tell me why'; and on being told of the intention to replace him with the Major-General he added 'Buggins's turn. Pridham is to remain where he is';[54] and so it came to pass – until the end of the war. This was a case where Cherwell's influence was wholly beneficial; and if any student of the material side of World War II wants to know the inside story of why, for example, between 30 and 60 per cent of the navy's armour piercing shell produced for that conflict were likely to fail, or why the army had no better anti-tank gun than the totally inadequate 2-pounder in 1939, or the story of the development of the Proximity (or VT) fuze he should certainly consult Pridham's unpublished memoirs. His influence in the technological field was widespread and wholly advantageous; and but for Cherwell's intervention and Churchill's prompt action it would have been lost.

114

The Home Theatre
1939-1942

0   50   100   150
Nautical Miles

Shetland Islands

North Rona

Orkney Islands

Cape Wrath

Pentland Firth

Scapa Flow

Stornoway

St. Kilda

Moray Firth

Rockall

WESTERN ISLES

Skye

Inverness

Aberdeen

SCOTLAND

Mull

Oban

Dundee

Greenock

Firth of Forth

Atlantic Ocean

Edinburgh

Glasgow

Bloody Foreland

Londonderry

Larne

Belfast

North Channel

Newcastle

Isle of Man

Irish Sea

Liverpool

Galway

IRELAND

Dublin

Limerick

Wexford

St. Georges Channel

Fishguard

Pembroke

Swansea

Cardiff

ENGLAND

Cork

Queenstown

Milford Haven

Bristol Channel

Bearhaven

Southampton

Exeter

Plymouth

Lands End

Falmouth

English Channel

MAP (2)   "BEAR HAVEN"
CORRECTLY SPELLED
"BEREHAVEN"   (BANTRY BAY)

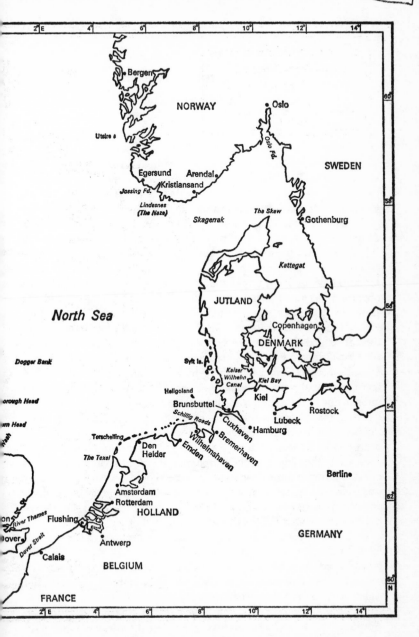

CHAPTER 9

The Admirals Afloat.
I. Home Waters and the Atlantic
1939-1942

So far we have been concerned mainly with Churchill's relations with
the admirals in Whitehall, but it is now time to consider how those who
were flying their flags afloat fared in their dealings with him. When
Churchill returned to the Admiralty in September 1939 he inherited
as Cs-in-C, Home and Mediterranean Fleets Sir Charles Forbes and Sir
Andrew Cunningham, and it is with them that we shall chiefly deal in
this chapter and the next. It is, however, first necessary to say a little
about British practice regarding the operational control of naval
forces. The Admiralty, unlike the War Office and Air Ministry, was an
operational centre as well as an administrative department, and the
Board of Admiralty was invested with wide powers of instruction to
and direction of naval forces. The extent to which those powers were
used depended chiefly on the personalities, preferences and outlook of
the First Lord and First Sea Lord. Before the outbreak of war Admiral
Pound wrote to Forbes describing his broad intentions. He proposed
that the normal practice should be to give the C-in-C all the available
information and leave him to order the necessary dispositions; but he
qualified that principle drastically by suggesting that, especially when
the fleet was keeping wireless silence, it should be 'recognized that at
times it will be necessary for the Admiralty to alter dispositions'. Forbes
at once saw the dangers in this proposal, and replied asking that 'if at all
possible information rather than an order should be passed';[1] but he
was in fact the admiral who first suffered from such practices – which
continued throughout Pound's time as First Sea Lord and were
particularly evident while Churchill was First Lord.

In October 1939 Pound sent Forbes a fuller description of his
intentions in the matter of operational control. 'All Commands are
treated alike', he wrote, '. . . Every C-in-C sends his forces to sea and
orders them to return to harbour when he likes. Naturally I reserve the
right to butt in if I consider it necessary, but I should never do so if it
could possibly be avoided . . . Another reason why it is fatal for the
Admiralty to try and control forces at sea is that in these days of W/T

[i.e. wireless] silence one often does not know where they are within 200 miles.'[2] Several points in this letter invite comment. Firstly Pound certainly did not in practice follow the intention expressed in the first sentence quoted; and interventions in Home Fleet operations were far more frequent than in those of overseas commands. Secondly Pound certainly did not eschew intervention 'if it could possibly be avoided'; nor did Churchill either as First Lord or as Prime Minister. More will be said on that score later. Thirdly it may be remarked that when Churchill was angered by what I had written in the first volume of *The War at Sea* about Admiralty interventions he took a diametrically opposite view to that expressed by Pound to Forbes – namely that modern conditions, and especially the maintenance of wireless silence, had made it *necessary* for the Admiralty to give orders, not only to Cs-in-C but possibly to individual ships or squadrons under their command.[3]

It is interesting to find that Forbes never changed his views on the danger of excessive Admiralty interventions; and other officers who served as Cs-in-C either afloat or ashore fully supported him on that score. For example when in 1942 Pound called a meeting of all Cs-in-C of Home Commands at the Admiralty Forbes pressed that 'a return should be made to the old Service custom of giving a C-in-C instructions and leaving him to carry them out'; and he quoted several examples of that principle being infringed. Pound then made the surprising statement that 'there was no intention of operations being centralized by the Admiralty'.[4] It is difficult both to reconcile Churchill's views on interventions with Pound's and to explain the wide discrepancy between the expressed intentions and the actual practices of the latter.

While Italy remained neutral most of the Mediterranean Fleet was called home or sent to hunt for German commerce raiders in the Indian Ocean and South Atlantic; so Cunningham had little to do except chafe over his forced inactivity. Forbes on the other hand was faced by many difficult problems. Scapa Flow in the Orkneys, which had been chosen rather belatedly in 1938 to serve again as the fleet's main base, was ill-defended against both air and submarine attacks, and after the sinking of the battleship *Royal Oak* inside the Flow by U.47 on 14 October 1939, and the damage done on 4 December to Forbes's flagship the *Nelson* by a magnetic mine laid by another U-boat off Loch Ewe on the north-west coast of Scotland, a long interchange took place between the Admiralty and Forbes regarding whether his fleet should be based on the Clyde or Rosyth instead of Scapa. Forbes held that the

Clyde was much too far away from the waters where his ships might at any moment be needed – namely the passages leading from the North Sea out into the Atlantic; while Rosyth, though far better placed strategically, had the disadvantage that it could easily be obstructed with mines and was more liable to attack from the air than Scapa. Damage inflicted on warships in Rosyth on 16 October had emphasized the latter danger. Forbes therefore wanted to get Scapa well enough defended for his fleet to return there, and he told the Admiralty that he 'totally disagreed' with their proposal that he should use the Clyde. This message seems to have annoyed Churchill, who visited Forbes on board his flagship in the Clyde on the last day of October 1939, accompanied by the First Sea Lord and the Deputy Chief of the Air Staff. Churchill opened the ball with the remark 'We made a perfectly polite signal to you for good reason and you replied "I totally disagree" '. After they had argued 'hammer and tongs' during the forenoon Churchill took Forbes aside and told him he was converted to the admiral's view, and that he now had to convert the other two.[5] So Forbes won his first argument with Churchill – which shows that by making a resolute stand straight away, which was not Pound's tactic in handling Churchill, he could be brought to accept an admiral's view. A big effort was accordingly made to put the defences of Scapa in order, and the fleet was able to return there in March 1940. Incidentally the government appointed Admiral Chatfield, who had been First Sea Lord 1933-38 and was Minister for Co-ordination of Defence in Chamberlain's War Cabinet in 1939, to inquire into the circumstances surrounding the sinking of the *Royal Oak*; and in his report Chatfield placed the main responsibility for the inadequacy of the defences of the anchorage squarely on the pre-war Board of Admiralty.[6]

The troubles which beset Forbes during the first phase of the war did not, however, end with the settlement of the issue of where his main base should be. In November 1939 he missed the *Scharnhorst* and *Gneisenau* on their homeward passage after they had made a raid on the lightly armed ships of the Northern Patrol;[7] and on several occasions he failed to intercept German warships or disguised merchant raiders on their outward or homeward passages by way of the northern passages to the Atlantic. Then came the German surprise attack on Norway when none of their naval forces sent to occupy the key ports (Bergen, Trondheim and Narvik) was intercepted while at sea except by submarines, though heavy losses were inflicted *after* they had reached their destinations. We now know that Forbes's chief handicap was that the Germans had broken our naval cypher, and so knew, at any rate approximately, what dispositions the Home Fleet was taking up. Thus there is substance in Forbes's complaint that 'It is most galling that the enemy should know just where our ships . . . always are, whereas we generally learn where his major forces are when they sink one or more of our ships.'[8] In the fleet there was much disgruntlement over these failures, which gained Forbes – most unfairly – the nickname of 'Wrong Way Charlie'.

It has already been told how the Norwegian campaign brought many new troubles, and heavy losses to the fleet; and it was then that the navy learnt the hard lesson that, so long as adequate air cover was lacking, control of coastal waters by warships in support of military operations was impossible. Forbes himself became very critical about the ineffectiveness of his ships' A-A gunnery; and it was in those months that the mistakes made by the Admiralty before the war in the design of such weapons and their control systems came home to roost. Rear-Admiral Tom Phillips, the Deputy Chief of Naval Staff, who had no first-hand experience of the deadly effect of unopposed dive-bombers on warships, insisted that all that was needed to deal with them effectively was greater courage and resolution; and he took it very badly when told that such ideas were unjust to those officers who had the experience, and were in fact far from the truth.*

It was during the invasion scare of the summer of 1940 that disagreement between Forbes and the Admiralty came to a head. The COSs proposed that most of the fleet should be scattered around east and south coast ports to counter invasion, and the War Cabinet approved such dispositions.[9] This led to the Atlantic convoys being practically stripped of their escorts, and so to the U-boats enjoying the period which their captains described as their 'happy time', when they could pick off unprotected merchant ships, whether sailing independently or in ill-defended convoys, with virtual immunity to themselves. On 28 September Forbes made his 'final appeal' to the Admiralty to reconsider these dispositions. He represented that, as most of his ships could reach the places where the enemy was likely to launch an invasion attempt within twenty four hours, the dispersal of his fleet around the coast was as unnecessary as it was harmful; and he argued that the duty of dealing with the first flight of an invading force should be placed squarely on the Army in accordance with its 'immemorial role', but in modern

---

* I had a stormy interview with Phillips on this matter when I brought back to the Admiralty first-hand reports of the effect of bombing off Norway in April 1940. Phillips *would* not accept that it was suicidal to send warships to operate off an enemy-held coast without air cover.

conditions assisted by the RAF. The Navy would in his view then be free to carry out its proper function of acting 'offensively against the enemy and in defence of our trade'.[9A] Today it is of course clear that, having won his sweeping victories in Europe, Hitler could achieve no further expansion westwards, because of Germany's maritime weakness. Though Churchill did not see this at the time Forbes undoubtedly did. Reviewing these problems many years later Lord Cunningham wrote 'How right he [Forbes] was . . . He was in my opinion quite one of the soundest and best of our war admirals, and was never given credit for his doings. Winston and Brendan Bracken disliked him.'[10*] Pound, however would not at the time accept such a view, and undoubtedly knew that there was criticism of Forbes in the fleet.

While the invasion threat was at its height in the summer of 1940 Churchill took, as was natural, the liveliest interest in naval dispositions and other measures to defeat it. Even before the fall of France he told A. V. Alexander that he was 'content with your proposed disposition of heavy ships in the West'.[11] The ships in question included the creation of a new squadron at Gibraltar (Force H) to replace French sea power in the western Mediterranean, and powerful Home Fleet units brought from Scapa Flow to Rosyth on the Firth of Forth in order, as Churchill put it, 'to cover the island'. Churchill was on sounder grounds in stressing that 'If we have to quit Gibraltar [because of Spain declaring war] we must immediately take the Canaries, which will serve as a very good base to control the western entrance to the Mediterranean.' 'All preparations,' he added, 'were to be made' to carry out that intention;[12] and the plan was therefore prepared by Admiral Keyes's Combined Operations command.

Churchill also produced many ideas about how, if the invasion forces sailed, they should be dealt with; and he fired a number of heavy broadsides at various aspects of the Admiralty's administration, planning and operational control. One of his brainwaves was to resurrect the use of fireships by means of which 'a sheet of flaming oil' could be 'spread over one or more of the invasion harbours'. But that idea was in fact already being put in hand by Lord Hankey, now Chancellor of the Duchy of Lancaster, who had been attracted by an expedient which he described as the use of 'Greek fire'; and experiments were

* Admiral K. G. B. Dewar, who although a controversial character, especially after the '*Royal Oak* Incident' of 1928, (see Roskill, *Naval Policy*, I, pp. 559-60) had a very good brain, wrote to the author in 1957 'Forbes's objections to immobilizing A/S craft in the anti-invasion ports while the U-boats created havoc in the Western Approaches, were therefore thoroughly justified.'

being carried out well before Churchill brought the matter up.[13]

In February 1947 Admiral Forbes met Churchill at a Navy. Club dinner at which the wartime Prime Minister was the guest of honour and made, in Forbes's words, 'a very good, human and friendly speech'. In discussing the anti-invasion plans of 1940 after dinner Churchill told the admiral that 'He himself had never believed that invasion was possible.' To which Forbes replied 'to the effect that he had camouflaged it very well.' Churchill then raised the question of how far south the C-in-C would have brought such units of the Home Fleet as were left to him 'if the Germans had invaded,' and Forbes told him that such a question, which had in fact been an issue between them in 1940, 'did not arise as I was certain the Hun would not invade us'. However he concluded his record of the encounter by remarking that 'We made it up'; and so ended a long controversy.[14]

Though no contemporary record of the reasons for the premature relief of Forbes has been found, in September 1940 Pound wrote to Cunningham that Admiral J. C. (later Lord) Tovey, who was in command of the Mediterranean Fleet's Light Forces, was to come home because 'there seems to be some chance CMF [i.e. Forbes] will be relieved in the near future – not because he has not done well but because there is a growing demand for younger people.'[15] However in 1942, when Churchill was pressing for Cunningham to replace Tovey in command of the Home Fleet and referred to the premature relief of Forbes as a precedent, Pound reminded Alexander that it had been done because he 'had reason to believe that he [Forbes] had not got the confidence of the Fleet, and I therefore recommended to you that it was desirable that he should be relieved and you accepted my advice'[16] – which was very different from what he had told Cunningham two years earlier.

Admiral Tovey was accordingly called home, was summoned to meet Churchill, and sent Cunningham an amusing letter about the encounter. 'You know the PM much better than I do,' he wrote, 'and you will understand how I loved him almost at first sight, but he made some such astounding statements about naval warfare . . . [that] I still don't know if he was wanting to find out if I was prepared to applaud everything he said or whether he really believes half what he says.' In expectation of a difficult interview Tovey had, however, 'schooled himself' to keep his sense of humour and 'moderate his language'. 'The PM,' he continued, 'was quite charming,' and told Tovey that 'he didn t mind my being absolutely outspoken, in fact he liked it.' As to the recent attacks on the French warships in Oran and Dakar, of which more later, Churchill had said that he considered Cunningham had been 'too pussy-foot' in his dealings with Admiral Godfroy, the commander of the French squadron at Alexandria, which got Tovey, who had of course been present during the negotiations, 'rather on the raw'.[17] None the less the offer of command of the Home Fleet was made. The interview took place at Chequers, with Air Marshal Dowding (C-in-C, Fighter Command) and Churchill's private secretary Eric Seal as well as A. V. Alexander and Admiral Harwood (ACNS, Foreign) present. Churchill then blamed the heads of the services, and not the politicians, for the poor state of the services in 1939; and when Tovey responded with some 'extremely generous' remarks about the pre-war COSs, Churchill and Alexander 'walked out of the room' – which suggests that Churchill's earlier assurance that he wanted Tovey to be 'absolutely outspoken' was subject to drastic qualifications. Next day Tovey was told that 'the change in command was postponed and he was to return to the Mediterranean'. Later, however, 'they changed their minds again', he wrote;[18] and so it came to pass that he took over from Forbes on 2 December 1940. Tovey's strength of character and outspoken manner were in truth such as made it certain that he would not take kindly to interventions in operational matters by Pound or Churchill.

In 1938 Churchill had attacked Neville Chamberlain's government fiercely for surrendering the right to use the three Naval bases in Eire which he himself had been instrumental in retaining under the 1921 Anglo-Irish Treaty.[19] Perhaps it was because the renunciation of those rights occupied a prominent place in Churchill's indictment of pre-war policy that, early in his premiership, he considered ways and means of reversing it. At any rate in July 1940 he considered the possibility of sending troops from Ulster across the western border into the Irish Free State, presumably to occupy Lough Swilly.[20] But the COSs had far too much on their hands at that time to look favourably on such an idea; nor did the Admiralty see any appreciable advantage in it – so long as the bases in Ulster were available. In the following November the British representative in Dublin, Sir John Maffey (Lord Rugby, 1947), had an interview with de Valera at which the question of the bases was raised; but he got little or no change. On reading Maffey's report Churchill wrote angrily to the Dominions Secretary 'So we are not only to be strangled by them [the Irish] but to suffer our fate without complaint.' Maffey, he directed, should be made aware 'of the rising anger in England and Scotland, and especially among merchant seamen' which he considered the attitude of the Eire government was stimulating.[21] In fact the fall of France had forced us to bring all our con-

voys in by the north-western approaches, and possession of the bases in
Eire would therefore have made little difference to their defence. The
Admiralty and COSs therefore damped down Churchill's ardour.

Churchill was, as already remarked, keenly interested in any 'naval
offensive,' and he strongly supported the recruitment of Commandos
for raiding operations. Early in March 1941 Admiral Tovey carried out
an attack on the Lofoten Islands off north-west Norway (operation
'Claymore'), with the primary purpose of destroying fish oil factories.
The Director of Combined Operations, Admiral of the Fleet Sir Roger
Keyes, the hero of the Zeebrugge raid of April 1918, had a big hand
in its planning and execution, and to Churchill's delight it was completely successful.[22] He signalled to Admiral Tovey 'I am so glad you
were able to find means of executing "Claymore". This admirable
raid has done serious injury to the enemy and has given an immense amount of innocent pleasure at home.'[23] But the Home
Fleet's next undertaking of that nature produced a very different reaction
from him.

Towards the end of 1941 a combined operation called 'Anklet'
against the island of Vaagsö in the same area was mounted. Rear-
Admiral L. H. K. Hamilton was in command, and the objectives of the
raid were described as 'limited'. Churchill was in Washington at the
time for the meeting with the American political and military leaders
known as the 'Arcadia' Conference, and when the results of the operation were telegraphed to him he answered on 29 December in very
critical language. 'I cannot understand,' he told the COSs, 'why on the
threat of dive-bombers arriving at Bodö [a small port further south] the
operation Anklet should have been turned into a "raid of short dura-
tion". After all these elaborate preparations you have certainly made a
very hasty departure. Pray let me have full explanation of what appears
to be a complete abandonment of the original plan.'[24] Apart from its
ungracious tone this message confirms the view expressed earlier,
namely that Churchill had not yet grasped that even minor combined
operations do require 'elaborate preparations' and prolonged training.
Admiral Phillips, the VCNS, sent a reply to the above message to
Pound, who was in Washington with Churchill, saying that 'Hamilton
was instructed by [the] C-in-C, Home Fleet, not to hesitate to withdraw if he considered [the] air threat serious.' He had not yet returned
to harbour, so a full report must be awaited.[25] On 5 January the COSs
telegraphed fuller information about the air threat and consequential
withdrawal of our forces, and Phillips sent Pound a long account of the
operation, including the statement that Tovey 'entirely approved of

[the] decision' taken by Hamilton.[26] Pound replied that he had told Churchill that he was 'entirely in agreement with the decision to withdraw',[27] but neither of these messages mollified Churchill, who returned to the charge in as strong terms as before, saying that the object of the operation was 'the interruption over an indefinite period of the German north and south traffic in iron ore and supplies against Russia'. If the assembly of a certain number of aircraft 'was to be held a good reason for an immediate retreat, this operation should never have been undertaken' he asserted; and the 'episode must therefore be judged a marked failure'.[28] Then he attacked Pound personally, telling him that his message to Phillips saying that he approved Admiral Hamilton's action, viewed with his own critical message about the operation, 'appears to indicate a relationship between us which I am sure does not exist'.[29] In other words Pound was reprimanded for showing his deputy that he disagreed with his touchy master.

On the 9th Pound sent Churchill two pages of explanation, insisting that 'Neither Tovey nor Hamilton are officers who would call an operation off before they were convinced it was necessary.'[30] He also offered an olive branch about his message to Phillips which had caused offence. Early in February, in answer to another critical letter, Pound told Churchill that it had been Tovey who originally suggested the operation; but Churchill merely grumbled 'It was very soon abandoned by him.'[31] Churchill also sent Pound a much wider ranging criticism of Tovey, saying that although he was confident that he 'would fight his ship or squadrons' 'he strikes me as negative, unenterprising and narrow-minded. He has protested against almost every positive proposal put to him. This however is entirely between ourselves.'[32] Obviously Churchill's confidence in Tovey had plummeted.

Whatever may be the rights and wrongs of the foregoing clash the Vaagsö raid produced excellent co-operation between the C-in-C, Home Fleet and the Director of Combined Operations. Before the forces sailed Tovey wrote a letter to Keyes ending 'Good luck to the expedition and your conception'; and shortly after it was over he wrote again telling the DCO that 'It was a great pleasure to all of us to work with your force', and paying tribute to 'the obvious efficiency and fine spirit' of the officers and men of the Special Service Brigade.[33] Thus one common source of friction in combined operations – namely disagreement between the commanders – was entirely absent on this occasion.

The interchanges between the admirals and Churchill over the withdrawal from Vaagsö have been recounted at some length because

they show how extraordinarily obstinate and ungracious he could be –
even over what now seems to have been quite a minor matter. A less
patient man than Pound might well have allowed this dispute to
develop into a major conflagration – just as 'Jacky' Fisher did in 1915.
A. V. Alexander noted in his diary a few months later 'Yesterday
Pound remarked to me "At times you could kiss his [Churchill's] feet –
at others you feel you could kill him" ';[34] which shows how severely
Pound's patience and loyalty were taxed.

In May 1941 Tovey's fleet, and many other ships, were involved in
the dramatic pursuit of the *Bismarck*, which began disastrously with the
sinking of the famous battle-cruiser *Hood* in the Denmark Strait
between Iceland and Greenland in the early hours of the 24th,* but
ended victoriously – though only by a very narrow margin – when the
German battleship was sunk about 650 miles west of Brest three days
later.[35] Churchill had of course been watching the progress of the
operation with intense interest and, in view of the high stakes involved,
considerable anxiety. When it seemed that Tovey's two battleships
(*King George V* and *Rodney*) might be forced to break off the pursuit
because of shortage of fuel he came up with one of the most extraordinary signals of the war – '*Bismarck* must be sunk at all costs and
if to do this it is necessary for *King George V* [Tovey's flagship] to
remain on the scene she must do so even if it subsequently means
towing *King George V*.'[36] It should be noted that, although this signal
was sent by Pound, Churchill himself admits that he originated it –
which shows how the former sometimes acted as mouthpiece for the
latter.[37] After Tovey had returned to harbour Pound apologized to
him for the despatch of this signal; but he surely should not have allowed
it to be sent. The post-mortem on the *Bismarck* operation also showed
Pound and Phillips in a very unfavourable light over the proposal to
bring certain senior officers to trial by Court Martial for not re-engag-
ing the *Bismarck* after the *Hood* had been sunk – despite the serious
damage sustained by the *Prince of Wales* and the wholly unfavourable

* Some officers considered that the Naval Wire Barrage weapons fitted in the *Hood*
caused her loss in May 1941 and Professor Marder has accepted their view (*Dardanelles
to Oran* p. 116 *note*). But it is far more likely that, as the Boards of Inquiry found, one
or more of her main magazines was penetrated by the *Bismarck*'s shells which, at the
range of the battle would have descended at a very steep angle and could have penetrated the old battle-cruiser's deck armour. Professor Marder evidently does not realize
that the *Hood*'s turrets were of post-Jutland design (15-inch Mark II), and it was
impossible for them to be blown up through a gunhouse fire penetrating straight down
to the magazines – as happened to the *Queen Mary*, *Invincible* and *Indefatigable* at
Jutland.

tactical situation at the time. Tovey, however, stepped in very firmly, and told Pound he would haul down his flag and act as 'Prisoners' Friend' if he persisted in such an intention – which killed it effectively.[38]

Throughout 1941 Churchill worked hard, and on the whole successfully, to bring the United States nearer to giving full support to the British cause. The famous 'Former Naval Person' to President correspondence, actually initiated by Roosevelt in September 1939, was the chief means by which he sought to further this purpose;[39] and now that it has been published almost in entirety one cannot but marvel at the skill with which he won the President's confidence and argued his country's case on a vast variety of subjects.[40] In February 1941 he was severely critical of what he regarded as an excessively discursive Staff Appreciation on Anglo-American naval policy and strategy written by Rear-Admiral R. M. Bellairs, who had been attached to Plans Division for the purpose, and which was intended as a guide to those who were to negotiate with the Americans. Churchill set out his own views on the subject forcefully. 'I think we should say,' he told Alexander and Pound, ' "We loyally accept the US Navy's dispositions for the Pacific. We think it unlikely that Japan will enter the war against Great Britain and the USA. It is still more unlikely that they would attempt any serious land operations in Malaya entailing movements of a large army and the maintenance of its communications while a US Fleet of adequate strength remains at Hawaii. It would however be a wise precaution . . . if the American Asiatic Fleet were somewhat reinforced with cruisers".' He considered that later on 'some enterprise with aircraft carriers supported by fast ships against the Japanese homeland towns might be attempted . . .' 'In the meanwhile,' he continued, 'apart from the admirable dispositions proposed by the US for the Atlantic we should be glad of assistance in convoys through the Pacific and Indian Ocean against individual Jap raiding cruisers.' But, he emphasized, 'The first thing is to get the US into the war. We can settle how to fight it afterwards'; and he considered Bellairs's paper, if forwarded, might prove 'a hindrance and not a help to the main object'. Nor could he see why 'even if Singapore were captured, we could not protect Australia by basing a fleet on Australian ports' – though where that fleet was to come from seems to have escaped his notice. 'As for India,' he continued, 'if the Japs were to invade it would make the Indians loyal to the King Emperor for a hundred years' – which shows astonishing ignorance of the strength of Indian nationalist feelings. Finally, he concluded, 'But why should they [the Japanese] be such fools as to get tied up with these vastly superior unbeaten naval forces on the high seas?'; which suggests that he was not only totally unaware of Japanese naval strength but ignored the vast distances over which the supposedly 'superior unbeaten naval forces' were scattered.[41] Churchill's main thesis, it may be remarked, was a close repetition of what he had written to Chamberlain in March 1939;[42] but he did at least foresee the famous raid on Tokyo by US Army bombers flown from aircraft carriers in April 1942. [43]

If Churchill was wildly wrong in his appreciation of Far Eastern strategy he was absolutely right in his insistence on the supreme importance of his personal exchanges with President Roosevelt. In April 1941 he told Lord Halifax, the ambassador in Washington, 'Do not discourage the President from posing his questions direct to me or allow any of the naval staff to do so . . .';[44] and in that same month, when the occupation of Iceland by American forces was being discussed, he minuted on a Foreign Office telegram about the transport of men and supplies to the island 'I would rather that telegrams of this sort should not be sent without me seeing them first. What does the convenience of shipping mean compared to engaging the Americans in the war?'[45] In May of that year the aftermath to the *Bismarck* chase produced further evidence of Churchill's determination to bring about active American involvement. When it became known that the *Bismarck*'s consort the heavy cruiser *Prinz Eugen* was at large in the Atlantic he told Alexander and Pound that 'the bringing of her into action and the search for her raise questions of the highest importance. It is most desirable that the US Navy should play a part in this. It would be better for instance that she should be located by a US ship as this might tempt her to fire on that ship, thus providing the incident for which the US Government would be so thankful . . . If we can only create a situation where the *Prinz Eugen* is being shadowed by an American vessel we shall have gone a long way to solve the largest problem.' The Admiralty's reply was to the effect that they had already asked the Americans that their forces operating in the most promising area (east of Newfoundland) should go to sea and try to locate the ship, and that their air patrols from Newfoundland should be co-ordinated with those flown by the RCAF for the same purposes.[46]

In the following month Churchill was angered by someone on staff 'starting the idea among the Americans that we should like their destroyer forces to operate on their side of the Atlantic rather than upon ours'. He considered that the culprit had committed 'a great disservice' and 'should be immediately removed from all American contacts': and he drove home his point by declaring that 'No question of naval strategy in the Atlantic is comparable to the importance of drawing the Americans to this side.' He asked that 'this should be accepted at once as [? a] decision of policy.'[47] Though Churchill's purpose is very understandable he did not take account of the fact that there was very heavy British as well as American seaborne traffic along the east coast of the USA; and the holocaust achieved there in 1942 by the U-boats, which Alexander told Churchill had 'been frightful',[48] shows that the staff's reasoning had some sound sense behind it. At any rate no answer appears to have been sent to this complaint by Churchill, and he seems to have allowed that particular issue to drop.

At about the time when the foregoing squall arose Alexander told Churchill that the US Naval Attaché had asked for details of our anti-submarine methods and particulars of successes achieved against the U-boats. The Admiralty's policy was, he said, 'to withhold as little as possible' from the Americans; but as the information requested had a very high security classification he proposed to ask them to restrict its circulation on a similar basis. To which Churchill replied 'Don't put yourselves in too cheap' – meaning presumably that some *quid pro quo* should be sought in return for information given.[49] But the arrangements to give everything they wanted to the Americans, finalized in September 1940 and recounted earlier, were in fact by that time working very smoothly – despite Churchill's initial reluctance to adopt such a policy.

Whilst discussing Anglo-American relations at this time it is relevant to mention that in September 1941 Churchill told the Admiralty that it was 'imperative that the campaign now under weigh in the US to discredit us and the Administration' – presumably the work of iso-lationist and pro-German interests – 'by alleging that we make in-sufficient or improper use of American supplies should be promptly and fully countered'. He required all departments to provide the Ministry of Information with the necessary ammunition 'to rebut attacks or promote an effective line of counter-propaganda'.[50]

To return to the summer of 1940 and events in Britain, although we can now see that, with Fighter Command of the RAF undefeated and strong naval forces concentrated in the narrow seas, a serious invasion using the ponderous barges assembled on the French Channel coast was simply not a practical operation of war, at the time the threat seemed real enough; and the loss by the BEF of practically all its equipment had left us desperately short of every type of weapon. Large purchases of small arms were accordingly made in USA, and Churchill took a very lively interest in their safe transport across the Atlantic. Twice in

February 1941 he was moved to send strong protests to Alexander and Pound about the measures taken to protect the ships carrying the weapons, and about the choice of the ports at which they could unload in greatest safety; but the Admiralty was able to assure him on both counts that their arrangements were the best possible.[51] Indeed the suggestion in his minutes that they were being negligent on such matters reads very oddly.

Hitler's attack on Russia on 22 June 1941 eased some of Tovey's difficulties – because much of the Luftwaffe's strength was transferred to the eastern front; but it introduced a wholly new and extremely arduous responsibility for the transport of enormous quantities of British and American war stores and raw materials to north Russian ports by the long, outflanked Arctic route. At first all went well – because the Germans did not attempt to interfere seriously with the convoys; but when they realized the scope and importance of the traffic they transferred powerful surface forces, and numerous U-boats and bombers to north Norway, and losses then began to mount. In July 1941 Churchill asked the Admiralty 'to send a small mixed squadron of British ships to the Arctic to form contact and operate with Russian naval forces', and Pound replied that it would be done as soon as we were confident 'that it is practicable to operate them there . . . No time is being wasted on our side.' But in fact the Russians proved so extraordinarily suspicious and uncooperative that the joint defence of the convoys in the White Sea visualized by Churchill was never fully achieved.[52]

Constant trouble with the Russians was experienced at both ends of the Arctic convoy route. For example in June 1942 Pound had reluctantly asked the head of the Soviet Mission in Britain for the recall of a certain Captain Chekin who had been 'abusive and insulting' in carrying out his duty of overseeing the loading of cargoes for Russia. After Admiral Kharlamov, the senior Russian officer in Britain, had been given particulars of the conduct complained of the guilty man was replaced.[53] The British mission in north Russia also experienced much obstruction over such matters as the despatch of a medical unit to care properly for our own sick and wounded men who had to be put ashore at Murmansk or Archangel, and who were suffering serious and unnecessary hardships in Russian hands. Only after prolonged negotiations and a long delay was the medical unit finally admitted in October.[54]

Pressure from Stalin to continue the convoys during the summer of 1942, when daylight was virtually continuous throughout most of the passage, caused Churchill to overrule Tovey's vigorous protests to

Pound about the virtual certainty that, sooner or later, a disaster would take place.[55] Though the controversy was conducted chiefly between Tovey and Pound, the latter passed on the C-in-C's views to Churchill, and it was at this time that Tovey's relations with the Prime Minister deteriorated sharply, and he described the admiral as 'a stubborn and obstinate man'.* The expected disaster duly overtook convoy PQ.17 in July 1942, when despite Tovey's prophetic warning that to order the convoy to scatter would be 'sheer bloody murder' Pound did precisely that because of the threat of attack by heavy German warships.[56] It was probably these events which caused Tovey to write to Cunningham 'To me it [the strategic control of the war] appears to have been based on expediency and bright ideas without any real governing policy behind it. WC as Prime Minister is magnificent and unique, but as a strategist and tactician he is liable to be most dangerous. He loves the dramatic and public acclamation. He has, to my knowledge, put up some wild schemes and, again without knowing details, I disliked intensely his original scheme for a second front [in 1942].'[57]

Tovey was in fact never a man to pull his punches,† which doubtless explains why Churchill, in whose eyes 'Jacky' Fisher's conduct in 1915 remained a haunting memory, viewed him with considerable misgivings. In June 1942 he wrote to Alexander about 'his naturally negative and unenterprising attitude of mind'[58] – which was a great deal less than fair – and in the following month he sent the First Lord and First Sea Lord a note objecting to a signal the admiral had made on the grounds that it 'might well read in the sense that Admiral Tovey is not prepared to obey the orders he might receive from the Admiralty'.[59] But Tovey also got into trouble with the top hierarchy in the Admiralty through a letter he sent them towards the end of that year. The Permanent Secretary replied in a style worthy of Pepys that Their Lord-

---

* I am certain that I found this criticism of Tovey by Churchill in a letter to Pound written in mid-1942. For obvious reasons I did not print it in my war history, but I quoted it in the second of my articles entitled *Churchill and the Admirals* (*Sunday Telegraph*, 11 February 1962). However on re-searching the First Lord's and First Sea Lord's papers and Churchill's Private Office Operational Files I have been unable to relocate it. Possibly it was destroyed during the process known as 'weeding' the official records, which was often carried out with scant regard for the historical importance of papers selected for destruction.

† Lord Tovey, as he became in 1946, told the author how when he had been Flag Captain to Admiral Sir John Kelly in the Atlantic Fleet after the Invergordon mutiny of 1931, the admiral had written in his confidential report 'Captain Tovey shares a characteristic with myself. In my case I call it tenacity of purpose, and in his obstinacy'! Tovey to Roskill 22 February 1961.

ships 'take exception to the terms in which your observations [probably about the need for more long-range aircraft for the Atlantic battle, to be referred to shortly] are couched . . . They have therefore ordered that your letter of 5 November be expunged from Admiralty records'; and that was evidently done.[60] Thus we shall never know what it was that aroused such indignation at the Board Room's famous table that the Grinling Gibbons carvings may well have trembled, and the wind vane over the fireplace have gone into violent oscillations.

In March and again in June 1942 Pound called the Cs-in-C of all Home Stations to the Admiralty for discussion of various matters which they had raised. Their principal complaints concerned, firstly, the tendency for everything 'to get even more centralized', with consequential increase of paper work, and, secondly, the constant shifting of Coastal Command aircraft from one command to another, which prevented their senior officers getting to know their naval opposite numbers well. An interesting point raised in these discussions was the objection of the Cs-in-C to what they called 'Private Navies'. In that category they certainly included the Combined Operations Directorate, of which Mountbatten had become the head in October 1941 in place of Keyes.[61] Though the creation of the new organization by Churchill, and the addition of Mountbatten to the COS Committee, did undoubtedly produce difficulties and duplication with the conventional departments, his drive, energy and originality offset such disadvantages as it may have possessed. In discussing the Cs-in-C's objections one has also to remember that the Admiralty was always very jealous of any person or office which tried to poach on what it regarded as its own preserves. Except for the choice of Mountbatten as CCO Churchill played no part in these discussions; and Pound probably preferred Mountbatten to Keyes, whose appointment he told Churchill 'I certainly do [? did] not like . . . but I did not feel very strongly about it.'[62]

The transfer to north Norway of strong German surface forces led to a chance for the Home Fleet to deal with the *Tirpitz* in the same manner as it had dealt with her sister ship *Bismarck*.

Early in 1942, when the *Tirpitz* was at Trondheim, Churchill told Pound that 'crippling this ship would alter the entire face of the naval war and that the loss of 100 machines [i.e. aircraft] and 500 airmen would be well compensated for'.[63] In March a chance of fulfilling that purpose arose, and at far less cost than he had been prepared to pay. Thanks to cryptographic intelligence the Admiralty was able to give Tovey warning of the intention of the ship to make a sortie from Norway to attack our Arctic convoys, and Tovey took his main fleet, including the new aircraft carrier *Victorious*, to sea to intercept her. In the initial stages his plan worked perfectly, and on 9 March he flew off a striking force of twelve torpedo-bombers with the object of damaging her as the *Ark Royal*'s had done to the *Bismarck*, and so enable him to bring his battleships into action to finish her off. Unfortunately the torpedo-bombers obtained no hits, and the *Tirpitz* returned to harbour undamaged.[64] This failure aroused understandable anger in Churchill's mind, coming as it did so soon after Japanese torpedo-bombers had inflicted fatal injuries on the *Repulse* and *Prince of Wales*, and he demanded an explanation from Pound. The truth was that Tovey's striking force was far weaker and much less well trained than the Japanese one had been, and was equipped with much less lethal weapons. Pound did his best to explain the difference in the circumstances which had prevailed on the two occasions, but this by no means satisfied the Prime Minister, and seems to have contributed to the scepticism which he later expressed about the value of the Fleet Air Arm – especially compared to his favoured Bomber Command.[65] In the following year Churchill again represented that 'the destruction of T [sic] remains an object of prime and capital importance' – which was certainly no exaggeration, though the Admiralty was of course very much alive to the need. They at once gave him a full statement of all measures being taken to achieve that object – including the projected attack by midget submarines.[66]

In 1942 our shipping losses rose catastrophically, partly because of the reluctance of the US Navy to introduce convoy off the east coast of America and in the Caribbean – a failure which Roosevelt attributed to his country's navy having been 'definitely slack' over preparing against such an offensive.* But the introduction by the Germans on 1 February of an entirely new cypher for communicating with their Atlantic U-boats had deprived us of the most valuable source of Intelligence, and so contributed to the holocaust.[67] Heavy losses were also suffered in the 'air gaps' south of Greenland and, to a lesser extent, off west Africa, which could not at the time be reached by British or American air-

* Roosevelt to Churchill 18 March 1942. *Loewenheim*, p. 196. On 12 March 1942 Churchill sent Hopkins (for Roosevelt) a message expressing his 'deep concern' over tanker sinkings in these waters and urging 'immediate convoys'. Roosevelt replied, not very helpfully, on 17th suggesting Churchill should 'have a talk with Admiral Pound' to see if the trans-Atlantic escort system could be completely revised so that ten destroyers could be added to the *patrols* on the east coast. This was of course not at all what the Admiralty, which had in fact supplied the figures in Churchill's message, wanted.

craft based on either side of the Atlantic. Though the 'Battle of the Air', as it came to be called, was fought mainly in Whitehall Tovey expressed strong views on the need for more and better aircraft for Coastal Command of the RAF. In essence the conflict was waged between those who held that the bombing of German towns was the primary strategic requirement, and the only 'offensive' strategy open to us at the time, and those who argued that if we lost the Atlantic Battle we lost the war, and that victory in that struggle therefore demanded the allocation of all the resources which they deemed necessary. The principal protagonists were, on the bombing side Churchill himself, supported by the redoubtable C-in-C, Bomber Command, Air Chief Marshal Sir Arthur Harris, who developed an extraordinarily close relationship with the Prime Minister – even to the extent of opposing the policy of the Chief of the Air Staff,[68] and Lord Cherwell, Churchill's chief scientific adviser. The result was that, as General Kennedy the Director of Military Operations at the time has written, 'for a long time he [Churchill] continued to believe that the war could be won by aircraft. So sure was he of this that the bombing policy of the Air Staff was settled almost entirely by the Prime Minister himself in consultation with Portal [CAS], and was not controlled by the Chiefs of Staff'.[69] On the opposite side were ranged A. V. Alexander and Pound, supported by Admirals Tovey and Noble, the C-in-C, Western Approaches; and they had of course the whole resources of the naval staff behind them. As to Churchill's views, he seems to have oscillated between anxiety about progress in the Atlantic Battle and the desire not to reduce the bombing of Germany. In August 1941 he told Portal 'I have certainly sustained the impression that the Air Ministry in the past has been most hard and unhelpful both to the Army and to the Navy in meeting their special needs';[70] but, as we shall see, in the following year he refused to meet the navy's 'special needs' at the expense of the bomber offensive.

Here we may retrace our steps to the origins of that conflict. Although it was Cherwell who initiated the inquiry which exposed the inaccuracy of our bombing in August 1941,[71] and although it is fair to remark that the inquiry stimulated the development of radio navigation, which was a vital aid to bombing accuracy, it was also he who, in Professor R. V. Jones's words, 'completed the shift in philosophy and morality from the selective bombing of key points such as oil plants to the area bombing of towns'.[72] Moreover concentration on Cherwell's inhuman purpose of 'dehousing' the German people quickly proved that his estimate of its effectiveness was wholly fallacious. Lord Tren-

chard, the originator and unremitting protagonist of Strategic Bombing, sent Churchill a stream of papers arguing his case at this time.[73]
Churchill however by no means accepted the whole of Trenchard's
thesis, minuting on one of his papers that he did not think 'we can
entirely neglect the needs of the Navy and of the Army as Lord
Trenchard seems to suggest', and on another of them telling Harris
'you will see how he flogs a good horse to death'.[74] None the less he
did become so deeply committed to the 'offensive' concept of the
bombing campaign that other strategic priorities, and in particular the
Atlantic Battle and the Far East, were given too little weight. For
example in July 1941 Churchill told Roosevelt 'Then, we must subject
Germany and Italy to a ceaseless and ever growing bombardment.' In
describing the Moscow meeting with Stalin of August 1942 he told the
President 'We then passed to the ruthless bombing of Germany, which
gave general satisfaction . . . I made it clear that this was one of our
leading military objectives'; while in the following November he
telegraphed 'I am most reluctant to reduce the weight of bombs we
are able to drop on Germany . . .'.[75] This constant refrain on Churchill's
part fully confirms Professor Michael Howard's statement that,
contrary to the urging of General Brooke the CIGS, he did treat the
bombing offensive as 'a thing apart' from other strategic needs; while
his reaction to the papers by Trenchard and Harris referred to above
shows, in the same author's view, the extent to which he was *parti
pris* on this issue.[76] It also explains why the heavy bombers and not the
forces engaged in the Atlantic Battle were given priority for fitting the
new centimetric radar sets which could have, and ultimately did, make
a vital contribution to the defence of convoys.[77] That, in brief outline, is
how, in the words of Professor P. M. S. Blackett (Lord Blackett 1969),
certainly one of the most brilliant scientists involved in the controversy
over deployment of our resources, 'the dehousing of the German
working-class population, with the object of lowering her morale and
will to fight, became official British policy until the autumn of 1943'.[78]
It is a severe indictment of Cherwell, and so of Churchill who at the
end of 1940 described the heavy bomber in a letter to Roosevelt as
'the weapon on which above all others we depend to shatter the
foundations of German military power',[79] and who held firmly to that
view in the critical year 1942. In fairness to Churchill it should, however, be recorded that there is some evidence that, although he had
approved the bombing policy pressed on him by Cherwell and Harris,
he did entertain misgivings about its inhumanity – though not apparently about its effectiveness.[80]

The 'Battle of the Air' began badly for the Admiralty when, in April 1942, Pound refused to take any action on a strong protest received from Sir Arthur Salter, the head of the British Merchant Shipping Mission to the USA, about losses suffered on that side of the Atlantic;[81] and in the same month Admiral E. J. King the formidable American Chief of Naval Operations and C-in-C, US Fleet, refused to help by transferring some long-range aircraft to the struggle.[82] Pound therefore asked Alexander to try and get the two squadrons needed from the RAF; but although the staff prepared a paper for the First Lord to use in discussion with the Secretary of State for Air, and in May the matter was considered by the COS Committee, no effective action emerged.[83]

Although early in the war Churchill had sung the praises of the British Asdic submarine detection equipment very loudly in a letter to Roosevelt,[84] in November 1941 he sent Alexander and Pound a bitter complaint regarding 'the failure of our methods, about which so much was proclaimed by the Admiralty before the war'.[85] Though it was certainly the case that the Admiralty's belief that the Asdic had mastered the submarine had proved much too optimistic Churchill had now veered too violently in the opposite direction; since without the Asdic the navy would have been as helpless against submarines as in World War I, and it did play a vital part in the detection and destruction of many U-boats. Churchill's disillusion with our anti-submarine measures probably contributed to the excessive confidence which he came to place in strategic bombing. For in June 1942 he told Alexander and Pound that the '1000 Bomber Raid' made on Cologne on 30-31 May 1942 was to be repeated that month, with help from Coastal Command, and that he 'must definitely ask for compliance with this request'.[86] In July Pound had correspondence and talks with Portal, the CAS, and agreed to withdraw a paper prepared for the COS Committee on the need for more long-range aircraft for the Atlantic battle. Pound's reason was that they had reached agreement on the principle that the RAF shared with the Navy the responsibility 'for the security of our sea communications within range of our shore-based aircraft', and the Air Ministry had accepted 'that there is indeed a very real need for immediate assistance from RAF in Home Waters'.[87] Pound told his colleagues on the staff that he had not got 'the slightest intention of asking for further help at the present time';[88] but in fact the escalating shipping losses soon forced his hand.

In that same month Churchill accused Coastal Command of inadequate and inefficient maintenance of its aircraft, and wrote that until that had been rectified 'there can be no case for transferring additional squadrons from Bomber to Coastal Command'.[89] At about the same time Pound insisted to Admiral Sir Reginald Drax, who had been brought in as a special adviser to him, that 'the battle of the air . . . has now been concluded satisfactorily from our point of view', and referred to there having been 'a real change of heart on the part of the Air Ministry'.[90] One may feel that, no matter how desirable were good relations at the top of the two services, this showed astonishing complacency – especially as it soon became apparent that Portal did not by any means have full control over Harris. In the following month Churchill pressed his view yet more strongly by telling Pound 'You must not trench so heavily on the reserves of the RAF',[91] and arguing that the patrols being flown over the U-boats' transit routes across the Bay of Biscay did not justify the 'inroads on our Bomber resources'.[92] This onslaught did at least provoke a strong riposte from Pound, who asked for the permanent transfer of the aircraft then on loan from Bomber Command.[93]

Portal undoubtedly intended to observe the promise he had given to Pound in April; but it was not until September that he was able to tell him that four long-range bomber squadrons had been transferred to Coastal Command for the Biscay patrols until such time as the strength of the latter command had been built up further.[94] In fact we now know that only for one fairly short period of ninety-four days, from 1 May to 2 August 1943, when Dönitz misguidedly ordered his U-boats to stay on the surface and fight it out with the aircraft, did the Biscay patrols achieve good results. Meanwhile the 'air gap' in mid-Atlantic remained unfilled, and that the U-boats concentrated their efforts there.[95] In October more bad news came from Portal – that the first of the new four-engine Lancasters were to go to Bomber Command;[96] and later in that month Churchill read to the COSs a paper entitled 'Note on Air Policy' which opened with the ominous words 'The bombing offensive against Germany and Italy must be regarded as our prime effort in the Air.'[97] Plainly the Pound–Portal agreement was proving a very weak reed for the Admiralty to lean on.

Air Marshal Harris lost no opportunity to press on Churchill what Bomber Command was doing to help in the Atlantic Battle – often short-circuiting the Chief of the Air Staff. Thus in June he sent Churchill a list of enemy or enemy-controlled merchant ships which had been sunk by mines laid by his command's aircraft. Churchill sent it on to Pound with a note saying 'These activities are valuable aids to the Navy'; and it is certainly the case that air minelaying later produced very good results – especially in the Baltic – which the navy could not reach with surface ships. But that was not the type of help the Admiralty was seeking in 1942.[98]

In August Harris sent Churchill another of the memoranda in which he argued with single-minded passion that only the bomber offensive against Germany mattered, and that all 'diversions' from that campaign, including strengthening Coastal Command, were wrong.[99] Churchill however did not go all the way with the C-in-C, Bomber Command, minuting that both Trenchard and he 'fall into the error of spoiling a good case by overstatement';[100] while J. M. Bruce, the Australian High Commissioner, was so shocked by Harris's paper that Churchill asked him to treat it as 'withdrawn'.[101] At about the same time, however, he asserted that the chief need was to increase Bomber Command's strength from thirty-two to fifty 'fully operative' squadrons at home, and approved two squadrons being transferred to it from Coastal Command to help reach that figure.[102]

By no means all the overstatements and exaggerations came from the Air side. In October Admiral Tovey wrote to the Admiralty that more and better air co-operation was essential if the acute shipping crisis was to be overcome – which was true enough. Inadvisedly he went on to describe the bombing of Germany as 'a luxury not a necessity', which caused Churchill to remark that the paper 'damns itself', and he saw no reason for circulating it – thus suppressing the views of one of the admirals most deeply involved in the Atlantic battle.[103]

In July 1942 Roosevelt asked Churchill for the transfer to the US Navy of the corvettes and minesweepers building in Canada on British account, to help solve the US Navy's acute shortage of such vessels. Churchill, advised by the Admiralty, replied that he was anxious to do all he could to help. But after discussing the matter with Harry Hopkins, Roosevelt's special emissary, he pointed out that 300 escort vessels were building in USA at the request of the British; and we could not tell where the U-boats would next strike – perhaps a discreet reference to the fact that this was the period when we were unable to read signals sent in the U-boat cypher. He proposed that the vessels building in America and the whole of our own production 'should be thrown into a common pool and assigned to the best advantage' – an idea which was theoretically attractive but hopelessly impracticable, since both parties were certain to claim that their needs merited the higher priority.[104] Three weeks later Pound reported that our own shortage of escort vessels totalled 342; but he admitted that the American shortage was some 70% larger.[105]

In October Lord Leathers, the Minister of War Transport, sent the Defence Committee (Supply) an urgent plea that 'the needs of the Navy' should be met, because 'the security of our sea communications is a condition *sine qua non* for the United Nations' and should therefore be given the highest priority for allocation of men and materials. But Churchill declined fully to accept such an argument.[106]

Although from the naval point of view there was little if any break in the clouds at the end of 1942, in October Churchill did tell Roosevelt 'First of all, I put the U-boat menace. This I am sure is our worst danger';[107] and in November he telegraphed to Harry Hopkins for the President asking for thirty Liberators fitted with the new centimetric Radar. Hopkins replied that twenty-one would be sent to the European theatre 'to operate under the control of General Eisenhower'.[108] Again this was of course not what the Admiralty wanted; but in that same month Portal accepted that the top priority was for long-range aircraft to fill the 'air gap', and the second was for them to have the new radar. [109] Then Churchill decided that *all* the new radar sets were to go to Bomber Command. Though Alexander protested on behalf of the Admiralty he considered no useful purpose would be served by taking the issue to the Cabinet, as Churchill had offered.[110] The First Lord probably realized that, if he took up the offer, Churchill himself would act as both judge and jury. All that he got was the laconic statement from Churchill that 'the best targets must be chosen' – which shows how ingrained the bomber offensive had become in his mind.[111] This failure by Alexander to represent the navy's view on a crucial issue strongly enough was without doubt one of the cases which caused Admiral Sir William Davis, who was serving in Plans Division at the time, to remark to the author 'I have heard him [Alexander] time and time again give in to Winston without a fight.'[112]

Although the many papers and letters exchanged over the Battle of the Air were generally couched in courteous language the minutes by the Sea Lords and Naval Staff give what was in all probability a far truer picture of the feelings aroused on that side of the house. The chief burden of trying to persuade Alexander and Pound to take a firmer line fell on the Directors of the Plans, Trade and A/S Warfare Divisions; and from them on the VCNS and ACNS (U-boat Warfare and Trade), Admirals H. R. Moore and J. H. Edelsten. But the strong feelings were very widespread in the Admiralty – because all the staff knew beyond doubt by the end of the year that the Germans were building U-boats much faster than we were sinking them, that our sea and air convoy escorts were increasing at a proportionately much slower rate, and that we were faced with defeat in the one battle which we simply could not afford to lose.[113] Perhaps a letter from Admiral W. J. Whitworth, Second Sea Lord 1941–4, to Admiral Cunningham illustrates best the strength of the feelings aroused. 'Our fight with the Air Ministry,' he wrote, 'becomes more and more fierce as the war proceeds. It is a much more savage one than our war with the Huns, which is very unsatisfactory and such a waste of effort.'[114]

Various proposals for reorganization of the British commands responsible for the Atlantic Battle were put forward in 1942. For example Sir Stafford Cripps (Minister of Aircraft Production 1942–5) proposed to Churchill the appointment of what Alexander described as 'a Super C-in-C', and suggested Admiral Somerville for the post. The First Lord objected on the grounds that it would cut across 'the whole system of naval control', and it certainly seems unlikely that it would have brought any material benefits.[115] In the following year a somewhat similar idea was put forward from Washington, as will be recounted later.

In conclusion of this brief summary it is difficult not to feel that Churchill's memories of 1915, which unquestionably produced a determination in his mind never again to have at the Admiralty a strong-willed First Lord (except of course himself), or a First Sea Lord who might prove a reincarnation of Jacky Fisher led to very serious mistakes in the realm of strategy and priorities in 1942 and early 1943.[116] Alexander and Pound simply were not a strong enough team to cope with Churchill himself, obsessed as he was by his concept of 'offensive' measures, and supported by Cherwell, Harris and the other advocates of strategic bombing. The Admiralty and naval staff certainly cannot be wholly acquitted of error – notably over their pressure for bombing the four principal U-boat bases in France (Brest, St Nazaire, Lorient and La Pallice), and for strengthening the air patrols over the Bay of Biscay. The former produced little effect on the U-boats themselves, which were protected by enormously thick concrete shelters, though the attacks did cause dislocation to maintenance and repair work;[117] while the provision of air escorts to cover the convoys in mid-Atlantic would have produced far better results than the transit route patrols – and ultimately did so. None the less it does seem fair to suggest that if the Admiralty's broad views had been accepted the Atlantic Battle could have been won at least six months earlier – with far-reaching effects on the whole course of the war, and indeed on the condition of post-war Europe. The tragedy of the failure to get adequate air escorts for the struggle at sea until the eleventh hour is increased by the fact that whenever a serious loss occurred to any convoy Churchill turned round and rent the Admiralty, accusing them of every kind of negligence or failure, and seeking punitive retribution against anyone he deemed culpable in a manner which can only be described as vindictive.[118]

Churchill had in fact far stronger grounds than such cases on which to attack the Admiralty – namely over the pre-war failure to provide efficient means for refuelling warships at sea – such as the Germans had developed. 'When I was at the Admiralty,' he told Alexander and Pound in March 1941, 'I repeatedly asked that more attention should be paid to the development of refuelling at sea'; and he considered it 'a scandal' that the German battle-cruisers could remain out many weeks while 'again and again our ships have to be called off promising hunts in order to go back to fuel 6–700 miles away'. In truth the 'neglect of this principle', which he described as 'a grievous drag on the power of the Fleet', derived from the centuries old possession of a chain of over-seas bases from which our ships were supposed to draw their fuel.[119] Not until World War II was the inadequacy of this reliance exposed.

By no means all Churchill's complaints were as justified as that one; and some of the brainwaves which he supported can justly be described as ludicrous. Such was the suggestion to build 'seadromes' on which the shore-based aircraft involved in the Atlantic Battle could land to refuel. Mountbatten became a strong advocate of that idea, known as 'Hab-bakuk'. But Alexander pointed out, perhaps a little sarcastically, that even assuming the problems of design, construction and mooring could be solved, to supply a platform 'suitably equipped and defended would require 35,000–65,000 tons of armour plate and 120,000 tons of struc-tural steel'; and it would take at least three years to build it after the design had been worked out. Moreover when all the difficulties had been overcome 'by routeing our trade close to Iceland' he wrote, 'we shall obtain all the advantages of a seadrome with the sole disadvantage of a slightly longer route'.[120] Nothing more was heard of that idea. But just as absurd in the sense of wasted effort was Churchill's sudden demand, again probably instigated by Cherwell, for a 'daily report on the number and total of unrepaired merchant ships in our harbours'. The answer sent was the tactfully expressed view that the staff had more important work to do, and the hope that the existing weekly summaries would suffice.[121]

Nor did Churchill show reasonable humanity over the need to give officers and men who had served more than four years, nearly all overseas, and were now in a ship refitting in USA, a chance to see their homes; for he wanted the crews used to man at once some of the ten coastguard cutters which Roosevelt had offered to help us in the Atlantic battle. Actually the Admiralty had earmarked those fully-trained crews to man the urgently needed new warships nearing completion at home. But Churchill deplored what he unjustly called 'an easy going view' of the Admiralty's responsibilities, and declared himself to be 'entirely out of sympathy with that kind of proposal'. Not surprisingly no answer was sent.[122]

Early in 1942 our Intelligence indicated the likelihood of a break for home being made by the powerful German squadron (*Scharnhorst, Gneisenau* and *Prinz Eugen*) which had been in Brest harbour since the previous May, and had always been a potentially serious threat to the Atlantic convoys. The Admiralty's appreciation was that they would try and force a passage up-Channel, choosing the conditions of time, weather and tide which were most favourable to such a purpose.[123] That was in fact to prove correct in all respects except for the anticipated time of passing through the Straits of Dover. Admiral Tovey however considered they were more likely to make for the Iceland-Faröes passage and thence into the North Sea, and that his best chance of intercepting them would be to the east of Iceland. When he told the Admiralty that he might only have the old and ill-protected battle-cruiser *Renown* and the carrier *Victorious*, while the German squadron might be reinforced by the recently completed *Tirpitz* Churchill challenged the statement strongly. 'What does T[ovey] mean?' he asked Pound. 'Surely he has *King George V* and *Duke of York*?' The First Sea Lord had patiently to explain that refits, repairs and the working-up of new ships meant that the Home Fleet was at a very low level of strength.[124] Though events were to prove Tovey wrong the exchanges quoted provide example of Churchill's lack of *rapport* with him – despite his recent, if lucky, success in sinking the *Bismarck*.

It was almost certainly Tovey's stand against continuing the Arctic convoys into the summer of 1942, his vigorous campaign for more long-range aircraft to join in the Atlantic Battle, and his opposition to Churchill's plan for a major combined operation against the Norwegian coast that year which caused the Prime Minister to seek a more amenable C-in-C for the Home Fleet.[125] In view of the strained relations which had developed between him and Admiral Cunningham in 1941, to be recounted in the next chapter, it is odd that his choice should have fallen on him. Cunningham himself provided the author with an amusing account of how the Prime Minister's plan developed when he

was brought home at short notice in April 1942 – ostensibly to relieve
Admiral Sir Charles Little as head of the British naval mission in
Washington. Cunningham was evidently on his guard, and scented
that the Prime Minister 'has undoubtedly some ulterior motive' –
which prognosis was to prove close to the mark.[126] 'A few days after
my arrival,' he wrote, 'I was invited down to Chequers for the night
and was taken into the map room after dinner for a *tête-à-tête* with W.
The conversation went something like this:-

WSC.   "Of course there is no reason why you should go to Wash-
        ington."

ABC.   "I thought that was the reason for my being brought
        home."

WSC.   "No, I want you to go to the Home Fleet."

ABC.   "But you have a very good Admiral there already Sir John
        Tovey."

WSC.   "Oh, I want you to relieve Admiral Tovey."

ABC.   (rather angry) "If Tovey drops dead on his bridge I will
        certainly relieve him. Otherwise not."

Then I was told I could go to Washington . . .'[127]

Churchill evidently did not quickly abandon his plan for a re-
shuffle of the top admirals, since on 4 June he wrote to Alexander
proposing that Cunningham should relieve Tovey in command of
the Home Fleet, that Tovey should take over the Western Approaches
Command at Liverpool, and Sir Percy Noble who had held the latter
command since February 1941, should go to Washington to replace
Little.[128] Alexander sent these proposals on to Pound, who replied that
he was 'in total disagreement' about relieving Tovey, and that to do so
would imperil the navy's confidence in the Admiralty's administration.
Though Little had, he wrote, 'done a great deal to forward this co-
operation [with the US Navy]' he was 'sure it requires someone with
Admiral Cunningham's prestige to bring it to a really satisfactory condition'.[129] However Alexander wrote in his diary that Churchill still
wanted Tovey to be relieved, because he had 'a poor opinion' of him.
'Crisis may loom ahead,' continued Alexander; but Churchill had
'promised to see Pound, and to try to see Cunningham again'.[130]
What actually happened was that Churchill wrote 'I will see 1st L[ord]
alone at No. 10' [his italics],[131] and one wonders why he wanted Pound
to be kept out of it. At any rate Churchill evidently gave way and
Cunningham went to Washington on 24 June and remained there until
November, when he returned to the Mediterranean as Allied Naval

Commander for the landings in North Africa. Also in November Sir Max Horton took over the Western Approaches Command, an inspired appointment, and Noble replaced Cunningham in Washington.[132]

One other incident concerning the return home of Cunningham in April 1942 must be recounted here. Very naturally he called at the Admiralty to see Pound, and he later described to Rear-Admiral J. H. Godfrey, who had been Director of Naval Intelligence since the beginning of 1939, how he found the First Sea Lord 'in great distress' – caused apparently by his troubles with Churchill. Pound asked Cunningham whether he ought to resign, and also told him that 'Winston was thinking of getting rid of him and putting Mountbatten in as 1st Sea Lord'. Such a proposal must have been highly embarrassing to Cunningham, since he himself was the obvious successor to Pound – if a change was to be made. Moreover Mountbatten's substantive rank was only that of Post Captain, though he had just been made an Acting Vice-Admiral on becoming Director of Combined Operations. Even if the report which had reached Pound about Churchill's plan was correct it is hardly conceivable that Mountbatten's appointment to the top naval post would have been acceptable to the service – or indeed welcomed by himself. Cunningham accordingly advised Pound 'to glue himself to his chair' – despite the fact that he was well aware of the disabilities from which he suffered; and it thus came to pass that Pound carried on.[133] What makes this whole encounter puzzling is that Churchill so often expressed his affection for Pound that it is difficult to believe that he was seriously considering replacing him.

Having introduced Admiral John Godfrey because of Cunningham's letter recounting his meeting with Pound it will be appropriate to bring in here the story of his downfall. As DNI he built up the Admiralty's Operational Intelligence Centre (OIC), from which the entire war at sea was directed, to a very high state of efficiency; and he brought into it and other sections of his division a large number of able men in many different fields. Though highly intelligent Godfrey was certainly not an easy man to work with; but he did win the loyalty and affection of his staff – all of whom seem to have admired him greatly. But he evidently got at odds with the Generals on the Joint Intelligence Committee (Major-Generals F. H. N. Davidson the DMI and Sir Stewart Menzies the head of the Secret Service), and in September 1942 Pound reported to Alexander that, after full investigation the VCNS (Vice-Admiral Sir Henry Moore) had reported to him that he was 'quite certain there cannot be that co-operation [on the JIC] which is most important for its proper functioning' as long as Godfrey represented the navy on it. He was therefore to be relieved.[134] In retrospect this was very unfair to Godfrey, whose departmental work had been admirable – as many of those who witnessed it have since testified;[135] and one does feel that Pound and Moore should have given him support rather than allowing the Generals to get him sacked. Godfrey was the only British admiral to receive no recognition at all for his war service.

The acute troubles which beset Britain at sea in 1941 and 1942 caused Churchill to resurrect what he considered to have been the mistakes made by the Admiralty over the pre-war naval building programmes. He recalled how in 1937 he had inveighed against giving the new battle-ships 14-inch instead of 16-inch guns, such as had been mounted in the *Nelsons* of 1924.[136] What he ignored was that, unlike the Germans, Italian and Japanese, British governments had always adhered strictly to the limitations imposed by the Washington and London treaties, and that it had proved quite impossible to get all the requirements which by the late 1930s were plainly desirable – namely at least twenty-nine knots speed, good armour protection, heavy A-A armaments and nine 16-inch guns – within the prescribed displacement of 35,000 tons.[137] In February 1942 Chatfield raised in the House of Lords the fact that little or no progress had been made with the *Lion* class battleships, which he had got authorized in 1938.[138] Churchill was furious, drafted a reply and sent it to Alexander and Pound to be checked, writing that 'I am not prepared to leave Chatfield unanswered.'[139] Though Pound did not accept all the strictures in Churchill's draft and was evidently anxious to avoid a controversy on issues which were by that time largely academic he did not succeed in tempering the Prime Minister's wrath. In the letter as despatched Churchill widened the issue by attacking Chatfield for not having included any destroyers in the 1938 programme, as well as for ordering the 14-inch battleships. Expectedly the admiral sent an angry reply, pointing out the effects of 'the infamous London Treaty' and stressing that in 1938 shortage of industrial capacity and of money had made it impossible to include all the ships the Admiralty would have liked to order.[140]

Chatfield next put down a motion for debate in the Lords on 'a programme of battleship contruction and its progress'. Alexander then met the admiral and tried to persuade him to withdraw the motion; but he refused to do so. The First Lord told Churchill that Chatfield had expressed 'great irritation' over the reply he had received when he had last tried to raise the matter – followed by 'a rude letter' from the PM – presumably the one referred to above. But he had none the less expressed 'a great liking for the PM and had no desire to embarrass him'.[141] Churchill however flatly refused to allow the matter to be debated openly in the Lords, and insisted that if the motion was allowed to stand the House would have to go into Secret Session.[142] The outcome was that when the motion was taken Lord Cranborne (Secretary of State for Colonies) proposed that the House should do so.[143] As no record of such debates was kept we do not know what was said. Subsequent events suggest, however, that Chatfield got little if any change. But the whole correspondence on this matter now reads distastefully, since even if Chatfield's motives were not wholly free from self-justification, he was genuinely concerned about our weakness in heavy ships; and his great services to the navy and the country as First Sea Lord 1933–8, which Churchill had previously recognized and had warmly commended in Parliament, should surely have deterred him from launching such a hurtful attack. His attitude showed some lack of the magnanimity which he himself preached; but, as Rhodes James has remarked, his magnanimity 'could be highly selective'.[144] Incidentally Lord Hankey, whom Churchill had ungraciously dismissed from the government in March 1942,[145] sent Churchill a paper on 'Capital Ships' at about the same time as Chatfield took the matter up. As he and Chatfield were old friends, and were both of them critical of some aspects of Churchill's methods and strategic purposes, it seems likely that they acted in collusion with each other.[146]

In October 1942 Churchill produced one of his wide-ranging papers on strategy entitled 'Policy for the Conduct of the War' setting out every one of the possible operations which the allies might adopt.[147] Pound asked the staff to report on it, and the very able Director of Plans Captain (later Admiral of the Fleet Sir Charles) Lambe wrote that, much as he admired 'the imagination and drive inherent in the document', he believed that 'in general tone' it was 'dangerous', because it regarded 'all projects that have ever been discussed as capable of fulfilment either concurrently or at short intervals'. 'If we try to be ready for everything' he argued, 'we shall achieve nothing.'[148] Pound told Alexander that, as the paper had not been circulated officially the COSs considered it unnecessary for them to comment on it. Alexander agreed, and Churchill's ideas were therefore not placed on the agenda; but his paper provides an interesting example of the way his ever-active mind would cause an immense amount of fruitless work to hard-pressed staff officers.

Despite the many difficulties and serious set-backs experienced in 1942 Churchill's mind turned to the possibility of launching an offensive either against north-western France or Norway – chiefly with the object of taking weight off the hard-pressed Russian army.[149] In May he asked for plans to be prepared for the latter,[150] and Admiral Sir Reginald Drax, an 'intellectual' among Flag Officers who had helped to prepare the navy's war plans as long ago as 1933,[151] was called back by Pound to review both alternatives. In an able paper he warned that 'Whoever invades across the sea gives hostages to fortune in doing so. It may be assumed that we must put into the selected area not less than a million men . . .'[152] Though the Norway plan had long held great appeal to Churchill the Admiralty considered it as impossible to carry out in 1942 as the cross-Channel operation. When Pound received Churchill's proposals regarding that plan he told the staff to dig out the records of the 1940 Norwegian campaign to help him show that the idea was impracticable. As an example of how far Churchill's schemes some-times departed from reality his idea was, according to Pound, that 'the initial expedition should consist of some 50-100 ships which should contain everything which would be required for about two months'. Pound rightly did not believe there were many places in north Norway where 'you can anchor twenty much less fifty or a hundred ships' because of the great depth of water in the fiords.[153]

As regards the cross-Channel assault, early in July Churchill told Roosevelt that 'no responsible British general, admiral or air marshal is prepared to recommend Sledgehammer as a practicable operation in 1942'.[154] The President, albeit reluctantly, accepted the substitution of the invasion of French North Africa, to be referred to in the next chapter, and it fell to Churchill to break the news to Stalin that there would be no second front in 1942 when he flew to Moscow from Cairo in August.[155] It is interesting to find that as early as June of that year Pound consulted all the Home Cs-in-C about the appointment of Admiral Sir Bertram Ramsay, of Dunkirk fame, as C-in-C, Expeditionary Force for an invasion operation. They all welcomed the pro-posal, and promised all the help they could give Ramsay. Churchill approved the appointment without hesitation.[156] Nor did the Admiralty have serious difficulty over getting the Prime Minister and Cabinet to accept their proposals for the 1942 building programme, though the former had doubts about the need for the large 'fleet type' destroyers proposed and was inclined to prefer smaller vessels for escort purposes. This programme was, however, the last one to receive a comparatively easy passage from Churchill, who had always wanted the ships which would in his opinion enter service most quickly.[157]

Towards the end of this very difficult year Pound sent Churchill a paper arguing that 'in the opinion of the Board [of Admiralty] the situation generally at sea is so serious that the Cabinet should be informed and the urgency of the Navy's needs reassessed',[158] and another one pressing for the new centimetric radar sets to be allocated to the ships and aircraft involved in the Atlantic Battle and not to Bomber Command.[159] The first paper produced a lengthy riposte from the Prime Minister who, among other points, blamed the Admiralty for 'the present unsatisfactory condition of the Fleet Air Arm' – which was by no means entirely fair – and deprecating 'all the arguments about the importance of sea power and sea communications' which he evidently regarded as academic. It thus came to pass that Coastal Command got none of the new radar sets until the following year. These exchanges show how very difficult it was to get from Churchill the priority needed to avoid losing, let alone winning the Atlantic Battle; and how he repeatedly accepted the needs *in principle* but refused as frequently to provide them at the expense of the bombing of Germany.

148

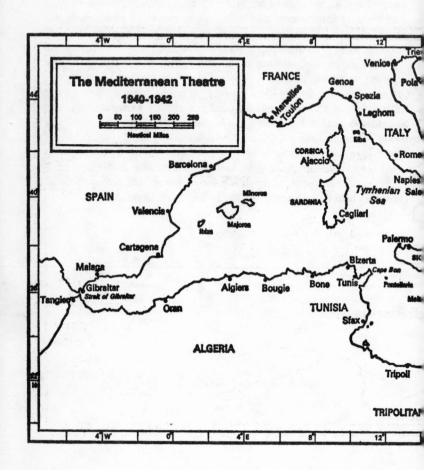

MAP ③

CHAPTER 10

The Admirals Afloat.
II. The Mediterranean
1940-1942

As soon as Mussolini began to make plain his intention to enter the war reinforcements were ordered to the eastern Mediterranean from all over the world, and by the end of May 1940 Admiral Cunningham again commanded a substantial, though far from modern fleet. Except for possession of the elderly aircraft carrier *Eagle* he was heavily out-numbered in all classes of ship by the Italian navy; and the Italians also possessed a huge superiority in shore-based aircraft. On 23 May the admiral telegraphed his broad strategic intentions to the Admiralty, who passed them on to Churchill.[1] This evidently provoked the Prime Minister into accusing Cunningham of being too 'defensive' – a suggestion which, to anyone who knew the admiral, was palpably absurd. He himself admits, in a marked understatement, that he was 'rather taken aback' by this suggestion, despite Pound telling him that he had tried to convince Churchill that there were no grounds at all for his accusation; but this early clash does once again illustrate his obsession with his own concept of 'offensive' measures – without much regard to the resources available. Early in June Cunningham signalled that control of the eastern Mediterranean and Aegean – which were the obvious first necessities – 'is not defensive' and that it 'by no means ex-cludes action in the central Mediterranean and against the Italian coast', which he hoped 'will be possible'.[2]

Meanwhile the naval staff were considering what should be done if France capitulated, and in mid-June Pound signalled that 'our Atlantic trade' would in that event have to be 'the first consideration', and that it might therefore be necessary to move the fleet from Alexandria to Gibraltar.[3] Next day Cunningham replied that such a move was certain to lead to the loss of Malta, though huge quantities of valuable stores could be saved if it were started at once.[4] Two days later he followed this up with a stronger message lest his initial reaction should 'have sounded somewhat acquiescent'. Withdrawal from Alexandria would, he now emphasized, involve 'such a landslide in territory and prestige' that he hoped 'it will never have to be taken'.[5] Churchill has written that he 'vetoed' this proposal; but in view of Cunningham's strong opposition this is surely too strong a claim;[6] and one can hardly blame the staff for investigating in advance what such a measure would entail, and ascertaining the C-in-C's views about it.

Towards the end of June, after the French government had signed an armistice with the Germans on the 22nd, the future of the French warships in African ports was urgently considered in London, and on the 29th the Admiralty told Admiral Sir James Somerville, who had been hastily sent to Gibraltar with a rather scratch collection of ships (known as Force H) how they proposed to handle the question of preventing the powerful French squadron based on Mers-el-Kebir near Oran falling into German hands. They proposed that its commander, Admiral Marcel-Bruno Gensoul, should be offered three alternatives – namely to steam to British ports, to scuttle themselves or to be destroyed by the British.[7] That afternoon Cunningham was told that it was 'under consideration to seize [the] French ships at Alexandria – simultaneously with [the] operation at Oran', the earliest date for which was the morning of 3 July. He was asked for his views on the 'best procedure to be followed' in order to achieve the purpose 'with minimum risk of bloodshed and hostilities on the part of the French'. Furthermore he was told that it 'would also be desirable to deal with [the] ships at Sfax [in Tunisia] in a similar manner to those at Oran immediately [the] operation at Alexandria has been completed'.[8]*

Cunningham's reply to these proposals was forthright. He signalled that he was 'most strongly opposed to [the] proposal for forcible seizure of [the] ships in Alexandria'; nor could he 'see what benefit is to be derived from it'. The points on which he pressed for 'urgent consideration' were, firstly, that the situation at Alexandria was 'quite different from elsewhere in [the] Mediterranean'. Secondly he asked 'What is [the] object of seizure?' If it was 'to prevent [the French] ships falling into enemy hands that', he declared, 'has already been achieved'. Thirdly he pointed out that if it was 'desired to obtain [the] ships for ourselves' it was 'unlikely to be attained by forcible seizure', since he was 'convinced that [the] French would resist most vigorously'. The probable outcome, he continued, would be 'for the ships to scuttle themselves at their moorings', so producing 'a harbour fouled with wrecks'. Fourthly he considered that repercussions throughout the Middle East theatre would be 'disastrous', particularly in the Suez Canal area and French Somaliland, where their co-operation was 'vitally

* The French squadron at Alexandria comprised the old battleship *Lorraine*, three heavy and one light cruiser and some minor vessels.

important', and in Syria where a 'friendly attitude is very necessary'. He represented that if on the other hand 'matters are allowed to pursue their present course at Alexandria' lack of pay and of food might well cause the ships to 'drop into our hands'. But he stressed that the foregoing arguments took no account of 'repercussions consequent on forcible action at Oran', which he was 'very much against . . . if it can possibly be avoided', chiefly because it would 'alienate the whole of the French element friendly to us'. As regards Sfax he had no reports of ships there and asked for information about them. In fact they were of minor importance.[9]

In their reply the Admiralty agreed that they would like 'to obtain [the] French ships at Alexandria for our own use if it can be done without bloodshed'. In that event we would accept those of their crews who wished to serve with the Royal Navy, while the reminder 'would be repatriated'. If we could not obtain the ships for our own use 'they must be dealt with' in one of two ways said the Admiralty. Either they could stay at Alexandria with skeleton crews and be 'immediately put in a non-seagoing condition', we giving a promise only to use them if the Germans broke the recent Armistice terms, or they must be 'sunk at sea'. Because action was to be taken at Oran on 3 July Cunningham was told to put the alternatives to Admiral René-Emile Godfroy, the commander of the French squadron, early that morning.[10] Cunningham has described this message as 'more consistent with the realities of the situation' than the earlier one.[11] As he was receiving all the signals sent to Somerville about the Admiralty's intentions at Oran he was fully informed about what was going on at the other end of the Mediterranean.

The second of July was a day of great anxiety for Cunningham, who had to inform all his senior officers of what was afoot and also prepare to seize the French ships if the British government insisted on it. He asked Admiral Godfroy to visit him on board his flagship the *Warspite* at 7 a.m. on the 3rd, as the Admiralty had instructed; but the unusual hour was of course bound to warn him that momentous events were in train. Godfroy and his Chief of Staff arrived punctually and were received with all the formalities normally accorded to a foreign Flag Officer – namely piping the side and the Marine guard and band paraded. Cunningham and his Chief of Staff Rear-Admiral A. U. Willis met the French officers at the gangway and took them down to the C-in-C's day cabin where they all sat in armchairs instead of around a table as at a formal conference. The object was of course to produce a relaxed atmosphere. Conversation was in English, which

Godfroy spoke fluently, except when an interpreter was needed to clarify some point. Godfroy's manner was, according to Cunningham, 'entirely helpful and cordial', but it was obvious to the British officers that he was under great strain.

Cunningham first read to the French Officers a message from his government expressing the desire that his ships should carry on the fight against the common foes, on which Godfroy merely commented that he would have preferred to receive this from his own government – which of course meant from Vichy. Cunningham then put to Godfroy the various proposals signalled to him – explaining that he had to ask for acceptance of one of them that day. He gave a promise that all the French officers and men who joined us would receive the same pay and be subject to the same conditions of service as their British counterparts. Those who did not wish to join us were, he said, entirely free to return to France – for which he would make arrangements as soon as it could be done. Godfroy was asked to explain these proposals to all his ships' companies, making it plain that they were free to decide as they wished. Finally he gave the admiral a guarantee that all the ships which joined us would be returned to France after the war.

In reply Godfroy represented, firstly, that his ships could not possibly fight under any flag except the French one, since the crews could thereby be classed as deserters; and, secondly, that he could not accept such a proposal without consulting his government. He was moreover sure that if his ships joined us the Axis powers would demand that equivalent ships should be transferred to them. Cunningham then pointed out that the terms offered were good, and that he himself could present them to the French crews over the admiral's head, though he was reluctant to do so. Godfroy admitted that this was so, and Cunningham then emphasized that the object was not only to prevent his ships falling into the enemy's hands but to preserve them for France. This argument plainly impressed the Frenchman, but as there was evidently no prospect of his accepting the conditions offered Cunningham passed on to the second proposal – namely that he should put his ships in a condition in which they could not go to sea and only keep on board skeleton crews, for whom we would provide pay and supplies.

Godfroy at once made it plain that he thought he could accept such terms, but asked to be allowed until 1 p.m. to think them over. Cunningham, knowing what was in train off Oran, insisted that he must have an answer by 11.30 a.m., to which Godfroy agreed. He was then told the third proposal, which was to take his ships to sea and sink them in deep water. Understandably it held no appeal for him. Cunningham brought the meeting to an end at about 8.30 a.m. by impressing on Godfroy that the decision was up to him, that it was a case of *force majeure*, and that he could honourably accept any of the alternatives offered. If it could not be the first one he hoped that it would be the second. He was optimistic enough to signal to the Admiralty an hour later that he expected the second alternative to be accepted.[12]

During the forenoon Cunningham waited in great anxiety for news about events at Oran, and was highly apprehensive about the effect on Godfroy if Somerville had to use force. At noon he received a bitterly disappointing letter from the French admiral saying that he could only accept the second alternative (demilitarization) if he was allowed to recommend it to his superiors. If he could not communicate with them he must therefore accept the third one (to sink his ships). In explaining his decision he made much of the concept of French 'sense of naval honour'. Cunningham at once sent a reply saying that he had no choice but to accept Godfroy's decision, and agreeing to his request for a forty-eight hour extension so that arrangements could be made for the safety and transport of his crews. He signalled this information to the Admiralty, emphasizing that there was no question of the French ships putting to sea without his consent, and that he wanted 'at all costs to avoid sinking the French ships in Alexandria harbour' or Godfroy being 'ordered to do so by his government'. In the meantime Cunningham was trying to persuade him to discharge oil fuel and carry out some measures of demilitarization. He concluded by telling the Admiralty that he was 'sure Godfroy has at the back of his mind that the Italians will break the armistice terms and thus enable him to fight again'.[13]

At about 2.30 p.m. Cunningham reported that he had succeeded in inducing Godfroy to discharge oil and remove his torpedo warheads, but he would not agree to only skeleton crews being left on board without the consent of his government.[14] Shortly before 5.30 p.m. he added that the cruisers were now discharging oil and the destroyers preparing to do so.[15] The Admiralty's reply was that 'crews should commence being reduced at once by landing or transfer to merchant ships', and ended with the minatory words 'Do not (Repeat) NOT fail'.[16] In retrospect Cunningham described this as 'a perfect example of the type of signal which should never be made' – because it showed no understanding at all of the 'explosive atmosphere at Alexandria or the difficult conditions in which we were working'. He did not believe at the time or later that it 'emanated from the Admiralty' – by which he meant of course that Churchill himself had inspired it. His supposition was almost certainly correct, but one does wonder why Pound apparently made no effort to get at any rate the last four words deleted.[17] Moreover as the message ignored the difference of time between London and Alexandria it did not reach Cunningham until long after dark. He assembled his Flag Officers on board the *Warspite* that evening, explained the situation and told them he intended to ignore the signal.

Just after the Admiralty's 'Do not fail' message was received a note from Godfroy arrived telling Cunningham that he had learnt about the 'ultimatum' presented to the French fleet at Oran, that his own Admiralty had ordered him to sail but that he had replied that to do so was impossible. On the other hand he had stopped the discharge of fuel in order that he might not 'incur reproach' for continuing to do so after being ordered to sail. Nor did a long and painful visit from Admiral Willis persuade him to budge an inch.

In the small hours of 4 July Cunningham told the Admiralty about these developments. He signalled that there were now three possible courses of action – to seize the French ships by boarding, to sink them by gun and torpedo fire where they lay, or to face Godfroy with a demand to intern or surrender his ships, which would probably result in his scuttling them. He did not think seizure would be successful, since the French had been thoroughly alerted. If he used strong arm methods it would 'lead to useless bloodshed on both sides', to the French ships being sunk in the most inconvenient places, and perhaps to our own ships suffering damage as well. Unless, he continued, 'Their Lordships see fit to direct otherwise' he intended to put the third alternative into force on the morning of the 5th. He concluded with the tactful but reproachful words 'I fear that in the sense of your 1824 of 3rd July [the 'Do not fail' message] I have failed.'[18]

That night Godfroy learnt what had taken place at Oran. Early on the 4th Cunningham received another note from him saying that he repudiated every undertaking he had given, and making it plain that he intended to go to sea – if necessary fighting his way out of the harbour. Cunningham at once reported this to the Admiralty, adding that he was now 'attempting to sow dissension' among the French crews but would 'sink him [Godfroy] if he moves'.[19] The French ships could be seen to be raising steam, and appeared to be cleared for action; while Cunningham made preparations to take the very step he had all along tried to avoid – namely engage in a battle in Alexandria harbour. There was now only one hope – that he could suborn the French officers and men from their allegiance to Godfroy during the six to eight hours before the ships would have steam. Every French ship had a British 'opposite number', and from the latter the Captains and officers at once began to use every possible form of persuasion on the crews of the former. To Cunningham, watching anxiously from his flagship, it soon became clear that, as he had put it 'the leaven was gradually working'.

A little before noon the Admiralty came up with another unhelpful signal saying that 'It does not seem at all certain that Godfroy in his present frame of mind will sink his ships unless you force him to do so by some threat. What threat do you propose?' They admitted 'the un-desirability of a battle in Alexandria harbour', but declared that 'the present situation could not be allowed to persist indefinitely'. They also asked whether Cunningham had considered taking his fleet to sea, leaving the French ships inside the harbour, so that his own could be 'suitably disposed for engaging them, and an ultimatum then de-livered'.[20] Cunningham must have thought such an idea little short of crazy, since it would enable Godfroy, if he wished to be really nasty, to do great damage to shore installations and to Cunningham's numerous supply ships. It actually crossed with a message from him telling White-hall that the 'situation [is] very tense', and chances of a negotiated settlement seemed remote; but he reported the efforts at persuasion then in progress.[21]

Early in the afternoon the French Captains were seen to be visiting Godfroy's flagship, and about an hour later a message came from the admiral asking Cunningham to receive him. The outcome was that he yielded to superior force and an agreement was quickly reached. Before 3.30 p.m. the C-in-C was able to report home that all oil fuel would be discharged from the French ships forthwith and that they would immediately be placed in a condition in which they could not fight. The discharge of crews was reserved for further discussion.[22]

That evening Cunningham sent a longer message explaining what he had done at each stage and why. He described the successful out-come of his propaganda campaign, and assured the Admiralty that as soon as the de-fuelling and disarming of the French ships was com-pleted he would 'feel quite free to take the fleet to sea to continue operations against the enemy'.[23] The reply came in the early hours of the 5th, when Alexander and Pound signalled their 'most sincere congratulations on [the] complete success of your negotiations'. The Prime Minister, they said, 'also wishes his congratulations to be sent to you'.[24] Though all thus ended happily one may doubt whether, if a less firm, patient and morally courageous man than Cunningham had been in command a disaster would have been averted.

Despite the congratulations sent from London subsequent events suggest that Churchill did not fully appreciate the great qualities shown by Cunningham on this occasion. As to the admiral's view of the Prime Minister, he evidently entertained some misgivings, since although he described him in his private correspondence as 'a great fighter' and 'a great leader' he qualified those eulogistic words by expressing doubts regarding Churchill's character and methods.[25]

To turn to Oran, the presentation of the British proposals to Admiral Gensoul, and the resultant tragic outcome has often been described and will not be fully recounted here.[26] But it must be mentioned that the use of force, which Somerville finally and most reluctantly adopted under heavy pressure from London, was not completely successful since the battle-cruiser *Strasbourg* (one of the primary targets) and three destroyers escaped from the harbour and returned safely to Toulon. French casualties were tragically heavy, forty-seven officers, 196 Petty Officers and 1054 ratings being killed and 351 more wounded. So ended what Somerville described as 'a filthy job', while Gensoul declared that 'If there is a stain on the flag it is certainly not ours.'

Several points which have perhaps not been given sufficient attention may be mentioned here. The first one concerns the choice of Captain C. S. Holland as the emissary charged with the very delicate task o presenting the British government's alternatives to Gensoul. Long afte r the war Admiral John Godfrey (DNI 1939–42) told Lord Cunningham that in May 1940 he had warned Pound that 'Holland's judgement about French officers had become gravely impaired';[27] but the warning was ignored. Secondly Cunningham thought that Somerville had erred in dropping mines in the approaches to the harbour while negotiations were still in progress, since it was all too likely to stiffen Gensoul's attitude. On the other hand it is certainly the case that Gensoul himself contributed greatly to the failure to achieve a negotiated settlement by sending the French Admiralty two very incomplete and highly misleading versions of the British alternatives as presented to him. The key passage in the first one read 'Ultimatum sent. Sink your ships in six hours or we shall use force. Reply: French ships will reply to force with force.'[27A] Nor could Gensoul himself ever produce a satisfactory explanation of how this crucial error came to pass.[28]

The tragedy of Oran (or Mers-el-Kebir as the French more correctly call it) is enhanced by our present day knowledge of how close things came to a satisfactory solution. On the morning of 3 July Pound drafted a signal authorizing Somerville to accept demilitarization of the French ships where they lay – which was precisely what Gensoul had offered in the final stage of the negotiations with Holland. However, the War Cabinet turned down Pound's draft on the grounds that 'this would look like weakening' – a reason which, as Professor Marder has remarked 'at first sight, almost defies belief'.

As regards the chief instigator of the operation it is beyond doubt that, as he himself has admitted, it was Churchill; and those who were with him at the time have borne witness to the strength of the emotion which the essential need, as he saw it, to eliminate a grave threat to our whole position at sea aroused in him.[29] That the decision also showed, not for the first or the last time, the streak of ruthlessness in his character is surely undeniable. Whether the violence was necessary or not will long continue to be debated; but for our purpose it is only necessary to note that Churchill acted against the strongly expressed views of all three admirals on the spot. Could it be, one wonders, the result of a sub-conscious regret that Asquith did not overrule de Robeck when in March 1915 he refused to renew the naval attack on the Dardanelles? At any rate Churchill's action, marvellously presented to a crowded and initially silent House of Commons on 4 July, finally won him the sustained applause of members of all parties. His masterly rhetoric eliminated the misgivings of many MPs who had felt serious doubts about what we had done.

Alexander and Pound fully supported Churchill in applying pressure to the admirals on the spot; but the latter continued to hold to the end of their lives that, given more time and patience, a peaceful solution could have been arrived at.[30]* Admiral Sir Dudley North, from the Gibraltar command rashly if courageously made his protest by letter – thereby bringing on his head a stiff reprimand and, in all probability, laying up a rod in pickle for his own back.

On 7 July, four days after Oran, the new French battleship *Richelieu*, which had escaped from Brest at the time of the French collapse and had reached Dakar in Senegal, was attacked by carrier aircraft and depth charges dropped from a motor boat.[31] Though we believed her to have been effectively immobilized repairs were in fact completed within about a year. Pound seems to have been uneasy about what we had done at Oran and Dakar, and anxious to avoid a repetition. Three days

---

* While working on my war history I had many interviews and much correspondence with Cunningham, Somerville and North, the three admirals concerned in the execution of the attack on Oran and related plans. None of them ever budged from the view that, given more time for negotiation, the tragedy could have been averted. On 9 January 1950 Cunningham wrote to Admiral Lord Fraser, then First Sea Lord, that '90% of senior naval officers, including myself, thought Oran a ghastly error and still do'. BM. Add. Ms. 52575.

after the attack on the *Richelieu* he wrote to Alexander suggesting that as she had 'been dealt with the moment appears opportune to review our policy . . .'; also 'that a halt now be called in our action against the French Navy, and that we should take steps to let our [new?] policy be known to the French authorities'. His reasons were, firstly, that French hostility could make Gibraltar and Freetown, Sierra Leone, untenable, so forcing us to occupy the Azores and Cape Verde Islands; secondly that enemy raiders could gain the use of French overseas bases; and, lastly, that the other new French battleship the *Jean Bart*, which had reached Casablanca from St Nazaire, was far from completed and would in any case be difficult to attack.[32] Alexander evidently sent these proposals on to Churchill; but he was already immersed in the attempt to instal General de Gaulle in Senegal known as operation 'Menace'; and as that undertaking affected profoundly the career of one of the three admirals involved in the action taken against French warships – namely Admiral North, the Flag Officer North Atlantic (FOCNA) at Gibraltar, it will be convenient to turn to his fate.

Early in May – two months before Oran – the Admiralty extended North's appointment – to his great satisfaction;[33] so the Admiralty must at that time have felt complete confidence in his capacity. When, however, he sent home his protest about Oran A. V. Alexander was evidently greatly angered. He strengthened Pound's draft letter in which North was told that, although the 'opinions of senior officers are always of value before an operation has taken place . . . Their Lordships deprecate comments on a policy which has been decided by the Admiralty in the light of factors which were unknown to officers on the spot'; and he told Churchill that he had proposed to Pound 'that it should be for consideration to supersede' North.[34] From these minutes it appears that if anyone was, as Pound's secretary told Professor Marder, made 'hopping mad' by North's letter about Oran it was Alexander rather than Pound.[35] Moreover the secretary's adjectival description is, in my view, totally inapplicable to Pound in any circumstances. Furthermore on the day after receiving Alexander's proposals Pound told him that 'It is desirable that officers should give their opinions before Admiralty orders are received as they may be in possession of information unknown to the Admiralty . . . It is also desirable that officers should represent their views even after orders are received if they think they are in possession of information which is not known to the Admiralty.' As there was 'no question . . . of the Admiralty orders not being carried out I do not think therefore, that there is a case for superseding FOCNA' concluded Pound.[36] That soberly worded minute surely contradicts the secretary's 'hopping mad' description.

Though the letter of reprimand sent to North on 17 July followed the lines of Alexander's strengthened minute he sent North's report and the Admiralty's riposte to Churchill that same day, together with the statement that whereas he himself had wanted to have the admiral superseded Pound 'did not think there is a strong enough case for this'.[37] One may feel that this action by Alexander was wholly unnecessary, since the Oran affair was over and done with. Churchill replied 'It is evident that Admiral Dudley North has not got the root of the matter in him, and I should be very glad to see you replace him by a more resolute and clear-sighted officer.'[38] This blast must have placed Pound in an awkward position, as he now knew that he had the Prime Minister as well as the First Lord against him on the question of replacing North; and that may help to explain Pound's later actions.

Professor Marder pays tribute to North's World War I service as First Lieutenant and Commander of the battle-cruiser *New Zealand*, and to the success he achieved in several important appointments in between the wars – including that of Chief of Staff to Admiral Sir John Kelly, who was given command of the Home Fleet after the Invergordon Mutiny of 1931 and certainly did not suffer fools or incompetents gladly.[39] Thus Marder's remark that North was 'widely regarded in the Service as the epitome of the courtier sailor' is a great deal less than fair to an officer whose association with the Royal Family derived from his distinguished service and attractive personality rather than from wealth or influence in high places. Be that as it may the admiral's aristocratic connections may have contributed to the prejudice against him shown by Alexander, who had worked his way up to the position of First Lord of the Admiralty by devoted service to the Labour Party and the Co-operative movement. One may guess that temperamentally he and North were poles apart at the time of the fracas.

We cannot here go into the details of the planning and execution of the combined operation against Dakar of August-September 1940, for which the reader may be referred to my own account and to Professor Marder's more detailed study;[40] but in view of its repercussions on certain admirals, and especially North, the background must be made clear. As regards action against French warships, on 4 July, the day after Oran, North was told that if we became involved in war with France, and *only then* 'inferior [French] forces were to be stopped and ordered into British-controlled ports'.[41] Three days later he was told

above: Inspecting Guard of Honour at launch of HMS *Warspite* at Devonport,
by Mrs Austen Chamberlain 26th November 1913.

below: On board HMS *Prince of Wales* for passage to Newfoundland
for Atlantic Meeting, August 1941.

above: Churchill with Admiral of the Fleet Sir Roger Keyes (DCO)
watching landing exercises c. 1941.
below: Commodore Roger Keyes (COS), Admiral Sir John de Robeck (Naval C-in-C),
General Sir Ian Hamilton (C-in-C Middle East Forces)
and General Sir Walter Braithwaite (CGS) at Gallipoli 1915.

above: King George VI and Admiral of the Fleet Sir Charles Forbes.
Visit to Home Fleet Flagship *Warspite* in Clyde, probably 28th February 1940.

below: Gneisenau in action with *Glorious* off north Norway, 8th June 1940.

above: HMS *Bittern* (sloop) hit and set on fire by German bombers.
Namsos, Norway, April 1940.
below: A British cruiser (Town Class) towing a tanker set on fire by German bombers
out of harbour. Probably Steinland. Norway, April 1940.

above: Alexandria harbour 21st May 1940 looking east. In background (L to R)
battleships *Bretagne* (Fr.), *Malaya, Royal Sovereign, Provence* (Fr.), *Lorraine* (Fr.).
Centre heavy cruisers *Tourville* and *Duquesne* (Fr.). Foreground three French destroyers, *Tigre* in centre

below: The attack on the French Fleet at Mers el Kébir. In the foreground the battleship
Provence; in the background the *Bretagne,* 3rd July 1940

left: The escape of the *Strasbourg* from Mers el Kébir, 3rd July 1940.

below: A seaboat being lowered from HMS *Foresight* with General de Gaulle and General Spears on board off Dakar, to confer with Admiral J. H. D. Cunningham on board HMS *Barham* (in background). 24th September 1940.

above: Heavy air attacks on Grand
Harbour, Malta, January 1941, when the
damaged carrier *Illustrious* was in
harbour.

left: Admiral Sir John Tovey (C-in-C
Home Fleet) with Captain J. C. Leach
on board *Prince of Wales*, 1941. '

above: Farewell to one of the escorting destroyers
on return from Atlantic Meeting, August 1941.
below: Suda Bay, Crete. Ships set on fire by air attacks, May 1941.
HMS *York* in centre.

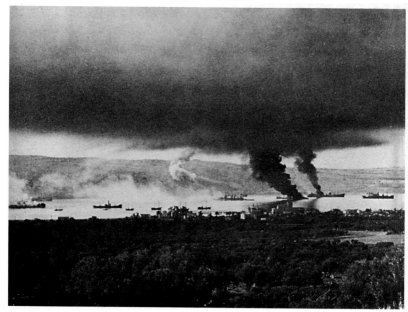

above: The ill-fated Convoy PQ17 assembling at Hvalfiord, Iceland, July 1942.
below: German photograph of British prisoners being marched through Dieppe
after the raid of 19th August 1942.

above: Admiral Sir Max Horton and Sir John Tovey (C-in-C Western Approaches and C-in-C Home Fleet) on board *King George V*, c. 1942.
below: Japanese photograph of sinking of *Prince of Wales* and *Repulse* off east coast of Malaya, 10th December 1941.

above: Sinking of HMS *Hermes* by Japanese carrier aircraft off Trincomalee, Ceylon, 9th April 1942.
below: With the Chiefs of Staff for Casablanca Conference, January 1943.
Left to Right: Air Chief Marshal Sir Charles Portal (CAS), Admiral of the Fleet
Sir Dudley Pound (CNS), Winston S. Churchill, General Sir Alan Brooke (CIGS),
Vice Admiral Lord Louis Mountbatten (CCO).

above: Admiral of the Fleet Sir Andrew Cunningham and Vice-Admiral Sir Algernon Willis with General Dwight D. Eisenhower. Algiers, 1943.

left: A U boat sinking after attack by a Sunderland of Coastal Command. (Note survivors in water bottom right).

that if French warships attempted the passage of the Straits of Gibraltar they were to be dealt with in accordance with the signal of the 4th.[42] On 12 July another message told the admiral that 'the Government reserved the right to deal with warships proceeding to enemy-controlled ports'. In other words North was not required to take action against a superior force, and if the destination of any French force was an enemy port the government would give orders regarding what was to be done about it.

As to the operation against Dakar, it is justifiable to quote Churchill's frank admission that 'I thus undertook in an exceptional degree the initiation and advocacy of the Dakar expedition.' In August Admiral Keyes, the Director of Combined Operations, pressed Churchill hard to entrust the planning of the operation to him, offering '2350 first class fighting men led by officers spoiling to fight', and assuring him that 'you will not hear anything more about difficulties, hazards and political dangers'. But Churchill was persuaded not to delay the departure of the troop convoys by accepting Keyes's offer, and in fact he had virtually nothing to do with 'Menace'.[43]

In his memoirs Churchill attributed the failure of the expedition to 'a chapter of accidents' over reports of a powerful French squadron consisting of three large cruisers and three super-destroyers from Toulon being allowed unhindered passage through the Straits of Gibraltar, and to muddles in London in the handling of reports of this movement. It must also be made clear that Churchill's statement in the House of Commons on 8 October 1940 that the French warships 'carried with them a number of Vichy partisans . . . sent to overawe the population, to grip the defences and see to the efficient manning of the powerful shore batteries', which he repeats in his memoirs, is wholly fictitious.[44] The French squadron was actually bound for Libreville in Gabon, far to the south of Dakar, and had only been allowed by the Germans to sail on condition that any British interference with its passage was resisted by force.* As Admiral Somerville had at the time only the battle-cruiser *Renown* and six destroyers, it is as unlikely that he 'could have stopped and parleyed with the French squadron pending decisive orders', as Churchill wrote,[45] as he could have won a battle with it if the Frenchmen carried out their orders to fight. However, the free passage allowed to the French squadron through the Straits of Gibraltar led to the relief of Admiral North, and so to what became the

* On the instructions given to the French admiral commanding the squadron from Toulon see Jacques Mordal (pseudonym for the well-known French naval historian Hervé Cras) *La Bataille de Dakar* (Paris, Editions Ozanne, 1956) pp. 122–4.

most protracted controversy of the post-war years.

If as is often said, in war time truth is the first casualty justice is always a close runner-up. Had the Admiralty merely told North that he was to be relieved of his command at some convenient date before the expiry of his extended term he would have had no more cause for complaint than had other senior officers of all three services who were unlucky enough to hold high commands early in the war, and suffered such treatment. Such were Admiral Forbes, Generals Mackesy and Wavell and Air Marshal Longmore. The fatal mistake by Pound was to lay at North's door an accusation of what amounted to dereliction of duty; and it is surely understandable that on reading such a charge the admiral should have done his utmost to vindicate himself through some form of trial or inquiry. The only person who seems to have realized that Pound was taking an unnecessarily dangerous line was Sir Archibald Carter, the Permanent Secretary of the Admiralty, who on 10 October minuted that he was 'anxious to avoid a full reasoned reply [to North's report of the 6th] since, simply as a matter of argument, I don't feel too confident that Sir Dudley North hasn't the best of it'.[46] Carter's misgivings were also expressed on two later occasions. On 12 October he minuted on Somerville's report of the 7th, in which the admiral said he wished 'to accept full responsibility' for the French squadron not being intercepted, 'I feel that to prevent any future misunderstandings it might be wise to define a little more closely the relationship between FOC. Force H [Somerville] and FOCNA [North]';[47] and the chain of command certainly was ill-defined. Alexander seems to have been more aware than Pound of the danger of making a charge amounting to dereliction of duty against an officer; but it was in the main Pound's terminology which was finally used in the letter sent on 15 October telling North that he had forfeited 'Their Lordships' confidence' owing to his failure 'in an emergency to take all prudent precautions without waiting for Admiralty instructions'. He was therefore to be relieved of his command.[48] A month later, by which time the quarrel was plainly coming to the boil, Carter minuted 'I have never been at all happy about this controversy.'[49]

Pound's case against North rested chiefly on the fact that the French cruisers might, after passing through the Straits of Gibraltar on 11 September, have turned north to one of the Bay of Biscay bases in German occupation – to permit which was contrary to Admiralty policy at the time; and that North ought to have taken precautions against such an eventuality by ordering Somerville's Force H to sea. But that force had been described by the Admiralty as a 'detached squadron', and they had often sent orders direct to its commander – not through North. It is moreover quite certain that, although North was senior to Somerville, the latter did not in any sense regard himself as being under the command of the former. Professor Marder asks 'Why did North not take precautions against a possible movement to the northward?';[50] to which the short answer is that he did do so – by ordering air reconnaissance to track the French ships only two and a half hours after the first sighting. He informed the Admiralty that he had done so, and only called off the air reconnaissance when it was clear that they were southward-bound.[51] Also, as he later told the Admiralty, his intelligence had always indicated that their destination was to the south; and as he knew that the Admiralty 'had at least as much information as I had, and probably more' it was reasonable to expect that he would be told if they considered the ships 'might be going north'.[52] Thus Pound's case against North, both on operational grounds and on the chain of command, was not at all strong; and although North did not make as much use of the chance to rebut the major charge against him as he could have done, the weakness of the case against him enhances the feeling that Alexander and Pound were determined to get rid of him, and were not too scrupulous about the arguments used to justify such action. They also completely ignored the uncomfortable fact that, if North had ordered Force H to sea (or had ordered Somerville to take such action), a battle might well have taken place off Gibraltar in which the powerful French squadron came off much the better.* Nor were the Admiralty and Foreign Office blameless for the long delay in the reports on the movement of the French cruisers being decyphered and circulated to those concerned.

There is of course absolutely no firm evidence indicating that North was, as he repeatedly argued, made the scapegoat for the failure of the combined operation against Dakar. Yet it is difficult to find a rational explanation for the complete about-turn executed by Pound towards him. Early in 1940 he wrote in very friendly language to North 'From what I hear, you have undoubtedly made great improvements at Gibraltar, and things are now running much more smoothly';[53] and, as already mentioned, he renewed North's appointment as FOCNA in the following May. In mid-July moreover he refused to accept the

---

* The French cruisers *Georges Leygues*, *Montcalm* and *Gloire* were fine modern ships displacing about 8200 tons and mounting nine 6-inch guns and four torpedo tubes each. The three 'super-destroyers' of *Le Fantasque* class displaced about 2600 tons and mounted five 5.5-inch guns and nine torpedo tubes. All six were much faster than the *Renown* and the mixed bag of six destroyers finally collected to accompany her to sea.

Alexander-Churchill proposal that he should be superseded because of his critical report on Oran. Furthermore on 22 September, eleven days *after* the French squadron passed through the Gibraltar Straits but about three days *before* the final failure at Dakar, he sent the admiral another friendly and chatty letter beginning 'My dear North'.[54] And, finally, the Admiralty allowed *sixteen days* (11 to 27 September) to elapse between the passage of the French squadron and calling for a report on his actions from North. The only reason ever offered in explanation of this prolonged silence is that 'the Admiralty was entirely taken up with the conduct of operation "Menace" at the time'[55] – which does not seem very convincing. Taken together the foregoing facts do suggest either that Pound's early opinion of North was badly at fault, which could be true as Pound was certainly by no means always a good judge of character; or that he was subjected to pressure from above – which can only mean Alexander or Churchill – to have him sacked, and yielded to it. On the evidence I have cited I cannot, with the best will in the world, find Professor Marder's account judicious or even acceptable.

Churchill's views of the effects of the arrival of the French ships on or near the scene of operation 'Menace' have already been quoted, and as he repeated them in his memoirs he obviously held to them after the war. Though there is his letter to North of 7 June 1948 disclaiming any responsibility for his dismissal, the fact that, as Professor Marder has discovered, he did originally intend to deal with the affair in his memoirs but 'cut this out *deliberately*' must leave one in some doubt whether he had a hand in the Admiralty's decision;[56]* for in view of Alexander sending North's report on Oran to Churchill, and the oft proven interest of the latter in the appointments of, and sometimes the dismissal of Flag Officers, it would be most surprising if he told the Prime Minister nothing about the decision to relieve the admiral.[57] Furthermore I note that in a letter I wrote to Lord Cunningham at the time when I was trying to build up a fair account of this fracas, and had access to the Churchill papers in the Cabinet Office, I mentioned that Sir James Butler and I had tried to get Churchill's side of the story from

---

* There is in the Prime Minister's Private Office papers the draft of a message to Admiral J. H. D. Cunningham, the Joint Commander with General N. M. S. Irwin for operation 'Menace', reading 'Arrival of French cruisers possibly with troops on board seems to me to destroy hope of a bloodless capture of Dakar.' It is endorsed in Churchill's hand 'Show me later' and was never sent. In fact the Joint Commanders represented that the arrival of the French cruisers 'should not have altered the military situation', and as de Gaulle had protested emphatically against cancellation of the operation the War Cabinet authorized them to go ahead.

him but that he had 'refused to give any opinion'.[58]

The story of North's interview with Pound after he had returned home, which Marder gives fairly fully, and of which the admiral gave me a long and vivid account, makes painful reading;[59] and North's conclusion that Pound was in 'a very exhausted and nervous condition, with an utterly washed out appearance', so accounting for his rudeness, is probably accurate. For Pound, as already mentioned, was certainly not a fit man, and it is well known that anyone who loses normal sleep as a result of osteo-arthritis is liable to have some very bad days. It is charitable to assume that North's interview took place on one of them.

After the war, when North was pressing for an inquiry to be held into the circumstances attending his dismissal, Lord Cunningham wrote to Lord Fraser, then First Sea Lord, accepting that the suggestion that North had been made a scapegoat for the Dakar fiasco was groundless. But, he continued, 'You know probably better than I that DP [Pound] was at times rather hasty in finding scapegoats – maybe prodded thereto by Winston. I can remember writing to him [Pound] on three separate occasions and telling him I thought he had been un-just.' To which Fraser replied that 'The thing that really upset the First Sea Lord was that North waited for instructions without putting him-self in a position in which he could carry out any instructions'; and Fraser recalled Pound saying to him 'How can I continue to place reliance on a Flag Officer who does not act because he is waiting for instructions?'[60] All of which of course begged the questions whether Somerville's force was or was not under North's command, and whether the Admiralty's instructions about intercepting French war-ships were clearly worded.

And so the controversy continued throughout the early 1950s with five Admirals of the Fleet (Lords Chatfield, Cork and Orrery and Cunningham, Sir John Cunningham and Sir Algernon Willis) trying firstly to get the Admiralty to grant an inquiry, in which they were unsuccessful, and then asking Harold Macmillan, the Prime Minister, to receive them as a deputation and to consider a memorandum they had prepared on the subject. The final outcome was that in May 1957 Macmillan, having himself studied the vast dossier which had ac-cumulated about the case, acquitted North of professional failure and assured the House of Commons that he had not been 'the victim of Service or political prejudice'. Though he thus skilfully exonerated Churchill of having played any part in North's dismissal it is hard to avoid the conclusion that there *was* 'Service prejudice' against him on the part of Alexander and Pound. However Macmillan's assurance that

North 'has nothing with which to reproach himself', and that 'there is no question of his professional integrity being impugned' satisfied the Admirals of the Fleet and ended the long controversy. The pity was that it had taken seventeen years to achieve that end, and it is difficult not to feel that the time when an *amende honorable* should have been made was during Churchill's second premiership – perhaps soon after my account was published in 1954.

To end on a personal note, during my research into the story of these tangled events Admiral Sir Rhoderick McGrigor, First Sea Lord 1951-5 asked me to come and see him about them. When I had explained the main points and shown him the principal signals which had passed between the Admiralty and Somerville and North about policy towards French warships he said 'Yes, it was much more the Admiralty's fault than North's.' Secondly Sir James Butler and I had an interview with Sir John Lang, the Permanent Secretary of the Admiralty, about my draft on the subject, and during it Lang produced from his safe Churchill's minute to Alexander suggesting the relief of North on account of his criticism of Oran, referred to above, and which I had of course not seen before. Lastly Lord Cunningham wrote to me that Macmillan's statement in Parliament had followed so closely what I had written in *The War at Sea* that 'There is no question but that the clearing of Dudley North's reputation has also put you all right as a historian.'[61] Cunningham also wrote when he had visited Admiral McGrigor to discuss the North case he found 'to my horror that North had applied in November 1943 when I was First Sea Lord for the case to be re-considered. I was never shown the letter!'; and he suspected that Alexander 'had kept it in his own hands'.[62] Be that as it may the evidence of Alexander's animosity towards North, cited above, is strong. How far he kept Churchill informed of what was done in the autumn of 1940 is likely to remain uncertain; but to do so would have been wholly in accord with his normal practice.

After the war a good many senior British officers felt that North's campaign for vindication was undignified, and that he should have accepted the treatment meted out to him without complaint. It appears that Professor Marder in his account of the expedition against Dakar and its aftermath was much influenced by those who held such views.[63] Yet once the guns have stopped firing there are surely grounds for reviewing quasi-judicial proceedings which, in the heat and pressures of war, may have produced injustice. The Admiralty's argument that to grant such an inquiry would open the floodgates to all officers who had been relieved of commands lacks conviction – because, so far as I know, none of them (except perhaps Admiral Harwood, about whom more will be said later) was told that they were being relieved for dereliction of duty. Furthermore if the normal procedure regarding the administration of justice is bound to be slow, there are surely good grounds for modifying the wartime principle that heads of departments must be allowed to get rid of officers in whom they have lost confidence as soon as possible. Thus if the Admiralty had been prepared to grant North the inquiry he sought soon after the war a great deal of ill-feeling and much tendentious writing would have been avoided.

One officer besides North suffered as a result of the French squadron making an unhindered passage through the Gibraltar Straits. Captain R. H. Bevan, the Director of Operations (Foreign), was on duty on the night of 10–11 September when a message from the Naval Attaché, Madrid, which bore the 'Immediate' priority and gave warning of the French ships' approach was received.* Bevan must surely have been aware of the latest, if ambiguous, developments in the Government's policy with regard to French warships, and also with the plans and progress of operation 'Menace'; but he may not have appreciated the possible significance of the French ships' movements in relation to the latter. He later told Pound that he was shown the signal at about 6 a.m. on the 11th and intended to take action on it when he began the day's work but forgot to do so.[64] He accordingly received a letter conveying to him 'an expression of Their Lordships' displeasure',[65] and was removed from his post; but as he was given command of a cruiser Pound cannot have taken a very serious view of his lapse. Churchill however took a very different line about what he described as 'a most serious and disastrous failure in responsibility . . . contributing to a far worse misfortune [presumably at Dakar, and to] a grievous breakdown in the staff system at the Admiralty'. He wanted Bevan to be placed on half pay unless he himself claimed the right to a Court Martial.[66] Alexander consulted the Admiralty's legal advisers, and as a result he pointed out to Churchill that, although there was no legal bar to trying the officer by Court Martial, 'the prisoner's right of a plea of mitigation of sentence would put the Board of Admiralty in an extremely awk-

* Warning of the passage of the French squadron from Toulon was telegraphed by the French Admiralty to their naval attaché at Madrid on the morning of 6 September, instructing him to inform his British opposite number in order that the British authorities at Gibraltar might be made aware of the movement. The French attaché reported back on the evening of 10th that he had carried out those instructions and had also informed the Spanish Ministry of Marine. These telegrams are printed in full as Annexe V of Jacques Mordal, *La Bataille de Dakar* but are not mentioned by Professor Marder.

ward position as he would certainly say he had already been punished'. To put him on half pay was, he wrote, 'certainly open to the same objection', and would moreover in the First Lord's opinion 'be likely to create a sense of injustice in the fleet'.[67] Churchill was not mollified by this argument, and questioned whether an expression of displeasure constituted 'a sentence'. He minuted to Alexander 'I consider the officer should be placed on half pay and trust you will be able to meet my wishes.'[68] Alexander passed this vindictive request to Pound, who stressed that the Board alone 'must bear the responsibility for whatever is done in the matter of discipline', and added that action such as Churchill had proposed would be 'not only contrary to naval justice but also to civil practice'.[69] On reading these strong objections Alexander passed them to Churchill, in suitably modified form, and added, a little unctuously, 'I am sure you know that there is nothing I would like to do more than to meet your wishes at all times,' but that all his advisers were opposed to the infliction of a second punishment.[70] All he got by way of reply was 'The premature infliction of a minor and altogether inadequate punishment is now held to bar proper disciplinary treatment of a gross case of neglect of duty in a Staff Officer. I greatly regret the result.'[71]

One other aspect of Bevan's lapse merits attention. The Madrid signal was certainly distributed to all senior staff officers on the morning of 11 September, and must surely have been 'on the file' when Pound presided over the usual 9.30 a.m. staff meeting. Yet neither the Assistant nor the Vice Chiefs of Staff apparently drew attention to it. Pound went straight from the staff meeting in the Admiralty to one held by the COS Committee at which Churchill was in the chair,[72] and it was apparently then that Pound first learnt about the arrival of the French cruisers off Gibraltar – not from the Madrid message referred to above but from the report of the patrolling destroyer which had sighted them, sent at 4.45 a.m. that morning and passed on by North to the Admiralty at 6.17 a.m. saying that he had ordered the destroyer to stop shadowing the French ships. Pound at once telephoned to the Admiralty to signal to Somerville that the Renown was to raise steam for full speed.[73] Though the minutes of the COS meeting throw no light on the matter it does therefore appear that the effect of the French cruisers' passage on operation 'Menace' was then raised; and in view of Churchill's great interest in the undertaking it is hard to believe that he was left in ignorance of what was happening 1000 miles away in the Straits of Gibraltar. As to Captain Bevan, though the initial error was certainly his it seems true to say that it was compounded by more highly placed officers on the staff; and therein may lie the reason why Pound considered a fairly mild reprimand adequate and stood out against any more severe punishment.

To return to the Mediterranean, early in October 1940 Cunningham ran another convoy to Malta from the east without loss, and at the same time brought some empty ships from the island to Alexandria. The escort of the latter ran into an Italian destroyer force, and after a spirited engagement sank two of its ships and damaged a third one. The latter was taken in tow by a consort in an endeavour to get her home again, and in the proposed communiqué about the battle which Cunningham telegraphed to the Admiralty he paid tribute to the gallantry displayed by the enemy ships, especially in their endeavour to save the damaged one. When Churchill read this magananimous suggestion he was greatly angered and told Alexander that the tribute was quite unjustified. 'This kind of kid glove stuff,' he wrote, 'infuriates the people who are going through their present ordeal at home [i.e. from bombing] and this aspect should be put to the admiral.'[74] An appropriate signal was accordingly sent; but Cunningham remained impenitent because, as he has written, 'on this occasion the Italian destroyers *had* fought well'.*

The period between June 1940 and January 1941 was one of high success for Cunningham and Somerville who, with greatly inferior forces, then established a clear ascendancy over the Italian navy. Sweeps were frequently made into the central Mediterranean, convoys were run to and from Malta without serious loss, Italian shore installations all over the theatre were bombed and bombarded, and in November 1940 their navy received a very nasty knock when Fleet Air Arm aircraft torpedoed three of its biggest ships in Tarantoharbour. In September the Admiralty passed to Cunningham Churchill's congratulations on his recent successes, and in November the admiral received even warmer congratulations from him over Taranto.[75]

Perhaps it was because of Somerville's strongly expressed views on Oran that Churchill evidently regarded him with a good deal less than complete confidence at this time. In November the admiral was charged with escorting from Gibraltar a convoy of three fast merchantmen (two for Malta and one for Alexandria) with very valuable cargoes, and encountered a powerful Italian force off Cape Spartivento, the southern tip of Sardinia. He at once set off in pursuit of the retreat-

---

* See *Odyssey*, pp. 278-9 for a detailed account of this action and for Cunningham's reaction to the Admiralty's reprimand – which he probably guessed to have emanated from Churchill.

ing Italians, but on realizing that they had the legs of his ships, and knowing that his primary responsibility was to ensure 'the safe and timely arrival' of the convoy, he broke off the pursuit early in the afternoon and returned to cover and protect the merchantmen. This action aroused doubts about Somerville's 'offensive spirit', and while the Admiralty had received only two signalled reports sent *while he was at sea* on which to form an opinion they decided to send out Admiral of the Fleet Lord Cork and Orrery to inquire into the admiral's actions.* While Somerville told Cunningham how 'amazed' he had been to receive a signal suggesting 'a lack of confidence in my leadership',[76] Alexander and Pound were preparing to have him relieved. Churchill supported such action, minuting 'Why not give Harwood his chance here?'; and Alexander so far prejudged the outcome of Lord Cork's inquiry as actually to nominate Harwood, who had made his name in the River Plate battle and was serving as ACNS (Foreign), to relieve Somerville.[77]

When Lord Cork had all the facts before him, including Somerville's full report, he had no hesitation in concluding that the admiral had acted perfectly correctly. Somerville wrote to Cunningham that Cork had 'asked me not to be too hard on the Admiralty, and said there were people inside and out of it (Tom [Phillips] and Winston!) ready to raise their voices without any knowledge of the facts . . . I believe he [Cork] considers the whole thing [i.e. the inquiry] was a bloody outrage'.[78]

Meanwhile an Italian broadcast which claimed that Somerville had run away from their fleet had stimulated Churchill to reconsider the position. He told Alexander and Pound that a Court Martial or Court of Inquiry, followed by the relief of the admiral, would inevitably be taken as justifying the claim they had made. 'Admiral Somerville,' he wrote, prejudging the result of the Inquiry, 'has clearly lost the confidence of the Board – it is quite sufficient to tell him to haul down his flag and relieve him by Harwood without giving any other reason than we think a change necessary on general grounds. This is in fact true because even before these two episodes [presumably Oran and the convoy action] confidence in him had largely departed . . .' He did not therefore want Lord Cork to be sent to Gibraltar; but Alexander replied that as he was about to arrive there, and Somerville knew all about the institution of the Inquiry, to cancel it and simultaneously

* Admiral Sir William Davis, who was in Plans Division and serving on the Joint Planning Staff at the time, is quite certain that the initiative in sending out Lord Cork came from Churchill; but Alexander's papers make it plain that he, very naturally, took the executive action about ordering the inquiry. Interviews 1975 and 1976.

order him to haul down his flag 'would entitle him to say that he had been unfairly treated'. Moreover if the change was made the Axis propaganda machine would, in his view, 'shriek their conviction' that such action provided 'complete support of their previous lying statements'. Churchill thereupon withdrew his request to cancel Lord Cork's mission, writing that 'should the Court of Inquiry consider the Admiral blameworthy and unless facts emerge which are very different to those on which we have rested, I hope the relief will take place this week'.[79] In the event the Inquiry produced, as we have seen, very different results from those anticipated by Churchill; but it was not until nearly two months later that he closed the argument by more or less admitting to Alexander that he had been wrong. 'I am glad to learn from the First Sea Lord,' he then wrote, 'that the letter relieving Admiral Somerville has not yet gone. In view of all the circumstances, I think the question might be reviewed.'[80] In fact of course that had already happened.

The Admiralty was not, however, prepared to admit that Somerville had acted entirely correctly – even after they had received both his and Lord Cork's full reports. For they told the former, with irritating didacticism, that 'No opportunity must be allowed to pass of attaining what is in fact the ultimate object of the Royal Navy – the destruction of the enemy's forces whenever and wherever encountered.' This was of course an echo of the teaching of the influential American naval historian Captain Alfred Thayer Mahan, which, though widely accepted as gospel at the turn of the century, has recently been subjected to penetrating criticism.[81] A curious aftermath of the Inquiry into Somerville's actions on the above occasion was that Pound wrote to Cunningham that 'I have never regretted the action we took' in sending out Lord Cork.[82] One wonders what benefits he considered to have accrued therefrom, and whether they could possibly be held to have offset the effects on the officers and men of Somerville's force of knowing that their commander's leadership had been seriously called in question.

In September 1940 Somerville had returned home briefly, and received from Pound 'some valuable tips about wild cat schemes Winston might broach' when he visited Chequers.[83] One such scheme, for the seizure of the small Italian island of Pantelleria between Sicily and Tunisia (operation 'Workshop') was being urged on Churchill by Admiral Keyes, the fire-eating Director of Combined Operations whom we encountered earlier. In October he argued strongly to Churchill that the 5000 Commandos he had raised and the Glen Line ships which had been converted to assault landing craft carriers should be used to assault either Pantelleria or some island in the Dodecanese.[84] At first Churchill strongly favoured the former plan. In November Keyes attended a meeting with him in the Down Street underground station deep shelter at which, according to the admiral, he 'blistered' the Joint Planning Staff for not carrying it out.[85] After the meeting had dispersed Churchill kept Keyes back and said to him 'I tell you frankly that I am not going to have anything to do with it unless you do it and lead it'; to which the admiral replied that he was very ready to do so.[86] In December Churchill accordingly signalled 'Personal and Most Secret' to Admiral Cunningham that Keyes would 'execute the operation with full control of all forces employed'. 'No doubt,' he went on, it was 'a hazard . . . But Zeebrugge would never have got past [the] scrutiny bestowed on this [operation].'[87] This reference to the Zeebrugge raid of April 1918, possibly prompted by Keyes himself, who constantly referred to it at this time, provides an interesting example of Churchill's highly selective interpretation of history; since long before 1940 it was well known that, for all the gallantry displayed, it failed to block the harbour to the passage of U-boats for any appreciable time – which was of course the object of the operation.

Towards the end of October Cunningham signalled that an eight day postponement of 'Workshop' (from 1st to 9th November) was essential.[88] This produced a furiously angry riposte from Churchill who, perhaps recalling a saying of Nelson's,* wrote to Alexander and Pound 'It does not seem to be appreciated by the Naval Staff that time is the essence of success in war.' He demanded 'a full explanation of the delays', and inveighed for two-and-a-half pages against the staff's 'negativism and undue yielding to difficulties and a woeful lack of appreciation of the time factor'. He therefore wanted a high ranking officer to be specially appointed whenever an operation was being planned, to carry the responsibility 'for any avoidable breakdown'. But in this case Churchill seems to have realized that he had gone too far, since after discussion he asked for his minute to be withdrawn and the original returned to Downing Street; but Alexander had a copy made, and it has survived in the First Lord's papers.[89]

---

* 'Time, Twiss, time is everything; five minutes make the difference between a victory and a defeat.' Nicolas, *Letters and Despatches of Lord Nelson*, IV, p. 290, note 6. Alternatively Churchill may have had in mind a saying of Drake's, which Keyes was fond of quoting to him – 'The advantage of time and place in all martial actions is half a victory which being lost is irrecoverable.' See Christopher Lloyd, *The Nation and the Navy* (Cresset Press, 1954) p. 26.

After the November postponement the plans for 'Workshop' were bandied to and fro between the special Planning Section formed in the Admiralty, the Inter-Service body set up to organize and conduct such undertakings and Keyes's staff* – with the admiral constantly chafing over the delays and pressing for a decision to go ahead with it. Late in December Churchill told General Ismay, his personal Staff Officer and head of the military wing of the War Cabinet secretariat, that 'constant reflection has made me feel the very high value of Workshop'.[90]

Cunningham, however, replied to the message of 11 December in which Churchill pressed on him the benefits which he expected to accrue from the successful execution of 'Workshop'[91] that he had 'never questioned the feasibility' of the operation but that his 'concern has always lain in its subsequent maintenance' at a time when he was already having trouble in meeting existing commitments, such as the supply of the army in the western desert and of Malta.[92] Pound for his part played his hand skilfully, by not offering any early opposition but taking the first clear opportunity to kill the plan when it was safe to do so without arousing Churchill's wrath. The chance arose at a meeting early in December, when Pound quietly remarked that 'Pantelleria had so far caused us very little trouble.'[93] At about that time Keyes told his wife that 'In all my stormy career I have never had more bludgeoning knocks than those of the last three weeks . . . However I am confident and determined, despite every kind of difficulty and obstacle, to strike a blow for the country which will make you proud.'[94] On the last day of the year the COSs, to Keyes's fury, decided to postpone the operation until late in February 1941.[95] During these exchanges Cunningham signalled to Pound that he hoped that Keyes would not be sent out to his station for 'Workshop', and Pound, rather rashly, showed the message to Churchill. 'He went off the deep end,' Pound wrote to Cunningham '. . . and sent a telegram from himself to you in which he said he very much regretted the expression. I told him it was quite wrong that he should send a telegram of that nature to you . . .'[96] – an interesting example of Churchill as Prime Minister acting as though he were still First Lord.

After it was all over Cunningham wrote to Pound 'I was indeed

---

* These bodies were, respectively, the Admiralty's Executive Planning Section (EPS) and the Forward Operational Planning Section (FOPS), which were of course additional to the normal naval staff divisions responsible for such matters and also the Joint Planning Committee. Thus Keyes's oft-repeated complaints about the extraordinarily cumbersome administrative and operational organization with which he had to cope certainly seem to have had substance in them.

thankful that Workshop was not carried out. I don't think there is much doubt that we should have lost both the Glen ships [*Glengyle and Glenearn*, which were to have carried the Commandos] and anything else lying off the island.'[97] Apart from the problem of maintaining the garrison after the capture of his objective Keyes certainly under-estimated the effects of the arrival in Sicily of German dive-bombers early in 1941; and when he sought support from Sir Charles Portal for his view that 'the risk of being knocked out by them is greatly exag-gerated', the CAS replied that he could not 'subscribe to the view that it would not be unduly hazardous to pass valuable ships through the Narrows' between Malta and Tunisia.[98] The outcome was that the Glen ships with the Commandos onboard were sent out to the Middle East via the Cape of Good Hope, and although Keyes com-plained bitterly that they were then 'frittered away and dispersed' they played a gallant part in the attempt to hold Crete in May 1941, and also carried out a useful raid during the brief campaign against Vichy French Syria in June. As regards 'Workshop' the retrospective opinion of Admiral Sir William Davis, who was lent to Keyes for the planning of the operation, is that 'at that time, with our almost total lack of resources, the plan was not a strategical starter. The COSs were right [to cancel it] and Keyes [and so Churchill] was wrong.'[99] But Admiral Davis also admits that 'Workshop never really had a chance, if for no other reason that the staff (i.e. the machine) were absolutely patholo-gically anti-Keyes and his DCO team. Fundamentally they resented a chap like Keyes being as it were a fifth wheel in the coach and NOT being subordinate to the Chiefs of Staff';[100] and that view does of course wholly substantiate the complaints made by Keyes at the time the operation was being planned.

Though Keyes was certainly not without vanity about his warlike achievements and capabilities, telling Eden that 'I know the Almighty has given me an instinct for war and the vision to see what is essential in its prosecution,'[101] neither was he blind to the dangers and diffi-culties of carrying out combined operations. Thus in his report on an exercise carried out at Scapa in August 1941 to prepare for the occupa-tion of the Spanish Canary Islands if the Germans attacked Spain and made Gibraltar untenable he wrote that 'Combined operations are immensely difficult to execute, and they certainly cannot be under-taken with the light-hearted optimism which I have heard expressed.' Indeed he compared the faults and failures displayed during that exercise with those which had destroyed the chance offered by the surprise landing in Suvla Bay, Gallipoli, in August 1915.[102] But the obverse to such sensibly cautious statements is his letter to Churchill of February 1941 claiming that 'If my force [the 'Workshop' one] had been let loose under my leadership in the Mediterranean, which it would [? could] well have been several weeks before the Germans arrived there [in Sicily] – but for the hostility and timidity of the CNS – I do not believe any limit could have been placed on what we might have achieved by a succession of assaults on islands large and small . . .'[103] Apart from the injustice of the attack on Pound what, one may ask, would have been the use of the 'islands large and small'? And how were they to be garrisoned and supplied when Malta alone was taxing Cunningham's resources to the limit? Yet Churchill shared with Keyes the addiction to the capture of widely scattered islands – sometimes, as we shall see, with disastrous results.

It will be convenient here to carry on the consequences of the Keyes-Churchill association to the end. Early in 1941 Pound wrote to Cunningham 'It is really a terrible business having R. K. mixed up with the business [of 'Workshop'] as DCO. He is a perfect nuisance . . . I firmly believe that the only thing he cares about is the glorification of R. K.';[104] and it is certainly a fact that he caused constant trouble and difficulties.[105] The second assault force he raised was sent to Freetown, Sierra Leone, in the autumn – in case seizure of the Portuguese Atlantic islands, namely the Azores and the Cape Verde group, proved essential.[106] Though Churchill had long been worried about Somerville's squadron 'lying under the Spanish howitzers at Gibraltar [sic]', and had urged occupation of the Azores rather than 'wait until a disaster has occurred' the Foreign Office considered that such action would precipitate a German invasion of the Iberian peninsula.[107] Churchill also told the COSs that the Germans were 'infiltrating the Cape Verde Islands, and that U-boats were probably working from bases in them' – which the COSs denied.[108] They, like the Foreign Office, were anxious not to give the Germans a pretext to occupy the islands, but a British expedition was none the less prepared to do precisely that. Though anxiety for the safety of Gibraltar and of the ships working from that base is, in the circumstances prevailing at the time, perfectly understandable the episode as a whole graphically illustrates Churchill's addiction to assaults from the sea, regardless of the operational difficulties involved and the possible politico-strategic repercussions.

Keyes actually considered his ships and men held at Freetown to be wasted, and pressed on Churchill that the purpose for which they were there could be achieved peaceably with President Roosevelt's co-operation – which at that time was in fact very unlikely to have been forthcoming. He wanted them to be recalled home in order to carry out 'large scale raids' against important German installations in France.[109] That there was something in Keyes's case is shown by the success of the raid on the German radar station at Bruneval on the Normandy coast planned and executed by his successor in February 1942.[110] But Keyes was denied such a chance to show what his men could do.

Although in February 1941 Churchill evidently lost patience with Keyes and returned a paper to him with the remark 'It is quite impossible for me to receive a letter of this character'[111] in the following month Ismay made, on behalf of Churchill and the COSs, an attempt to re-define his duties and responsibilities in such a way as would eliminate the friction between him and the service staffs. The draft of the new directive stated that he was responsible 'under the Minister of Defence and the Chiefs of Staff' for 'the command, and training in irregular warfare generally'. After exchanges over the amendments asked for by Keyes a satisfactory compromise was achieved.[112] But the friction with the COSs, the Joint Planners and the Service staffs did not abate, throughout 1941 Keyes bombarded Churchill with complaints and requests for interviews, and by September it was plain that such a state of affairs simply could not be allowed to continue. Accordingly the COS secretariat tried to produce a statement regarding 'the proposed inter-service organization dealing with Combined Operations'. But the new title of 'Adviser on Combined Operations and Commandant of Combined Training Centres' proposed for Keyes was too plainly a demotion for it to have any appeal to him; so he bluntly rejected the proposal.[113] Churchill wrote to him 'My dear Roger, I am sorry that you do not feel able to fall in with the proposal which the COS have made to you. I have really done my best to meet your wishes. I have to consider my duty to the State which ranks above personal friendship. In all the circumstances I have no choice but to arrange for your relief'.[114] A short time later Keyes was told officially that he would be relieved on 19 October by Captain Lord Louis Mountbatten, who would be given the rank of Commodore First Class and be known as 'Commodore, Combined Operations.'[115] In the following month Pound told Cunningham 'Roger Keyes is making himself very unpleasant because he has been removed from being Director of Combined Operations. Force Commanders objected to his being entitled to tell them what to do.' He repeated the story of Keyes's refusal of the new post offered to him, and ended with the remark that Keyes 'never had much brain but whatever he has got left is quite addled'.[116] The other COSs also apparently welcomed Keyes's departure, General Dill, the

CIGS, telling Churchill that 'you can't win World War II with World War I heroes'.[117] So ended one of his less happy experiments in admirals' appointments.

In the autumn of 1941 Mountbatten paid a visit to the USA and met all the leading Americans, including the President. After his departure Admiral H. R. Stark, the Chief of Naval Operations, sent Pound a glowing tribute to the British emissary. 'He has been a great help to all of us,' he wrote, 'and I literally mean ALL . . . his sincerity, frankness and honesty have not only won our liking but our deep respect.' Pound sent this eulogy to Churchill, who asked if he could send it to the King.[118] With a man of such markedly higher intellectual calibre holding the appointment vacated by Keyes, in March 1942 Churchill and the COSs evidently felt confident enough to appoint him Chief of Combined Operations [CCO] and to give him the rank of Acting Vice-Admiral and equivalent though honorary rank in the other services. He also became a permanent member of the COS Committee.[119] Thus was initiated a new era in Combined Operations, to which we will revert later.

Even after he had been relieved Keyes continued to send protests to Churchill and other Ministers, claiming that he had been driven out by intrigues against him on the part of the naval staff in general and Pound in particular.[120] Nor did Churchill's assurance that he was quite sure he had not been a victim of intrigue mollify him. Churchill did however say that there was 'widespread prejudice' against appointing retired officers to executive posts, and of retaining them in such capacities when nearly seventy years old; and he admitted that Keyes's high rank and his personal association with himself had 'also caused embarrassment and friction'.[121] In that connection it is relevant to quote the view of General Sir Ian Jacob who, as Military Assistant Secretary of the War Cabinet 1939–46, was singularly well placed to observe these events. Churchill, General Jacob remarks, 'was no real exception to the normal human failing . . . of applying ideas formed in the young and most active period of life to situations existing in old age . . . Some examples will illustrate the fact'. After mentioning Churchill's pressure for the Baltic incursion which he had strongly favoured in World War I, Jacob continues by recounting the appointment of Keyes as DCO in World War II because he had 'greatly impressed Churchill by his fire and dash in the first war. . . . He did not look around for the modern Keyes until it had been found that things didn't work under Keyes any longer . . . The same tendency was evident when he selected Lord Cork and Orrery to command the naval side of the Narvik expedition. We had suffered greatly in the first war from "dug-outs" – and here was the same tendency to bring back men for jobs which they would have been ripe to undertake twenty-five years earlier.'[122] To which I would only add that there is no record of Pound ever having protested against such appointments; and that he was subject to the same failing remarked on by Jacob is supported by his bringing in various retired officers to advise him on particular subjects, and by his appointment of Admiral Sir Frederic Dreyer as Chief of Naval Air Services in 1942.

Not only were these attempts to draw new wine from old bottles immensely frustrating to the proper staff, because they often produced duplication of work; but the implication that the rising generation possessed no men of comparable qualities was as unfair as it was untrue. As to Pound himself there can be no doubt that he was sorely tried by Churchill. In March 1940 (before the French collapse) he wrote to Cunningham 'I find Winston admirable to work with [as First Lord]';[123] but by the following December he had evidently modified his view substantially. 'The PM is very difficult these days, not that he has not always been,' he told Cunningham. 'One has however to take a broad view because one has to deal with a man who is proving a magnificent leader, and one just has to put up with his childishness as long as it isn't dangerous. Also with a man like that it is not good policy to present him with a brick wall unless it is [about ?] a thing which is really vital';[124] which was a pretty fair summary both of Churchill's character and of Pound's way of handling him.

To continue with Mediterranean operations, in July 1940 Somerville sent home a series of signals about his future plans and the risks he considered acceptable – especially with regard to the valuable aircraft carrier *Ark Royal*. Churchill at once demanded to see the answer it was proposed to send, and put up his own ideas for the reinforcement of Malta with modern fighter aircraft. After ascertaining Pound's views Alexander replied stressing the handicap under which both Cunningham and Somerville worked because of the impossibility of protecting their ships with shore-based fighters 'as we do in the North Sea when ships are in the bombing area'. As to the problem of Malta's defences, Pound proposed to send aircraft and A-A guns out by the Cape route, as did Cunningham. This idea evidently angered Churchill who sent five pages of riposte, the general tone of which was to accuse the Admiralty of timidity. For example 'Anyone', he wrote, 'can see the risk from air attack which we run in the Central Mediterranean. From time to time and for sufficient object this risk will have to be faced. Warships are meant to go under fire'; and he once again claimed that if only his proposal of 1939 to re-armour the old R. Class battleships and to increase the elevation of their guns had been accepted 'we could assault Italy by bombardment with comparative immunity' – which was of course wildly optimistic.[125] Evidently Churchill's next thought was that he had overstepped the mark in this case, because his paper is endorsed 'Cancelled. Original returned to No. 10.' But later in the month he wrote again saying that he had re-read the accusatory minute and returned it to Alexander as 'I wish it to remain on the record';[126] and he kept up the pressure for fast mechanized transport ships to be passed straight through the Mediterranean to Malta and Alexandria.[127] In fact operations to fly Hurricanes to Malta from the west were carried out in August and November 1940, and in the latter month the first through-Mediterranean transports arrived safely.[128] But it was not until May 1941, by which time stronger escort forces were available, that Churchill's pressure for the use of the shortest possible route for supplies urgently needed in Egypt was really put to the test in the famous 'Tiger' convoy of five fast merchantmen loaded with tanks, aircraft and guns.[129] Only one of the transports was lost, and this success produced warm congratulatory messages from Churchill to Somerville and Cunningham.[130] If his own courage and persistence were the decisive factors it is only fair to record that our shortage of modern ships, and especially of aircraft carriers, was such that the desire of the staff and of the admirals concerned that they should not be risked except in a really worthwhile cause showed sensible prudence rather than the pusillanimity of which Churchill accused them.

In January 1941 Churchill attacked Pound about 'the valuable ships in Malta under various conditions of repair'. 'Admiral Cunningham,' he continued, 'does not seem to have been much concerned with the fate of all these ships'; an accusation which, to anyone who knew Cunningham and appreciated his acute shortage in virtually all classes of warship, was palpably absurd.[131]

In the following month Somerville carried out a skilfully planned, though in fact not very effective bombardment of Genoa with Force H.[132] Churchill was delighted, and signalled 'I congratulate you on the success of the enterprise against Genoa'; but the sting was in the tail of the message, reading 'which I was very glad to see you proposed yourself'[133] – an obvious reflection of his doubts about Somerville's 'offensive mindedness' which had arisen in the previous November as a result of his brush with the Italian navy off Cape Spartivento. In March the Commandos who had recently arrived in the Middle East carried out a raid known as operation 'Pitch' on the small Italian-held island of

Castelerizo off the south-west coast of Turkey. The Italian reaction was stronger than expected, air cover was lacking and the Commandos had to be taken off after suffering considerable casualties. Typically Cunningham himself took the responsibility for this failure and for the 'lack of resolution and judgement displayed by some of those concerned', though he admitted that the admiral to whom he had entrusted the planning E. de F. Renouf had proved to be a sick man.[134] Churchill, however, first told Eden, the Foreign Secretary, who was in Cairo at the time, that he was 'perplexed and somewhat unsettled', and asked for answers to a long string of questions about the conduct of the operation;[135] and when he read the War Office report he told Ismay that he was 'thoroughly mystified' and wanted the COSs 'to have it probed properly'.[136] On reading Cunningham's signalled report his mystification changed to anger, and he demanded of Alexander and Pound 'What disciplinary or other measures are going to be taken on this deplorable piece of mismanagement after we have had eighteen months' experience of war?'[137] Alexander sensibly remarked on this example of Churchill's addiction to head-hunting that a considered view must await receipt of the full reports by the three Cs-in-C;[138] and nothing more was heard of it – probably because this minor operation was soon overshadowed by the ordeals of the Greece and Crete campaigns.

Though 1940 had ended well for Cunningham, whose relations with Churchill had obviously improved since their clash over the French fleet in July, the New Year was only a few days old when the Luftwaffe came to the aid of Germany's increasingly shaky ally; and the specially trained dive-bombers which had just arrived in Sicily inflicted an unpleasant check on his fleet's increasing command of the central Mediterranean by sinking a cruiser and seriously damaging one of our few and precious modern aircraft carriers, the *Illustrious*. This was the first time that the Mediterranean Fleet had experienced what the Home Fleet had learnt off Norway fifteen months earlier – namely the deadliness of the German dive-bombers except in the face of adequate fighter protection.

The sharp deterioration of our situation in the central Mediterranean early in 1941, with the Germans installed in Sicily and Tripoli, and Malta gravely imperilled, caused Churchill to ask for a study to be made of the possibility of capturing Sardinia 'as a foothold in this vital area'. He also reverted to the means whereby the A-A armaments of our ships could be made more effective, and urged again that the best answer lay in Lindemann's rocket weapons and Long Aerial Mines – which all experience had shown to be useless.[139] The fundamental need was in fact for a tachymetric system of A-A fire control, as indeed had been recommended by the powerfully constituted Naval Anti-Aircraft Gunnery Committee of 1921, but whose conclusions were ignored in the late 1920s. Unhappily such a failure simply could not be rectified quickly in time of war.* The staff considered at length what could be done, and the outcome was the long overdue decision to form a Gunnery and Anti-Aircraft Warfare Division, and to appoint a new Assistant Chief of Naval Staff to supervise all aspects of weapon development. In retrospect it seems astonishing that it had taken nearly two years of war to institute those very desirable measures. Churchill expressed satisfaction with these proposals, and perhaps the most important result was to expedite the fitting of the new short-wave radar sets to all ships' weapon systems.[140]†

We cannot here devote space to a full discussion of the arguments for and against sending military aid to Greece in 1941, but it is worth recalling that as early as June 1940 Cunningham had strongly urged that Crete should be occupied 'whatever the political situation' in order that he should have the use of the fine harbour of Suda Bay on the north coast of the island.[141] In terms of strategy his proposal had a great deal to commend it; but the political situation in Greece did not permit its adoption until after Mussolini had launched his wanton and unprovoked attack on that country at the end of October 1940. Thereafter the despatch of troops, aircraft and all sorts of equipment to Greece loomed large in the deliberations of the Middle East Commands and in London; and Churchill's strongly worded messages to General Wavell in January and February 1941 must have played a considerable part in forcing the hands of the theatre commanders.[142] But no matter how strong were the political arguments for sending aid to Greece, in terms of strategy such action now seems to have been little short of lunacy; for it not only prevented the army pressing on to capture Tripoli but, as the decision was taken just when Somerville's and Cunningham's forces were meeting off that port, it frustrated the

* A tachymetric system actually measured the course and speed of an enemy aircraft and fed the results into the control system; but in about 1928 the Royal Navy went for the simpler and cheaper but far less efficient 'Course and Speed' system which in effect used guessed data. The German and American navies both developed efficient tachymetric systems by 1939. See Roskill, *Naval Policy*, II, pp. 333-4.

† The author of this history can claim to have had a share in these developments, which resulted from a series of meetings with Admiral Fraser, the Controller of the Navy, and the DNO. Most of the ideas came from Captain G. M. Langley, who became the first Director of the new Staff Division. During a quiet visit to my home the need for a Gunnery and A-A Division was agreed and its organization outlined.

chance to cut the main Axis supply route to Africa.

Early in March Cunningham signalled his apprehensions about the Greek commitment to the Admiralty. Enemy air attacks were, he said, likely to cause heavy losses to the troop and supply convoys, our defences were very weak, and he did not possess anything like the forces needed to meet all his responsibilities; but he ended with the words 'We are, I am convinced, pursuing [the] right policy and [the] risk must be faced up to.'[143] Cunningham later recorded in his diary that he 'was against it' [the expedition to Greece] but acquiesced for political reasons put forward by Eden, the Foreign Secretary, who had been sent to Cairo by Churchill to discuss the matter.[144] Although the next phase began with Cunningham's greatest success in the Battle of Matapan on 28 March 1941 he was soon beset by many difficulties and problems besides those concerned with the transport of some 58,000 soldiers and large quantities of stores and equipment to Greece.

In April a report from Malta that air attacks on an Italian convoy bound for North Africa and a night search for it by destroyers had achieved nothing produced a typical Churchillian blast. 'This is a serious naval failure,' he told Alexander and Pound. 'Another deadly convoy has got through. We have a right to ask why did not the Navy stop them.' Pound told Alexander that the sea and air forces based on Malta were so slender that 'I think it must be brought home to the PM that success can never be guaranteed in naval operations at night.'[145] In fact Churchill's complaint was quickly proved to have been premature, since the next reports were that the convoy had turned back to the north when attacked by our aircraft, but was then located and totally destroyed by the destroyers at their second attempt. On being told of this success Churchill minuted 'Yes, brilliantly redeemed. But what about the next [convoy]?' – as though anyone could predict its movements in advance.

In that same month a long interchange of signals took place between Cunningham and the Admiralty on the need to deprive the enemy of the use of Tripoli harbour, the chief port of entry for supplies and reinforcements for Rommel's Afrika Korps. On the 15th the admiral was told that 'drastic measures are necessary to stabilize the position in the Middle East', and that 'the general plan' was to use the battleship *Barham* and an old light cruiser to block the harbour.[146] This idea must surely have derived from Keyes's blocking raid on Zeebrugge on St George's Day 1918 which, as we saw earlier, had made a great impression on Churchill. On the same day that the forgoing message was sent to Cunningham Pound signalled to him that 'Instructions have been received from H. M. Government that the navy must do everything possible to prevent supplies reaching Libya from Italy'[147] – a directive in which Churchill's hand can surely be detected. The implication that Cunningham was either insufficiently aware of the need or was doing too little about it was surely rather extraordinary. He replied tactfully that he had 'seen fit to query Their Lordships' decision [about using the *Barham* as a blockship] and most earnestly request reconsideration'.[148] He also assured London that 'we are not idle with regard to [the] Libya situation', and that no one in the theatre 'will say that [the] navy has let them down out here'.[149]

On 16 April the COSs signalled to the theatre commanders the directive which Churchill had issued two days earlier, part of which read that 'It becomes the prime duty of the British Mediterranean fleet . . . to stop all seaborne traffic between Italy and Africa', and that the blocking of Tripoli 'would be well worth a battleship on the active list'. The mention of UP (Unrotated Projectile or rocket) weapons and Long Aerial Mines in the directive for use in the defence of Malta points to Cherwell's hand, as those devices had always been among his favourite developments.[150] That evening Pound sent a rather apologetic addendum admitting that Cunningham's commitments 'are greater than I imagined', and that when his earlier message was sent he had 'no knowledge of destroyer operations on [the] Libyan coast' or of the need to run another convoy to Malta.[151]

Cunningham next reinforced his protest against using warships to block Tripoli by telling Pound that for reasons of secrecy he could not call for volunteers for such an operation, but would have to send the ships in about two-thirds manned and without the crews knowing that their ships, and in all probability many of their lives were to be sacrificed. Such an idea was utterly abhorrent to him, and would, he considered, seriously jeopardize, if it did not destroy 'the whole confidence of the personnel of the fleet in the higher command, not only here but at home also'.[152] In the end the Admiralty agreed to Cunningham's alternative, which was to take the whole fleet to sea and subject the port to a heavy bombardment. That he did on the night of 20-21 April, and without loss though we now know that the effects were much less than was believed at the time.[153] The Admiralty next signalled fantastic proposals regarding how the Axis convoys to Tripoli should be attacked by day and night, including the idea of basing a battleship on Malta – apparently in ignorance of the island's acute shortage of oil fuel.[154] The admiral was, he admits, now 'beginning to feel seriously annoyed' by this constant instruction on how to do his job; and another

'Personal' signal from Churchill doubtless did little to smooth his ruffled feathers.[155]

The whole interchange about Tripoli has been recorded at some length because it does illustrate very clearly the danger of over-centralization, especially when a very powerful Minister of Defence is using an acquiescent First Lord and First Sea Lord as his mouthpiece. Much signal traffic and the generation of considerable heat would have been avoided had the COS Committee and Admiralty merely expressed their broad strategic intentions and priorities and left it to the man on the spot to carry them out as he thought best.

Shortly after the bombardment of Tripoli Lord Salisbury (Secretary of State for Dominions) sent Churchill a letter in which he praised 'our wonderful sailors afloat' but attacked the Admiralty in very strong terms, chiefly on the grounds that they did not like risking their ships, and had 'boasted that our Fleet did not receive a scratch' in the Battle of Matapan (28 March 1941). Churchill sent this polemic on to Alexander and Pound with a note describing it as 'an important outside opinion'; but of all the many strictures they had received from Churchill's hands none raised their hackles as much as this one. The First Lord and First Sea Lord were both of them deeply shocked, which, considering the very heavy losses of all classes of warship suffered since 1939, is hardly surprising. The reply they sent described Salisbury's attack as 'based on prejudice' and exhibiting 'looseness of thought'; and Alexander also said 'I feel I must resent the inference . . . that the bombardment of Tripoli was due to the impetuousness of the man on the spot acting against the judgement of a nervous Admiralty . . . it is quite wrong for these armchair critics to assume that the Admiralty are never responsible for the initiation of such operations . . .' But all that he got by way of an answer was a message from Churchill's private secretary saying that his master 'thanked him for his full reply'.[156]

To return to Cunningham's fleet, its commander was allowed little time to brood on the idiosyncracies of the high command, because the expected crisis produced by the call to evacuate some 58,000 soldiers and as much of their equipment as could be saved from Greece, and then to repeat the process from Crete – and with virtually no air cover – soon arose. In between the two evacuations he and Somerville, much helped by unexpectedly low visibility, managed to execute Churchill's courageous decision to pass straight through the Mediterranean the convoy of five fast merchantmen with sorely needed tank and aircraft reinforcements referred to earlier.

Whereas over 50,000 soldiers were safely brought away from

Greece, though at a heavy price, the defence and subsequent evacuation of Crete presented far more difficult problems – chiefly because the only first-class harbour, Suda Bay, was on the north coast and within easy range of the German bombers. While Cunningham was straining every nerve to get reinforcements and supplies to Crete, and losses were mounting all the time, he was harassed by extraordinary interference from London – in one notorious case by the Admiralty directly contradicting his orders* – and by high-level messages from the COSs, in which Churchill's hand may surely be detected, to the effect that greater efforts were needed and greater risks must be accepted. Cunningham, who reasonably found such prodding 'singularly unhelpful', replied with exemplary patience, and continued to do all that was possible;[157] but after 27 May further reinforcement of the island garrison proved impossible. The evacuation that followed greatly increased the toll exacted from the over-driven ships. It ended on 1 June with the rescue of some 16,500 soldiers; but about 5000 had to be left behind. At the end of what Cunningham called this 'disastrous period in our naval history' he wrote to Pound offering to give up his command – an offer which was not accepted despite the strained relations which had developed at the height of the battle.

The next offensive by the army (operation 'Battleaxe') was launched on 15 June 1941 after heavy pressure on General Wavell by Churchill. It failed and led to the relief of the General soon afterwards. He was one of the truly great leaders of World War II, but had never managed to establish a satisfactory rapport with Churchill, who neither then nor later appreciated his qualities. Though the German attack on Russia on 22 June brought some temporary relief in the Mediterranean as in the Atlantic Battle, the land campaign soon produced a whole crop of new problems for Cunningham – chiefly brought about by the Axis occupation of the airfields in Libya and Crete, which made the running of convoys to Malta and all operations in the central basin of the Mediterranean far more hazardous.

In September 1941 fighter reinforcements and stores were again sent to Malta from the west (operation 'Halberd'), and Somerville ended a signal setting out his intentions by saying 'I do not intend to fall into the trap of being led away from [the] convoy by an enemy who has the means and desire to avoid action and whose object may well be the reduction of [the] convoy escort in order to facilitate air and submarine attacks.' Doubtless he was remembering the criticisms

* By ordering the transport *Glenroy*, which Cunningham had ordered to withdraw to turn north again. Cunningham merely ignored the order. See *Odyssey* pp. 374-5

levelled at him for his conduct during the Malta convoy of November 1940, referred to earlier. Churchill sent this to Pound with a minute 'What do you say about this? I don't much like it myself.'[158] Pound replied that the Fighting Instructions had been amended since Lord Cork's inquiry into Somerville's actions to make clear that other considerations might modify the absolute priority given previously to 'the safe and timely arrival of the convoy'; but he considered Somerville's signal 'had better not have been sent'.[159] In the event the operation was successful, only one of the nine supply ships in the convoy being lost; so the circumstances envisaged by Somerville did not arise. This success brought Somerville the first message of completely unqualified congratulations from Churchill for 'the skill and resolution' displayed in 'the latest of a long series of complicated and highly successful operations for which you and Force H have been responsible'[160] – a somewhat abrupt change from the attempt to have the admiral relieved some nine months earlier.

In October a long interchange of signals took place about the next step if the imminent new land offensive (operation 'Crusader') produced a great victory. Churchill was very keen to follow up such an event by invading Sicily (operation 'Whipcord'); but the theatre commanders insisted that this would only be possible if Benghazi had been regained and the capture of Tripoli was 'reasonably certain in a short time'.[161] Cunningham held that the capture of Tripoli alone 'goes a long way to securing the through-Mediterranean route', but stressed the heaviness of the commitments already facing him.[162] Finally the Admiralty told him that in view of the difficulties he had represented 'the COSs no longer recommended Whipcord. Prime Minister has accepted this conclusion and operation is therefore abandoned.'[163] This is an example of Churchill's readiness to accept service advice if represented strongly and persistently enough, though the failure to destroy Rommel's Afrika Korps in 'Crusader', did of course make the decision inevitable, because the enemy retained possession of the vital airfields in western Libya.

The foregoing set-backs did at least make clear how inaccurate and ineffective Bomber Command's attacks in the Mediterranean theatre had been, though Churchill seems to have accepted the Air Ministry's wartime propaganda about them – a subject to which we will revert later. The through-Mediterranean route thus remained firmly closed, while the worsening conditions in the Middle East were producing most serious misgivings in London and Cairo. The problems of this time were so many and so difficult that in October Pound, reverting to his thoughts of June 1940 about withdrawing the fleet from the Eastern Mediterranean, asked Cunningham what the effect would be of removing all capital ships and carriers from, firstly, his fleet and, secondly, from Somerville's squadron. Cunningham replied that such a proposal aroused his 'most serious misgivings', and the idea was evidently taken no further.[164] If it had got to Churchill's ears one cannot doubt that he would have refused to countenance such a retreat.

In November the critical situation in the western desert, and consequential increase of peril to our whole position in the Middle East caused Churchill to adopt the same line about stopping Axis supplies reaching Benghazi as in the case of Tripoli in the previous April; but this time his language was more moderate and there was no suggestion of using blockships. On 23 November Pound signalled to Cunningham that he had 'just been discussing with the Prime Minister the situation in the western desert', and stressed the importance of 'keeping the enemy short of petrol'.[165] Cunningham replied direct to Churchill that he was 'naturally very much alive to [the] vital importance of [the] Benghazi supply route', and that Pound would presumably have told him of 'the dispositions which were already in hand to deal with [the] situation'. But he stressed, as often before, the weakness of air reconnaissance from which he suffered.[166] When Pound applied more pressure Cunningham told him that he was sending two light cruisers and two destroyers to Malta to step up his offensive against the Axis convoys.[167] In fact considerable successes were achieved against the enemy supply convoys in late November and December; but thereafter the offensive declined, partly because of increased enemy air strength in southern Italy and Sicily and the severe bombing which Malta was suffering, and partly because heavy losses were suffered by the striking forces working from that island and from Alexandria.

On 11 December Churchill gave a packed House of Commons one of his periodical *tours d'horizon* of the military situation. Though it had all the masterly touches and the breadth of treatment to which the House had become accustomed, he was in fact far too optimistic about events in the western desert, telling Members that the enemy was 'retiring to a defensive line west of the Tobruk forts', and that 'the establishment of our air power far forward . . . enables the great supply depots of Tobruk, which have been carefully built up, to furnish support for the second phase of our offensive . . .'[168] His omission of any mention of the fact that it was the navy which had kept Tobruk supplied provoked Cunningham into telling Pound that 'I fear the PM's speech on the supplies of Tobruk made all out here in the service angry'; so he had signalled home the losses suffered during these operations. To date they amounted to twenty-seven White Ensign ships sunk and a like number damaged – quite apart from the heavy losses of merchant ships.[169] The total disregard of the naval effort was certainly a serious lapse on Churchill's part. As to the general situation, the truth was that by the end of the year a new crisis was plainly imminent in the Middle East theatre.

The early months of 1942 produced no easement of the severe trials undergone by the Mediterranean Fleet, which had produced such strained relations between its commander and the Prime Minister, and further heavy losses were suffered in attempting to run convoys to Malta from the east while the Afrika Korps held the vital airfields in Libya. Cunningham's privately expressed feeling was that Churchill was 'a bad strategist but doesn't know it, and nobody has the courage to stand up to him'. He considered that the movement to get him 'to do his Prime Minister's job and not be Minister of Defence is absolutely right';[170] but there was of course never the slightest prospect of Churchill relinquishing powers which his earlier experiences had convinced him to be essential to the energetic and fruitful conduct of the war. Nor is it possible to conceive anyone else taking on the post of Minister of Defence with Churchill as Prime Minister, since such a division of supreme responsibility simply would not have worked.

The March 1942 convoy to Malta, which actually brought the island little relief and at heavy cost, was the last operation conducted by Cunningham, since Pound had told him that it was desired to send him to Washington as head of the British Admiralty Delegation and as his personal representative on the Combined Chiefs of Staff's Committee. Cunningham told Pound that he was 'ready to go on [as C-in-C, Mediterranean] if desired', but that 'if you felt a change was desirable out here [and] to make it without consulting me I was perfectly ready to go'. Recent losses had, he continued, exterminated the battle fleet, but there were still some 25,000 naval officers and men on the station, and he would have preferred 'someone better experienced and better known to the personnel' than the Admiralty's nominee Admiral Sir Henry Harwood as his successor.[171] Both the offer and the warning in Cunningham's letter were ignored, and in April he returned home. His first encounter with Churchill has already been described; but the Prime Minister was evidently not deterred by the flat refusal he then returned to the suggestion that he should relieve Admiral Tovey. In June he wrote that, although he accepted that Cunningham should pay 'a short visit to Washington' he hoped that 'in say a couple of months be will be put in his rightful place as Head of the Home Fleet'.[172] Why Churchill should have regarded that fleet as the 'rightful place' for Britain's foremost fighting admiral instead of the Mediterranean, where very important events were pending, is obscure. However, Pound reacted strongly against relieving Tovey prematurely, and told Alexander that such treatment of a man who had proved himself 'a capable . . . and successful leader would cause the Navy to lose all confidence in Admiralty administration'. He was 'entirely in disagreement with the contention of the Prime Minister' that the appointments he had proposed 'are in the true interests of the Service'.[173] This was one of the strongest protests Pound ever wrote; and it was evidently effective. In confirmation of the tight hold Churchill kept over all Flag appointments, it is appropriate here to mention that in September 1942 he and Alexander, the latter plainly acting on Pound's advice, had a long exchange about the next holders of the Gibraltar and Malta commands and various sea-going appointments. Although Churchill questioned the adequacy of the officer chosen for Malta the Admiralty's view finally prevailed.[174*]

Cunningham's relief as C-in-C, Mediterranean, Admiral Harwood, had been specially promoted for his conduct of the River Plate battle in December 1939, although he had in fact been previously marked down to be passed over for Flag rank.[175] Since December 1940 he had been serving in the Admiralty, without any marked distinction, as Assistant Chief of Naval Staff (Foreign). He was given the rank of Acting Admiral for his new post – a double step which his experience can hardly be said to have justified, since his only sea-going command had been that of a small cruiser squadron. The Mediterranean command with its immense strategic and political implications and the paramount need for inter-service co-operation at the top level was of course a wholly different and far larger responsibility. Harwood's appointment was almost certainly proposed by Pound to Alexander and approved by Churchill, who seems still to have regarded him as an 'offensively minded' admiral with the exaggerated aura of the River Plate battle

* The appointments discussed were those of Admiral S. S. Bonham-Carter as relief for Admiral Leatham in Malta, whether Admiral Edward-Collins should stay on at Gibraltar though as Vice-Admiral, Gibraltar instead of as Flag Officer, North Atlantic, and the future of Admirals H. M. Burrough, who was required for the invasion of North Africa, Philip Vian, I. G. Glennie and C. H. J. Harcourt. Vian and Glennie were both in urgent need of rest after having gone through a very hard time in the Mediterranean, and that was arranged. Harcourt was to be given command of the 18th Cruiser Squadron. All these proposals for changes in Flag appointments were submitted by Alexander to Churchill.

still glowing round his head – a concept of his abilities which was to prove wholly misconceived.

By April 1942 the air bombardment of Malta had reached such a high degree of intensity that not only was its continued use as a base, even for submarines and aircraft, becoming very dubious, but its surrender, due to inadequate defences and starvation of the populace, could no longer be ignored. Drastic action was plainly essential, and Churchill asked Roosevelt for the loan of the aircraft carrier *Wasp* to fly in Spitfires from the west. Roosevelt accepted the proposal, subject to a satisfactory explanation regarding why the old, slow and ill-manned *Furious* could not be used. This alternative originated from Admiral E. J. King, the C-in-C, US Fleet and Chief of Naval Operations, who had always wanted to deploy his service's full strength in the Pacific. After a lengthy interchange with London Roosevelt made the *Wasp* available, and her first trip got all but one of the forty-seven Spitfires embarked safely to their destination. But the Axis reaction was so strong that a repetition was plainly essential. Roosevelt agreed, and in May the *Wasp* and *Eagle* together flew in sixty-one more Spitfires successfully.[176] This was a case where the intimate personal relationship established by Churchill with Roosevelt, about which he had told Cunningham very privately in April 1941,[177] proved vital. But after the June convoy from the east had failed a new attempt to revictual the island became more necessary than ever; and that had to be done from the west. We will revert shortly to that undertaking.

In July Churchill told Alexander and Pound that he had the impression that Harwood and the ships based on Alexandria 'are doing very little in this fight, either in cutting off the enemy's supplies or in actively bombarding the enemy bases'. Alexander replied giving particulars of exactly what Harwood's fleet had done recently; and there the matter rested – for a time.[178] In July Harwood protested about the lack of RAF co-operation with his ships in their endeavours to achieve the purposes by which Churchill set such store; but that whole issue was bound up with the question of diverting Bomber Command aircraft from the strategic bombing campaign, which has already been recounted. However, Admiral H. R. Moore, the VCNS, considered that the time for 'more talks and compromises' on this issue had passed, that the Admiralty should take the matter to the War Cabinet 'and have a show-down'. 'Without doubt', he wrote, 'there would be an unholy row, but good might come of it.'[179]

The August convoy to Malta from the west (operation 'Pedestal') achieved some success, five out of fourteen ships, including a vital tanker, getting through; but the losses incurred by the powerful escort forces were very heavy, and although the fall of the island was now less likely its defence was by no means yet assured.[180]

Tobruk, which had been successfully defended from April to December 1941 during a siege lasting 242 days fell to Rommel's new offensive with heavy losses and immense booty to the enemy on 20 June 1942 – to the great chagrin of Churchill and the intense disappointment of Cunningham, who had just returned home. 'There is no question,' wrote the latter, '[that] we were outmanoeuvred and outfought.'[181] The disaster also shattered Churchill's confidence in General Auchinleck. In September Harwood tried to restore the situation by launching a sea-borne raid on Tobruk combined with a surprise land attack (operation 'Agreement'). It accomplished nothing and heavy losses were suffered. Churchill's opinion of Harwood at once slumped. 'I was not favourably impressed by Admiral Harwood's account of the Tobruk operation,' he told Alexander and Pound; 'We certainly suffered very heavy losses for little or no result.'[182] The naval staff prepared a reply, but as Harwood's report had not yet been received Pound adopted stalling tactics. 'Keep it until asked for' he wrote; and by late November Churchill accepted that the issue was 'dead'. However, as we shall see later, this failure probably remained in his mind.

Churchill also at this time resurrected his old animosity against the French warships under Admiral Godfroy, now known as 'Force X', which had been immobilized in Alexandria since July 1940, and again he wanted them to be seized. 'Superior force is a powerful persuasion' he wrote to Pound; and he wanted to bring two of the Eastern Fleet's battleships from East Africa to the Mediterranean to supply the necessary force. 'I hate to see ships idle at a crisis' was his comment on the work of Somerville's fleet. But Pound refused to accept the need for Somerville's battleships to be transferred to the Mediterranean, because their presence 'is not necessary to deal with [the] Vichy ships'.[183] Actually Harwood was not idle about putting pressure on Godfroy, and at the beginning of December sent him a long and reasoned statement on why he should join the Allies; but he told Cunningham that the Frenchman was 'very tiresome, he won't take the slightest risk and wants 100% certainty [presumably of Allied victory] so that not only his conscience but that of his officers can feel perfectly clear'.[184]

In his Washington appointment Cunningham evidently anticipated trouble with Admiral E. J. King, USN and took steps to forestall it – including adequate financial provision in that notoriously expensive city. After a severe tussle with Churchill and the Treasury he got what he wanted, and so, in the words of one of his staff, he was able to appear on the stage where important Inter-Allied issues were to be discussed 'as the victorious commander which he was'. But the trouble with King was not slow in developing. After formal calls had been exchanged Cunningham asked for an interview to discuss naval problems – only to be told that King was very busy and could not offer him an appointment until six days ahead. Cunningham thereupon called a meeting of the Combined Chiefs of Staff and explained to his Army and Air Force colleagues that he was sorry to waste their time but had important naval matters to discuss. The gambit apparently worked.[184A]

The chief problem for discussion was of course the planning of operation 'Torch', the Anglo-American landings in French North Africa which Churchill had got the initially reluctant Americans to accept instead of the cross-Channel assault.[185] But King continued to prove very difficult and uncooperative. In August Cunningham wrote to Pound that he had just had 'a very stormy interview' with him about the comparatively trivial issue of submarines for the Mediterranean.'He was abominably rude,' continued Cunningham, 'and I had to be quite firm with him and I told him that the remarks he made got us no further in winning the war . . .'[186] At the previous meeting of the Combined Chiefs of Staff King had been 'quite impossible and just objected to everything' he wrote. Cunningham was convinced that he was 'dead against' operation 'Torch', but he had found Admiral W. D. Leahy, President Roosevelt's personal Chief of Staff, 'a steadying influence' and a supporter of the undertaking. But he warned Pound that King was 'determined not to place any US ships under British command'.[187]

Early in September Churchill submitted to Roosevelt his proposal that Cunningham should be appointed Allied Naval C-in-C for 'Torch' and that Admiral Ramsay of Dunkirk fame should be his deputy. Both would of course come under the orders of General Dwight D. Eisenhower, the American soldier selected as Supreme Commander. By that time Cunningham's firm but tactful handling of King was bearing fruit, and the CNO 'not only readily agreed to the American Naval Task Force under Rear-Admiral H. K. Hewitt being under Cunningham's command but also told Cunningham 'to send home any American Flag officer who he thought incompetent', because he (King) 'would know that Cunningham was right and would not argue'.[187A] That highly satisfactory dénouement makes one feel that the decision to send Cunningham to Washington at such a critical juncture was a wise one.

In October Cunningham accordingly returned to London, where the detailed planning was carried out, and from there he reached Gibraltar on 1 November. Ramsay stayed in England in order to supervise the final arrangements, and the operation was launched on 7 November. Although a good many troubles were experienced in both the Algerian and Moroccan landings, the achievement of complete strategical surprise was a remarkable accomplishment and undoubtedly contributed greatly to the rapid success of the assaults.[188] A month later Cunningham told Pound 'I am finding Eisenhower and the Americans increasingly easy to deal with. The former particularly so,'[189] which was in very marked contrast to his experience in Washington; and that happy state of affairs was to continue until the end of Cunningham's second term on the Mediterranean station.

Churchill naturally took a very great interest in the planning and execution of operation 'Torch'; but after it was launched Cunningham was evidently plagued by what Ramsay described as 'tiresome signals sent to you without my being consulted'. He said that 'they usually emanate during the night from CNS [Pound] himself', apparently without the ACNSs (Home) and (Foreign) even being consulted. Ramsay was highly critical of the part played in these matters by Admiral H. R. Moore, the VCNS, whom he described as 'a weak little man' – which was a good deal less than fair to Moore.[190] For Churchill and the British COSs however, the acceptance of 'Torch' instead of the cross-channel invasion in 1942, for which the Americans and Russians had both pressed, was a personal triumph crowned by its successful execution. It was marred only by the rejection of the proposal to carry out an assault at Bône well to the east of Algiers, which Cunningham had favoured and which might have greatly expedited the conquest of Tunisia and so the conclusion of the African campaign.

194

The Indian Ocean & Pacific Theatres
1941-1943

- ▬ ▬ ▬ South West Pacific Command Area
- ─ ─ ─ ABDA and ANZAC Boundaries
- ▪▪▪▪▪▪▪▪ Other British and American Naval Commands

Archangel

Leningrad

Riga

Odessa

Istanbul   Batum

Alexandria
        Cairo

Basra

Aden

Bombay

Calcutta   Akyab   Rangoon   Bangkok

Madras
Trincomalee

Colombo

Maldive

Seychelles   Addu Atoll

Kilindini

Mozambique   Diego Suarez

Mauritius

EAST INDIES COMMAND BRITISH

Cape
Town   Durban

SOUTH
ATLANTIC
COMMAND
BRITISH

Crozet

Kerguelen

Vladi

Peking

Nanking
Shanghai

Forme
Hong Kon

PHILIPPINES

ABDA AREA
15th Jan-25th Feb 1942

Singapore
SUMATRA   BORNEO

Batavia
Java

ABDA
15th Jan 1942
24th

4th April 1942

AUST

SOUTH
Perth

Albany

MAP 4

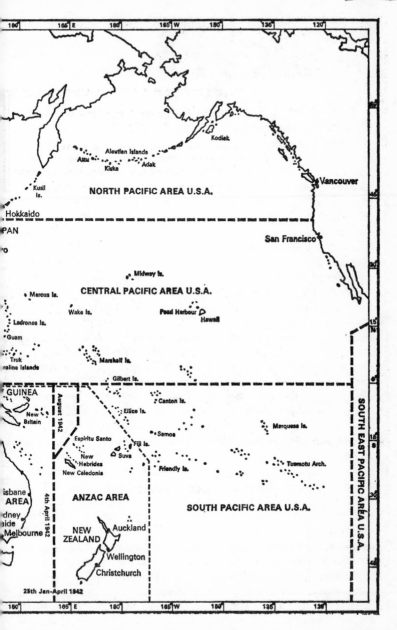

The Indian Ocean and the Far East
1941-1943

Churchill's pre-war blindness with regard to the Japanese threat to the vast British interests east of Suez, about which the Service Staffs were so deeply worried, has already been mentioned; but the outbreak of hostilities in Europe by no means altered his stance. In September 1940 he told Alexander, the First Lord, that 'The NID [Naval Intelligence Division] are very much inclined to exaggerate Japanese strength and efficiency.'[1] Although in February 1941 he admitted to President Roosevelt that 'the weight of the Japanese Navy, if thrown against us, would confront us with situations beyond the scope of our naval reserves' he qualified those apprehensions by adding 'I do not myself think that the Japanese would be likely to send [the] large military expedition necessary to lay siege to Singapore.'[2] As late as August of that year he still felt that Japan 'would lie quiet for a while', but he was prepared to send out a modern battleship, which he considered 'might indeed be a decisive deterrent';[3] and early in November he told Roosevelt 'We are sending that big ship you inspected [the *Prince of Wales*] into the Indian Ocean as part of a squadron we are forming there. This ought to serve as a deterrent on Japan.'[4] It is therefore plain, firstly, that it was Churchill, not the naval staff, which underrated Japanese prowess and efficiency; and secondly that the deterrent concept dominated his thinking on Far East strategy almost to the eleventh hour. Without doubt this misjudgement arose chiefly from the deep impression made on him by the effect on the Home Fleet's dispositions of the presence of the very powerful German battleship *Tirpitz* in Norwegian waters; and he sought to draw an analogy between her influence and that which a single British battleship would have on Japan – despite the fact that conditions in the two theatres were of course very different. Looking back on the events of this period Churchill remarked in his memoirs that 'I am sure that nothing we could have spared at this time . . . would have changed the march of fate in Malaya';[5] but the very large, though not properly trained or equipped land and air reinforcements which were rushed to Singapore after the Japanese attack surely gives the lie to Churchill's comment. What 'we could have spared' depended of course on getting priorities right; and the Far East stood low in that respect.[6]

Towards the end of August 1941 Churchill reverted to the deterrent concept, telling Pound that 'It should become possible in the near future to place a deterrent force in the Indian Ocean', and that if it were done it 'should consist of the smallest number of [the] best ships . . .' Pound replied that, depending on the situation and if war had not broken out with Japan, 'it may be found desirable to send *Nelson, Rodney, Renown* and an aircraft carrier to Singapore in the first instance as they would [then] form a greater deterrent'; but if war broke out 'they would have to retire to Trincomalee'. He proposed to send the four old R. Class battleships to the Indian Ocean.[7] Churchill reacted strongly against the idea of placing slow and obsolescent ships where they could not fight the Japanese and would not prove a deterrent to them; and he went on to produce his old grievance about the *King George V* class, our latest and treaty-limited battleships, being weaker than the German *Bismarcks*.[8] The discussions on this issue in the COS and Defence Committees have been dealt with elsewhere;[9] but we may here quote the account of one such meeting which Rear-Admiral T. S. V. Phillips, the Vice Chief of Naval Staff, sent to Pound, for whom he was deputizing, on 17 October 1941. 'The Prime Minister', he wrote, 'at once raised the old question of sending out the *Prince of Wales* and gave the Defence Committee all the arguments that he has used before. He was also most scathing in his comments on the Admiralty attitude to this matter. The First Lord and I defended the position as well as we could, but the Prime Minister led the other members of the Defence Committee to the conclusion that it was desirable to send the *Prince of Wales* to join the *Repulse* and go to Singapore as soon as possible. The Admiralty expressed their dissent.'[10] Such was the background to the shocking disaster which was to destroy British prestige throughout the East and, in the long run, must surely have contributed to our loss of empire.[11]

As late as September 1941 Admiral Sir Geoffrey Layton, the C-in-C China, circulated a memorandum within his command stating that 'In the event of war with Japan . . . it is the intention to send a powerful British fleet to the Far East with the intention of operating from Singapore.' The maximum scale envisaged was, he continued, six battleships, one battle-cruiser, one aircraft carrier, thirteen cruisers, thirty-four destroyers and ten submarines.[12] Though Layton was of course merely repeating the intentions communicated to him from London his memorandum does show how extraordinarily long-lived the concept of a 'main fleet for Singapore' was; since by the autumn of

1941 it was absolutely plain that, so heavy had been our losses in other theatres, there was no possibility of such a fleet being conjured into being – at any rate in a short time.[13]

Early in October Pound signalled to Cunningham that the *Rodney* and the four R. Class battleships were to go to the Indian Ocean 'and possibly further East as soon as possible', and that the *Nelson* would follow them as soon as she had been repaired.[14] Churchill at once told Pound that 'this major Fleet movement has not yet been approved by me or the Defence Committee. No action must be taken pending [a] decision'[15] – an example of the tight control he maintained over naval dispositions. At the end of that month he told the Prime Minister of Australia, who was understandably anxious to know whether a 'main fleet' would materialize in the Far East, that the *Prince of Wales* and *Repulse* were to meet in the Indian Ocean 'in order further to deter Japan'.[16] However on 11 November Churchill sounded a note of caution, telling Pound 'I do not quite see what all this haste is to arrive at Singapore for a pow-wow. This is one of those cases where I am for "Safety First".' Pound replied that the *Prince of Wales* would now reach Singapore about 6 December instead of the 1st, on which Churchill minuted 'Good'.[17]

The commander chosen for the embryo Eastern Fleet was Rear-Admiral T. S. V. Phillips, who had been serving as Deputy (later Vice) Chief of Naval Staff since the beginning of the war; and he was given the rank of Acting Admiral on taking up the appointment. Phillips was a very able, hard-working staff officer, but not a patient or tolerant man. He was indeed subject to fits of violent anger if he thought his ideas were being obstructed, or if he did not agree with some proposal. Pound had complete confidence in him, and so did Churchill in the early days; but in the autumn of 1940 Phillips opposed retaliatory bombing of German cities, and early in the following year he argued strongly against the diversion of forces from Cyrenaica to Greece – which was actually done in March. The author of the entry on Phillips in the Dictionary of National Biography, Admiral H. G. Thursfield, who was an intimate friend of his, wrote that 'contact with the Prime Minister practically ceased' from that time. Though Churchill's Principal Private Secretary John Colville has told the author that he 'never heard him speak of Phillips with anything but admiration, and indeed affection'[18] the recollections of officers who were serving on the naval staff at the time confirm both the breach between Phillips and Churchill and that the cause of it was his too outspoken criticism of Churchillian strategy.[19]

Although no written record of the preliminaries to Phillips's appointment has been found it is certain that Pound initiated it, and that Alexander consulted Churchill; for the Prime Minister always insisted on being consulted about Flag Officers' appointments. But Phillips had no sea-going war experience, and was 'a prisoner of his fiercely expressed [pre-war] convictions . . . to the effect that bombers were no match for battleships'.[20] At the time of the Norwegian campaign he repeatedly argued that all that was needed to defeat the dive-bomber was more resolution on the part of commanding officers, and he would not listen to those of the staff, of whom this author was one, who tried to convince him that, far from warships being able to defend themselves against air attacks, fighter cover was essential if heavy losses were not to be incurred when operating within range of the dive-bombers. Lord Cunningham confirmed to the author much later that Phillips had 'told Winston that the ships were much too frightened of air attack'. 'This', he added, 'accounted for quite a lot';[21] and certainly the appointment of an officer of such strongly expressed convictions to the Eastern Fleet command was, after the experiences of Norway 1940 and Greece and Crete 1941 ominous in the extreme. Admiral John Cunningham, who had commanded a cruiser squadron in the Norwegian campaign put his finger on the basic cause of this trouble when in the following year he wrote to his namesake Sir Andrew that he had done 'all in my power to warn them [the Admiralty]'. 'I think,' he continued, 'the real trouble is that people who don't *know* are afraid of being accused of being afraid and so will not be honest in their weighing up of the risks against the possible advantages';[22] and that diagnosis may well have been applicable to Phillips.

Phillips's appointment, and the double step in rank awarded to him, also aroused caustic comments from other admirals. 'I shudder to think,' wrote Somerville, doubtless with his experiences in Force H in mind, 'of the Pocket Napoleon [Phillips was of very short stature] and his party. All the trials [?] to learn and no solid sea experience to fall back on. They ought to have someone who knows the stuff and can train that party properly on the way out.'[23] Early in November Churchill telegraphed to General Smuts, the South African Prime Minister, that Phillips was on the way to the Far East in the *Prince of Wales*. 'He is a great friend of mine and one of our ablest officers,' he added, and having been VCNS since the beginning of the war 'he knows the whole story back and forth'. This was of course a great exaggeration of Phillips's experience, which had been entirely confined to Whitehall. However Churchill told Smuts that the admiral had 'a great desire to have the honour of meeting you,' and asked Smuts to accede to his request.[24] One can only presume that Churchill's eulogy of Phillips was a throw-back to the early days of the war, because it is wholly contradicted by those who knew him well and have recorded the evidence of the breach between them mentioned above. Smuts however accepted Churchill's suggestion, with the result that Phillips left his flagship at Freetown and flew to Pretoria. Presumably he and Smuts discussed the problems which faced the admiral, but unfortunately no record of their talks was preserved. Smuts did however telegraph to Churchill a few days later a prescient warning of the danger he foresaw in the movement of such an exiguous force into what might soon prove to be the front line at Singapore.[25]

Alexander and Pound, or his deputy Phillips, certainly put up a strong resistence to the pressure applied by Churchill, whom Eden supported, to send the two capital ships to Singapore; but they gave way in the end, and Pound took the responsibility for the disaster that followed on himself – despite the fact that a much greater share of it properly belonged to Churchill.[26] By contrast with Pound's unselfish loyalty Churchill himself blamed Phillips in retrospect, declaring that his idea always had been that the *Prince of Wales* and *Repulse*, accompanied if possible by a carrier should go to Singapore, should be known to have arrived at Singapore, and 'should then disappear into the immense [eastern] archipelago'. The last thing that any member of the Defence Committee wanted, he argued, was 'anything like the movement which Admiral Phillips thought it right to make' in order to intercept a Japanese invasion force. However, his naval historical assistant assured him that until a late stage the documents reiterated that the purpose of the movement of the two ships was to act as a deterrent against Japanese aggression. The idea that they should disappear among the islands occurred to no one until early December – by which time it was too late.[27]

After the disaster Somerville protested to Cunningham 'Why the hell didn't they send *someone* out there who has been through the mill and knows his stuff?';[28] and Churchill also evidently considered that Phillips's inexperience had been a contributory factor. On learning that when the *Tirpitz* escaped damage at the hands of Home Fleet carrier-borne torpedo–bombers she used a smoke screen to shield herself, he asked Pound if Phillips could have done the same. Pound replied that this was so, but he presumed Phillips had preferred to keep a clear field for his A-A gunfire rather than obscure it with smoke.[29] If Pound's surmise was correct it lends support to Phillips's oft expressed conviction that heavy ships' A-A armaments could provide effective defence, mentioned above.

A fortnight before the disaster in the Far East the battleship *Barham* met her end off the Egyptian coast at the hands of a skilful and determined U-boat commander.[30] Alexander at once told Churchill that the loss of three capital ships in such a short period made it essential to hasten completion of the *Anson* and *Howe*, the last two of the *King George V* class; and he asked for '1A Priority' to be given to that purpose. Churchill's reply was prompt – and satisfactory. 'Certainly,' he told the First Lord, 'and for repairs to *Nelson*' – which had been damaged in the September 1941 convoy to Malta.[31]

It is unnecessary here to recapitulate the tragic story of the loss of Malaya and Singapore, out of which few of those involved emerged with credit. When Phillips arrived in the *Prince of Wales* he took over the appointment of C-in-C, Eastern Fleet from Sir Geoffrey Layton – who had in fact been on the station in command of a very exiguous China Fleet since July 1940, and certainly was far more familiar with local conditions and problems than Phillips – to whom he was moreover far senior in substantive rank. Phillips's arrival and assumption of command can hardly have been welcome to Layton, but he never made any comment on it – or on the ironical fact that immediately Phillips lost his life the Admiralty appointed him in his place. But the forces at Layton's disposal were then even more inadequate, and he could do little except try and stem the process of dissolution before leaving for Ceylon, the base on which it was hoped to rebuild our strength.

The disasters of December 1941 naturally made it essential to reorganize the command of such naval forces as remained in the Far East. When the American-British-Dutch-Australian (ABDA) command area was set up under General Wavell early in January 1942 the American Admiral T. C. Hart, who had been in command of the Asiatic Fleet based on Manila and had escaped to Java by submarine, was the obvious nominee. But President Roosevelt soon telegraphed to Churchill that he had asked to be relieved on grounds of ill health. After a long interchange of messages between Washington and London it was agreed in mid-February that the Dutch Admiral C. E. L. Helfrich should become Acting naval C-in-C, and he held that hopeless position until the disintegration of the ABDA command.[32]

Early in 1942 Churchill sent Pound a blistering minute about the failure of the navy to stop Japanese forces moving by sea down the west coast of Malaya after the fall of Penang; and Pound's reply, to the effect that the Admiralty was not fully informed about what was happening but the available small craft were doing their best provoked an even angrier riposte. 'This is really not good enough,' wrote Churchill; and he described the Japanese command of the west coast cf Malaya as 'one of the most astonishing lapses recorded in Naval history'. Though he apologized for being 'disagreeable' he insisted on 'a far more searching inquiry' being instituted.[33] By 24 January, the date of Churchill's second minute, it was of course far too late to stimulate local efforts by any form of inquiry into past failures. Pound replied, patiently as always, giving what information he had and pointing out that the crux of the matter was Japanese air superiority. On 9 February, only six days before the surrender of Singapore, Churchill, probably realizing that disaster was irremediable, dropped his complaints.[34] The reports from survivors, when they did reach the Admiralty much later, made it plain that some discreditable incidents took place at Penang and other west coast ports – notably the widespread desertion by crews of the very miscellaneous collection of small craft which had been hastily commissioned, and the failure to destroy such vessels before they could fall into Japanese hands.[35] But it was gradually discovered that the discreditable incidents were to some extent offset by examples of outstanding courage and self-sacrifice.[36]

After it was all over Admiral Layton wrote an extremely forthright report on the fall of Singapore and other events within his command, in which he was highly critical of almost all service and civilian leaders from all the countries involved in the disaster. In such circumstances there is of course always a tendency to blame the other fellow, and Layton's polemic would best be ignored were not his impartiality shown by the fact that he reported that, among those whom he found unequal to their task, was the naval C-in-C, East Indies, Vice-Admiral G. S. Arbuthnot.[37]

Towards the end of February 1942 Churchill asked General Wavell, who had just become C-in-C, India on the disintegration of his ABDA command, whether the 'key situation' of Ceylon did not require 'a first rate soldier in supreme command', and whether General Pownall would be the right man for the job.[38] Wavell agreed about Pownall, but in the meanwhile Admiral Layton had arrived in Ceylon – and had found something of an Augean stables there. He reported to Pound that he had been 'profoundly shocked by [the] state of unreadiness and unjustified complacency in nearly all circles', and was convinced that the change foreshadowed in Churchill's message to Wavell was 'not only desirable and necessary but imperative and urgent'.[39] On reading this message Churchill discussed the matter with Pound, and proposed that Layton should be appointed in supreme command of all forces and authorities in Ceylon.[40] The appointment became effective on 5 March; and was without doubt one of the best Churchill ever made. Quite soon after taking over his new responsibilities Layton told Pound that he had 'weathered the storm' which he had expected to arise, and that 'after a slight outburst [presumably on the part of the Civil authorities] they had accepted the situation in what I can only describe as a very good spirit . . .'[41]*

When Layton's War Diary covering the final phase of the operations in Malaya reached London Alexander suggested to Churchill that it should be circulated to the War Cabinet, as had been done with the reports sent in by the other commanders concerned in the disaster, including General Wavell;[42] but Pound considered it would be a mistake – probably because of the admiral's strictures on officers of the other services and on civilians, most of whom were of course in no position to defend themselves.[43] On reading the diary Churchill's reaction was to tell Alexander that 'It is singular that Admiral Layton makes no reference to the failure to provide defences for the Singapore Fortress from land attack'; and he quoted Layton's caustic statement 'so the Army retired to Singapore which the Japanese reduced, for all that it was heavily fortified and nominally defended by 100,000 troops, in a matter of forty-eight hours by the simple expedient of landing in the least likely places'. 'This,' remarked Churchill, 'seems to be the only reference to the fortification of the Island or to the gorge [sic] of the Fortress. It is an extraordinary instance of a mental blind spot which affected all concerned.'[44] That minute is of interest in showing how obsessed Churchill was by the view that Singapore was 'a fortress' – which an island the size of the Isle of Wight with about a million inhabitants living on it certainly was not;[45] and if it came to 'blind spots' Churchill himself had certainly not been free of one about the likelihood of Japanese aggression and the defence of Malaya. He saw no advantage in circulating Layton's report, and ordered it to be 'put by till the end of the war'; and that was done.

---

* When I was investigating Admiral Layton's activities as C-in-C, Ceylon I was told an amusing story about how the recently appointed Civil Defence Commissioner Mr (later Sir Oliver) Goonetilleke complained to the Governor (Sir Andrew Caldecott) that Layton had called him 'a black bastard'. To which the Governor replied 'My dear fellow that is nothing to what he calls me!' An excellent account of Layton's impact on the preparation of Ceylon for war is to be found in E. F. C. Ludowyk *The Modern History of Ceylon*. (Faber. 1966).

For Pound, whose health and vigour were steadily deteriorating, the early months of 1942 must have been a bitter experience – especially as he was under attack from within the navy for being too subservient to Churchill. Early in March he wrote a curious letter to him about their relations, explaining how he had been able to accept responsibility for almost everything that appeared ill-judged or even disastrous, including the loss of the *Prince of Wales* and *Repulse*, but objecting to Mountbatten being given a double step in rank on his appointment to succeed Keyes as Director of Combined Operations.[46] This was certainly an odd issue on which to take up the cudgels with the Prime Minister, but it does make plain how unshakable was Pound's loyalty to him.

Early in March Churchill sent the COSs a minute saying that he was 'increasingly impressed with the disadvantages of the present system' in the Eastern Command area of having Naval, Army and Air Force officers 'equally represented at all points [i.e. in the command hierarchy]'. He claimed that it had 'resulted in a paralysis of the offensive spirit, due to the fact that the Officers of the three Services together nearly always, except in the higher ranks, present the sum of their fears and difficulties'. He therefore wanted to move in the direction of appointing Supreme Commanders 'in particular areas and for special tasks' – a subject to which we will revert later.[47]

In that same month Leo Amery (Secretary of State for India) suggested to Churchill that there was a good deal to be said for a suggestion put up by Mountbatten that 'we or the Americans might get busy with commerce raiders against Japanese shipping'. Churchill passed the proposal to Pound with the remark 'Our Q-ships [i.e. U-boat decoy ships] might at last come into their own';[48] which shows how his thoughts constantly tended to revert to World War I. In fact the successes then achieved by Q-ships had been so widely advertised that the Germans were accepting no risk of encountering them again, but sank any vessel which was acting suspiciously on sight. Yet the idea held such appeal for Churchill that a lot of labour, money and lives were wasted early in the war on trying to repeat such a ruse. However, Churchill accepted Pound's refusal to adopt the Mountbatten-Amery proposal.

In March 1942 the Admiralty sent to the Defence Committee their latest assessment of Japanese naval building, and Churchill read with incredulity the estimate that nine capital ships and two aircraft carriers were on the stocks; but he admitted that if this was so 'the future is indeed serious'. Though he now executed a sharp about-turn regarding Japanese sea power, writing that 'we must on no account under-rate' it, he asked for a catalogue of facts about their ship-building and industrial capacity. When Alexander produced a statement reviewing the capital ship position on both sides, and included the German 'pocket battleships', he minuted 'It is a pity to exaggerate the German and Japanese strength and minimize our own. The case [wd] be stronger if [?] restated and under-rated.'[49] After the staff had produced answers to all his inquiries he returned to the charge on the question whether Japanese ships were built more quickly than British ones. The Admiralty reply was to the effect that our own production did not compare unfavourably with theirs.[50]

In April further heavy blows were suffered by the Eastern Fleet when the Japanese carrier striking force swept across the Bay of Bengal and struck at Ceylon. The small aircraft carrier *Hermes*, two heavy cruisers and various lesser ships were sunk, and Somerville was lucky to escape complete disaster to his elderly and heterogeneous fleet. Indeed Admiral Willis, his second-in-command, considered that he accepted too heavy risks at the time by cruising to the east of the Maldive Islands and seeking an opportunity to use his few carrier aircraft to attack the very powerful enemy at night.[51] The correct strategy then was, in Willis's opinion, to preserve his ships as 'a fleet in being', and to keep out of the way to the south-west while advertising his presence by bogus wireless signals sent by small ships placed further east to lead the enemy on a false scent.[52] Be that as it may, on 7 April the Admiralty gave Somerville discretion to withdraw to East Africa – which he did, though not until more losses had been suffered.[53] It was lucky for him that the Japanese did not press their advantage but withdrew from the Indian Ocean to strike against the US navy once again. The outcome was the decisive battle of Midway, fought on 4 June, which put an abrupt end to the Japanese period of maritime dominance.

Churchill was highly critical both of Somerville's actions at this time, and of his strategic proposals. With regard to the latter he told Alexander and Pound that the admiral's intentions 'would seem to involve an immense dispersion of our limited aircraft and A-A [defences]. I do not think we could accept the views of Admiral Somerville as governing the strategic mission of the Eastern Fleet.' He considered that by his requests for reinforcements Somerville was 'asking for everything and giving the least possible'; and he castigated his proposal to develop bases in various islands in the Indian Ocean on the grounds that 'nothing could be more foolish than to squander our resources all over the places he mentions and not have one which is strong and well protected'.[54] Though Churchill certainly had a point in his complaint about trying to defend a lot of scattered island bases the trouble was that, as Somerville did not possess a 'Fleet Train' of supply ships to enable him to stay at sea for long periods, such as the Americans had developed in the Pacific, he had no alternative but to try and solve his logistic problems from shore bases; and that being so it was obviously necessary to defend them. Regarding the losses suffered from the Japanese carrier air attacks on 5 and 9 April Pound was able to provide Churchill with satisfactory notes for the speech he was intending to make in the House of Commons on these disasters;[55] but in June Churchill returned to the charge against Somerville, telling Alexander that 'No satisfactory explanation has been given by the officer concerned of the imprudent dispersion of his forces in the early days of April. . .'[56] Once again the Admiralty had to explain the difficulties of the man on the spot.

Soon after the disasters of early 1942 the famous '1000 bomber raid' on Cologne took place on the night of 30-31 May – though the magic figure of 1000 bombers was only achieved by the RAF recalling aircraft from, among other sources, Coastal Command. Among the top soldiers and sailors involved in the struggle to avert complete disintegration in the Far East such operations caused much heart-burning. Wavell, who had become C-in-C, India again in February 1942, wrote to the COSs that 'It certainly gives us furiously to think' when, after attempting to deal with the Japanese foray into the Indian Ocean with only a score of light bombers, 'we see that over 200 heavy bombers attacked one town in Germany';[57] while Admiral Willis, the second-in-command of the Eastern Fleet, wrote to Admiral Cunningham that he wondered whether we were not 'a bit over-insured at home, especially in regard to the air'. 'If only,' he continued, 'some of the hundreds of bombers who fly over Germany (and often fail to do anything because of the weather) had been torpedo aircraft and dive-bombers the old Empire would be in better condition than it is now.'[58] But the origins of the shortage of such aircraft went back a very long way – to the addiction of the Air Staff to the conventional bomber and their dislike of torpedo aircraft and dive-bombers. But Churchill was unsympathetic to the views expressed by Wavell and Willis, writing that 'it is not possible to make any decisive change. All that is possible is being done . . . We have built up a great plant here for bombing Germany, which is the only way in our power of helping Russia';[59] which begged the question why some of the products of the 'great plant' could not be sent to India without vitiating seriously our aid to Russia.

Even before the battle of Midway Churchill was again showing impatience over what he regarded as unjustifiable inactivity on the part of the Eastern Fleet. The battleship *Valiant* had been badly damaged by the Italian midget submarine attack on ships in Alexandria on 19th December 1941, and in the following April the Admiralty proposed that, while she was being repaired at Durban, those of her crew, many of whom were survivors from recently sunk ships, who had served overseas for more than two years should be brought home and given some leave. Churchill at once scolded Alexander and Pound severely 'This ought not to have been done in view of the urgent need,' he wrote; and 'It was a wrong thing to do, without the consequences being considered and reported' – presumably to himself. The First Sea Lord's reaction was however strong – and humane; and Churchill did not press him further.[60]

In the following month Churchill proposed to send the four R-class battleships to Australia – more as a sop to that country's clamour for naval forces than for any sound strategic reason; but the staff resisted the idea and Churchill did not press it.[61] After Midway, however, he increased the pressure, telling Alexander and Pound that Somerville had 'two first class carriers and *Warspite*. He has been doing nothing for several months and we cannot really keep this fleet idle indefinitely' – an accusation which provoked a protest from Alexander that, although the fleet in question was at present on the defensive 'it does not follow that it is not performing an important role'.[62] But Churchill constantly complained about 'idle ships' being 'a reproach' during this period,[63] causing Pound to remark to Cunningham that only politicians supposed that ships were doing nothing unless they were always 'rushing about'.

In July Churchill told Alexander and Pound that 'a great easement has come to us in the Indian Ocean' – which was true enough; but he was over-optimistic in expecting that 'at any time now the Japs may involve themselves with Russia'; and he disliked a request received from Admiral E. J. King USN that the Eastern Fleet should make a lunge towards the remote Portuguese island of Timor in the Eastern Archipelago, which he described as 'very dangerous action'. With the first battle of Alamein in progress in the western desert he wanted instead 'to re-assert our sea power in the Eastern Mediterranean' by bringing most of Somerville's fleet through the Suez Canal to that theatre, 'and thus make impossible any attempt to throw an enemy army across from Greece on to the Egyptian shore'. Such a move would, he continued, at least show Admiral King that 'our ships could not be accused of standing idle while the Americans were moving [in the central Pacific]'. He wanted this idea 'to be examined by the Naval Staff most earnestly and in a forward spirit' in case the Alamein battle 'should turn in our favour'. That the staff did; but Pound's answer poured cold water on the whole idea, which would destroy the build-up of the Eastern Fleet in order to counter an illusory threat; and Churchill again accepted the Admiralty's view.[64]

Despite the Anglo-American agreement at the Atlantic Conference of August 1941 that the defeat of Germany should be given top priority, and the reaffirmation of that strategic principle at the first Washington ('Arcadia') conference of the following December, Admiral King constantly tried to get a higher priority for the Pacific war. Though King was certainly no Anglophil it seems that his chief reason was to win the greatest possible share of the credit for victory over Japan for his own service, rather than share such credit with the British – as was bound to be the case in the European war. Early in 1943 Field Marshal Sir John Dill, whom Churchill had sacked as CIGS and sent to Washington as head of the British Joint Staff Mission in November 1941, telegraphed home that King had complained to him 'rather plaintively' that we had never given sufficient weight to the Japanese menace – which was true enough of Churchill from about 1936 to 1941 but was not true of the British COSs. King had put forward to Dill what he called 'a concept' that one quarter of America's and Britain's strength should 'be devoted to holding Japan' and the remaining three quarters to defeating Germany. King said he had tried 'to sell this idea to the President'; but Roosevelt was evidently un-impressed – presumably because it infringed the spirit if not the letter of the Argentia and Arcadia agreements. The naval staff told Pound that such an idea was 'a most illogical employment of our combined forces', which could only be decided 'by a joint agreed assessment of strategic requirements'; and there the matter was left – without it even being put to Churchill, who would no doubt have rejected it out of hand.[65]

By the autumn of 1942 the heavy losses and damage suffered by the US Navy's small number of fleet carriers produced a suggestion from the British mission in Washington that an offer of two of our own ships of that class 'would be most opportune'. The staff raised no serious objections, so Churchill telegraphed to Roosevelt that we were pre-pared to send out the *Illustrious* from the Eastern Fleet and the *Victorious* from the Home Fleet after the invasion of North Africa, provided that the Americans would lend the small and lightly built carrier *Ranger* to the Home Fleet.[66] Then the mission telegraphed that it was plain that the American navy was lukewarm about the idea, and had emphasized 'the disadvantages of a mixed force' – an excuse which savours of Admiral King's reluctance to have any British ships in the Pacific. Churchill thereupon told Roosevelt that he bowed to his wishes, and only the *Victorious* was sent.[67] She reached Pearl Harbor early in March 1943; but by the time she had been re-equipped the crisis had passed and little use was made of her.[68]

In the summer of 1943 German U-boats again entered the Indian Ocean and sank a number of ships in the Mozambique channel. General Smuts, the South African Prime Minister had wanted to seize bases in Mozambique, then a Portuguese colony, to facilitate the work of our sea and air escorts; but the Foreign Office opposed such a step because of its possible repercussions on Portugal and so on the great combined operations in the Mediterranean.[69]

Churchill was angered by the losses and told Alexander and Pound 'I am shocked at this new disaster . . . Where are the destroyers which belong to the Eastern Fleet? Are they all sharing the idleness of that Fleet?' Pound replied, patiently as ever, that we had driven the U-boats from the North Atlantic, which was 'the one place they can beat us', and that to win the war they must return to that theatre. We had, he continued, strengthened the patrols and hunting groups in the Bay of Biscay, and to strip them in order to reinforce the Indian Ocean would be 'playing the enemy's game'.[70] Churchill however kept up the pressure, and Pound had to explain that 'we are endeavouring to carry out large scale operations [in the Mediterranean] as well as protecting our trade'. But for those operations a dozen more escorts would, he said, have been available. A few days later he told Churchill 'I am personally satisfied that everyone is thoroughly aware of the situation, and that everything possible is being done to minimize our losses'. It was, he continued, 'only the people on the spot who can decide what is the best way of using the reinforcements when they receive them'.[71] All of which suggests that Churchill never really understood that no nation with world-wide trade to defend can possibly be strong everywhere and all the time. Incidentally this must have been one of the last minutes Pound sent to Churchill, since it was early in the following month that he suffered the stroke which caused him to resign.

The surrender of the Italian fleet in September of that year produced some euphoric ideas in Churchill's mind. He telegraphed to Alexander from Quebec, where the 'Quadrant' conference was in progress, proposing that most of their navy's strength (five capital ships, one fleet and five escort carriers, six cruisers or A-A cruisers, one or two destroyer flotillas and at least six submarines) should leave Britain in mid-November and go to the Indian Ocean by way of the Panama Canal 'stopping on the way to take part in some American operations against Japan'. 'The war is still going on,' he pointed out, rather unnecessarily, 'and the Navy ought to continue to take a leading part in it.' The First Lord replied stressing all the responsibilities nearer home which still remained, such as the Arctic convoys; but the staff considered that 'a balanced force' of less strength than Churchill had proposed could be ready to leave by 1 December. Then Churchill switched to advocacy of an amphibious assault on Sumatra, (operation 'Culverin'), which we will encounter again later; and as that necessitated the ships going out by the Suez Canal he dropped the 'British Ocean Force' idea.[72]

If it was chiefly the alleged 'idleness' of Somerville and the Eastern Fleet which produced Churchill's expostulations and exhortations in 1942-3, he was equally caustic about the work of the Fleet Air Arm, comparing its cost in men and material, and its accomplishments, unfavourably with those of Bomber Command; but as such complaints affected the navy as a whole, and not only the Eastern Fleet, we will revert to them later. Though it doubtless did nothing but good for the service staffs to have a Minister of Defence who took a lively interest in even the day-to-day minutiae of their affairs, perusal of the stream of minutes and memoranda, often written in hectoring language, which descended on the Admiralty at the time of its greatest trial between December 1941 and June 1942 does make one feel that Churchill sometimes carried his principle of exercising what he has called 'a close general supervision over everything that was done or proposed' too far; and one wonders whether the physical and mental exhaustion which Pound increasingly showed at this time was not exacerbated by the bombardment to which he was subjected. After all the worst disaster for which he must accept responsibility – namely the scattering and subsequent near destruction of the Arctic convoy PQ. 17 – took place in July 1942. Though it is of course true that the service chiefs and the commanders of large forces in war must possess high stamina and be capable of standing up to great strain, perhaps one of Churchill's greatest mistakes lay in his overlong acceptance of a First Sea Lord who did not possess those qualities in sufficient measure.

CHAPTER 12

The Mediterranean
1943-1944

In August 1942 Churchill flew to Cairo and thence to Moscow – primarily to break the news to Stalin that there would be no 'second front', in the sense of a cross-Channel invasion, during that year. From Moscow he returned to Cairo to reorganize the military command in the Middle East prior to the launching of the offensive which was to culminate in the Second Battle of Alamein (23 October–4 November). Early in the following year he became greatly perturbed about the Axis seaborne traffic to Tunisia, on which the supply and reinforcement of their armies in North Africa chiefly depended, and he made it plain to Pound that he considered the navy was not doing enough to disrupt the enemy convoys.[1] This issue came to a head when the Eighth Army captured Tripoli on 23 January 1943. Montgomery had conceived a strong dislike for Harwood and complained to Churchill that the navy had been dilatory over the clearance of Tripoli harbour, which the Germans had blocked very thoroughly before evacuating it, and through which the Eighth Army commander wanted supplies to be brought in as quickly as possible. The complaints reached the Admiralty in the form that 'The Army Commander sent for the [naval] C-in-C's Chief of Staff [Rear-Admiral J. G. L. Dundas] and after a very cold and critical reception including sceptical remarks in regard to the navy's intended hours of work gave him a message to the C-in-C containing the following extract "The Naval Party which arrived up here to uncork the harbour arrived with totally inadequate resources as regards personnel, equipment and explosives."'

Early in January Pound sent Alexander a strongly worded defence of Harwood who, he wrote, 'has done very well in opening up Tobruk, Benghazi etc. and in getting them going so quickly . . .'; and he attributed the absence of more offensive naval operations to the inability of the RAF to provide air cover while the great land battle was in progress.[2] A reply to Churchill was accordingly drafted in these terms, but as the file copy is unsigned we cannot be certain that it was sent. It declared that Montgomery's statement quoted above was 'quite unfounded', that the army did not appreciate the difficulty of underwater salvage work, and that 'there has been no delay and no lack of material on the spot'.[3] However, less than a week after the preparation of the exculpatory document Alexander telegraphed to Harwood offering him the appointment of Second-in-Command, Eastern Fleet. The bait was that, whereas the eastern Mediterranean Command, the title of which had been changed to Levant Command in February, was in effect a shore appointment with no proper flagship for a C-in-C, the Eastern Fleet's second-in-command was flying his flag afloat. It is impossible to say whether Harwood would have accepted the change without demur if Pound had left the matter as stated in Alexander's offer because on 13 February he followed up that message with a long, and one may feel quite unnecessary letter of explanation. This missive was in many ways a repetition of Pound's mistake in sending Admiral North an explanation of why he was to be sacked;* and the outcome was rather similar.

Pound began by saying he would 'be glad to see your Flag flying afloat again', and could well have stopped there. Unfortunately he went on to tell Harwood that when Richard Casey, Minister of State in the Middle East since March 1942, had been in London he had told Churchill 'that the Naval representation on the C-in-C Middle East Committee was not as strong as that of the other Services'; and although he and the First Lord had 'resisted any idea of a change of command' their representations had been weakened by the suggestion 'that the Navy had not done enough during the advance of the Eighth Army' – which obviously must have come from Montgomery. When Churchill arrived back in England he had, Pound continued, 'once again raised the question of your relief', and had asked him 'to see the CIGS and hear what the Army felt'. General Brooke 'was quite definite that the Army had lost confidence that the Navy would in all circumstances give them the necessary support'; and the clearance of Tripoli was, he declared, 'largely responsible for this'. Pound went on to say 'that the story as a whole leaves one with the definite impression that insufficient supervision had been taken on the highest level'; he particularized on the clearance of the harbour in some detail, and ended with the conclusion that he had therefore 'come to the conclusion that a change in command was desirable'.[4] In view of what Pound had written to the First Lord in defence of Harwood only a few weeks earlier this was an extraordinary volte-face on his part.

It is hardly surprising that Pound's letter should have produced eight foolscap pages of angry reaction from the victim, who declared that

* See pp. 161-163.

when Churchill left Cairo for Tripoli, if not earlier, he had made up his mind that he wanted him to be relieved. Harwood attributed this chiefly to Churchill's 'venom' against the French squadron at Alexandria, about which he himself 'had to bear the full blast'. He went on to discuss his relations with Montgomery, who he declared had developed 'a bias against me personally' as a result of the abortive and costly raid on Tobruk already mentioned. The admiral insisted that the operation had in his view always been 'a desperate gamble [undertaken] to help the Army', which was in a very difficult situation at the time, and that the other two Cs-in-C, as well as Montgomery himself, were fully apprised of the risks and had accepted them. 'The views so freely expressed' by Montgomery were, Harwood submitted, 'not only ill-informed as regards the unblocking operation, but were prejudiced so far as I am concerned'. As regards Brooke's statement that the army had lost confidence in the navy Harwood declared that 'quite frankly and simply [it] is not true'. All reports which had reached him were 'in exactly the opposite strain'; and he strongly rebutted the charge that there had been any lack of foresight or avoidable delay over the clearance of Tripoli harbour.[5]

Pound annotated this explosive missive in his own hand. He asserted, firstly, that Churchill and the French squadron 'did not come into it' – a somewhat dubious statement since in February Churchill ordered Casey to tell Admiral Godfroy that he and his men would get no more pay as long as they remained inactive, and also took steps to prevent his use of French funds in Egypt.[6] Secondly Pound asserted that Montgomery 'never said anything about Tobruk' – though we know the General had been highly critical of that operation. Lastly Pound wrote, presumably for Alexander's benefit, that 'There is no security of tenure of an appointment', and if another man 'can do it better' the incumbent 'must give way' to him. Also 'it is wrong for the Admiralty to keep people in appointments if they consider they are not maintaining the prestige of the Service as high as possible'. The outcome was that the relief of Harwood stood.

Meanwhile Sir Andrew Cunningham had met Harwood who of course gave him the same *pièce justificative* as he had written to Pound; whereupon Sir Andrew somewhat rashly took up Harwood's case with the First Sea Lord, saying that in his opinion he had been perfectly right to oppose Churchill's desire to use strong-arm methods against the French squadron in Alexandria. Indeed Sir Andrew said that he himself had expressed the same view to Churchill during his recent visit to North Africa. As to Montgomery's complaint about the clearance of

Tripoli harbour, Cunningham declared very firmly that 'This I know is quite untrue. In my opinion Tripoli was most expeditiously cleared – .' To which Pound replied in much the same terms that he had given to Harwood himself, adding the sharp rebuke that he was 'surprised at your [Sir Andrew] expressing such a definite opinion about the relief when you only know one side of the case'.[7]

To sum up this fracas, there is little doubt that Harwood was never a big enough man for the job given to him – an error of judgement for which Pound must carry the chief responsibility, though Churchill had approved the appointment. Furthermore his health was never robust and at the end broke down completely. Certainly he was unlucky in that his Chief of Staff, Admiral Dundas, was also not a fit man. He was invalided home and died soon after the war. But Montgomery did develop an unreasonable prejudice against the naval C-in-C, possibly because, in contrast to the General's addiction to physical fitness, he was a corpulent man and did not look well in the naval hot weather rig of white shorts. As an epilogue to this unhappy tale it can be said with confidence that close investigation of the clearance of Tripoli does not reveal any serious neglect or delay on the navy's part.[8] The conclusion surely is that Montgomery used that accusation as a pretext for getting rid of an officer from another service – whose position in the command hierarchy was moreover superior to his own.

After the capture of Tripoli congratulatory messages were being sent by the military to all and sundry, and Commodore H. G. Norman, the naval C-in-C's additional Chief of Staff in Cairo, was at the time lunching with Montgomery and his staff. When Norman suggested that some mention might be made of the navy's support of the Eighth Army during its long advance he received a heavy kick under the table from General de Guingand, Montgomery's Chief of Staff. After lunch the General told Norman that it was hopeless to ask for any such recognition until Harwood had left. Then he would see that it was done. He was as good as his word, and the signal was sent on the very day Harwood was replaced.*

After the disappearance of Harwood from the scene relations between the navy and army improved – partly because on 20 February 1943 Sir Andrew Cunningham relinquished his title of Allied Naval Commander, Expeditionary Force and resumed his more famous position as

* Admiral Norman told the author this story when he was helping with the account of the Harwood-Montgomery imbroglio and the clearance of Tripoli harbour published in The War at Sea, II, pp. 435-7.

C-in-C, Mediterranean. It should, however, be noted that at first the limit of his command area was just to the east of Sicily, but in June it was extended to 20° East (about the longitude of Benghazi) in order that he might be responsible for the convoys coming from both east and west for the invasion of Sicily. Everything to the east of those boundaries came under the new Levant Command, about which more will be said shortly. The assumption by 'ABC' of command of the naval forces with which Montgomery had to co-operate quickly showed him that he now had to deal with a man of far higher calibre than Harwood. Though sparks sometimes flew between Montgomery and Cunningham, and the latter considered General Alexander handled his irrepressible subordinate too tenderly, no trouble of real importance arose between them at first.[9] In fact Cunningham's forces played a great part in preventing any appreciable number of Germans escaping from Tunisia when the trap finally closed on them in mid-May. The Sicilian channel was quickly cleared of mines, and on the 15th Cunningham reported home that 'the Mediterranean was clear'. Apart from the immense saving of shipping the relief of Malta was the chief benefit derived from the victory in North Africa. Churchill sent Cunningham very warm congratulations 'upon the admirable work done by the Navy during the whole Tunisian campaign and particularly at its conclusion –'; and he asked for his 'thanks and congratulations' to be conveyed to all officers and men under the admiral's command.[10] The contrast to his opinion of the navy's part in the clearance of Tripoli is striking.

The concentration of naval forces in the central Mediterranean at this time inevitably brought about a decline in the importance, and the strength, of the Levant Command, and may perhaps have given the residue the impression that the war had passed them by and that their efforts could be relaxed. If that is so a heavy price was to be exacted before the end of the year. The junction of the forces placed under Eisenhower for operation 'Torch' with those coming from the Middle East under General Alexander evidently raised in Churchill's mind what he described in the draft of a speech he proposed to make in the House of Commons as 'the modern ideas of Unity of Command between various allies and also between the three services'. Pound evidently scented danger in the last six words and suggested their omission. 'Unity of command as between our own three services', he wrote, 'is in my opinion uncalled for owing to the admirable way in which our three services co-operate, and does not conduce to efficiency' – an odd comment when one takes account of the fact that it was produced just when the Harwood-Montgomery rumpus came to a climax.[11] However, in the masterly survey of the recent Casablanca Conference and the progress of the war which Churchill gave to an enthralled House of Commons on 11th February he described the new command organization for the Mediterranean theatre but kept off what Pound regarded as dangerous ground.[12]

In the spring of 1943 the approach of victory in North Africa caused the COSs to alter the command organization in the Mediterranean by separating the eastern from the central and western theatre – which was obviously going to be the more important – and downgrading the former. Churchill very naturally took a lively interest in who was to be given the Eastern Mediterranean command; but Pound was slow to put forward names. His first choice was the surprising one of Rear-Admiral A. F. E. Palliser, who had been Phillips's Chief of Staff at the time of the disaster of December 1942 off Malaya; but for unspecified reasons that fell through.[13] Then Pound proposed Rear-Admiral G. J. A. Miles, who was head of the naval mission in Moscow; but Ismay told Pound that the Prime Minister would 'almost certainly want a note about him' before giving his approval.[14] If one was sent it has not survived, and the matter is only of interest in showing how Churchill insisted on vetting all Flag appointments himself. What finally happened was that, after an interim period during which Admiral Sir Ralph Leatham, who had been Flag Officer, Malta for most of 1942, held the Levant Command it was taken over by Admiral Sir John Cunningham.* In March he wrote to his namesake Sir Andrew, who was then Allied Naval Commander under General Eisenhower in the western theatre, that he knew nothing about the circumstances behind Harwood's relief; and the offer of the Levant Command had come 'as a surprise' to him – the more so because 'feelers' had recently been put out to him about his relieving Somerville in the Eastern Fleet. Because Harwood's supersession had taken place so soon after Churchill's return home John Cunningham 'imagined that his venom had in some way been stirred up' – which showed that he was far from knowing the whole story. But his interviews with Alexander and Pound about his new appointment had shown that they both 'seemed to anticipate difficulty' in getting Churchill's agreement to it.[15]

Here it may be relevant to mention that not only were Sir Andrew and Sir John Cunningham unrelated but in character, temperament and methods they were completely disparate. I served under both of them

---

* Sir John Cunningham was no relation to Sir Andrew, who later became Admiral of the Fleet Viscount Cunningham of Hyndhope.

when they were Post Captains and I a junior Lieutenant, but I did not get to know either intimately until after the war. As a Captain Sir Andrew was plainly a first-class seaman but also a martinet – though with a sense of humour; while Sir John, who obviously had by far the better brain, seemed somewhat fussy and pedantic. For instance he always dotted the i's and crossed the t's in any paper one submitted to him for signature. I was pondering on how to describe their differences as full Admirals when an officer who had served a great part of the war on the staff of both of them provided me with exactly what I was fumbling for in my mind. 'It would be difficult', wrote Admiral Sir Manley Power, 'to find two men less alike than "ABC" and John D. Cunningham. The former fiery, aggressive, active and intolerant; the latter quiet, thoughtful, rather lethargic, very kind but possessed of an acid tongue. "ABC" scintillating, successful and inclined to be schoolboyishly boastful. John D. with an unlucky series of operations – Norway, Dakar and the Dodecanese – behind him very cautious, cynical and suspicious of adventure.' On changing from Sir Andrew's to Sir John's staff Power might well have recalled the young Henry V's remark on finding himself King 'Not Amurath an Amurath succeeds';[16] or, as Power puts it 'I found myself translated suddenly from reining in a champing charger to goading a reluctant draft horse.'[17] In those pithy metaphors one may surely find a clue to the reason why Churchill never took to Sir Andrew (nor he to Churchill), and why he did not place Sir John among the brightest luminaries of the naval firmament of the period.

To return to the central Mediterranean, Sir Andrew Cunningham set up his headquarters in Algiers after the success of 'Torch', and it was chiefly from there that he and his staff strove to produce an agreed inter-service plan for the invasion of Sicily (operation 'Husky') – and with very little time available to complete so important and intricate a job. Expectedly Montgomery proved the chief stumbling block, and in April Cunningham told Pound that 'we are arriving at a state of dead-lock over "Husky" – I am afraid Monty is a bit of a nuisance'.[18] The General had in fact refused to give his attention to the draft plan until the Axis forces had been cleared out of Tunisia; and when he did study it his criticism of splitting the assault into two parts – one at the south-east corner of Sicily and the other on the north coast near Palermo – was forthright. So the whole plan had to be recast – to Cunningham's great annoyance. In retrospect however the admiral's Staff Officer Operations Captain Power considered that Montgomery was right in insisting on concentrating all his forces on the southerly assault; but avoidable friction was in his view produced by him expressing his views 'in [an] insufferably imperious manner' and in conveying them to the naval staff 'in a series of bombastic signals'. It is certainly the case that the changes, tiresome though they were, could have been made more easily had Montgomery studied the plan when he first received it, and had he thereafter shown more tact.[19] But, as has been said of Churchill himself, Montgomery was never a man who exactly ran around with an oil can.[20]

Late in June 1943, Andrew Cunningham wrote to Pound that 'the soldiers seem to think that they will be landed at the exact spot they expect to be, that the weather will necessarily be perfect, and that naval gunfire will silence all opposition . . .'. The thought of having to turn back and delay all the ships and landing craft, over 2000 in all, if the weather should make the landings impossible he found 'a bit hair-raising'.[21] Having been present at Gallipoli in 1915 the admiral was only too well aware of the hazards involved in large scale amphibious operations.

While these negotiations were in progress Cunningham had Churchill as his guest at Algiers, and described his eight day stay as 'much too long in these busy times and a perfect nuisance, interfering with the work'. But he admitted that Churchill was 'very amusing and his memory is quite amazing', though he found the late hours which he kept 'a bit wearing'.[22] Evidently Churchill bore the admiral no ill will for his refusal to fall in with his plan that he should relieve Admiral Tovey in the Home Fleet, mentioned earlier.

The invasion of Sicily in July 1943 and the landings in Salerno Bay in the following September (operation 'Avalanche') have been the subject of many books and need not detain us; but the Italian surrender signed on 3 September, just when the latter operation was about to be launched, produced repercussions which come very much within the scope of this book, since it caused Churchill's attention to revert once again to the Aegean Islands and thence to the Dardanelles, and to the possibility of bringing Turkey into the war. That such prospects had long been in his mind is shown by the mention of Turkey becoming a favourably disposed non-belligerent or even an ally in his long letter of 2 February 1943 to Roosevelt; and he also there mentioned her possible help 'to Great Britain in her *necessary attack on the Dodecanese*, and later upon Crete, which General Wilson [C-in-C, Middle East] has been directed to prepare *during the present year*' (italics supplied).[23]

On 1 August General Wilson telegraphed home in optimistic terms about the prospects for successful action in the Dodecanese produced by the Italian surrender; but he stressed that his command was not in a position 'to act quickly' because 'our resources have been drained to supply North Africa'. On reading this message Churchill ignored the General's caveat and sent the COSs a minute saying 'Here is a business of great consequence to be thrust forward by any means . . . This is no time for conventional establishments but rather for using whatever fighting elements there are . . . I hope the staffs will be able to stimulate action which may gain immense prizes at little cost, though not at little risk.'[24] Next day the COSs ordered the landing ships and craft which had been allocated to Mountbatten's South-East Asia Command, to be held in the Mediterranean; but they warned the C-in-C, Middle East that no other resources could be provided. However on the 21st, largely as a result of protests from Mountbatten, the assault shipping was released, and on the last day of the month the Middle East commanders told the COSs that this decision made any assault from the sea in their theatre impossible – except for minor raids.[25] However, Churchill was not prepared to accept such negativism, and told the Cs-in-C 'This is the time to play high. Improvise and dare.'[26] Thus was the stage set for a costly tragedy.

On 7 October Churchill urged on Roosevelt the importance of capturing Rhodes; but the President replied that he was not prepared to instruct Eisenhower to carry out 'diversions which limit the prospects of the early successful development of the Italian operations'.[27]

Before recounting the sequel it must be made plain that the three Cs-in-C in the Middle East (Admiral A. U. Willis from 14 October, General Maitland Wilson, and Air Chief Marshal Sholto Douglas) were a theoretically equal triumvirate – as had been the case since the beginning of the war; but Churchill's messages about the Aegean operations were nearly all addressed to the General only – which suggests that he regarded him as a sort of Supreme Commander. This misconception certainly caused difficulties to the other Cs-in-C.[28] Another source of confusion was that whereas Douglas was subordinate to Air Chief Marshal Tedder, the Air Officer Commanding the Mediterranean theatre, Willis and Wilson were independent Cs-in-C. Moreover relations between Douglas and Tedder, notably over the provision of aircraft for the Levant Command, were far from cordial – as both have made plain in their memoirs.[29] Furthermore Tedder was in general hostile to naval needs, and favoured the concept of an independent air strategy applied by means of strategic bombing. One may reasonably feel that Churchill as Minister of Defence and the British COSs ought to have made sure that the chain of command was clear before encouraging operations in the eastern theatre on a considerable scale.

The key to the Aegean was the island of Rhodes; but the Germans acted very quickly, and disarmed the large Italian garrison. As the forces necessary to assault it simply were not available in the Middle East, the commanders decided to occupy Cos, Leros and a number of smaller islands instead; but with the Luftwaffe firmly in possession of command of the air the supply of the assault forces was bound to prove difficult.

Admiral Willis, who had held an important command for the landings in Sicily and at Salerno, had to take over the Levant Command at short notice because Sir John Cunningham was required to relieve his namesake Sir Andrew, who was to return home to become First Sea Lord in place of the dying Pound. On 16 October, just after Sir Andrew had taken over as First Sea Lord, Churchill wrote to him that he had so far only approved Sir John becoming *acting* C-in-C, Mediterranean but was 'quite willing to discuss a permanent arrangement'. Three days later he told Alexander that he agreed to Sir John being made C-in-C, but added 'Pray let me have your proposals, together with the scope of his command, which should certainly cover the entire Mediterranean.'[30] That idea, however, held no appeal to the Admiralty, presumably because Admiral Willis had already been appointed C-in-C, Levant. In any case with so much happening in the western and central basins it would surely have been difficult for one man to carry responsibility for the eastern theatre as well.

It was not a happy moment for Admiral Willis to take over the Levant Command. Not only had the American COSs shown at the Casablanca Conference of the previous January that they were totally opposed to any ventures in the eastern basin, but he found himself saddled with responsibility for operations in the Aegean in the initiation of which he had taken no part. What this meant became clear to him at a meeting at General Eisenhower's headquarters at Tunis on 9 October, which he attended only as a silent observer – because he had not yet taken over the Levant Command. Six days previously the Germans had recaptured the island of Cos by a surprise attack, so depriving the Middle East forces of the only airfield from which effective cover could be given in the Aegean. After some debate the conference decided to hold on to Leros and Samos, although success now depended on the provision of long-range American Lightning fighters from the Mediterranean command. Six squadrons of these excellent aircraft had been diverted to that purpose on 6 October; but on the 10th, before Willis took over the Levant Command, they were withdrawn on the grounds that they were required to escort heavy bombers in attacks on targets in north Italy. Though Churchill took the matter up with Eisenhower, and wrote strongly to President Roosevelt about it, he failed to get this decision modified.[31] Churchill's account of these events leaves one in no doubt that he bitterly resented this thwarting of his hopes; for he commented that 'The American staff had enforced their view; the price had now to be paid by the British.' On the other hand it can surely be argued that he should have made certain that the necessary forces would be made available before he spurred the Middle East commanders into action.

Early in October, by which time it was plain that the improvisations adopted to meet Churchill's insistent desire to occupy some of the Aegean Islands were proving quite inadequate, he telegraphed to Sir Andrew Cunningham 'It seems of the greatest importance to use naval forces freely against the impending attack on Leros, which may be decisive . . . on the fate of the fortress.'[32] He wanted Cunningham to fly to Cairo to consult on the matter with Eden and the Middle East Commanders; but he totally ignored the fact that the diversion of naval forces to the Aegean, which had in fact taken place on a considerable scale, could not bring about the desired result as long as the Germans enjoyed command of the air over the waters in question.

Among the naval forces transferred to the Levant Command losses mounted steadily to the German dive-bombers and to the minefields which we could not clear because the sweepers could not be protected from air attack. Indeed with the German bombers substituted for the Turkish shore batteries the situation was remarkably similar to that which had prevailed in The Narrows of the Dardanelles when we were trying to clear the minefields in March 1915.[33] Furthermore to sailors of long war experience, and Admiral Willis was one of them, the situation was developing in exactly the same way as off Norway in 1940 and Crete in the following year; and the warships' crews were beginning to question why, at this late stage, they should be called on to undergo a repetition of those ordeals.*

Willis accordingly proposed that an increasingly costly and probably fruitless venture should be abandoned, as the Cs-in-C, Middle East

---

* Admiral Willis's memoirs contain a nice story of a young sailor seeing an old hand inflating his lifebelt before their ship left Alexandria for the Aegean. On the former asking why he was doing so the latter replied 'Mark my words, Son. This is the only fucking air support we'll get this trip.' 'I took care,' comments Willis, 'that this story reached the ears of the Air Marshals.'

had authority to do; but Wilson and Douglas, who unlike Willis had of course initiated the operation, refused to agree. Then it was found that Leros was not being properly prepared for defence, and reinforcements and a new commander were sent there; but the destroyer carrying them was sunk. The situation, as Willis reported home, was now steadily deteriorating, and by the time the CAS pressed Tedder to provide the necessary air cover it was too late. On 12 November the Germans succeeded in assaulting Leros from the sea and with paratroops, and four days later the garrison capitulated. General Wilson telegraphed the bad news home, saying that the surrender had taken place 'after a very gallant struggle against overwhelming odds', which was in fact excessively flattering to the forces engaged.*[34] The troops on the other Aegean islands were then withdrawn.

Most of the responsibility for this failure must surely rest with Churchill, whose addiction to the capture of islands which would certainly prove difficult to supply was remarked on earlier.[35] That he strongly resented Roosevelt's refusal to help is proved by the telegram about holding Leros which he sent to the President late in October; for he told him (misquoting St Matthew) that 'the dogs under the table eat of the children's crumbs'.[36] Furthermore his hope of bringing Turkey into the war, which was the principal plank on which he rested his case, was an illusion; for the Turks could not have defended themselves as long as the Germans held Greece and most of the Aegean Islands. When in 1944 the Germans were forced to withdraw from Greece the islands fell into our hands virtually uncontested.[37] However, when on 20 November Churchill and the First Sea Lord arrived in Alexandria on board the *Renown* for the Cairo Conference, and were met by Admiral Willis, the Prime Minister uttered no word of reproach about the frustration of his hopes.[38] Yet the Aegean fiasco was a tragic, and one may feel wholly unnecessary ending to a year which had brought important and long-awaited successes.

While the Aegean operations were in progress in the eastern Mediterranean a great deal had happened in the central basin. The seaborne assault at Salerno on 9 September 1943 was successful, though only by a very narrow margin; but it was not until 1 October that

---

* Apart from poor resistance by the garrison there was a bad naval failure to interfere with the German seaborne landings. Losses in this short campaign were four cruisers damaged (one beyond repair), six destroyers sunk and four damaged and two submarines sunk. Army losses were about 4800, and are made the more poignant by the fact that they included four battalions which had gone through the long siege of Malta and had been sent to the Middle East to recuperate.

Naples was captured and the port was quickly reopened in order to bring in supplies for the army. Then came the winter, with terrible weather in the mountainous regions of southern Italy, and by the beginning of the New Year the Allies' Fifth and Eighth Armies were completely held up on the Garigliano and Sangro rivers. This resulted in a plan being made, with Churchill's strong support, to land a fresh assault force at Anzio (operation 'Shingle') behind the main German defences, with the object of forcing them to withdraw to the north of Rome. But great difficulties were experienced in collecting the necessary landing ships and craft for the new operation; and those recently allocated to Mountbatten for the offensive across the Bay of Bengal, already discussed, had to be recalled for the purpose. Churchill's account of the conference in Eisenhower's villa at Tunis, where he was recovering from a sharp attack of pneumonia, on Christmas Day 1943,[39] is amplified most amusingly in the unpublished memoirs of Admiral Sir Manley Power, who was at the time Deputy Chief of Staff (Plans) to Sir John Cunningham. It was Power who produced, at very short notice, the paper about the situation regarding assault ships and craft which so commended itself to Churchill that (to try and reproduce his inimitable lisp) he referred to it as 'Thish is jusht what I want. Now gentlemen [to all the top service people present] can any of you take exsheption to theshe cogent argumentsh for retaining theshe vital veshells for thish great adventure?' – namely the assault at Anzio.[40] When none of the very distinguished company could pick the smallest hole in Power's paper Churchill telegraphed its contents home to the Chiefs of Staff, mentioning the name of its author – to Power's dismay. This of course produced a good-natured blast from Sir Andrew Cunningham when Power returned home at the end of the year – to the effect that he had usurped the functions of the COSs.[41]

The encounter between Power, who was only an Acting Captain at the time, and Churchill shows how his confidence could be won even by quite a junior officer who not only showed great knowledge and clear thinking, and the ability to express them on paper, but was prepared to give as good as he got in cut and thrust argument. Though allowance must be made for the fact that Power was an essential instrument in furthering Churchill's strong desire to carry out the amphibious assault at Anzio there is no doubt that he was much impressed by the young Captain. So much so that Power actually spent that Christmas evening sitting next to him on a sofa, drinking brandy and listening to 'a fascinatingly varied monologue from this extraordinary man' who, only a few days earlier, was alleged to have emerged from his coma long enough to mutter 'I shupposhe it ish fitting I should die beshide Carthage'.*

Early in January 1944 Power was called to a high-ups' conference at Marrakesh, where Churchill was convalescing, and when he demanded an appreciation of the Anzio operation Power refused to produce such a document behind his C-in-C's back. Whereupon Churchill ordered, and signed, an appointment placing Power on his own staff! After strongly protesting about this irregularity Power wrote the document explaining how the difficulties could be overcome – which so delighted Churchill that he asked the young Captain to lunch and put him on his left. Churchill next announced that the naval C-in-C was arriving and advised Power to meet him; on hearing which the latter said 'But he's not my C-in-C any longer since this morning!' Churchill then told General Hollis of the COS's secretariat to tear up the appointment to his own staff, Power reverted to his original status, and had to placate his C-in-C about these extraordinary goings on. Fortunately John Cunningham, who understood Churchill's methods very well, was tolerant about his Staff Officer's adventures in the field of Grand Strategy and in negotiations with the top hierarchy.[42]

The Anzio landings took place on 22 January 1944, the weather was kindly, complete surprise was achieved, and the assault forces were put ashore with only slight losses. Then, to Churchill's intense chagrin, the American general in command did not at once advance and seize the key Alban hills which commanded the approach to Rome. Instead he merely dug in and prepared his beachhead for defence against the expected counter-attack. As Churchill put it in a typically picturesque if somewhat mixed metaphor 'I had hoped that we were hurling a wild cat on to the shore, but all we had got was a stranded whale.'[43]

The German reaction was swift and violent, the beachhead was soon sealed off, and not until late in May did the Anzio forces break out and join hands with the Fifth Army advancing northwards. Rome fell on 4 June and then the advance became rapid – until General Alexander's forces were drastically reduced in order to reinforce the landings in the south of France (operation 'Anvil', later renamed 'Dragoon') which, on American insistence, had originally been planned to take place simultaneously with the Normandy landings, but which had to be post-

* See Lord Moran, Churchill; The Struggle for Survival 1940–1965 (Constable, 1966), pp. 148–58 for his doctor's account of his illness at Tunis and convalescence at Marrakesh. He does not mention the anecdote recorded by Admiral Power, so it may, like many Churchill anecdotes, be apocryphal. Power has told the author that he got the story from Commander 'Tommy' Thompson, Churchill's 'Flag Commander'.

poned until mid-August.

The long hold-up at Anzio and the diversions to 'Anvil' were bitter disappointments to Churchill, who had always wanted to press the Italian campaign to a successful and final conclusion; but he never made any complaints against Sir John Cunningham, whose staff had planned and executed operation 'Shingle' perfectly.

In September 1944, following a visit by Churchill, Sir John wrote to Sir Andrew Cunningham, that the Prime Minister had 'certainly put his finger well into our pie while he was here [presumably a reference to the conference at Marrakesh described by Power]. I think it was a pity he stayed so long with Alex[ander] who at the time was in one of his depressed moods – the result was that the PM formed very wrong impressions and became thoroughly indoctrinated with all the worst Eighth Army theories . . . [they] regard it as the Navy's sole job in life to be the answer to their prayer "Give us this day our daily bread" . . . They seem to lose all power of movement as soon as they get away from the sea, and to be disinclined to move at all unless they have got at least sixty days' supplies within a couple of miles of the front line.'[44]

As Churchill has himself published highly critical remarks about the scale of transport and supplies demanded by the army for the assault at Anzio it seems that the naval C-in-C's strictures were not without foundation.[45] Nor were the old inter-service jealousies entirely stilled at this time, as is shown by the entry in Sir Andrew Cunningham's diary towards the end of 1944 that he had received reports of the Air Ministry trying to take over all the Malta airfields. 'It is in fact well known,' he wrote, 'that they think of ousting the Navy from Malta by claiming all the airfields, and they are occupied in trying to establish posts for air marshals after the war.'[46] But Malta always had a special place in Cunningham's affections, and indeed in those of all naval men of the period, because of the gallantry of its people during the long siege of 1940-3.

In mid-June 1944 a successful combined operation mounted from Corsica won the strategically important island of Elba, thereby strengthening our hold on the Ligurian Sea and putting an end to tiresome attacks by German light craft on our vital coastal traffic. A month later the Allied armies captured Leghorn which, though badly wrecked, was soon restored sufficiently to serve as a valuable advanced base for the supply of the Fifth Army. Ancona on the Adriatic coast was captured a few days later, and served a similar purpose for the Eighth Army, besides facilitating offensive operations against German bases and coastal traffic on the Dalmatian coast. In mid-July the armies reached the 'Gothic Line', the last major German defence position in Italy running from just south of Spezia on the west coast to Pesaro on the Adriatic; but thereafter the reduction of General Alexander's strength, reluctantly accepted by Churchill on the recommendation of the COSs 'in the broadest interest of Anglo-American co-operation', and only after he had deployed all his gifts of eloquence and persuasion in the endeavour to convert President Roosevelt to his strategic purposes, brought the Army's offensive to a halt.[47]

Meanwhile early in February 1944 Churchill had proposed to the COSs that about a month after the invasion of Normandy an operation should be mounted to seize Bordeaux by a *coup de main*, and then follow it up with armoured divisions which he suggested moving initially to Morocco for the purpose. All this was to be done, he wrote, 'without prejudice to "Anvil"' (the invasion of the south of France), to which these forces were not allocated. 'It is silly', he continued, 'to go on as we are butting at only one place without trying to reap the immense opportunities which will be open almost everywhere else.' After receiving a prod from Churchill the COSs replied very dubiously regarding the possibility of capturing Bordeaux in the manner suggested, because it lies fifty miles up the River Gironde; but they tried to placate Churchill by admitting that his idea 'offers very great attractions'. In April Churchill renewed the pressure, arguing that as 'Anvil' in its original form was now dead his proposal, known as operation 'Caliph', should be carried out. Though the COSs tactfully agreed 'in principle' the project never reached the stage of detailed planning; and it was in fact plain that we did not possess anything like the shipping and landing craft needed – quite apart from the difficulty of mounting yet another combined operation.[48] In retrospect this certainly seems to have been one of Churchill's less practicable strategic brainwaves.

The scene now shifts to the Levant and the Aegean Islands from which we had been ignominiously expelled in November 1943. In the autumn of the following year the Germans began to reduce their island garrisons, and early in October they started to withdraw from Greece. On the 15th British warships, soon followed by supply ships to relieve the starving population, entered Piraeus, the port of Athens. The approaches to the Dardanelles, on which Churchill had so long cast covetous eyes, now came under Allied control; but as Turkey still remained neutral, and the need to supply the Russian armies through the Black Sea ports had been reduced in importance as a result of the great victories on the eastern front, the chance, and indeed the need, to exploit that route came too late to influence the land campaigns.

On the Greek mainland a terrible period of civil war between the various political factions began with the German withdrawal, and Churchill rushed in British troops to prevent the Communists gaining control of Athens. The Americans, still blindly unaware of Stalin's expansionist aims, and highly suspicious of British 'imperialism', refused any support for the measures Churchill deemed essential;[49] and apprehensions about our intervention were also aroused at home. However, when Churchill put the issue to the House of Commons on a vote of confidence on 8 December he was supported by a large majority (279–30). As he has himself given a graphic description of his courageous visit to Athens in order to find a satisfactory, if temporary, political solution there is no need to repeat the story here.[50] The ships in the eastern basin organized the liberation of Athens, the clearance of the numerous minefields in the Aegean and the supply of the Greek people with such promptitude and efficiency that no word of criticism or complaint was directed at the navy by Churchill.

Throughout this period Churchill's relations with the admirals responsible for a very wide variety of operations – from the major amphibious assault at Anzio to the activities of the coastal craft and other vessels in the Ligurian Sea, the Adriatic and Aegean were perfectly cordial. The year 1944 thus ended on a note of high success in the Mediterranean theatre, though Churchill never budged from his view that the diversion of forces from Italy to the 'Dragoon' landings was a major strategic error.

CHAPTER 13

Home Waters and the Atlantic Battle
1943-1944

In 1942-3 Churchill was under very heavy pressure from Stalin to increase and expedite the transport of supplies to Russia, and his patience, which was never an outstanding feature of his character, had plainly reached breaking point by the beginning of 1943. He then told Alexander and Pound that 'M. Maisky [the Soviet ambassador in London] is not telling the truth when he says I promised Stalin convoys of thirty ships in January and February . . . M. Maisky should be told that I am getting to the end of my tether with their repeated naggings and that it is not the slightest use trying to knock me about any more.'[1] The idea of Maisky knocking Churchill about certainly conjures up visions of an amusing scene. But when Pound told Churchill that, although the next of the new series of Arctic convoys (known as JW.52), would sail on time, only sixteen of the twenty ships intended to go would for various reasons be ready, he laconically minuted 'Lamentable' on the letter.[2] However, when Pound suggested that Admiral H. R. Stark, the commander of the US naval forces in Europe, should attend the meetings of the Anti-U-boat Warfare Committee in order to extend and improve British-American collaboration Churchill readily agreed.[3] In that same month Cherwell produced a paper on the growth of the U-boat fleet and the rate of shipping losses it was inflicting, and a long interchange between Churchill and the Admiralty ensued which shows very clearly the outlook of 'The Prof' on the bombing controversy. The Bay of Biscay air patrols were not, in his view, 'comparable in value with the immediate attack on Germany . . . It is difficult to compare quantitatively the damage done to any of the forty odd big German cities in a 1000 ton [sic] raid . . . with the advantage of sinking one U-boat out of 400 and saving 3 or 4 ships out of 5500. But it will surely be held in Russia as well as here that the bomber offensive must have more immediate effect on the course of the war in 1943.'[4] Such views probably carried considerable weight when the continued heavy shipping losses suffered early in the year intensified the long controversy over long-range aircraft for Coastal Command. At about this time the question of obtaining the use of air bases in Eire came up. The Admiralty would of course have liked to gain such facilities; but the general view was that we should 'accept Eire aerodromes as a gift but not fight for them'; and there the matter was left.[5]

One result of the catastrophic losses suffered in 1942 and early 1943 was that the question of establishing a unified and centralized command for the Atlantic Battle was debated in Parliament; but the Admiralty had no use for such a proposal.[6] Then in April H. L. Stimson, the American Secretary of War, proposed the appointment of a Supreme Commander to direct all the Allied forces engaged in the Atlantic Battle. Pound wrote to Churchill that he was 'definitely against' such an idea, and held that extension of the Western Approaches Command's area of responsibility further west and the establishment of the Allied-U-boat Advisory Board (an Anglo-American body) would meet the needs adequately.[7] A short time later Sir Charles Portal, the CAS, told Churchill that the organization and control of the American air forces stationed on their east coast were so fragmented and inefficient that he favoured the idea of 'Unified Air Control', but only after the Americans had established 'a strong and effective air command analogous to our Coastal Command and under the operational control of their Navy Department'[8] – which perhaps gave too roseate a view of the advantages of the British system. However, Pound went along with Portal and told Churchill that if a British officer was appointed Supreme Commander friction with the Americans was inevitable, and to appoint an American to the post was 'unthinkable' because there was none equipped with the necessary knowledge and experience.[9]

As one surveys the vast mass of paper produced by the Admiralty, Air Ministry and other authorities on the Atlantic Battle at this time, and reads Churchill's reactions to such of them as reached him, it seems clear that, whereas on many difficult strategic issues he knew exactly what he wanted, he suffered from a distinct dichotomy on this one. For example only about three months after he had refused to countenance any reduction of the bombing offensive or the allocation of the new radar sets to Coastal Command he telegraphed to President Roosevelt that he proposed to tell Stalin that 'We are crippled for lack of [the] shipping' needed to launch the 'second front' in 1943; and a few weeks later he told Roosevelt 'I am extremely anxious about the shipping situation.'[10] This state of affairs was of course exactly what the naval staff had foreseen, and had represented, six to nine months earlier; and it is reasonable to feel that a stronger stand by Alexander and Pound would have brought Churchill to see what lay ahead at that time. This was, perhaps, the most far-reaching and tragic strategic error which can, at any rate in part, be laid at Churchill's door, since it was shortage of shipping that delayed every offensive by the United Nations in every theatre up to mid-1944, and so prolonged the struggle at the cost of inestimable suffering to the peoples of the occupied countries. The failure undoubtedly derived in part from the fact that by 1943 Pound was a very sick man indeed, and quite unfit to carry his great responsibilities. Captain (later Admiral of the Fleet Sir) Charles Lambe, the Director of Plans at this time, told the author that he was asked by some of the top members of the staff to represent this state of affairs to Sir Stafford Cripps, whom Lambe knew well, in the hope that he would pass it to Churchill.[11] But as the Prime Minister was then on bad terms with Cripps, as a result of his criticisms of the organization for the higher direction of the war, such an approach was not likely to achieve its purpose.* In any case the approach ought surely to have been made by A. V. Alexander, and not by a Captain RN, no matter how highly the latter was regarded.

In fact the turning point in the Atlantic came in May 1943, by which time two squadrons of very long-range American Liberators had been allocated to and manned by Coastal Command. They and the recently arrived escort aircraft carriers at last covered the 'air gap' south of Iceland, and it was chiefly their work and the fact that, after a long period of inability to decypher the German U-boat command's signals in 1942, we again broke the cypher early in the following year, that brought the decisive victory of May 1943 over the U-boats.[12] This climacteric did not of course make all shipping safe all over the world, and whenever losses occurred Churchill sent Alexander and Pound unfairly critical notes about them. For example when a convoy suffered heavily off Sierra Leone he wanted Admiral Edelsten, the ACNS responsible for trade defence, to be replaced by Admiral Somerville, who was then C-in-C, Eastern Fleet, 'at the earliest moment'.[13] Pound put things into better perspective by telling Alexander that since the institution of convoy in the area in question only eight out of 743 ships sailing in convoy had been sunk, and that as Edelsten 'bears no responsibility' for the recent losses the question of his relief should not be linked with them. Churchill thereupon gave way;[14] but the incident does illustrate his tendency to seek a scapegoat whenever things went wrong.

* On Cripps's criticisms of Churchill's war direction, culminating in his resignation of the office of Lord Privy Seal and from the War Cabinet in November 1942 see Churchill, *Second World War*, IV, pp. 497-503. Cripps accepted the Office of Minister of Aircraft Production without a seat in the War Cabinet.

The extent and decisiveness of the victory of May 1943 was, very naturally, not fully appreciated at once in London, and in July Pound gave orders that no ship involved in the Atlantic Battle was to be diverted or paid off without his approval.[15] In the same month, however, Cherwell produced statistics showing that whereas in the first half of 1942 every U-boat operating in the Atlantic had sunk two ships, in the corresponding period of the following year their accomplishments had only been half a ship each. Churchill asked if the Admiralty agreed, and on being told that Cherwell's figures were 'substantially correct' he sent his congratulations.[16] Yet in that same month he told Pound he was 'shocked' by long-range German aircraft sinking several large ships in a homeward convoy off western Spain, and Pound had once again to explain that, with the invasion of Sicily demanding huge resources, we simply could not be as strong everywhere as we would have liked.[17]

A curious feature of this period is the frequent pressure by the Admiralty for the RAF to bomb the German U-boat bases in western France, despite the fact that recent experience had proved that it was sea and air convoy escorts which inflicted most of the losses, and that the Air Staff were sceptical of such attacks achieving much against U-boats protected by very thick concrete shelters.[18] It was Professor P. M. S. Blackett who at this time produced the soundest and best argued case for the employment of our sea and air forces in the Atlantic Battle, and who instituted what came to be known as 'Operational Research' to arrive at scientifically based conclusions on such matters as the optimum size of convoys.[19] Unhappily he never gained the Prime Minister's ear to the extent that Cherwell did. At any rate the second half of 1943 provided clear indications that, although losses might occur on some distant route at any time, the main battle in the North Atlantic had been won.

While the Atlantic Battle was moving to its climax Churchill became highly critical of the work of the Fleet Air Arm. We saw earlier how in July 1942 Pound made Admiral Sir Frederick Dreyer, a retired officer with no experience of naval air work, Chief of the Naval Air Services – though without a seat on the Board.[20] Hostility to this extraordinary appointment, surely one of Pound's worst misjudgements of senior officers, was soon aroused in Parliament and the Press; and it finally became clear that Dreyer would have to go. Intimation of this intention produced, however, several long letters of self-justification from Dreyer to Pound; and he even tried to get his case placed before the Prime Minister, whose reaction was deservedly severe.[21] 'It is high time', wrote Churchill, 'that the experiment of employing him at the head of the FAA was brought to a close';[22] and when Dreyer tried to get in touch with Churchill himself through Ismay he brought on his head a stinging rebuke from Pound, including a peremptory order to return the official papers evidently still in his possession.[23] Admiral D. W. Boyd, who had wartime experience of naval air work, was appointed Fifth Sea Lord with responsibility for the FAA and with a seat on the Board on 14 January 1943, and Dreyer disappeared from the scene unlamented – except by Pound who wrote a consolatory letter to his old friend.[24]

Churchill, however, remained antagonistic towards the FAA, and in July he wrote to Alexander that it was 'a rather pregnant fact' that it had lost only thirty killed out of a strength of 45,000 in the three months ending 30 April[25] – a suggestion which reminds one of his protest to Wavell over the evacuation of British Somaliland in 1940, and Wavell's reply that 'a big butcher's bill was not necessarily evidence of good tactics' – which Churchill never forgave.[26] In the case of the FAA casualties Admiral Boyd wrote 'I am naturally astonished at the spirit of the PM's minute'; but after the staff had all expressed their indignation it was decided not to send a reply. This appears to be a case where judicious stalling by Pound averted a row with Churchill.[27] None the less his scepticism regarding the work of the FAA was evidently not assuaged, and the new Fifth Sea Lord had a difficult time with Cripps, the Minister of Aircraft Production, as well as with Churchill. Boyd was forced to admit that his department of the Admiralty was desperately short of good men, because 'all the real cream [of the FAA] were expended in the first two years of the war'.[28] Though he probably had the heavy losses suffered in the Norwegian campaign of 1940 chiefly in mind in truth the trouble went much further back – to the loss of nearly all the navy's senior aviators when the RNAS was taken over by the RAF in 1918.[29]

In addition to his attack on the Fleet Air Arm in mid-1943 Churchill proposed a large reduction in the navy's requirement for more men; and it was of course true that after nearly four years of war the Empire's resources of personnel were strained to the limit. However, with the great combined operations of 1943–4 in the offing theAdmiralty became extremely worried over the prospect of a heavy cut being imposed;[30] but when in mid-July Alexander and Pound presented the navy's case Churchill agreed to hold his hand.[31] His recommendations finally amounted to 190,000 men being allocated to the navy, which was only 2000 less than the Admiralty had asked for, and the Board readily accepted the compromise.[32] This is a case where the production of a well-presented case caused Churchill to change his mind, and Alexander expressed gratitude for his understanding.[33]

Churchill also took a very close interest in the naval building programme for 1944, deprecating the tendency to go for 'bigger and better destroyers' and wanting to stick firmly to what he called 'the hunter class' of vessel.[34] 'The short term programme', he wrote, 'must not be prejudiced by these remote constructions.'[35] It is fairly plain that, whereas by 1943 the Board of Admiralty was very naturally mindful of the post-war strength of the navy, Churchill still wanted our limited building and engineering capacity used for such ships as were likely to be finished in time to take part in the war. It is interesting to find that in the report of the Admiralty's Future Building Committee, which was circulated early in 1943, the Deputy First Sea Lord, Admiral C. E. Kennedy-Purvis, described the aircraft carrier as now being 'the core of the fleet'.[36] Though some members of the staff wanted the description of the new arm watered down Kennedy-Purvis refused to alter it. When, however, in the following year Cherwell sent the First Sea Lord a paper on the impossibility of battleships surviving heavy bombing attacks, Sir Andrew Cunningham replied that Cherwell 'had written much the same before the war';[37] which makes it appear that Cunningham was by no means wholly in agreement with his deputy on this issue.

In October 1943 the Admiralty wanted to scrap most of the elderly American destroyers which had come to us as a result of the 'destroyers for bases' deal of 1941 and which were requiring constant refits, as well as some worn out British ships. Churchill at once objected that 'I do not consider you have any right to strike off these forty vessels', though he was prepared for them to be paid off and kept in reserve unmanned. Alexander replied that to keep such ships in service was 'doubly wasteful' – both of manpower and repair facilities; to which all he got from Churchill was 'Noted'.[38]

In November 1943 Churchill returned to the charge about the navy's building programme and manpower needs. He told Alexander he was 'at first sight wholly in favour' of building light fleet carriers instead of ships of the much larger and more expensive fleet class, and he would discuss the whole matter with the First Lord and Controller; which shows that he still clung to some of the responsibilities for detailed naval affairs which he had carried as First Lord. But he was horrified by the request for 288,000 more men for the fleet and 71,000 for the shipyards in 1944, and considered that, in view of the many far-reaching changes which had taken place in the war at sea 'one would expect . . . it would be possible to make very sensible reductions even in the existing personnel of the navy'. The correspondence continued into the New Year, when Alexander offered to cut the light fleet carriers from the eight approved in 1943 to four, or even to two.[39] In fact a compromise was reached, and six ships of this class had entered service by the end of the war, two of them as 'maintenance carriers'.

Admiral Sir Bruce Fraser succeeded Sir John Tovey as C-in-C, Home Fleet on 8 May 1943, and Tovey took over the Nore Command, which was to play a big part in the invasion of Europe. Churchill had entertained a strong admiration, even affection for Fraser ever since he had proved a patient, adaptable and very successful Controller of the Navy during Churchill's tenure as First Lord. Towards Tovey he felt, as was mentioned earlier, much less warmly, and it is amusing to find that in the following year, when difficulties with Admiral E. J. King, USN, were becoming acute, Churchill put forward a proposal to send Tovey to Washington in place of Sir Percy Noble, who had been head of the British naval mission for two strenuous years and was pressing to return home. Churchill, obviously recalling his brushes with Tovey over the Atlantic Battle and the Arctic convoys in 1942, evidently considered he would prove a worthy opponent to the redoubtable 'Ernie' King. 'Admiral Tovey', he told Alexander 'would put up a splendid fight there [in Washington].'[40]* But in the end it was Sir James Somerville who relieved Noble, while Tovey received a cordial message from Churchill thanking him 'for the excellent work you have done for us at the head of the Home Fleet', and expressing the hope of visiting him in his new command.[41] As in Somerville's case, one does feel that Churchill's judgement of admirals' qualities or failings were subject to somewhat violent oscillations.

Plans to launch a cross-Channel invasion took up a great deal of the time of Churchill and the COSs in the period covered by this chapter, and it is well known how, despite pressure from Stalin and from the American COSs, Churchill won his case for the next amphibious assaults to take place in the Mediterranean theatre at the Casablanca Conference of January 1943. However, planning for the cross-Channel operation went on all the time, and included an emergency strike

---

* In 1944 I was serving in the British Mission in Washington, and was sent back to London to explain the difficulties we were having with King to Admiral Cunningham. After hearing me out Cunningham said 'Roskill, we'd get on better if you'd shoot Ernie King!' To which I, knowing 'ABC' quite well, replied 'Is that an order, Sir, or merely a suggestion?'; whereupon he good humouredly turned me out of his office.

(known as 'operation Sledgehammer') if the situation on the Russian front deteriorated markedly. In August 1943 it became necessary to consider who should be appointed Allied Naval Commander, Expeditionary Force (ANCXF) for the major assault, now scheduled for 1 May 1944, and Pound put forward, rather surprisingly, Admiral Sir Charles Little as his first choice.[42] Little was an able officer of high intelligence, and had done well as C-in-C, China 1936-8 and as Second Sea Lord, with responsibility for the whole of the navy's personnel, during the first two years of the war. Then he had gone to the USA as head of the British Naval Mission, and thus lacked recent sea experience. Churchill replied (from the Château Frontenac, Quebec where the first Quebec Conference was in progress at the time) that he was 'both surprised and concerned to learn that the proposals for the appointments of Admiral Little and Air Chief Marshal Leigh-Mallory were made to the US COSs without my being consulted as Minister of Defence', which practice had, he continued, 'been the invariable rule'. He then went on to criticize Little severely, saying that 'I do not consider him in any way fitted for operational affairs, or indeed for any matters requiring capacity, originality or breadth of mind' – which was a good deal less than fair to the admiral. However Churchill was certainly right to declare that he was 'sure that Admiral Ramsay would be a far better appointment for this purpose on account not only of his natural abilities but [of] his unique experience in conducting a great overseas descent'. He would therefore only allow Little's appointment to stand until the Supreme Commander was designated; and he was very resentful about why 'the two appointments should figure in the Report of the COSs', because they 'can only be made between Heads of Governments with their approval'.[43] On the day before he received this blast Pound had in fact written to Churchill that the command appointments for 'Overlord' had been approved by the Combined COSs 'before you spoke to me on the subject'. He was 'satisfied that, at the present time, the arrangement by which Admiral Little is naval commander is best'; but if a change appeared desirable later he would 'bring it to your notice at once'.[44] Presumably in deference to Churchill's wishes the appointments were not mentioned in the final report of the Combined COSs;[45] and early in October Pound evidently warned Little that his appointment was not to stand. A week later he was told the news tactfully in an official Admiralty letter.[46] Little took the disappointment very well, saying that he would 'still serve the Board in any way it chooses', and they would hear no more from him on the subject of the disputed appointment.[47] The argument about who should command the naval side of the Expeditionary Force became entangled with other Flag appointments, notably the relief of Somerville by Fraser in command of the Eastern Fleet; but those problems will be recounted later. In October 1943 Sir Bertram Ramsay was officially appointed ANCXF, and as Little was by that time C-in-C, Portsmouth, the shore command which played the greatest part in the launching of 'Overlord', he was in the position to fulfil the promise given by his predecessor to give Ramsay, if he were appointed ANCXF, all possible help.

On 20 February Churchill wrote to Alexander and Cunningham that he had understood 'it was settled that Admiral Ramsay should return to the Active List before Operation Overlord'. Cunningham replied that, as far as he could recall no definite decision had been made, but that when it was discussed the 'repercussions, particularly on the promotion of junior officers' had been pointed out. This was a fair point, as the permitted number of Flag Officers on the Active List was limited, and if Ramsay were included in them others would suffer. Churchill replied that, as he had believed the matter to be settled, he had mentioned it to Ramsay over dinner; and so it had to stand.[48] It is, however, difficult not to feel that Churchill acted too precipitately in 'jumping the gun' over a matter which concerned not only the Admiralty's reputation for fairness in promotions but the future careers of many senior officers. The official letter telling Ramsay of his reinstatement was not sent until 30 March – which suggests that the Admiralty continued to feel uneasy about the matter.[49]

It was while Churchill was in Washington after the first Quebec Conference that Pound told him, with moving dignity, that he had suffered a severe stroke (which his medical advisers had actually long foreseen) and which necessitated his immediate resignation. He died in London on 21 October 1943 (Trafalgar Day). Enough has been said, here and elsewhere, about his qualities and failings to make it unnecessary to reopen the question. Churchill's tribute that he was 'my trusted naval friend' may serve as his epitaph.[50] In his memoirs Churchill argued that his offer of the post of First Sea Lord to Admiral Sir Bruce Fraser, then in command of the Home Fleet, arose from doubts regarding whether A. V. Alexander's first choice Sir Andrew Cunningham 'could . . . be spared from this scene [the Mediterranean] at a time when so much was going forward and all operations expanding'.[51] But there is strong evidence that this was less than the whole truth, and that Churchill did not want Cunningham as his principal naval colleague, presumably because he scented danger on account of the fearlessness with which 'ABC' had expressed his views on many of Churchill's 'prodding signals' and wildcat strategic ideas during his first term as C-in-C, Mediterranean. It probably does not go too far to suggest that Churchill considered he might prove another Jacky Fisher, and so lead to a repetition of the explosion of May 1915. Support for this view is provided by Alexander telling Cunningham after the war that, when he was pressing the admiral's claims to the office of First Sea Lord, he became aware of what he called 'Churchill's fear of the Board of Admiralty'; or, as Cunningham himself put it, he was 'apparently frightened that my arrival at the Admiralty would mean a very independent line' being taken by the Board.[52] According to Alexander when Churchill finally gave his consent to the appoint-ment he said 'All right. You can have your Cunningham, but if the Admiralty don't do as they are told I will bring down the Board in ruins even if it means my coming down with it.'[53] Though the sug-gestion of 'fear' on Churchill's part is surely an exaggeration the rest of the anecdote, taken with other evidence regarding the effect on Churchill of the events of May 1915, and the fact that from the begin-ning of the war he was determined not to have strong men as First Lord and First Sea Lord, rings true. In the end Sir Andrew Cunningham took over the vacant desk on 15 October 1943 – in time to pay a brief visit to his dying predecessor.[54]

Here it is relevant to mention a disagreement between two top admirals into which Churchill did not enter at the time, though it probably played a part in his later proposals regarding Flag appoint-ments. On 3 April 1944 carrier aircraft of the Home Fleet made a strong attack (operation 'Tungsten') on the giant battleship *Tirpitz*, which was lying in Altenfiord, north Norway, and still constituted a serious threat to our Arctic convoys. Considering the strength of the defences and the difficulties always experienced in carrying out air operations in those high latitudes, because of the very uncertain and variable weather, the attack was a success. Fourteen hits and one very near miss were obtained; but the bombs then carried by naval aircraft were not heavy enough to do lethal damage to the very stoutly built and heavily protected battleship.[55] Cunningham's whole instinct always was that once an enemy had been damaged a second blow should be struck as quickly as possible, before he had been allowed time to recover from the first; and on Fraser's return to Scapa he accordingly pressed him to repeat the attack as soon as possible. Cunningham's diary recounts what followed:

13 April 1944

I called up Bruce Fraser about repeat 'Tungsten', and found him in a most truculent and obstinate mood. He had held a meeting with his admirals and captains and made the decision that 'Tungsten' was not to be repeated. I reasoned with him and pointed out that Cs-inCs' decisions were not irrevocable and that the Admiralty must be allowed some voice in what operations were to be carried out. He did not admit this and said if we were not satisfied we must get another C-in-C, and in fact indicated he would haul his flag down if ordered to repeat 'Tungsten'. I told him to sleep on it and call me up in the morning.

I do not know what the underlying reason for this attitude is, to me a most untenable position to take up, but it may be that he resented very much being practically bludgeoned into 'Tungsten' originally and is determined to resist further pressure.

14 April

Called up Fraser 0945 and discussed the repeat 'Tungsten' operation. I understood him to acquiesce. BUT later [I was] told by VCNS [Admiral Sir Neville Syfret] Fraser refused to carry out the operation and if ordered [to do so] would haul down his flag. That of course could not be tolerated, but I held up the Admiralty signal ordering him to carry out the operation and drafted one to him to come to London and see me and discuss things. This to give him another chance.

Later. I found wiser councils [sic] had prevailed . . . and some manoeuvring on a lower level [had] made Fraser more tractable.

In fact the second-in-command, Home Fleet, Admiral Sir Henry Moore, sailed again on 21 April to repeat the attack, but on arriving at the flying-off position he found the weather conditions wholly unfavourable, and after waiting as long as his destroyers' fuel endurance permitted he diverted his aircraft to other targets. It is difficult to assess the rights and wrongs of this squall at the top of the naval hierarchy. Perhaps it was merely a case, in Kipling's words, where 'two strong men stand face to face, though they come from the ends of the earth';[56] but it does remind one of the rows between admirals earlier in the twentieth century, some of which have been mentioned here,* but which did not, fortunately, often recur during World War II.

As the build up for operation 'Overlord' (known as 'Bolero') went on in 1943 and 1944 Churchill very naturally took the liveliest interest in every aspect of the vast undertaking, and his minutes and memoranda poured in on the Admiralty and the COS Committee in an unceasing

* See pp. 21-22.

stream. For example in February 1944 he wrote to Cunningham at length on 'the great importance of a bombarding squadron', stressing that 'high velocity [naval] guns are particularly suited for the smashing of concrete pill boxes'. 'Here is the true use', he continued, 'for the *Ramillies* class', which he wanted deployed close inshore for the purpose. In fact, however, naval guns were not particularly well suited for such purposes, because of their flat trajectories – as had been demonstrated at Gallipoli in 1915. Though the handicap could be lessened by the use of reduced instead of full charges Cunningham replied that the waters off the assault beaches were too shallow to permit the use of heavy ships close inshore, and he preferred to use smaller ships whose rate of fire was higher.[57] As was his wont Churchill was not easily put off, and in March he demanded that Cunningham should send him a statement of the ships he intended to employ for bombardment. They did include four battleships and two heavy gun monitors, for use at long ranges, as well as many cruisers, destroyers and gunboats to work closer inshore.[58] It is noteworthy that Cunningham's replies to Churchill's minutes were usually a good deal shorter and more firmly worded than Pound's had been.

Perhaps the most important issue concerning the launching of the 'second front' was whether the assault should take place in the Pas de Calais area, where the sea passage was shortest and continuous air cover could be provided from home bases but the defences were strong and the beaches ill-suited to landing craft, or whether it should be made further west on the Normandy coast in Seine Bay. In the early discussions the Pas de Calais was, as Sir James Butler has recorded, 'generally favoured' by the Army and Air Force; but Mountbatten 'thought it entirely unsuitable and all along advocated the Cherbourg area'.[59] In the end he won his case, and in July 1943 General F. E. Morgan, the Chief of Staff to the Supreme Allied Commander (as yet undesignated) recommended that, after taking full account of the advantages of the Pas de Calais, 'our initial landing on the continent should be effected in the Caen area . . .'[60] The other vital issue was that, as there was no adequate harbour in the vicinity of the assault area, and the early capture of Cherbourg could not be guaranteed, the assault forces 'would have to take their harbour along with them'.[61] This was the genesis of the famous 'Mulberry' project. The original idea dates to the end of 1941, when Mountbatten joined the Combined Operations headquarters. It was revived, in a rather different form, by Commodore John Hughes-Hallet who had been lent to General Morgan by the DCO. Mountbatten gave the concept his enthusiastic support and drove ahead with the plans and experiments needed to bring it to fruition. For example in August 1943 he circulated a paper pointing out that, as the enemy would appreciate the impossibility of maintaining the invasion force except by using a harbour 'It is, therefore, of vital importance that we should be able to improvise port facilities at an early date'; and he went on to specify 'the basic requirements' to produce the 'Mulberries' and make them effective.[62] Mountbatten's part in these vitally important issues is relevant to this study because, when he reviewed his relations with Churchill in retrospect, he wrote that the more he thought about the matter the more he believed 'that what really attracted him to me was the fact that he knew I was fighting on my own a strong battle . . . to get the site of the invasion shifted from the Pas de Calais to the Arromanches area . . . He was also wildly enthusiastic about the "Mulberry" harbours.'[63]. Though the various factors which gave Churchill such great confidence in the young admiral can hardly be dissected and analysed, there can be little doubt that his part in the planning and preparations for 'Overlord' was very influential.

The assault was launched on 6 June and achieved both strategic and tactical surprise.[64] Even Stalin was moved to express to Churchill his admiration for the success of an undertaking unlike any other in the history of warfare for 'its vast conception, and its masterly execution'.[65] Soon after the initial assaults had succeeded Churchill renewed his pressure for more heavy bombarding ships; but Cunningham replied that 'The position in Overlord is satisfactory', though he was resentful of the American Admiral E. J. King having transferred most of his country's ships to support the projected landing in the south of France. Churchill wrote that he was 'quite ready to complain' about this provided that 'our house is in order' regarding making every possible ship available.[66]

On 19 June a quite unseasonable but violent gale struck the assault area, created havoc among the hundreds of landing craft crowded inside the artificial harbours, and did such severe damage to the American one that its use was abandoned. It may have been the strain produced by this untoward event which produced a tiff between Churchill and Cunningham on the 22nd. 'I had some firm exchanges with the PM about bombarding ships,' wrote the latter in his diary. 'He must poke his nose into what doesn't concern him. However he got little change out of me. He suggested I made him complain to the President about Admiral King's unilateral action in removing his forces from Overlord. I told him quite plainly that I had not wished or asked him to signal to the President.'[67] Next day, answering an inquiry about the effects of the gale, Cunningham replied that 'we have received a setback amounting to between one and two weeks'; and in fact, thanks to emergency measures, the full rate of unloading was restored before the end of July. Churchill was of course watching the situation anxiously, and Cherwell evidently produced for him some alarming statistics. Churchill told Alexander and Cunningham that he had received complaints from the American Army, and wanted 'a sort of Inspector Admiral for landing craft repairs' to be appointed 'with authority to push people around'. When Alexander deprecated such an idea Churchill wrote 'I am disappointed by your Minute' and asked for figures showing losses and repairs.[68] Admiral W. F. Wake-Walker, the Controller of the Navy, thereupon told Cunningham that '. . . The fact is it [the repair situation] was never bad, and if the Americans are pleased it is because they have just discovered what they could have discovered before, and it would have been better if they had done so before they started complaining. I still have not the least idea where the PM's figures came from, nor what they represent. I think they are probably on a par with a good many of the Paymaster General's [i.e. Cherwell's] statistics as regards value.' A more tactfully worded reply was sent by Alexander to Churchill.[69]

Also in July 1944 Churchill resurrected a World War I idea for using light nets to catch U-boats, and when Cunningham said that their use inside anchorages would hamper our own craft he minuted 'Well, do not say I did not tell you.'[70] In fact the numbers of escort vessels and Coastal Command aircraft deployed to deal with the U-boats coming from their bases in western France was so great that few of them even reached the assault area, and the damage they did was insignificant.[71]

After the Anglo-American forces had broken out of the beach-heads on 25 July a very rapid advance across western France followed. Paris was liberated a month later and Brussels was captured on 3 September. Churchill quickly demanded 'What are the Navy doing on the west flank of the Armies? I should have thought they would have been very lively all along the Atlantic shores of the Brest peninsula . . . As it is they seem to be doing very little except to fight on the NE flank . . . Admiral Ramsay must not weary of well doing . . . I am convinced that opportunities are passing.' Cunningham sent, what was for him, a fairly long answer covering one and a half pages and ending 'I think you will see from the above that without advertising its operations [probably a dig at the RAF's publicity campaign] the Navy is playing a full part on the West flank of the Armies and will continue to do so.' To which Churchill answered 'Thank you.'[72] The First Sea Lord soon followed that up with an account of successes against the U-boats, on which Churchill minuted 'Good'.[73]

The diversion of a large proportion of General Alexander's forces from Italy to the landings on the south coast of France frustrated one of Churchill's most strongly held strategic purposes – namely to launch an assault across the Adriatic to the Istrian peninsula, and thence advance through the 'Ljubljana Gap' to the Danube valley which, as he well knew, commands the whole of central Europe. Early in September he told the COSs that 'It remains however common to all contingencies that we should have powerful forces in Austria and from Trieste northwards at the close of the German war, and should not yield Central and Southern Europe entirely to Soviet ascendancy or domination. This is a matter of high political consequence, but also has serious military potentialities.' It was therefore in his view wrong further to weaken Alexander's army because 'The possibility of making an amphibious descent from Ancona or Venice – if we get it – upon Istria, holds a very high place in my thoughts.'[74] The COSs however warned him that 'We feel bound to say that we do not think the US Chiefs of Staff will be impressed with the military value of an assault on Istria.'[75] Though Churchill deployed all his formidable forensic and rhetorical gifts in that cause the American President refused to yield.[76] Roosevelt held firmly to his own COSs' view that absolute priority should be given to the expulsion of the Germans from France. Which of them was right on this issue will long be debated, but it is fair to mention that the communications through the Ljubljana Gap were so primitive that it is very doubtful whether they could have supported a large army; but Churchill was always inclined to ignore, or at least play down logistic considerations.*

The Admiralty took no part in the strategic argument except in so far as it came before the COS Committee; but Churchill's idea to switch the 'Dragoon' assault to the Bay of Biscay with the object of capturing Bordeaux aroused no enthusiasm in naval circles because the reorganization required would have been impossible in the short time available. Doubtless it was this disagreement and the many other

* The distinguished American historian Samuel Eliot Morison, author of the multi-volume *History of United States Naval Operations in the Second World War*, comes down strongly against the likelihood of the strategy favoured by Churchill achieving success. He points out that the communications he proposed to use were easily defensible. See Morison's study *American Contributions to the Strategy of World War II* (Oxford UP, 1958), pp. 33-5.

difficult issues which were putting such a great strain on the Prime Minister at this time which caused him to show himself at his worst. Extracts from Cunningham's diary will illustrate what this meant. On 6 July he wrote 'Meeting with the PM to discuss Alexander's operations in Italy and strategy for the war against Japan. There is no doubt the PM was in no state to discuss anything. Very tired and too much alcohol. Meeting started unprofitably by Brooke [CIGS] calling him to order for undermining Generals in command by his criticisms at Cabinet meetings [phraseology slightly amended]. This obviously hurt him badly. But he was in a terrible mood. Rude and sarcastic. I had a couple of blows up with him . . .' On 1 September Cunningham wrote 'In closed session [of COSs] I brought up and spoke strongly about the PM's private telegram to [General] Alexander asking him if he was getting proper naval support . . .'; and on the 8th 'COS meeting at 1030 followed by one with PM. He was in his worst mood. Accusing the COSs of ganging up against him and keeping papers from him and so on . . . The worst of it is his feeling against the Americans [doubtless over 'Dragoon'] whom he accuses of doing the most awful things against the British.' Yet only a few days later at the second Quebec Conference the same diarist recorded 'had a meeting with the PM at 1830 and found him in a mood of sweet reasonableness' – a change which he repeated almost verbatim at the end of October.[77]

Though Churchill was as bitterly disappointed by his failure to get the Americans to accept his strategy for the Italian campaign in 1944 as he had been by their refusal to help in the Aegean operations of the previous year he was certainly right in his assessment of Soviet aims in central Europe; and despite all the efforts he had made to support the Russians in their vast land campaigns he undoubtedly wanted their final frontier to be fixed as far to the east as possible. The great victories won by the Soviet armies in 1944 and their steady advance westwards naturally brought such matters into the strategic and diplomatic foreground. Early in the year lengthy exchanges took place between Churchill and the Admiralty and between him and Roosevelt about the transfer to Russia of some of the Italian warships which had come into our hands after the fall of Mussolini – as had been agreed at the Teheran Conference. A Soviet request that they should be handed over *in Russia* raised strong objections in London – because it would be very difficult for us to steam them there ourselves, and if the Italians were ordered to do so they would probably mutiny.[78] Churchill finally proposed to offer Stalin one of the old *R. Class* British battleships and eight elderly destroyers, to which the Americans were asked to add a cruiser, instead of the Italian ships – an offer which Stalin accepted 'with a growl' as Churchill put it.[79]

Other troubles with the Russians arose over the savage sentences imposed on British sailors and merchant seamen who had been arrested for offences such as drunkenness while in Russian ports. The Admiralty naturally wanted such victims of Soviet 'justice' to be released and sent home; but when Eden suggested a strongly worded telegram to Stalin on the subject Churchill minuted 'Alas I cannot send such a telegram. It would embroil me with Bruin on a small point when so many large ones are looming up. He would only send an insulting argumentative answer.' So Eden was told to 'go on barking away through the diplomatic channel', and 'to keep Parliamentary questions [on the subject] going'.[80] Trouble about handing over the ships continued however. In May Churchill told Alexander and Cunningham 'Do not hesitate to be blunt with these Russians when they become unduly truculent . . . It is for the Russians to show gratitude rather than for us to show deference . . . There are all sorts of ways of making people feel you resent their insults' – an art at which Churchill was of course a past master.[81] But he was insistent that when the ships to be handed over actually sailed from British ports to north Russia they should be provided with adequate escorts, since the loss of any of them was bound to produce serious repercussions.[82]

Relations with Russia certainly deteriorated sharply in 1944, largely as a result of Soviet intransigence over the future of Poland and their callous refusal to help when the Warsaw rising took place in July; but the convoys to north Russia none the less continued, and with only slight losses.* Long term mistrust of Soviet intentions was not, however, limited to Churchill, since in October Cunningham recorded in his diary that Portal, Ismay and he had strongly objected to a paragraph in a paper by Eden on the dismemberment of Germany saying that the COSs 'must not consider Russia as a possible enemy'.[83] Nor were British anxieties mollified by Roosevelt's very evident belief that he could handle Stalin better than anyone else, and that British imperialism was a greater threat to the ideals he stood for than Russian expansionism.

Operation 'Dragoon' finally took place on 15 August – nine weeks after the Normandy landings; and one may doubt whether it had appreciable influence on the strength of German resistance in the west.

* Ten convoys comprising 286 ships sailed for north Russia in 1944 and only three merchantmen and three escorts were sunk. See Roskill, *War at Sea*, III, Part II, Appendix R.

Cunningham recorded a conversation with Churchill towards the end of the year during which he implied that the historical verdict on 'Dragoon' would be unfavourable – to which the admiral replied that 'it would depend on who wrote the history'. Thereupon Churchill declared 'that he intended to have a hand in that'[84] – an intention which he amply fulfilled, though without by any means achieving universal acceptance of what he wrote.

On 4 September Montgomery's 21st Army Group captured the great port of Antwerp, and found it virtually intact. Here then was the opportunity to solve the long-standing and serious difficulty of supplying the Anglo-American armies through the distant ports of western France or through the recently captured but badly damaged ports on the Channel coast. Cunningham and Ramsay at once appreciated the vital importance of the army rapidly clearing the enemy from the banks of the Scheldt, so that the eighty miles of estuary and river could be swept clear of mines and ships of all types sent up to the port. But Montgomery's eyes were fixed on the possibility of his 'narrow front' thrust eastwards to the Ruhr and on to Berlin; while Churchill merely urged on Cunningham, after Dieppe had been captured on 1 September that 'the most active policy should be pursued by the Navy'[s] aid and share in every military success' – a need of which the First Sea Lord was very much aware. He accordingly replied that 'this is also the Navy's wish and active steps to that end are constantly being taken'.[85] On the 7th Cunningham wrote in his diary '. . . Again impressed on the COSs that Antwerp, though completely undamaged, was as much use to us as Timbuctoo unless the entrance and other forts were silenced and the banks of the Scheldt occupied. I fear this is being overlooked by the generals.' Nearly a month later he wrote that, after a visit by Ramsay, 'The fact appears to be that Montgomery has not given the clearing of the estuary of the Scheldt the attention it should have had and Ike [Eisenhower], though realizing the urgency has not succeeded in compelling Montgomery [to do so].'[86] At a conference in France attended by General Brooke on 6 October 'Bertie Ramsay', wrote Cunningham, 'did some straight talking about Montgomery's failure to clear the estuary of the Scheldt. Eisenhower apparently took the blame on himself. He would . . . It is extraordinary that the generals will pay no attention to our warnings . . .'* Ramsay's forcefully expressed views on the opening of the Scheldt may provide

* In his memoirs Montgomery admits that he erred over delaying the clearance of the banks of the Scheldt. *The Memoirs of Field Marshal Montgomery* (Collins, 1958) p. 297.

the clue to a cryptic entry in Cunningham's diary for 7 November. 'The PM', he wrote, 'wants Ramsay away from SHAEF [Supreme Headquarters Allied Expeditionary Force]! Why?'[87] Unfortunately no answer to his question has been found.

Though Churchill had left for the second Quebec Conference on 5 September and did not return until the 25th, and doubtless had many other important issues on his mind, if ever there was a case in which he should have given firm strategic directions to Montgomery, through Eisenhower and the Combined COSs of course, it was surely this. But the messages sent from Quebec contain no insistence from him on the importance of clearing the banks of the Scheldt, and it was not until the end of November that the army completed the job and the river was open to traffic.* If failure to give the Atlantic Battle the necessary priority in 1942 was the most grievous strategic error by the Allies, the long delay over opening the Scheldt two years later was of little less importance because, had it been avoided, it too might well have shortened the war.

On 2 January 1945 the invasion forces suffered a tragic loss when Admiral Ramsay was killed in an air crash in France. A. V. Alexander at once proposed Admiral Sir Harold Burrough as his successor. He had done very well in the critical Malta convoy of August 1942 and had been in command at Gibraltar since December 1943; but Churchill at first jibbed at the necessity 'to keep this large independent staff in existence now that the cross-Channel operations can quite properly return to the Admiralty and normal authorities'. His further remark that 'it is affectation to pretend that a C-in-C in the Navy should be appointed who counts equally with General Montgomery' certainly shows extraordinary blindness regarding the vast and vital responsibility such an officer carried for the supply and support of the Allied armies in western Europe. It also reinforces the view expressed earlier that, despite describing himself as a 'Former Naval Person' in his telegrams to Roosevelt, his outlook always remained basically military.† Cunningham was much annoyed by Churchill's attitude to Burrough's appointment, remarking in his diary 'How he [Churchill] works in complete ignorance [of] and disregard for facts beats me.' But after

---

* For a full account of the question of clearing the Scheldt, and of the operations ultimately undertaken to get the river open to shipping see Roskill, *War at Sea*, III, Part II, pp. 142-53. The best general account of the whole story of the major error made by the Army after the capture of Antwerp is Cornelius Ryan, *A Bridge Too Far* (Hamish Hamilton, 1974), Part I.

† See p. 20.

he and Alexander had talked the matter over with Churchill, and had explained the problems faced by the navy, he declared himself 'quite agreeable to the immediate filling of Admiral Ramsay's post by Admiral Burrough'. Eisenhower, who had shown himself 'well disposed about this' was, Churchill wrote, to be notified 'in the regular way'.[88] So ended the last serious dispute to arise over the planning and execution of operation 'Overlord'.

CHAPTER 14

The Indian Ocean and the Far East
1944

The succession of defeats and disasters suffered early in 1942 culminated, as we saw earlier, in the withdrawal of the Eastern Fleet from Ceylon to Kilindini (Mombasa) in Kenya, where it was at least well placed to safeguard the convoys to the Middle East. But the heavy calls for naval support for the great combined operations of 1943 in the Mediterranean led to its strength being so drastically run down that no offensive operations were possible, and it was not until September that Admiral Somerville was able to move his main base back to Ceylon. Even so reinforcements substantial enough to enable control of the Indian Ocean and Bay of Bengal to be regained did not reach him until early in the following year.

The many troubles which had beset the South-East Asia Command as a result of the disasters of 1942 raised doubts at home about whether the system whereby the Commanders-in-Chief of the forces of the three services formed a co-equal trinity was sound; and it was Leo Amery, the Secretary of State for India, who first suggested that the appointment of a Supreme Commander would bring about an improvement.[1]

In June 1943 Ismay drafted a telegram on the subject for Churchill to send to Roosevelt. In it Air Chief Marshal Sir Sholto Douglas was named as the first choice for Supreme Commander of the 'East Asia' theatre with the American General J. W. Stilwell as his Deputy. The Naval and Air Cs-in-C proposed were Sir James Somerville and Sir Keith Park, and although no name was put forward for the Army C-in-C Ismay suggested that, because only small American land forces were engaged, it should also go to the British. The organization of the High Command should, he suggested, 'follow as closely as possible, *mutatis mutandis*, the [General Douglas] MacArthur model' of the South-West Pacific Command. This draft evidently did not appeal to the Admiralty, since it was revised to include the statement that as the C-in-C, Eastern Fleet, Admiral Somerville 'has some responsibilities wider than those comprised within the East Asia Command, his relationship to the Supreme Commander should be the same as that which Admiral Cunningham bears to General Eisenhower' in the

Mediterranean theatre.[2] This was an issue which was to gain great importance placed in the foreground of the negotiations at an early stage; for the MacArthur and Eisenhower commands were organized and operated on totally different principles, the system of the former being authoritarian and highly centralized while the latter treated his service Cs-in-C as his trusted collaborators and was on intimate and cordial terms with all of them.

On 19 June Churchill telegraphed to Roosevelt in the sense of Ismay's second draft.[3] The President replied agreeing to a British Supreme Commander but rejecting Sir Sholto Douglas for the post. He also emphasized that Chiang Kai-shek was 'Generalissimo of the China Theatre', presumably to make it clear that he would not come under the new Supremo.[4] This qualification caused Ismay to suggest naming the new command area 'South-East Asia' instead of 'East Asia', a proposal which was accepted by Churchill, so leaving Chiang's position, by which the Americans set great store, unchanged.[5]

There now followed a prolonged interchange about who the new Supreme Commander should be. Sir Charles Portal, the CAS, was prepared to release Air Chief Marshal Tedder from the Mediterranean air command provided that Douglas succeeded him.[6] Field Marshal Sir John Dill, the head of the British Joint Staff Mission in Washington, represented that Sir Andrew Cunningham was 'the best man for the post', because he was on intimate terms with General Wavell, who had just been designated Viceroy of India, and with General Auchinleck, who was to succeed Wavell as C-in-C, India; and Cunningham also enjoyed 'great prestige' with the Americans.[7] Roosevelt telegraphed to Churchill describing Cunningham as 'especially acceptable'; but he was insistent that the command organization should follow the 'Eisenhower pattern'.[8] In mid-July Churchill decided not to persist with Douglas's nomination, because it would 'give great offence' to the Americans, but refused to release either Cunningham or Tedder from the Mediterranean[9] – despite Roosevelt having pressed for the former 'with complete and spontaneous unanimity on the part of all my advisers'.[10] In response to a request from Churchill the COSs next submitted the names of a number of possible candidates for the new appointment, with Somerville included among them.[11] However Churchill now had General Sir Oliver Leese in mind, and wanted Orde Wingate, whom he described as 'a man of genius and audacity', to command the army designated to reconquer Burma.[12]

In August Churchill asked Attlee, the Deputy Prime Minister who was in charge in London during the Washington or 'Trident' Conference, to consult Amery and Eden about Mountbatten's name being put forward, remarking that 'he knows the whole story from the top, he is young, enthusiastic and triphibious';[13] but Attlee replied that the view of those he had consulted was that Cunningham 'would be a better choice for this post'. However Churchill telegraphed that same day that Cunningham had told Pound 'it is not his line of country'.[14]

The way was now clear for Churchill to propose Mountbatten's appointment to the Americans, and that he did at the first Quebec or 'Quadrant' Conference.[15] On 15 August he telegraphed to Attlee that 'the reactions here to Dickie's proposed appointment are extremely favourable', whereupon the War Cabinet gave it their formal approval, subject only to the views of the Dominions being ascertained.[16] As their reaction was as favourable as that of the Americans Churchill submitted Mountbatten's name to the King, who 'cordially approved' the appointment and asked for his 'hearty congratulations' to be conveyed to his cousin. Mountbatten wrote to Churchill to thank him 'for giving me the finest chance any young man has ever been given in war', and describing how his 'worst fear' had been allayed by 'a typically thoughtful signal' he had just received from Somerville.[17] On reading Somerville's message Churchill wrote to him that it was 'up to the level of all your conduct in this war. There will be plenty of honour for all.'[18] Obviously the clash of November 1940 over the admiral's conduct of the action off Cape Spartivento, leading to Lord Cork's inquiry, was forgotten or forgiven.*

Although, as was told earlier, Pound had protested to Churchill about Mountbatten being made an Acting Vice-Admiral on appointment as Chief of Combined Operations, he did not apparently demur at his being given the higher rank of Acting Admiral on becoming a Supreme Commander, though he was insistent that his new rank should not be confirmed – presumably because to do so would affect, and possibly dislocate other promotions.[19] The appointment was accordingly announced by Churchill on 31 August, and was well received in the British Press and in Parliament, though protests soon appeared in some organs of the American Press.

The COSs next considered the organization and responsibilities of Mountbatten's staff. Their conclusions were, firstly, that he should form 'a relatively small, inter-service, inter-Allied personal staff which, with the assistance of the [service] Commanders-in-Chief and their staffs will formulate higher policy and outline plans'; and, secondly, that 'detailed planning should be the responsibility of the Naval, Military

* See pp. 169-70.

and Air Commanders-in-Chief under the general co-ordination of the Supreme Commander'.[20] It will be told later how things did not work out as the COSs had envisaged.

The big question mark in Royal Navy circles, and indeed in the COSs' organization, was of course how Mountbatten's elevation to the top of the Inter-Allied command hierarchy would be taken by the two very experienced admirals already on the station – Sir James Somerville, who had been in command of the Eastern Fleet since March 1942 and Sir Geoffrey Layton, the C-in-C, Ceylon from about the same date; for whereas Mountbatten was only forty-three years old and had not yet flown a flag afloat the average age of the service Cs-in-C in the South-East Asia Command was fifty-seven; and Somerville and Layton both had recent sea experience as Flag Officers. At first the auguries for harmonious co-operation appeared excellent. Somerville wrote to Pound that 'Dickie Mountbatten's appointment as Supreme Commander came as a bit of a surprise, but we all feel that his imagination and drive will be of the greatest value'; but he did add a warning that the new Supremo's command organization should follow that set up by Eisenhower in the Mediterranean, and should at all costs *not* be on the MacArthur model – which the British COSs had in fact favoured.[21] However Somerville told Pound he was confident that difficulties would not arise on that score because 'in all my past dealings with Dickie I have found that we see very much eye to eye.'[22] At about the time he wrote the foregoing letter Somerville assembled in Delhi all the small corps of naval staff officers responsible to him and for working with the Army and, in the words of one of those present, 'told us in his inimitable language that we had *got* to make the new set-up work, and that anyone who failed in that respect would be for the high jump.'[23] Lastly we have seen how Somerville's congratulatory message to Mountbatten himself eased the chief anxiety of the latter. In his reply Mountbatten wrote 'Your typically thoughtful, charming and helpful telegram did more than anything else to reassure me and make me feel that after all the Naval aspect of my task was going to be made pleasant and easy for me';[24] and in his next letter he set out his hopes and intentions more fully. The latter included an expression of the desire 'to keep my staff as small as possible', and not to set up 'a separate and independent Naval Staff'.[25] Unfortunately Mountbatten's subsequent actions hardly conformed to the intentions expressed in the second part of that letter; and when Somerville saw Churchill's directive to the Supreme Commander, which included the statement that he would be provided with 'a battle fleet of sufficient strength to engage any force which the Government consider the Japanese might be in a position to disengage from the Pacific theatre',[26] he at once protested to Cunningham, who had just taken over as First Sea Lord.[27] The basic trouble arose from the fact that Somerville's responsibilities extended far outside Mountbatten's command area. They included Aden and the Persian Gulf in the north, almost to the Cape of Good Hope in the south, and to Australia in the east, as well as the safety of the convoys to the Middle East whose route ran along the coast of East Africa. The naval staff considered that the sentence to which Somerville objected should be amended to read *tout court* that 'The Naval C-in-C will be provided with a Battle Fleet.'[28]

Cunningham accordingly sent a note to Churchill pointing out that 'ambiguity exists over the command of the battle fleet shortly to be assembled in Eastern waters', and giving his opinion that command of that force 'must come primarily under the Naval C-in-C if he is to carry out the duties with which he is charged'.[29] Four days later Alexander told Churchill that 'matters had come to a head', because whereas 'Mountbatten holds that the whole of the Eastern Fleet . . . is under his command at all times and for all purposes', Somerville held that his position was analogous to that of the C-in-C, Mediterranean *vis à vis* General Eisenhower, the Supreme Commander of that theatre. 'The sooner these contentions are settled', he wisely concluded, 'the better';[30] but that was more easily said than done.

Churchill accordingly tried his hand at eliminating the ambiguity complained of; but his draft affirmed that 'For all purposes of SEAC the Naval C-in-C and all his forces are under the Supreme Commander', and that when 'the three Cs-in-C sit in consultation with the Supreme Commander he has the power of over-riding decision and there is no question of a junta or committee'. Although Churchill did continue that 'All the above is without prejudice to the over-riding authority of the Admiralty over all ships and commanders at sea in respect of all purposes not specifically delegated to SEAC', the Admiralty was told they were 'responsible to the War Cabinet for not issuing over-riding orders to the Eastern Fleet obstructive of the purposes of the Supreme Commander.'[31] It is therefore plain on which side of the fence Churchill stood. Cunningham, however, now changed his mind, and represented that the original paragraph of the directive should stand. Relations between the Supreme Commander and the naval C-in-C must, he sensibly remarked, 'be interpreted with elasticity and good will', and cases where a conflict of responsibilities might arise 'are not capable of precise definition and must be settled . . . in a spirit of give and take.'[32] Churchill agreed and said that if differences arose 'the Minister of Defence as representing the War Cabinet [i.e. himself] would have to intervene.' But, he continued, 'I have not the slightest doubt that in all major matters affecting sea power the Admiralty view would be endorsed by the War Cabinet' – which went some way towards accepting Somerville's case.[33] In the end a signal was sent to Somerville which would, it was hoped, eliminate all friction and disagreement; for it told the naval C-in-C that he must accept the relevant paragraphs of the Prime Minister's memorandum 'as the authoritative guide' on the matter in dispute.[34] Plainly Cunningham was giving the Supreme Commander as much support as he could. Unfortunately Somerville continued to argue that his fleet only came under Mountbatten for the purpose of combined operations initiated and executed by the latter, and that the staffs of the three Cs-in-C, and especially their Planners, should act as advisers to the Supreme Commander rather than a separate staff set up by the latter.

There now followed a long series of letters from Somerville to Cunningham on the issues which had arisen. Some of them certainly dealt with matters of principle – notably his responsibility to the Admiralty for operations outside the SEAC command area, and the need for the separate 'War Staff' which Mountbatten soon set up.[35] But others show a surprising pettiness on Somerville's part, notably over his objection to the Supreme Commander visiting ships of the fleet and addressing their officers and men without his agreement. On Mountbatten's side there may have been some lack of tact, for example over the publicity given to operations carried out by 'Mountbatten's fleet', and over his proposals regarding the procedure to be followed when he visited British warships. According to Somerville the latter included the granting of a 'make and mend' (naval terminology for a half holiday) or 'some other relaxation of routine' to mark the occasion.[36] But because of Somerville's objections the Supreme Commander initially only visited the American aircraft carrier *Saratoga* and the French battleship *Richelieu*, both of which had joined the Eastern Fleet.

Cunningham continued to try and smooth things over, telling Somerville that for operations arranged by the Supreme Commander his ships were 'definitely under him', as was the admiral himself; but he was also 'responsible to the Admiralty generally for the Eastern Fleet area', and that although Mountbatten 'had asked to have the whole Eastern Fleet area placed under him', he had 'made him see this was ridiculous'.[37] However, Somerville, who was always a prolific letter writer, continued to press his views on Cunningham well into the New Year.[38] Cunningham did his best to pour oil on troubled waters, telling Somerville that 'I think you must give the Supreme Commander a little rope' in the matter of visits to ships, and that even if he had gone rather far in such a matter 'I think you must look at his difficulties'.[39] He evidently wrote to Mountbatten in the same vein on the same day, and the Supreme Commander replied gratefully saying that he had shown the letter to Somerville and they both agreed 'that there will be no difficulty in finding a *modus vivendi*', which would be worked out after his headquarters had moved from Delhi to Ceylon in April.[40] None the less difficulties between them continued, and in June 1944 Somerville wrote to Cunningham that, with regard to visits to ships 'I have given him [Mountbatten] every opporunity', and he had visited six ships of his fleet. 'These squabbles all seem very trivial', he continued; but in the matter of the Supreme Commander's staff he felt 'there is a main principle at stake'.[41]

Churchill seems to have known little about the strength of the feelings aroused between the two admirals, but in March 1944 A. V. Alexander told him that after some correspondence Somerville had agreed to relieve Sir Percy Noble, who was pressing to return home after two arduous years in what the First Lord described as 'the uncongenial and wearing appointment' of head of the British Naval Mission in Washington – a change which, he wrote, the Prime Minister had actually approved some time earlier. Cunningham had meanwhile signalled to Somerville that the offer of the Washington appointment 'was in no way a suggestion that it was time you were relieved in [the] Eastern Fleet'; but he must realize 'that officers who are qualified to fill the appointment [in Washington] are very scarce'.[42]

Churchill, however, now objected to the change, and Alexander had to send him a long explanation of the reasons why it was necessary – the chief one being that, as Churchill had already agreed, the principal naval command was bound to become the Eastern Fleet in the near future, and he had approved that Sir Bruce Fraser should move to it from the Home Fleet. It was therefore 'important that he should get there as soon as possible'.[43]

Meanwhile the great American offensive across the central Pacific had made the Japanese bases in the Marshall and Caroline Islands insecure, and in February 1944 they moved their still powerful main fleet to Singapore. We sent air reinforcements to India in case another foray was made into the Indian Ocean, as the Japanese had done in

April 1942. Though the COSs were not apprehensive about such a possibility Churchill was far from satisfied with the counter-measures taken.[44] On 1 April he told Cunningham that, even if the Japanese soon withdrew their warships from Singapore, as the First Sea Lord considered likely, 'I see no reason for moving the Eastern Fleet to the Pacific for a good many months to come . . . I should deprecate recalling Admiral James Somerville and sending out Admiral Fraser until we can see much more clearly than we do what is best to do'.[45] He preferred to await 'the general agreement . . . on our strategic policy', which had of course been the subject of his meeting with the Americans at Cairo and Teheran known as the 'Sextant' and 'Eureka' Conferences of November–December 1943.[46] Churchill wanted Fraser to be consulted about the change – to which Alexander replied that he and Cunningham were 'not quite clear' why his views were required, as he was 'proposed for the post of C-in-C, Eastern Fleet on his merits'.[47] Cunningham's diary shows that it was he who inspired this riposte, because he regarded the idea of submitting a C-in-C designate to what he called 'a strategic means test' went dangerously close to a revival of the time when admirals' appointments depended on their holding 'correct political views'.[48] In that same month Churchill made his strategic purpose clear by telling the COSs that he was 'determined that an amphibious operation should, if possible, be carried out by the South East Asia Command during the autumn/winter of this year (i.e. 1944)'.[48A]

Next Somerville, in Churchill's words, 'added new claims to our confidence by his brilliant attack on Sabang' in Sumatra – the first offensive blow struck by the re-formed Eastern Fleet – on 19 April 1944. 'Why', asked Churchill, 'do we want to make a change here at all? It seems to me he [Somerville] knows the theatre, has the right ideas about it and is capable of daring action.' He found it hard to believe that the admiral wanted 'to give up his fighting command' and go to Washington[49] – which was an accurate assessment of Somerville's personal inclinations, though he told Cunningham he would of course go anywhere he was required.[50] Alexander answered Churchill's objections to the changes by telling him that he was sure Fraser would show no less 'aggressive spirit' than Somerville, and that he was 'an officer of great merit fully competent to take command of the Eastern Fleet'. Though Somerville had 'no desire to take up the most uncongenial and expensive appointment' in Washington, 'he has', the First Lord continued, 'the knowledge and the good humour to deal with Admiral King'; and in view of his long service in the tropics he considered that he should be given a job in a less trying climate. As the Admiralty was planning 'for an Eastern War which may last two or three years' he pressed for the changes to be made before 'critical operations are in progress';[51] but the Prime Minister still refused to give way.

Churchill's views on the command changes discussed above were almost certainly coloured by his strong desire to launch offensive operations against the Japanese across the Bay of Bengal. The first one considered was an amphibious attack on the Andaman Islands (operation 'Buccaneer'), and he was horrified when he learnt that Mountbatten considered a striking force of some 50,000 soldiers necessary to attack an enemy believed to number only about 5000. Though Ismay was able to show that the figure of 50,000 was misleading because the assault and immediate follow-up forces would only number some 18,000 men, Churchill considered the demand for a superiority of more than 3 to 1 'the grossest libel ever uttered against our soldiers' – which again illustrated his tendency to belittle the hazards of combined operations.[52] Early in the New Year he pressed Mountbatten on the subject, telling him 'I am sure Wingate would not endorse such absurd propositions';[53] and he asked the Admiralty for a comparison with the strength used by the Americans in their assaults on enemy-held islands in the central Pacific. The reply was that a similar superiority had been deployed by them – which Mountbatten was able to confirm in general. But Churchill evidently remained unconvinced, since he closed the argument with the comment 'Noted. There is no doubt that a steam hammer will crack a nut.'[54]

The Americans, however, were totally unenthusiastic about the 'Buccaneer' plan, wanting instead to get the Burma Road reopened to facilitate the transport of supplies to the Chinese Nationalist Army – whose effectiveness they consistently overrated. After long and complicated negotiations 'Buccaneer' was cancelled.[55]

Churchill's favourite plan was however to launch a major amphibious assault against Sumatra, which commanded the approach to the Malacca Strait from the north, and so the road to Malaya and Singapore (operation 'Culverin'). His addiction to historical analogies made him view this undertaking as 'the "Torch" [invasion of French North Africa] of the Indian Ocean'.[56] Though the plan soon had to be scaled down to an attack on the north-west tip of the island only, because of lack of shipping and trained troops, the Joint Planners considered that even this would have serious effects on operations in the Arakan and for the reconquest of Burma.[57] Churchill, who was in Quebec for the 'Quadrant' Conference, was provoked into writing a long riposte attacking the staff's 'negativism', describing 'Culverin' as 'the largest diversionary action open to us with the forces available in 1944', and asking for the plan to be examined by Mountbatten and Wingate.[58] But their report made it plain that very large forces would be required even for the modified undertaking.[59] Incidentally Cunningham believed that Churchill's opposition to the relief of Somerville derived, at any rate in part, from his support for 'Culverin'.[60]

The key to all such undertakings as Churchill favoured was of course held by the Americans, who were totally opposed to this strategy, for reasons already stated;[61] and the British COSs realized that the Americans 'Pacific Strategy' was bound to win the argument – if only because they were providing nearly all the forces needed for it. After a meeting of the COSs with Churchill and other Ministers Cunningham grumbled in his diary 'We had hoped to get some decision on Far East strategy, but we were treated to the same old monologue of how much better it was to take the tip of Sumatra and then the Malay peninsula and finally Singapore than it was to join the Americans and fight Japan close at home in the Pacific.'[62]

On 17 May Somerville followed up his attack on Sabang by a much heavier blow against the port and oil refineries at Soerabaya in Java[63] – which strengthened Churchill's reluctance to change the C-in-C of the fleet. Somerville's telegrams, he wrote, showed that he was 'keen and sprightly in the last degree', while Fraser still had to account for the *Tirpitz*.[64] He felt that 'in both cases . . . you have the right man in the right place'; and as regards Admiral King being 'so difficult, why not let him be dealt with through other channels than our Admirals?' he asked. But Alexander and Cunningham could also be stubborn, and the former replied that the Home Fleet was so much reduced that the second-in-command, Sir Henry Moore, could well replace Fraser; and as regards Admiral King it was 'not feasible to deal with him in any other way than through the Admiral appointed to the Combined COS organization'.[65]

Still Churchill would not budge, and he next wrote resentfully about the Admiralty telling him what was necessary for the effective prosecution of the war against Japan, and also complained with regard to switching admirals about when 'they are on the top of their form . . . in order that they should dance attendance on Admiral King'[66]. Not until early June did he give way, and approve all the changes desired by the Admiralty.

The other serious difficulty in the South-East Asia Command

concerned the size and composition of Mountbatten's staff, and especially his 'War Staff Group'. Shortly before the Supreme Commander decided to move his headquarters from Delhi to a more convenient and congenial setting at Kandy in Ceylon in April 1944 Admiral Layton wrote in astonishment to Cunningham that the first estimate of the numbers involved had been 4000, but that it had now been increased to 7000. 'It does make one wonder', he continued, 'if it is right that one Commander should collect together 7000 able-bodied men and women to plan and supervise operations the scale of which is not yet settled . . . It seems to me that no one tries to put any brake on these things except James [Somerville] when he visits Delhi.'[67]

On 21 June Cunningham wrote in his diary that he had received 'A signal from Mountbatten that he and James Somerville have had a royal row. I am afraid it was bound to happen that way';[68] and the row was about the Supreme Commander's staff. Fortunately a *deus ex machina* arrived in Ceylon that same month in the person of Captain (later Admiral of the Fleet Sir) Charles Lambe, who was a close personal friend of Mountbatten's and had come from the important post of Director of Plans in the Admiralty to take command of the aircraft carrier *Illustrious* in the Eastern Fleet. In Lambe's words 'In June 1944 . . . I flew from Colombo to Kandy as an emissary from Somerville to Mountbatten to try and persuade the latter to abolish his separate planning staff [he then names the two officers on it who were the chief cause of trouble]. I have always believed I was successful'*[69] – a claim which is supported by Somerville's biographer, and led to Mountbatten adopting the 'Eisenhower model' of planning staff rather than the 'MacArthur model'.[70]

One other matter must be cleared up before leaving the somewhat distasteful subject of the quarrel between Somerville and Mountbatten, and that is whether the latter had power to ask for the relief of any service C-in-C whom he found inadequate to his responsibilities or wished to get rid of for some reason or other. Mountbatten told the author that he asked for and received such authority from the Com-

* Lambe had expressed his opposition to 'Mountbatten's super planning staff' earlier in a minute to the First Sea Lord dated 12 February 1944. Air Marshal Sir Guy Garrod, who became Allied Air C-in-C, SEAC, in succession to Air Chief Marshal Sir Richard Peirse, wrote to the author after reading Captain Lambe's letter 'I can claim to have influenced the Supreme Commander in the same direction as Lambe . . . My impression is that what Admiral Mountbatten had in mind shortly before June 1944 was to undo the close integration that existed between his planners and those of the Cs-in-C, and make his own planners independent and superior . . . Fortunately he was persuaded to take the opposite course.'

bined COSs at the Quebec Conference before accepting the appointment of Supreme Commander; but on questioning the three British
COSs concerned (Lords Cunningham, Alanbrooke and Portal) they all
firmly denied having given their agreement to such a request – chiefly
because the relief of a C-in-C did not depend on them but on their
Ministers or, in the final issue, on Churchill as Minister of Defence.[71]
It is true that Mountbatten asked for and obtained the relief of the
first Army C-in-C in his command, General Sir George Giffard, on
the grounds of his inadequacy; also that his successor Sir Oliver Leese,
with whose performance Mountbatten had not been wholly satisfied,
was replaced when he showed extreme lack of tact in his proposal to
sack General Slim, whose 14th Army had just completed the reconquest
of Burma.* It is also the case that the first Allied Air C-in-C, Sir
Richard Peirse was replaced at Mountbatten's request, but in that
instance the reason was highly indiscreet conduct. With Somerville
matters came to a head in June 1944, when he sent to the Admiralty his
views on the controversy in which he was engaged. Mountbatten
thereupon wrote to Ismay to the effect that he could not allow the
prevailing state of affairs to continue[72] – which was no doubt the 'royal
row' to which Cunningham referred to his diary. Fortunately Mountbatten's Chief of Staff, General Pownall, was in London at the time, and
he advised the Supreme Commander to hold his hand, because the
COSs were so fully occupied with preparing for the invasion of
Normandy that they could not give proper time to such a matter; and
Sir Bruce Fraser was in any case likely to take over the Eastern Fleet in
the near future. Pownall's chance to resolve the issue arose a short time
later when, at a meeting at Chequers, Churchill expressed a desire to
extend Somerville's appointment because 'he knew conditions there so
well'. Pownall replied that 'From the point of view of personalities I
think there should be a change'; and the Prime Minister 'hoisted this in'
and withdrew his proposal.[73]

Churchill was as confident of his judgement on the correct strategy
to be adopted in South-East Asia as he had been with regard to the
right man for the naval command. In July he told the COSs that
'Nothing could be worse than having our armies bogged down in
North Burma . . . the troops are ours, and we have the military direction of forces in this theatre. There is no doubt which way Admiral

---

* See Ronald Lewin, *Slim: The Standard Bearer* (Leo Cooper, 1976), Ch. 14 regarding
the extraordinary story of General Leese's attempt to get Slim replaced by General Sir Philip Christison in May 1945, and its frustration by Alanbrooke, the
CIGS.

Mountbatten's views lie'[74] – by which he meant of course an amphibious assault across the Bay of Bengal. But the trouble was that not only was Mountbatten dependent on American transport aircraft, but the Americans were obsessed with the potentiality of Chiang Kai-shek's forces, and felt no enthusiasm at all for Churchill's strategy – for which large numbers of assault vessels urgently needed in other theatres would be essential.

On 23 August 1944 Admiral Fraser took over command of the Eastern Fleet from Somerville, and two months later Alexander told Churchill that as the C-in-C of that fleet could not control both the Indian Ocean and Pacific forces the creation of a new command for the latter was essential. Admiral Fraser was therefore to be appointed C-in-C, British Pacific Fleet and would arrive at Sydney, Australia, in the *King George V* early in December, followed shortly by the rest of the ships allocated to him. By July 1945 a large fleet (four battleships, six fleet and four light fleet carriers, sixteen cruisers, forty destroyers and ninety escort vessels) would be assembled for the new command. Alexander proposed to Churchill that Admiral Sir Arthur Power should become the C-in-C, Eastern Fleet, which would be less powerful than Fraser's but would include three amphibious assault forces. Churchill approved the new dispositions in principle but followed his usual practice of asking for alternative names for the command and for a report on Power, before he approved the appointment.[75] As this minute shows exactly the qualities he looked for in a C-in-C it is worth quoting. 'It is important', he wrote, 'that the appointment should be filled by an officer who will work in the closest harmony with [the] C-in-C SEAC' [i.e. Mountbatten, the Supreme Commander], and also that he has the qualities needed for a theatre in which audacity and the powers of improvisation are essential.'[76] On reading this minute Cunningham wrote in his diary 'Gave Power a good write-up, which he richly deserves';[77] and on receiving that eulogy Churchill approved the appointment.[78] The title of C-in-C, East Indies, which had been in abeyance since June 1942, was revived for Power, and it is fair to record that not only did he have no difficulties with Mountbatten but he considered his predecessor's disagreements had 'not shown James Somerville at his best'.[79]

The agreement that the British fleet would join the Americans in the Pacific was reached at the second Quebec or 'Octagon' Conference in September 1944; but Admiral King was so plainly opposed to British participation in the final victory over Japan that at a meeting of the Combined COSs Cunningham asked him outright whether he was trying to reverse Roosevelt's acceptance of Churchill's offer 'with both hands'. When Somerville and Noble met in Cunningham's office in October he recorded that 'Noble says King is already showing signs of going back on the Washington [? Quebec] agreement about the fleet working in the Pacific . . .';[80] but a month later he wrote 'Telegram from Ernie King. He agrees almost entirely to our views, which is a great relief.'[81] The plans which had long been gestating, and in which Churchill had taken an intimate interest, were now able to go ahead at full speed.[82] But things did not go smoothly between Fraser and Cunningham during the build-up of the fleet in Ceylon, its move to Australia and the preparation of an advanced base at Manus in the Admiralty Islands. In mid-November the new C-in-C wrote what Cunningham described as 'an unpleasant letter complaining that the Admiralty consistently turned down all his proposals', and suggesting he should 'select someone whose judgement you would trust and advice you would follow'.[83] This fracas may have been a continuation of the trouble between them over the attack on the *Tirpitz*, recounted earlier; but if that is so it soon simmered down, and after reaching his new command Fraser sent Cunningham a number of cordial and co-operative letters.[84]

If 1944 saw many disappointments in the South-East Asia Command it produced the first decisive defeat of the Japanese army at Kohima in March;* and that opened up the possibility, which General Sir William Slim exploited so brilliantly, of breaking through to the Irrawaddy valley and then driving south to Rangoon. But, as regards amphibious operations, Churchill and Mountbatten suffered a series of frustrating setbacks. That the Americans were right to concentrate on the 'Pacific Strategy' is now plain; and although Churchill was very reluctant to abandon operations like 'Buccaneer' and 'Culverin', the British COSs knew that the American view would, and indeed should prevail. Where the Americans went wrong was in the belief that by reopening the Burma Road a great victory over the Japanese would be brought about in the vast spaces of inland China; but Roosevelt never came near to understanding what a weak reed Chiang Kai-shek was to lean on. On the other hand Churchill's strategic purposes were undoubtedly influenced by his traditional regard for British imperial interests – which were of course both anathema and a source of suspicion to Roosevelt and to many of his most influential advisers.

* See Arthur Swinson, *Kohima* (Cassell, 1966) for an admirable account of this close-run battle. General Slim's *Defeat into Victory* (Cassell, 1956) has his equally admirable account of the whole campaign for the liberation of Burma.

At the end of 1944 Churchill told the COSs that he wanted 'as large a fleet as possible in the Indian Ocean', which would of course have ruled out the transfer of the ships already earmarked for the British Pacific Fleet; and he again produced his analogy about the Japanese fleet at Singapore having the same influence as the presence of the *Tirpitz* in north Norway had on the Home Fleet's dispositions and operations. But Cunningham was totally opposed to having our main fleet based on Ceylon. 'Surely', he remarked, 'our object should be to defeat Japan as soon as possible'; and that was in his view more likely to be achieved by accepting and supporting the Americans' Pacific strategy. Churchill however, remained unconvinced, and he argued that the threat to Ceylon and to our trade in the Indian Ocean presented by the Japanese force at Singapore was real. Early in the following year he brought the question up yet again; but the COSs supported Cunningham, General Brooke the CIGS remarking that the Pacific strategy could 'bring victory six months earlier' than an advance across the Bay of Bengal to Sumatra, Malaya and Singapore.[85] In the end it was in the main their view which prevailed.

Looking back today it seems possible that, if Mountbatten could have been given the amphibious forces and equipment he needed, the liberation of Malaya and Singapore might have been expedited; but as the forces could only have been provided at the expense of the great operations in train in Europe, and those proved no walk-over, it is difficult to criticize the strategy adopted – except for the American emphasis on the Burma Road supply line to China. As to the personalities involved it is surely true to say that Mountbatten handled the extraordinarily intractable problems which faced him, and the temperamental and often difficult subordinates given to him, with a combination of tact and firmness, and of imagination with realism which it would be hard to better.

CHAPTER 15

The Months of Victory
January-August 1945

To conduct a world war is of course far easier in terms of strategy and tactics, though not in terms of international politics, when one is winning than when the tide is running strongly in the enemy's favour. Thus it is not surprising that the stream of exhortatory, deprecatory or minatory minutes and memoranda which Churchill addressed to the First Lord and First Sea Lord from 1940 to 1944 should have been reduced to a trickle in 1945; for the Prime Minister was then concerned chiefly with what the fruits of victory in Europe would be, and how they could best be garnered to the advantage of the western democracies. Moreover the prospect of a General Election and all the problems of demobilization and resettlement had suddenly become urgent and occupied much of Churchill's time and thoughts.

From the navy's point of view the imperative duties of the Home Commands were to keep the allied armies supplied and to cope with the inshore campaign by U-boats equipped with the Schnorkel device, which enabled them to recharge their batteries while submerged; and the Admiralty was also apprehensive about the threat from U-boats of revolutionary design, which were capable of far higher underwater speed and which were known to be in large-scale production. If a substantial number entered service in time they might well regain the initiative which the conventional boats had been deprived of in 1943.[1] The anxiety felt on this score is reflected in Cunningham's diary for 22 January 1945, when he wrote that 'It looks as though he [Churchill] is waking up to the U-boat threat. He talked of increased bombing of the assembly yards.'[2] In fact the bombing offensive did contribute greatly to delaying the completion of these dangerous enemies, and the threat to the dominance of the home-based sea and air escorts happily never materialized.

Admiral Sir Max Horton, who had held the crucially important Western Approaches Command since November 1942, continued to conduct the British side of the Atlantic Battle (which was far greater than the American share) with exemplary skill and resolution, and A. V. Alexander wanted ultimately to reward him with the command

of one of the three main home ports; but Cunningham considered him
to be 'much too senior' for such a post.[3] In fact no further naval appointment was offered him, and shortly after the German surrender he was
placed on the retired list.[4] There seems to have been a certain lack of
rapport between Cunningham and Horton, which is not altogether
surprising as both were very strong-willed men.[5] Cunningham proposed to reward Admirals Sir William James and Sir Percy Noble
with the somewhat honorific titles of Vice- and Rear-Admirals of the
United Kingdom; which was not a very satisfactory recognition of
their distinguished war service. But none of those proposals appears to
have been put to Churchill.[6]

The sharpest clash of this period was not between Churchill and
any admiral but between him and Air Chief Marshal Tedder, the
Deputy Supreme Commander to Eisenhower; and it only falls within
the field of this study because Cunningham wrote in his diary how 'A
violent memo. against Tedder was considered at [the] COS [meeting]
. . . in private session' on 12 April. 'It is curious', Cunningham
soliloquized, 'that with all his [Churchill's] great qualities, when he
deals with personalities he gets childish. He is such a bad "picker" [of
men] too. Montgomery he has fairly well sized up, but he is completely bluffed by [General Sir Harold] Alexander' – whose abilities
Cunningham had considered overrated ever since he was appointed
C-in-C, Middle East in August 1942, and whom Churchill now
wanted to replace Tedder. Cunningham next recorded that the
COSs had suggested that Churchill 'should withdraw his minute
[about sacking Tedder] but he refused, so we also stuck to our guns'.[7]
In the end no change was made, so Churchill evidently did give
way.[8]

Another issue deriving from the Atlantic Battle was the old question
of relations between Coastal Command of the RAF and the Admiralty,
and in March Cunningham recorded that the Sea Lords had reached a
'gratifying agreement' on the policy to be adopted. Briefly stated it
was that 'the Admiralty should make no claim to have the Coastal
Command turned over to the Navy. They should request that the
same system should be extended to foreign stations'; that 'they should
have a voice in the training [of aircrews], and that there should be some
permanency in the Coastal Command personnel'.[9] This substantial
change of front on the Admiralty's part was confirmed a few months
later, when the Sea Lords unanimously recorded their preference for
the prevailing system rather than attempt to gain complete control of
Coastal Command.[10] This decision went of course against Churchill's

own pre-war proposal, described above,* and against the views some admirals had expressed earlier in the war;[11] but its wisdom can hardly be called in question. A second, and in some respects more intractable problem concerning the final phase of the Atlantic Battle was the constant difficulty experienced in getting the Russians to co-operate properly. In April 1945 Alexander wrote to Churchill complaining that the Russians were obstructing the battle against the U-boats by refusing to grant visas for British and American technical experts to go to the Polish base of Gdynia, which had recently been captured along with much German equipment; and they had also rejected our proposal to lay a deep minefield in Kola Inlet, to make the approach to Murmansk more dangerous to the U-boats. The First Lord suggested that a telegram should be sent to Stalin on these matters, but Churchill replied 'I do not wish at the moment to send this telegram myself . . . I think the matter should be pressed through the regular channels.'[12] In truth satisfactory co-operation with the Russians was never achieved – to the great resentment of the naval staff and of the officers and men engaged in the very arduous work of carrying supplies to North Russia.

On 21 May Cunningham wrote in his diary that 'It seems certain we are to have a General Election', and was very critical of Churchill's letter to Attlee of the 18th in which he had tentatively proposed a referendum as a 'means of taking the nation's opinion' about extending the life of the present Parliament.[13] He considered that such an idea smacked of 'Fascist or Nazi procedure'.[14] Next day the First Sea Lord wrote that A. V. Alexander 'has much complaint over the behaviour of the PM in this General Election matter. He says Beaverbrook and Brendan Bracken have won and persuaded him to issue the ultimatum to the Labour Party.' Alexander deplored 'the break up of the Coalition in this unfriendly atmosphere', and that the *Daily Express*, Beaverbrook's paper, had published a 'pure invention' that he himself was 'thinking of leaving the Labour Party'. 'I am afraid', Cunningham concluded 'the two Bs are a pretty dishonest pair'.[15]

On 24 May the last war time Board of Admiralty meeting with Alexander in the chair took place, and Cunningham 'said a few words regretting his departure'. To the naval members of the Board Alexander had proved a solid and steady, if uninspiring leader, who was generally guided by what now appears to have been sound common sense. Only in the case of Sir Dudley North does he appear to have

* See p. 86.

shown personal animosity towards an admiral. Over lunch at Claridge's Hotel Bracken told Cunningham that he was not coming to the Admiralty 'though it was a near thing', and that 'Oliver Lyttelton was to be First Lord'. But when the composition of the Caretaker Government was announced on the 26th it was Bracken who was appointed. Cunningham disliked him because, as he wrote in his diary, 'he is Winston's creature and this is obviously Winston's way of trying to gain closer control of the Admiralty'. But he admitted that Bracken 'is not afraid of standing up for his department' – which may have been an oblique reference to A. V. Alexander sometimes failing to do so. As Bracken hated Sir James Grigg, the Secretary of State for War, Cunningham anticipated that 'there will be wigs on the green'.[16] However, a few days after he made these caustic diary entries he recorded that at his first interview with his new Minister he had found 'nothing to take exception to. In fact he talked great sense';[17] but when on the last day of the month Bracken sent for Cunningham's own secretary without offering any explanation the admiral, not altogether surprisingly, wondered what he was up to.[18]

In July Cunningham attended the Potsdam Conference, and recorded that at one of the Anglo-American dinners Admiral Leahy, Roosevelt's personal Chief of Staff, got very tipsy, while his American opposite number the erstwhile redoubtable and anglophobe Admiral King 'fell on my neck and besought me to call him Ernie' – in striking contrast to his earlier conduct; while Churchill was 'now most optimistic [presumably about the early defeat of Japan] and was placing great faith in the new [atomic] bomb'.[19]

The long awaited General Election took place on 5 July 1945, though the counting of Servicemen's votes delayed announcement of the result until the 26th. The outcome was a drastic drop from 432 to 213 Conservatives elected and an equally large increase in Labour representation from 154 to 393. Churchill has recorded the bitter chagrin he felt over his rejection by the people whom he had led for more than five crucial years, and at once tendered his resignation to the King.[20] Cunningham attributed the landslide to four causes. Firstly the people had undergone such hardship that they were anxious 'to try someone else'; secondly the view was widely held, 'not without reason, that the PM was becoming a dictator'; thirdly there was widespread dislike of Churchill's 'favourite sons', and of Beaverbrook in particular; and lastly dislike of 'the attempt by the Conservative Party to cash in on Winston's reputation as a great war leader before it waned'. He recorded, however, that Churchill's 'farewell statement to the nation was to my mind very dignified'.[21] Though there certainly was a measure of truth in Cunningham's analysis of the reasons for Churchill's defeat the causes probably went a good deal deeper. For one thing whereas the Conservative organization had not attempted to prepare for a return to party politics, and most Labour members of Churchill's government had loyally observed the wartime truce, Dr Hugh Dalton, though a Minister in that government, had for the previous two years or so been actively engaged on getting the Labour electoral machinery into order – as he himself has admitted.[22] Secondly, although Servicemen would cheer Churchill to the echo on every occasion when he addressed them, as he did in the ruins of the great Roman amphitheatre near Carthage in June 1943,[23] collectively they did not trust him to lead the type of post-war government they looked for, and to bring about the social changes they had been promised. Though it is difficult to quantify it seems possible that the Army Education Corps (AEC) and the Army Bureau of Current Affairs (ABCA), which organized lectures and discussions and distributed a monthly pamphlet to all units of all three services, exercised a good deal of subtle political influence; since many of the speakers and much of the literature distributed had a marked left-wing bias. To give only one example D. N. Pritt, a brilliant advocate and passionate friend of the Soviets, admits in his autobiography that after Hitler attacked Russia he was 'in tremendous demand to address meetings'.[24] The Government was of course not unaware of Pritt's activities, which were sponsored by G. E. C. Wigg, a Labour MP (Lord Wigg 1967). In 1942 Sir James Grigg, the Secretary of State for War, told Churchill that he was 'shocked that people of this sort [Wigg] found their way into the AEC'. The question of allowing Pritt to continue to lecture to men of the fighting services came before the Cabinet several times, and in March 1943 they decided that 'a person who had taken so prominent a part in advocating opposition to the war could not expect to be given facilities to lecture to HM Forces'.[25] None the less, if my own experience is anything to go by, the AEC and ABCA were very influential political propagandists, and probably contributed a lot to the Servicemen's votes being cast against Churchill in the 1945 General Election.

Early in August 1945 Churchill wrote to Cunningham beginning his letter for the first time 'My dear Andrew', and telling him that his 'earnest desire' was that his 'three great friends the Chiefs of Staff should receive some recognition on my initiative of the work we have done together in these long and anxious years'. He hoped therefore that Cunningham would agree to the submission of his name to the King for a Barony in the Resignation Honours – a proposal which, he said, Attlee, now Prime Minister, had approved.[26] Cunningham accepted the honour on behalf of his service rather than himself; but when in the following November he learnt about Attlee's proposals regarding hereditary honours – namely Viscounties for Brooke, Montgomery, Alexander, Portal and himself and Baronies for Fraser and Tedder, he told the First Lord, now A. V. Alexander again, that he regarded the recognition accorded to the navy, which 'had held the fort in bad times' as quite inadequate; and that if he accepted the honour he would 'appear to my brother officers as a grabber of all the honours that are going'. He urged that Tovey and Somerville should be given Baronetcies, and wrote that Portal agreed with him.[27] In December he followed up these representations with a letter setting out the same arguments more fully;[28] and it may have been thanks to his efforts that Tovey did get a Barony in 1946; but Somerville received no hereditary honour, and the disproportion between those given to sailors and airmen and those bestowed on soldiers was not rectified.

The Eastern and Pacific fleets, had been steadily building up since the success of the invasion of Normandy and became the principal naval commands after the surrender of Germany on 7 May 1945. At the beginning of that year Churchill was, among many other tasks and problems, watching anxiously the progress made towards regaining command of the Bay of Bengal as an essential preliminary to launching amphibious operations against Rangoon (operation 'Dracula') and then on the west coast of Malaya in order to recover Singapore.[29] On 11 January he attacked Cunningham about a report, actually unfounded, that a Japanese squadron had sailed from Singapore for those waters.[30] 'What do you say about this?' he asked; and then added, somewhat unnecessarily, 'You are responsible for the security of the Indian Ocean. I understood you were going to form a second fleet in the IO before sending the present fleet away [to the Pacific]. Let me know the disposition of the fleet and how you propose to guard against the Jap intervention on the coast of Burma . . .' Cunningham replied that the Japanese force in question had actually gone north-east towards Saigon, and went on to explain the build-up of the East Indies fleet. 'With the state of the Japanese fleet as it is and under existing circumstances of a strong [American] offensive in the Philippines* I consider it most improbable that the Japs would send major units into the

* The great American assault in the Philippines, soon followed by the decisive defeat of the Japanese navy in the succession of fights known collectively as the Battle of

Indian Ocean, or if they did the fleet . . . is adequate to deal with them
. . .' Churchill thereupon withdrew, somewhat apologetically, writing
'I have the greatest confidence in your judgement and am prepared to
accept your decision. I thought it very necessary however to refer
the matter to you and am glad you see no danger. Please report in a
fortnight.' When that period had elapsed Cunningham told Churchill
that the Japanese squadron had returned to Singapore, and he had 'no
reason to alter the opinion expressed in my minute of 12th January'.[31] The difference in tone between this minute and many of
those which Churchill had flung at Pound earlier in the war is striking.

While this exchange was in progress Admiral Layton, who had just
returned from Ceylon and was to take over the Portsmouth Command,
called to see Cunningham and gave his opinion of all the Flag Officers
on the East Indies station -- which was highly critical of all of them,
including A. J. Power the new C-in-C;[32] but Layton was, as we saw
earlier, always prone to pass harsh judgements on his colleagues and
contemporaries.

Late in 1944 the threat of Japanese suicide bombers ('Kamikazes') first
became apparent when the RAN cruiser *Australia* was seriously damaged
off Leyte Gulf. Churchill took up with Cunningham the possibility
of offering the Americans the latest of Cherwell's A-A devices, known
as the Type K rocket, which could be fired up to 24,000 feet where the
head then separated and discharged wires suspended by parachutes with
mines attached. This was actually an army weapon, and a variation of
the 'Long Aerial Mine' of the early days of the war.* The naval staff
declared that as we had 'no intention of using them ourselves', and
preferred to stick to the conventional and well tried Bofors and
Oerlikon guns, it seemed wrong to offer the rockets to the Americans.
Cunningham agreed, however, that they should be told about the
rocket weapon and 'all its drawbacks', whereupon Churchill told him
that 'your criticisms are so damaging that it is not worth my while
telegraphing to the President' -- which was a very different line to that
which he had taken as First Lord in 1939-40 when he had literally
forced the navy to mount such weapons -- despite the very serious
dangers they introduced to the ships themselves. This time he merely
wrote that 'it wd be a pity if naval thought on this matter were not

Leyte Gulf, took place on 20 October 1944. In January 1945 MacArthur was about to
assault Luzon, and it is presumably this offensive to which Cunningham was referring.
See Roskill, *War at Sea*, III, Part I, pp. 207-29.
* See pp. 85 and 180.

active', and asked whether a shell could be made 'which cast out, like a star, obstructions or splinters in all directions'. He asked Cunningham to 'set your best brains to finding a remedy for this great danger'.[33] All of which was a perfectly reasonable request, though the 'best brains' of both naval men and scientists had been wrestling with this problem ever since the inefficiency of our A-A gunnery had become apparent early in the war.

Relations between Cunningham on the one hand and Mountbatten and Fraser on the other remained uneasy during the early months of 1945. For example on 6 March Cunningham wrote in his diary that two 'infuriating signals' had come in, one from Fraser who was 'trying to be a law unto himself' and the other from Mountbatten whom the First Sea Lord accused of 'allowing himself to be made a cats paw of [sic] to help the elements in the [US] Navy Dept who wish to prevent the fleet operating in the Pacific'.[34] Next day he wrote that 'a pretty sharp rap on the knuckles' had been sent to Mountbatten at his instigation 'for addressing the US COSs', and that the British Joint Staff Mission in Washington had been told that 'we are totally opposed to Mountbatten's suggestions'.[35] Though it is not clear which signals and suggestions are referred to in these diary entries they do suggest that Cunningham disliked Mountbatten holding the position of a Supreme Commander – a point which he has confirmed.[36] As General Sir Henry Pownall, Mountbatten's Chief of Staff, said to me when trying to help me understand the difficulties experienced by the South-East Asia Command 'Mountbatten was a man who had his own circle of intimate friends and advisers, and Cunningham was definitely not in that circle'.[37] As to Fraser, relations between him and Cunningham soon improved, despite the latter sending 'a pretty strong signal' about the C-in-C BPF making appointments of officers without Admiralty approval.[38] Early in April Cunningham recorded that 'Bruce Fraser had obviously made a very good impression in Australia'.[39]

Meanwhile on the other side of the Atlantic Somerville had, in Cunningham's words 'had a royal row with [Admiral E. J.] King, chiefly about bases in [the] Pacific and [the] British [Pacific] Fleet'.[40] Here it is relevant to remark that, although Somerville's staff sometimes found his peculiar brand of bawdy humour, and his repartee heavily larded with obscenities, tedious and overdone, he was the most successful of all British admirals in handling 'Ernie' King. In 1945 I was his Chief Staff Officer for administration of the British Mission and for all activities concerned with weapons, and I clearly recall how the Admiralty was then applying very heavy pressure on us to get the

BPF equipped with American proximity (or VT for Variable Time) fuzes for their A-A armaments. Churchill had interested himself in this question as early as January 1944, when he inquired if the Admiralty was satisfied with the situation regarding allocation of these new and very effective devices.[41] When I went to negotiate with King's staff for the BPF's allocation I came up against a brick wall of refusal, so I raised the issue to Somerville at one of his weekly staff meetings. He asked for a brief on the subject, which I quickly provided, and the very next evening when we met at a cocktail party he said to me 'Well, Stephen, I've got your VT fuzes.' I was so astonished that I asked how he had done it. He said 'Well, as today was a public holiday I thought it would be a good chance to catch Ernie so I asked for an appointment and got it. I then said to Ernie "Look here, this VT fuze business in which we helped you with the design, has always been on a fifty-fifty basis when they got into production. Your staff is quite willing [which was not at all true] but they say there's a funny old bugger up top that's stopping it – and that's you!" ' Whereupon King had yielded – perhaps in astonishment at Somerville's mode of addressing him. I think the similar anecdote described by Somerville's biographer referring to Bofors guns for the BPF must actually be the one I have described, because he could hardly have used the same gambit twice.[42]

To turn from the admirals' problems and relations with each other and with London to strategy in Mountbatten's command area, even before the reoccupation of Rangoon in May 1945 he was planning for the major amphibious assault on the Malay peninsula which would culminate in the capture of Singapore. In February 1945 he gave orders to prepare to assault Phuket Island off the north-west tip of the Malay peninsula before the 'burst of the monsoon' in late April or early May – because there was an airfield on it from which cover could be given to the main assault further south (operation 'Zipper'). In order to expedite the latter Mountbatten agreed to abandon the Phuket Island plan and to rely on air cover being supplied by the squadron of four light fleet carriers in the East Indies fleet.[43] But Fraser had asked for those ships to join the BPF in June in order to replace the fleet carriers which had suffered damage from Kamikazes in the Okinawa operations of March–April, and to strengthen his carrier air power for the final assault on Japan.* Early in May Mountbatten told the COSs that the reconquest of Burma and the recovery of Rangoon completed the first part of the

* The *Indefatigable*, *Formidable* and *Victorious* were all hit by Kamikazes in April–May 1945, and the *Illustrious* developed defects from earlier air attacks. See Roskill, *War at Sea*, III Part II, pp. 343–53.

directive given to him in October 1943, but that the success of 'Zipper' depended largely on his having the light fleet carriers to provide air cover.[44] The COSs however decided, much to Mountbatten's wrath, that those ships must go to the Pacific, and arranged for him instead to have nine of the slower and less efficient escort carriers. Mountbatten signalled home that, although the removal of the light fleet carriers was 'most serious' he was prepared to go ahead with 'Zipper' using the substitutes allocated to him;[45] but he seems to have regarded the transfer to Admiral Fraser's BPF as an act of deliberate animosity towards him by Cunningham. Mountbatten was also offended by Hong Kong, the liberation of which was plainly imminent, being given to Fraser instead of it being placed in his sphere of responsibility.[46] Even though Cunningham did not like Mountbatten's appointment I find it difficult to believe that he acted maliciously in such matters.

In the event the dropping of the two atomic bombs on Japanese cities on 6 and 9 August certainly expedited, and perhaps brought about the surrender of Japan, and the instrument was formally signed in Tokyo Bay on board the USS *Missouri* on the 14th. The landing of Mountbatten's amphibious force at Penang on 28 August–2 September and the reoccupation of Singapore on 3–4 September were unopposed.

On 9 September the much debated and often changed Operation 'Zipper' finally took place in the Port Swettenham–Port Dickson area; but the deficiencies in planning which it exposed, and for which General Slim, who had only returned to the theatre to assume command of the Allied Land Forces SEAC on 16 August, cannot be held responsible, were so serious that chaos resulted in the approach waters and on the beaches. If determined Japanese resistance had been encountered a disaster might have resulted;[47] but in the event the troops were put ashore without loss, though casualties among the landing craft were heavy. Three days later Mountbatten accepted the surrender of all Japanese forces at a formal ceremony in the Singapore Municipal Buildings. Hong Kong was reoccupied on 30 August by Fraser's fleet, and another surrender ceremony took place there on 16 September. Thereafter Mountbatten's and Fraser's fleets were fully occupied in recovering Allied prisoners and carrying in supplies to the starving people of the whole, vast area. The post-surrender problems which arose, and which were by no means trivial, form no part of this narrative.

Churchill's object that British forces should liberate the whole of the territories lost in 1941–2 was thus achieved. But that accomplishment did not, as some hoped, lead to a restoration of European supremacy in South-East Asia; since Asiatic nationalism, which had been greatly strengthened by the series of defeats we suffered at Japanese hands, quickly became a very powerful force, and the governmental system of the whole area was revolutionized during the next ten years or so. If the Rising Sun flag of Japan had set in August 1945 so had the era of the white man's dominance.

Conclusion

No one who lived through the Second World War, and especially the years 1939–41, is ever likely to forget the debt which the world owes to Churchill for his incredibly swift transformation of a divided and discomfited people into a united, determined and resolute entity. The speeches whereby he chiefly accomplished that metamorphosis, whether made in the House of Commons or on the radio, were perhaps the most remarkable example of sustained oratory ever to have been produced. True enough they were generally prepared and rehearsed with all the care and attention which an actor would give to his appearance on the stage for the first night in a leading part, and that as a result they could at times show a lack of spontaneity; but his delivery, with its use of histrionic devices such as the 'calculated pause' followed by a chuckle, and then the unforgettable phrase or metaphor for which he knew his audience to be waiting with baited breath, showed a mastery of the rhetorical art which has rarely been equalled and is unlikely to be surpassed. If there is substance in Gilbert Murray's castigation of the preference of rhetoric to truth as 'the damnable vice'[1] Churchill's rhetoric was at any rate a masterly performance.

Churchill enjoyed several great advantages over his predecessors of World War I and of more recent times. For he not only had a virtually united Parliament to support him but the declaration of war had eliminated at a stroke all the doubts and hesitancies which had so puzzled and confused the British people for the past two decades. Gone were the superficially attractive but misleading shibboleths about achieving peace through 'Collective Security' and 'Disarmament by International Agreement'; and they were replaced by the simple need to wage war with all the strength and resolution of which the nation was capable. Churchill of course fully realized this, and it has truly been said that 'never before have words', such as he used in the summer of 1940, 'proved such potent instruments of war'.[2] Furthermore his accession to power came so suddenly, and after so long an exile in the political wilderness, that the burdens of office sat astonishingly lightly on his shoulders – despite his assumption of them at a time of acute crisis. No doubt his very obvious enjoyment of power contributed to the ease with which he bore the burdens. He was moreover determined to wield the power as *he* wished – subject of course to the will of Parliament, though to a lesser degree than he himself made out, and to the advice tendered by his political and service colleagues. As self-appointed Minister of Defence as well as Prime Minister his domination of the war-making machinery became as complete as his domination of the Admiralty had been at the beginning; and his interests were by no means confined to the great issues of strategy, diplomacy and supply. Even after he became Prime Minister he continued to put probing questions about the minutiae of naval administration – such as asking the First Sea Lord and Controller 'Have you got over the difficulty of 4.7 [inch] ammunition?' and telling them to distinguish in their reports on reserves between 'what is fired and what is lost when ships are sunk – which actually eases [the] reserve position'.[3] It is plain that it was a bitter disappointment to him when he found that, because of their vastly greater manpower and output, his Russian and American allies had displaced him as the chief architects of policy and strategy.

Churchill was of course a romantic by temperament, and he viewed the naval service through romantic eyes, remembering its contribution to the creation of the Empire by which he set such store, but ignoring the less creditable aspects of that achievement. To him the twentieth-century navy was personified by the power and dignity of Jellicoe's vast battle fleet, the dashing thrust of Beatty's fine-lined battle-cruisers with the probing light cruisers in their van, and numberless fussy little destroyers bustling hither and thither about the great ships. One may doubt if Churchill knew anything about the less romantic sides of the naval service at that time – such as the hellish heat and dust of the boiler rooms whose voracious furnaces devoured hundreds of tons of coal per hour when at high speed; or what it was like in the foetid atmosphere of the men's mess decks after days at sea with every aperture closed; or the exhausting routine of coming into harbour tired out and having at once to embark 1000 tons of coal. It is true that the gradual conversion to oil-firing, in which Churchill played a big part, mitigated some of the least attractive features of lower deck life. But his view of the twentieth-century navy was in general gained from the Admiralty's luxurious yacht or, when he went on board the warships, that seen or heard from the quarter-deck or in the cuddy, rather than the lower deck – as indeed was that of virtually all senior officers of the period. But Churchill's romanticism about the navy remained unchanged; and it was coloured by the views and outlook of the admirals who commanded it. As some of them behaved idiotically and also showed great mistrust towards or dislike of Churchill, it is not surprising that one finds again and again that his romantic view of the service came into conflict with his anger towards some of its senior officers. If ever there was a 'love-hate relationship' it is in my view to be found in Churchill's attitude towards senior naval officers; and it has been remarked above how some quite small incident or success could cause his opinion of one of them to rocket upwards as fast as some alleged failure would cause it to plummet to the depths. It is for this reason, combined with Admiral Pound's weakness in judgement of character, that Churchill's assessments of admirals' qualities and defects were sometimes wide of the mark.

It is curious that, of the admirals who held high commands or carried great responsibilities during the war, the number who both won and retained Churchill's confidence was about equal to the number to whom he never gave his unstinted trust. In the former category Admirals Pound, Fraser and Mountbatten were outstanding examples; and I would have included Admiral Ramsay with them had he commanded one of the major fleets. Those who came in the second category were Admirals Forbes, Tovey and Sir Andrew Cunningham; and I think Sir John Colville right to say that, of the wartime COSs Cunningham alone 'was impervious to Churchill's spell'.[4] Some admirals, such as Harwood, Somerville, Sir John Cunningham and Willis oscillated between the two categories at various times, according chiefly to how 'offensively minded' Churchill considered them. Doubtless the reasons for the high regard in which Churchill held some officers and the dubiety he showed toward others were complex; but the tact which they showed in reacting to his demands and exhortations, as well as their resolution in battle, were certainly important factors. The admirals I have included in the second category were perhaps too outspoken in their criticisms of some of his ideas, and too forthright in their replies to his signals and letters; for Churchill never took kindly to servicemen who opposed him on any score – which was no doubt a result of his experiences during, and study of, the first war.

Churchill's concept of strategy was, from the beginning of both wars, 'offensive'; and he never seems to have understood that, as long as we were desperately short of the sinews of war and of trained men to exploit them, to press for large-scale offensive operations was to court disaster. Fortunately, although he could be stubborn and obstinate to a degree, he could be deflected from such purposes if stood up to resolutely enough. None the less his erroneous strategic concepts, such as his blindness to the threat from Japan and his share in the responsibility for the disasters in Greece and Crete in 1941, brought very serious consequences in their train. As regards the Far East he took decisions which destroyed not only Britain's position in the entire area but that of other European powers as well; while the attempt to defend Greece probably delayed the clearance of the Axis armies from North Africa by some two years, and brought many trials and disappointments in its train.* His dedication to the bombing of Germany instead of first securing the safety of our sea communications, dealt with fully above, must also be classed as a major strategic error; and his addiction to the capture of widely scattered islands led to the dissipation of valuable resources. Last among his major mistakes and misjudgements may be placed his acceptance at Casablanca early in 1943 of the 'Unconditional Surrender' dogma, which was 'difficult to define and impossible or at least impracticable to implement';⁵ and the less far-reaching but deeply distressing fiasco in the Aegean in the autumn of the same year. In sum it is hard not to accept the conclusion of that astute American scholar and critic James McGregor Burns that Churchill 'lacked the steadiness of direction, the comprehensiveness of outlook, the sense of proportion and relevance that mark the grand strategist'.⁶ On the one hand his dealings with President Roosevelt in the early years generally, though not always, showed a grasp of correct priorities and essential measures, as well as a deep understanding of the vital importance of at least benevolent neutrality on the part of the USA. On the other hand his concept of an everlastingly united 'English Speaking People' was as much a chimera as Hitler's 'Thousand Year Reich'.

It was of course Churchill's erratic and idiosyncratic strategic purposes, from the Baltic operation 'Catherine' of 1939 to the proposal to switch the 'Dragoon' landings from the south of France to the Biscay coast in 1944, which caused many of the clashes between him and the top admirals; and when one adds to the wasteful expenditure of effort on such undertakings as 'Catherine' the frustration and muddles caused by his constant interference in operational matters the reasons why some admirals came to view his activities with misgivings, if not positive mistrust, are readily understandable. Perhaps this was the price which had to be paid for his dynamic leadership and his political achievements; but if that is so the price was not negligible.

* A. J. P. Taylor in *Four Faces*, pp. 43-6 enlarges on these major errors by Churchill. I agree with his arguments except that the statement that Churchill 'never relinquished his ultimate object of a Balkan offensive' shows misunderstanding of his purposes in that theatre.

As to his dealings with senior naval men it is of course obvious that war cannot be waged successfully by kid glove methods, and that the inefficient or unfit must be got rid of as quickly as possible. Yet Churchill wielded the executioner's axe so indiscriminately, and with so little attempt to ascertain whether his intended victims really were incompetent, that the injustices perpetrated were not few; and even today his treatment of some officers, and his invariable search for scapegoats when anything went wrong, leaves an impression amounting almost to vindictiveness – a fault which both A. V. Alexander and Pound also sometimes displayed. With Churchill the tendency to seek scapegoats was especially marked where his involvement in any operation was both deep and *personal* – as was the case with Narvik, Oran and Dakar in 1940.

The dreadfully late hours kept by Churchill, and his inconsideration towards the hard worked staff about them, added greatly to the strain imposed on the latter and to the misgivings senior officers felt about his methods. Lord Hankey recorded in his diary how in August 1942 some naval Captains were discussing this matter in the United Services Club, and one of them – probably Ralph Edwards or William Davis, both of whom have appeared in this narrative – came up to him and asked whether during the previous war the Cabinet had 'to meet in the middle of the night, and keep all the staffs waiting about until they had finished'. Hankey replied that late meetings had been very rare, and had never gone on after midnight.[7]

Churchill's outstanding moral and physical courage cannot of course be questioned. As to moral courage, his readiness to face difficult or unpopular issues constituted an essential element in his leadership. His physical courage is also proved up to the hilt; and, as Pascal remarked, 'Courage is the only sentiment which is almost as contagious as fear.' Churchill's courage certainly was contagious, especially in 1940–1 when it was most needed; but what is puzzling about that element in his character is his frequently demonstrated *enjoyment* of war. Professor Marder remarks how evident this was during a Channel crossing in 1940, and concludes, with perhaps a hint of reproach, that 'It would be foolish to deny that he enjoyed the war' – a view with which I am in full agreement.[7A] His determination to get himself put ashore soon after the Normandy landings of June 1944 ('I had a jolly day on Monday on the beaches and inland' he told Roosevelt) and his conduct at the crossing of the Rhine in March 1945 confirm that physical danger was positively exhilarating to him.[8] Yet such a view of warfare must surely raise some pretty big psychological questions.

In all the British fighting services of World War II there were, fortunately for the country, men of all ranks who possessed physical courage as great as Churchill's, or even greater. They generally volunteered for 'specially hazardous operations', or joined the Commandos or parachute regiments. I knew personally a number of officers who risked their lives in such a manner, and I believe their motives were as mixed as are most human motives. Some, like Commander Sir Geoffrey Congreve Bt., and Colonel Geoffrey Keyes probably wanted to show they were as brave as their fathers – General Sir Walter Congreve, VC and Admiral Sir Roger Keyes (Lord Keyes 1943) of Zeebrugge 1918 fame; and they both paid for such ambitions with their lives. Others, like Captain R. E. D. Ryder, VC, who led the raid on St Nazaire in March 1942, acted I believe out of a deeply felt if never expressed love of their country, and a desire to help it to the limit of their capacity. Such motives show of course complete selflessness.

I can think of two admirals of the twentieth century, both of whom I knew, who positively enjoyed war – Sir Roger Keyes and Sir Walter Cowan, who joined the Commandos though far beyond retiring age and served with them in the Middle East;[9] and Churchill's admiration for such men was probably not unconnected with the fact that their physical courage and their attitude towards war were similar to his own. Sir Andrew Cunningham, Sir Philip Vian and Lord Louis Mountbatten were also naval leaders possessed of outstanding courage, as were many who held lower rank; but such men did not show actual *enjoyment* of war as did Keyes and Cowan – and Churchill. I believe that the vast majority of servicemen of that era regarded their part in the war as an unpleasant duty which had to be accepted and seen through to the end. Their fundamental hope was to carry out their jobs with credit, often unobtrusively, and then to return home 'to enjoy the blessings of the land with the fruits of their labour' – and the company of their loved ones.* I think that such men contributed just as much to victory as did the more ostentatiously courageous; but Churchill always admired the latter, and possibly never fully appreciated the contribution of the former.

Churchill, as we have seen, kept very tight control over naval dispositions, over operations and over the appointments of senior officers, and was full of confidence in his ability to assess senior officers' qualities and deficiencies accurately. One example of his supreme

---

* See John Verney, *Going to the Wars* (Collins, 1955) for a brilliant account by one such officer who volunteered for hazardous service though in no doubt regarding his long-term hopes.

confidence in this matter may be mentioned. In June 1941 he wrote to Sir Archibald Sinclair, the Secretary of State for Air, 'I do not see how you can expect me to bear my responsibilities if my very clearly and courteously expressed wishes are not treated with proper respect and consideration. As Minister of Defence I am bound to take a direct part in all high appointments in the Fighting Services. No important appointment has been made by either of the two other services during my tenure without my being consulted . . .'[10] This self-confidence led him to initiate, or at any rate approve, some thoroughly bad appointments, such as that of Harwood as C-in-C, Mediterranean, and Edward-Collins to the Gibraltar command, and to toy with other nominees (notably Wingate to command the Burma army) which would have been equally unsuccessful, if not disastrous. The same feature of Churchill's character caused him to depreciate the qualities of others who in his view showed too much independence or a tendency to disobey orders. He was always on the look out for, and reacted very quickly against anything that could be described as obstinacy – plainly a reaction, possible subconscious, against 'Jacky' Fisher's behaviour in 1915. For example in 1940 he accused Admiral Fraser, the Third Sea Lord and Controller of the Navy, of '*deliberately* disobeying my orders and *obstinately* holding on to your naval repairs' instead of giving priority to repairing merchant ships[11] – which was especially absurd in the case of Fraser, who was always very attentive to Churchill's ideas and wishes.

We have seen how Churchill insisted that no major warships should be moved without his or the Defence Committee's approval; also that he himself frequently proposed changes in dispositions, such as bringing the Eastern Fleet's big ships through the Suez Canal to the Mediterranean in July 1942 or sending the same fleet to the Pacific west-about by the Panama Canal in September 1943. In effect he tried to remove all issues of naval strategy from the Admiralty and take them into his own hands. He also took a most lively interest in, and scrutinized minutely, each year's naval building programme, sometimes criticizing the Admiralty's proposals. For example in 1941 he was adamant that no big ships which would not complete in the following year could be approved, and that the designs of anti-U-boat vessels and minesweepers should be kept as simple as possible; and in 1943 he was critical of the Admiralty's proposal to build large Fleet-type destroyers.[12] His purpose obviously was to ensure that the country's limited capacity in materials, labour and money was used to the best advantage; and his long experience as First Lord had of course given him formidable knowledge of the way building programmes were framed, and what options were open with regard to them. Lord Fraser has remarked that 'he rarely pressed his case if sound arguments were put up against it';[13] but the despatch of the *Prince of Wales* and *Repulse* to Singapore in 1941 and the Aegean fiasco of 1943 surely lay that opinion open to challenge.

Churchill's extraordinary persistence in argument has often been remarked on, and there is ample evidence, some of which has been quoted here, that he would press a case both orally and in writing day after day and week after week, even if he did usually give way in the end – provided of course that his opponent had not already given in from sheer exhaustion, as Pound did on some occasions. As regards criticism of his proposals, anyone bold enough to do so too strongly was likely to receive very short shrift. If he persisted dismissal or rustication to a remote station was virtually certain – as in the cases of Captains V. H. Danckwerts and A. G. Talbot:* Robert Rhodes James has remarked on his 'habit of taking criticism personally',[14] which was certainly my own experience when he scanned the proofs of the first volume of my *War at Sea*. If the magnanimity which he preached could be highly selective, only rarely did he exhibit lasting rancour towards his critics.[15]

Admiral K. G. B. Dewar, no mean observer of the period and of its chief actors, wrote about recent studies of Churchill that they had shown 'strange ambivalence' in that they 'tried to differentiate between him as National Leader and as a strategist who sometimes usurped the functions of the COSs', in 'wanting to attack anywhere and everywhere regardless of any foreseeable object or long term policy'; and he gave Churchill's attitude to the convoy strategy and the bombing of Germany as examples.[16] I think there is a good deal of merit in that observation, and the research carried out for my war history and this book has produced much evidence in support of it.

In his attitude to the Indian Empire Churchill was incorrigible. On one occasion after the war when he met Mountbatten, who had recently returned home after completing the agreement for the independence of India and Pakistan, at Buckingham Palace and the admiral 'advanced towards him in a gay and friendly manner as usual', he said 'in a very gruff voice "Dickie, stop. What you did in India is as though you had struck me across the face with a riding whip"'; and walked away from his old friend, who was one of the admirals he most admired. They had no further communication until Churchill wrote to offer Mountbatten the post of First Sea Lord in 1955.[17]

* See p. 94.

It is of course impossible to weigh the benefits gained by the navy from his prodigious energy and fertility of ideas against the difficulties, troubles and losses incurred through what were, at any rate in part, his mistakes; but it is clear beyond doubt that almost all admirals who had personal contacts of any length and intimacy fell under the spell of his personality; and the fact that the second war at sea against Germany was so much better conducted than the first one may reasonably be attributed in part, though not entirely, to his leadership. Ronald Lewin, whose book will long remain one of the best studies of Churchill in the Second World War, has written that 'as a manager of war he was nonpareil';[18] and although parts of this study may make the reader feel that such a judgement requires some qualification it can hardly be seriously challenged. Furthermore whereas Franklin Roosevelt suffered from a dichotomy between the ideals for which he stood and the military need to win the war as quickly as possible and at a minimum cost in lives, and that dichotomy flawed his strategic judgement, Churchill suffered from no such complications. His purpose always was 'victory – victory at all costs, victory in spite of all terror; victory, however hard the road may be . . .';[19] and he carried with him in pursuit of that single-minded aim not only the navies of the Empire and Commonwealth but virtually the whole British people.

The fact that so many books and articles have been written about Churchill is proof enough of the fascination of his character, and because history is, in the words of the famous Dutch historian Pieter Geyl, 'an argument without end', the debate about his conduct of the war will doubtless continue. It may therefore be appropriate to conclude by reverting to Churchill's novel *Savrola*, mentioned for its value as a self-portrait at the beginning of this study, and to quote the eulogy by Thomas Babington Macaulay, the historian whose style influenced Churchill profoundly, of the statesman on whom he modelled so much of his political and strategic philosophy – William Pitt, Earl of Chatham. For in that work Churchill presents his hero as having Macaulay's essay on Pitt open at the 'sublime passage' which follows:

'And history, while for the warning of vehement, high and daring natures, she notes his many errors, will yet deliberately pronounce that among the eminent men whose bones lie near his, scarcely one has left a more stainless, and none a more splendid name.'*

* Quoted in *Savrola* (Hodder and Stoughton, Sevenpenny Library Ed.), p. 39. Originally published in Blackwood's Magazine, 1897. The quotation is taken from Macaulay's essay on the elder Pitt.

A Historical Controversy

One of the most difficult problems which every historian has, in my opinion, to decide is how much weight he should give to the various forms of oral and written evidence which come into his possession. As to the former, interviews can certainly be valuable; but such evidence must none the less be treated with caution – especially if the person interviewed has an interest, even perhaps a sub-conscious one, in propagating some particular point of view, or if he is speaking from memory of distant events. For memory, it is well known, is a most fickle jade. Written evidence, in the form of contemporary letters and diaries, may also be useful, but can be subject to distortion or prejudice similar to that sometimes encountered in oral evidence; while official minutes of high-level meetings are often as notable for what they omit as for what they record; since secretaries of such bodies as the Cabinet or Chiefs of Staffs' Committee tend to play down the differences of view or opinion expressed, and to give the impression that all discussions were harmoniously conducted. Such an impression can of course be very far from the truth.

One form of oral evidence which I have come to treat with caution is that which emanates from the Private Secretaries of or Personal Assistants to great men; since persons holding such posts are not likely to take an objective view of their masters' methods and actions. Nor can one expect a person who is so placed to press his master hard on a point of disagreement between them, since if such action were persisted in the master would be likely to replace the servant with someone more amenable.

My scepticism regarding this form of historical evidence derives in large measure from the fact that I possess a number of letters from private secretaries to the great, and such like individuals which can be shown to have pressed on me a very one-sided view on controversial issues. Some written statements from prominent men of World War II which I possess are equally partial and subjective, and in at least one case can be proved to be totally untrue. The laws of libel are such that to publish documents of that nature could land author and publisher in the law courts; and having been involved in one very protracted legal fight (Broome versus Cassell and Irving), and having received a threat of action for libel regarding a piece I did once publish, I have become very cautious in such matters. I have therefore put all such documents in safe hands, whence they will be made available to historians of the future when death has eliminated all risk of legal action.

The foregoing thoughts have been provoked by the extent to which Professor Arthur Marder has evidently placed confidence in and reliance on evidence emanating from such sources as the Private Secretary to Churchill as First Lord of the Admiralty 1939–40 and on those who served Admiral Sir Dudley Pound as Private Secretary or Personal Assistant when he was First Sea Lord 1939–43.* In 1972 Marder published an article entitled 'Winston is Back' in a Supplement to the *English Historical Review*, and he republished the article (with a number of corrections and insertions) in his book *From the Dardanelles to Oran* two years later. Both contained extracts from a letter written to him in September 1971 (over 30 years after the events discussed) by Sir Eric Seal, who was Private Secretary to Churchill as First Lord. In passing it may be remarked that Sir John Lang, the very able and clear-headed civil servant who was for a large part of World War II head of the Admiralty's War Registry (WR), which was responsible for the distribution of all incoming and outgoing signals, and later Permanent Secretary of the Admiralty, described Seal as 'an able man' but also 'a very assured person and apt to be certain of the rightness of his view'.[1]

To save the reader trouble I first reproduce below the very carefully worded summary of the cause and effects of the Admiralty's interventions in the Norwegian campaign, some of which were mentioned in Chapter 8, and the relevant extract about it from the letter which Sir Eric Seal wrote to Professor Marder.

(A) *The War at Sea*, Vol. I, p. 202.

After discussing Admiral Pound's intentions regarding control of the

---

* Marder cites, and quotes from letters written by Admiral Sir Ronald Brockman (Secretary to Admiral Pound), Rear-Admiral J. W. A. Waller (Personal Assistant to Pound), Sir Eric Seal (Private Secretary to Churchill), Captain G. R. G. Allen (Naval historical assistant to Churchill post-war) and Captain J. S. S. Litchfield (Joint Planning Staff under Pound) in his article 'Winston is Back', republished from the *English Historical Review*, Supplement No. 5 (1972) in *From the Dardanelles to Oran* (Oxford UP, 1974) pp. 169–70.

fleet as expressed in his pre-war letter to Admiral Forbes already quoted I continued as follows:

'The reader will therefore ask why it was that, throughout the campaign discussed in this chapter [i.e. the Norwegian campaign], the Admiralty's actions ran contrary to the First Sea Lord's expressed intentions. There can be no doubt that the powerful personality of the First Lord was a large factor in bringing this about. Mr Churchill used, during critical periods of naval operations, to spend long hours in the Admiralty Operational Intelligence Centre and the tendency for him to assume control therefrom is easily to be understood. Many of the signals sent during such periods bear the unmistakable imprint of his language and personality and, admirable though their purpose and intention were, it now appears plain that they sometimes confused the conduct of operations and increased the difficulties of the Commander-in-Chief. Mr Churchill makes an interesting comment on this question. Dealing with the cancellation of the attack on Bergen he says 'Looking back on this affair, I consider the Admiralty kept too close a control upon the Commander-in-Chief, and after learning his original intention to force the passage into Bergen *we should have confined ourselves to sending him information.'** It may, however, be considered that this comment does not go deep enough, since not only was the action taken by the Admiralty in respect of the Bergen attack by no means an isolated example of intervention from Whitehall at this period, but it fails to expose the inevitably difficult position in which a Naval Commander-in-Chief is placed if his plans and intentions are at any time to be altered or cancelled by his superiors ashore. The whole question is one which must be approached with caution . . . '

(B) *Sir Eric Seal to Professor Marder 8 September 1971*†

(Insertions made by me are in square brackets and are italicized). Arthur J. Marder, *From the Dardanelles to Oran* (Oxford UP, 1974) pp. 169-70.

'It is perfectly true that he [Churchill] spent a good deal of time in the War Room, which had a tremendous fascination for him. To infer from this that he assumed control is, in the circumstances, almost malicious. It is certainly utterly unwarranted and false. I made a careful search of all the signals sent by the Admiralty between 7 and 19 April [1940], and there were only two

---

* Churchill, *Second World War*, I, p. 470. Italics supplied here. Note the plural pronoun in the italicized sentence; also the principle stated by Churchill corresponds exactly to Admiral Forbes's expressed wish. See pp. 116-17.
† Reproduced by kind permission of the author.

with characteristic marks of Churchill's phraseology, which I may say I am pretty competent to detect! One is an appeal for fuller current information [*probably Admiralty signal timed 0148 of 28 April. Note the date. S. R.*], which was I think dictated in the First Sea Lord's presence, but which was sent off from my office as a personal message, and the other is referred to by Roskill on page 186 [of *The War at Sea, Vol. I*] who clearly did not recognize the First Lord's hand. It is an appeal to the C-in-C [*Home Fleet*] to reconsider the proposed attack on Trondheim ['*Hammer*'], which contains the characteristic Churchillism '*Pray therefore* consider this important project further.' Roskill omits the underlined words, without realizing that Pound would never have used this phrase, although his Secretary actually sent the message off.'

Well, well! Let us review the available evidence regarding Churchill at the Admiralty in 1939–40.

Marder declares that 'The fact is that, notwithstanding his great influence as First Lord (for better or worse) he did *not* dominate his professional advisers', and that, remembering the criticism which he brought on himself by his involvement in the Dardanelles campaign of 1915, he 'leaned over backwards now . . . not to lay down the law upon strategy or operational matters to the sailors';[2] but he admits that later as Prime Minister 'he interfered, or tried to interfere, with naval operations much more than when he was at the Admiralty'.[3] That Churchill did as Prime Minister act as Marder states is beyond argument. To quote A. J. P. Taylor 'He also intruded into the detailed operations of war and, when told that Hitler constantly interfered with his generals replied "I do the same".'[4] The question at issue is therefore whether or not he acted in a similar manner as First Lord. Common sense surely suggests that as a departmental head he would have had more inclination to interfere, more information to act on in that manner, as well as more time to devote to naval problems and operations, than when he came to hold the vastly greater responsibilities of Prime Minister and Minister of Defence; but more than the application of common sense may reasonably be required to disprove Marder's assertion and to contradict the evidence supplied to him largely by officers and officials of the Private Secretary–Personal Assistant type.

Let us look first at Churchill's own definition of his responsibilities and actions as First Lord of World War I. 'I accepted full responsibility', he wrote, 'for bringing about successful results, and in that spirit I exercised a close general supervision over everything that was done and proposed. Further I claimed and exercised an unlimited power of suggestion and initiative over the whole field, subject only to the approval and agreement of the First Sea Lord on all operative orders.'[5] Such terms of reference were, one may reasonably feel, cast very widely, and Marder has himself written that they prescribed 'too inflated a conception of his functions'.[6] On returning to the Admiralty in 1939 Churchill had evidently not modified his view of his responsibilities, since he wrote in his memoirs that 'By the Letters Patent constituting the Board the First Lord is "responsible to Crown and Parliament for all the business of the Admiralty", *and I certainly felt prepared to discharge that duty in fact as well as in form*' (italics supplied).[7] With regard to the methods used in discharging his responsibilities Churchill wrote 'All I wanted was compliance with my wishes after reasonable discussion'; but, as Mr Taylor has remarked 'it was compliance he wanted all the same, and those who opposed his ideas too persistently paid the penalty' – of dismissal or rustication.[8]

Professor Michael Howard has described Churchill as 'an imperious Prime Minister',[9] and the same characterization applies I am sure to his time as First Lord – though I would incline to call his direction of affairs authoritarian. But it can reasonably be argued that for the Admiralty as it was from 1832 to 1967 to function efficiently an authoritarian at its head was essential, especially in time of war. In support of that suggestion we have the example of the Arthur Balfour-Admiral Sir Henry Jackson régime of 1915–16 as a warning of the consequences of ineffective direction of naval policy.[10] Nor is Churchill the only First Lord to have held the concept of his functions quoted above; for there is an interesting precedent in Sir James Graham (1792–1861), who was also one of the few persons who have held the office of First Lord twice (1830–4 and 1852–5). His second term of office covered the Crimean War, and it was during that conflict that he told the House of Commons 'from time to time it is indispensable that the First Lord should in his private room constitute a Board, give an order, and sometimes, even without that form, give directions to the Secretary to issue a circular, he himself being responsible for the character of that order'.[11] Though Churchill certainly never claimed, nor behaved as though he claimed such wide personal powers as Graham they can both be reasonably described as authoritarian.[12]

Furthermore, as was remarked earlier, in World War I Churchill certainly did not always observe the qualification to his power of obtaining 'approval and agreement of the First Sea Lord' – notably over the signals sent at the time of the escape of the *Goeben* and *Breslau* to Constantinople, and over naval reinforcements for the Dardanelles. Obviously it is important to consider, when judging Marder's thesis about his not dominating his professional advisers in 1939–40, whether Churchill's conduct on returning to the Admiralty differed materially from his own description of his methods during his first tenure of that office. Here Marder's article under analysis is of great help, since careful study of it strongly suggests that there was only one major change – namely that in World War II he rarely, if ever, drafted Admiralty signals and telegrams in his own hand – as he certainly did on occasions in the first conflict.[13] But, as we shall see, he undoubtedly dictated messages sent in the Admiralty's name in the second conflict, though he generally showed them to the First Sea Lord and had them sent *in their joint names*. The events of 1915 obviously had instilled in his mind the need for caution in exercising his responsibilities – though one may doubt whether he actually viewed them very differently.

In a legalistic sense the statutory responsibilities of the First Lord under the Letters Patent appointing all members of the Board of Admiralty were of course quite unchanged. But the whole of Marder's chapter under scrutiny surely indicates that neither Churchill's view of his responsibilities nor his methods of carrying them out seriously differed in 1939–40 from what they had been in 1914–15. The accounts given by Marder of his views and actions on the recruitment and promotion of personnel; his advocacy of dummy warships for deception purposes; the strong support given to Professor Lindemann's 'Naval Wire Barrage' and other costly futilities designed to improve A-A defence (about which Churchill certainly overruled the naval staff division responsible); the counter-measures to the magnetic mine; the controversy on capital ship construction; his anti-U-boat policy and strategy (which was based on a premise quickly proved false, namely that 'hunting' was superior to 'convoy and escort'); his persistent and public exaggeration of our successes against the U-boats; his early attempt to pressurize the Irish Free State government to give us the use of the bases surrendered in 1938; his better advised attempts to get the Home Fleet's main base at Scapa properly defended; his fantastic 'trench-cutting tank' proposal; his strong support for operation 'Royal Marine', the dropping of fluvial mines in German rivers and canals; his ideas for catching German surface raiders; his great part in preparing for 'operation Catherine', the naval incursion into the Baltic about which Admiral Pound wrote 'I have had a long fight [with Churchill]' and 'much money and energy has been expended';[14] his pressure to cut off Germany's supply of Swedish iron ore – and many other examples, some of them mentioned by Marder and others cited here, surely confirm the applicability of his World War I description of his responsibilities to the second conflict. Indeed it would detract from the impulse which Churchill indisputably applied to all aspects of the sea affair in 1939 to suggest otherwise.

The opening of the Norwegian campaign on 7 April 1940 brought about a clear change in and extension of Churchill's methods – partly because continuous land, sea and air operations replaced the earlier occasional engagements at sea like the River Plate battle on 13 December 1939, and partly because Churchill probably saw in the new clash a parallel with the Dardanelles campaign of 1915, its lost opportunities, and above all its disastrous effects on his own career. It is chiefly over the conduct of the Norway operations, and my carefully worded criticism of Churchill's interferences in them, that Marder has based his attack on me. Whereas Marder writes about Churchill's alleged determination 'not to lay down the law upon strategy or operational matters to the sailors', and that 'the only exceptions were his personal intervention in the *Altmark* episode [of 17 February 1940] and *possibly* [Marder's italics] in one or two instances during the Norwegian campaign'[15] I suggested that his interferences were much more frequent, and that they sometimes had unfortunate results. In this connection it is interesting to remark that when Churchill sent the proofs of Vol. I of my *War at Sea* to Captain G. R. G. Allen, the officer who had acted as naval assistant to him when writing his memoirs, with the object of rebutting my case, Allen drew his attention to the fact that he himself had already placed on record his retrospective view that the Admiralty interfered unduly with the commanders of operations during the Norwegian campaign.[16]

To enable the reader to understand this controversy I must digress for a moment to describe the conditions under which I worked when I joined the Cabinet Office Historical Section in 1949, and the state of the Admiralty's records at that time. Though the Operational Intelligence Centre (OIC) had been closed down soon after the end of the war (and, most unfortunately, its daily War Diary had been destroyed), the War Registry (WR) was still functioning, though only on a skeleton basis and in normal working hours. The vast accumulation of In and Out signals which had passed through the WR during the war was still intact, and was preserved in basement rooms in the Admiralty. As these signals were arranged in daily bundles chronologically it was not difficult to locate the 'office copy' of any signal. Unfortunately *all* these signal bundles have been destroyed fairly recently during the process known as 'weeding' departmental papers before they are transferred to the Public Record Office. This holocaust is likely to prove a severe handicap

to historians of the future, who will only be able to find signals if for
some reason they were enclosed in an Admiralty 'docket' which has
been preserved or in private papers.

In my time in the Cabinet Office there were, however, two very
important exclusions from the signals collected and preserved in the
daily bundles referred to above. The first was that the office copies of
signals bearing the highest security classification of 'Hush. Most Secret'
or 'Personal and Private from First Lord and First Sea Lord' were kept
in the specially secure section of the Admiralty's Record Office known
as 'the cage'. Though I had to obtain permission on each occasion that
I needed access to such signals it was never refused to me. The second
exclusion was that no signal bearing the 'Special' (later 'Ultra') endorse-
ment, meaning that its contents were derived from cryptographic
intelligence or other very secret sources, were included in the daily
bundles.* They were kept in the office of the Head of War Registry,
and the right of access to such signals accorded to me meant that I could,
and quite often did, ask to see ones of particular interest – though I was
not allowed to quote from them.†

However, the Admiralty was at the time very sticky about me taking
any of their papers, most of which were still in their original 'dockets',
over to the Cabinet Office for study, and of my having copies made of
any of them. It was only after an appeal to the Permanent Secretary
that I obtained permission to remove not more than three dockets at a
time; and I was only allowed to have copies of papers made provided
that the typing was done in the Admiralty's own Record Office and I
returned the copies to the department when I had finished with them.
This was of course long before the days when Xerox copying or
micro-filming made the reproduction of documents so much quicker
and easier.

In defence of the Admiralty's stickiness over the loan and copying of
documents two points must in fairness be stressed. The first is that the
'Fifty Year Rule' regarding the release of official papers was then still in
force, and no one could foresee that under the 1967 Public Record Act
the 'closed period' would be reduced to thirty years, and that some
though by no means all of the World War II records would be released
simultaneously. Secondly, considerations regarding the security of

* F. W. Winterbotham in *The Ultra Secret* (Weidenfeld and Nicolson, 1974) is wrong
to say that such prefixes only applied to signals derived from cryptanalysis.
† Commander P. K. Kemp, who was Head of the Admiralty's Historical Section
1950-68 wholly confirms my recollections of the organization of the Admiralty's
signals at the time in question. Letter of 11 November 1976.

wartime cyphers were still regarded as being of paramount importance, and thence arose the segregation of all messages sent in high grade cyphers under special security restrictions.

Quite early in my research I realized that Churchill's method of communicating with the C-in-C, Home Fleet, Sir Charles Forbes, was a matter of great historical interest and importance, but a very tricky one for me to handle. I had much correspondence and several meetings with Forbes on this matter, especially after Admiral Sir Ralph Edwards, who was then Third Sea Lord, had lent me his two diaries referred to earlier. I then realized the extent of Churchill's interference in the Norwegian campaign (and not only in the naval side of it by any means), and sought out the signals to which Edwards made reference in his diaries. In passing I would remark that both here and elsewhere I have quoted from the Edwards diaries completely accurately, and not 'with extreme inaccuracy' as Marder has written in obvious ignorance of there being two diaries kept by the same person.[17] The copy of the Edwards diary from which they are taken, which he had specially made for me and which has his own marginal annotations, I have fortunately preserved, and in 1976 I produced it for perusal by Marder in my College.[18]

As already stated Marder's attack on my account of Churchill's interference in the Norwegian campaign, and especially the Narvik operations, is based chiefly on letters sent him by Sir Eric Seal. He mentions that Churchill 'was gravely upset' by my account, which is correct. The proofs of *The War at Sea*, Vol. I had been sent to him, then again Prime Minister, by Sir Norman Brook the Secretary of the Cabinet.

To turn to Seal's letter to Marder of 8 September 1971 he is of course wholly wrong to say that I did not recognize that the prefix 'Pray therefore . . .' to a message signified a Churchillian origin. No one who served on the naval staff 1939–41, as I did, could possibly be unaware of that fact, because Churchill's 'prayers', as they were colloquially called, constantly streamed in to us. It was purely for syntactical reasons that I omitted the words in the message quoted by Seal.

In the same letter to Marder Seal tells how he was given the help of Commander G. A. Titterton of the Admiralty's Historical Section (HS) to search the signal files; but Titterton knew little or nothing about the Norwegian campaign. He had been working for the Admiralty on the Naval Staff History of Mediterranean operations – and without any marked distinction or success. The officer of the HS who *was* very familiar with the Norwegian campaign, and possessed a vastly superior intellect to Titterton's, was Commander L. J. Pitcairn-

Jones; and he and I worked in intimate and cordial collaboration and never disagreed on any important issue. When I sent him the draft of my chapter on the campaign he replied 'May I congratulate you on the ground you have covered so adequately and concisely. I think our main conclusions agree remarkably.'[19] I was abroad at the time the Seal-Titterton 'search' took place in the autumn of 1953, and was never consulted about it. Nor was I told it had taken place on my return, which suggests an odd degree of secrecy on the part of the Admiralty. I can now only guess that Titterton and not Pitcairn-Jones was chosen to help Seal because Pitcairn-Jones's health was not robust at the time; but the fact that Seal says there were only two Churchillian messages (Titterton mentions four) strongly suggests that they missed the whole of the 'First Lord and First Sea Lord. Personal and Private' messages which passed between the Admiralty and Admiral of the Fleet Lord Cork and Orrery, the Flag Officer, Narvik, most of which were only to be found in the closely guarded Record Office 'cage' referred to above, and which were sent in the private cypher line arranged by Churchill for such communications to which Edwards refers in his diary. Marder remarks that 'the signals exchanged between Churchill and Cork' between 19 April and 23 May 1940 'have been brought together' in a certain PRO file.[20] But recent inspection of that file shows that the first 'First Lord to Lord Cork, Personal and Private' message was sent late on *17 April*.[21] and the first message by the same channel in the reverse direction was sent next day[22] – that is to say one and two days *before* the period referred to by Marder begins. However, *all* the signals which passed between the Admiralty and Lord Cork are not originals but typed copies which lack some or all of the indications regarding Priority, Security Classification, Distribution and Approving Authority which would have been shown on the originals. I am convinced that these typewritten copies are those which I had made and returned to the Admiralty as described above; for at the time I was concerned chiefly with the text of such messages. I cannot explain why it is that after 20 April originals have been preserved but not before that date. Furthermore some of the type-written copies which from their wording must have been initiated by Churchill only show 'Admiralty to Flag Officer, Narvik' as the address. Although therefore caution is necessary in the use of the PRO file in question the best analysis I can give of its contents is as follows:

(A) First Lord *or* First Lord and First Sea Lord to Lord Cork – eighteen when Churchill was First Lord. There are also three sent after he had become Prime Minister; but on Marder's thesis they should be excluded.

(B)   Cork to First Lord – twenty-five when Churchill held that office. There are also two sent after Churchill became Prime Minister and seven after A. V. Alexander became First Lord; but again they should be excluded if, following Marder, we consider only the period when Churchill was First Lord.

Confirmation of the suggestion that the Seal-Titterton 'search' never located the Personal and Private messages is provided by the fact that, in contrast to Seal's assertion that he found only two characteristic 'Churchillisms' almost *all* the Personal and Private Out messages contain unmistakeable and easily recognizable Churchillian phraseology. To give some examples: 'Pray [how could Seal have missed that prefix?] regard this telegram as my own personal opinion . . .';[23] or 'It seems to me that you [Lord Cork] can feel your way and yet strike hard';[24] or, with regard to General Mackesy 'If this officer appears to be spreading a bad spirit . . . do not hesitate to relieve him or place him under arrest';[25] or 'Here it is [at Narvik] we must fight and persevere on the largest scale possible';[26] or 'I must regard the next six or seven days as possibly decisive';[27] or 'I shall be glad to share your responsibilities'.[28] On 7 May a message referring to 'conveying the troops in HM ships or merchant ships close to the landing places as was done at Gallipoli', though sent 'from First Sea Lord' strongly suggests a different originator.[29] But perhaps an earlier Personal and Private signal from the First Lord to Lord Cork shows how wrong that author is to ascribe such messages only to Churchill's time as Prime Minister; since it told the admiral in detail and at considerable length exactly how, in Churchill's view, Narvik could and should be captured.[30] This message was in truth a remarkable parallel to one sent by Churchill during the Dardanelles campaign, which a critic quoted by Marder has stigmatized as 'one of those peculiarly objectionable messages in which the man on the spot is not only urged to attack but told how to do it . . .'; and, as was remarked about the earlier signal, this one 'in its easy and superficial reference to very difficult tasks, bears the unmistakable impress of the First Lord's hand.'[30A]

Doubtless many of the 'prodding' messages such as are quoted above would have encouraged early and positive action by the local commanders – had it been possible in the prevailing weather conditions and with the resources available; but there are several instances where remote control of this nature proved positively dangerous. Such were

the messages cancelling Admiral Forbes's intended attack on Bergen on
9 April, and those sent direct to Captain Warburton-Lee over the heads
of the C-in-C and Admiral Whitworth mentioned in Chapter 8.
And although Forbes erred in sending his two battle-cruisers to
counter what proved to be a false report of an enemy landing in Iceland
instead of using them to cover and escort the very vulnerable troop
convoys during the evacuation of Narvik,[31] there is substance in his
complaint that the successes achieved by *Scharnhorst* and *Gneisenau*
during their sortie of 4–13 June 1940 and the narrow escape of the
troop convoys from disaster arose chiefly from the divided control
between himself and Lord Cork, and 'the Admiralty not keeping me
informed of Lord Cork's programme'.[32] Support for this suggestion is
provided by Lord Cork's protest to Churchill that whereas one of his
messages was sent in the cypher 'which I believed ensured private
communication with yourself' the Admiralty had answered it in a
cypher which included the C-in-C, Home Fleet in the addressees![33]
Why Cork should have wanted to keep Forbes in the dark about the
evacuation is inexplicable; but it does emphasize the total lack of co-
ordination between the two commands brought about by Churchill's
stream of 'Private and Personal' messages to Cork. In final proof of
Churchill's part it may be remarked that on 14 May he signalled
'Private from Prime Minister' to Cork saying that although he was
leaving the Admiralty 'I shall, as Minister of Defence preserve the close
personal contact with you which I trust has been a help'[34] – a sentiment
which Alexander told Cork he 'fully shared' with Churchill.[35] Four
days later Cork signalled to Churchill 'I thank you for your assistance
and assurance of continued close interest which in the past has been
of the greatest help';[36] and on the 21st the admiral assured him that the
'desire not to fail you is uppermost in my mind'.[37] None of the foregoing messages were repeated to Forbes – which may not have mattered. But on 4 June Cork signalled to Churchill *only* that '4500 men
[were] embarked last night without incident'.[38] This was the start of
the evacuation, and it seems quite incomprehensible that Cork should
not have informed Forbes about it, and that the Admiralty did not
pass on his message to the C-in-C.

The foregoing extracts from the many signals which passed between
London and Narvik between 17 April and 4 June 1940 surely make it
clear, firstly, that the relationship between Churchill and Lord Cork
was of an extraordinary nature, and included constant interference by
the former in operational matters; and, secondly, that Seal's attack on
me was quite unwarranted. It has of course never been suggested by

me that only Churchill interfered in naval operations – either as First Lord or Prime Minister. Rather is it well known, and I have repeatedly emphasized it, that Pound was extremely prone to 'back seat driving', sometimes with disastrous results.[39]

On the qualities and failings of Admiral Sir Dudley Pound as a C-in-C afloat and as First Sea Lord, and in particular his relations with Churchill, I can claim some first-hand knowledge; for I served two years as First Lieutenant and Gunnery Officer of Pound's flagship the *Warspite* in the Mediterranean, followed after promotion to Commander in 1938 by a few months as her Executive Officer and Second-in-Command. From that appointment I went directly to the Admiralty almost simultaneously with Pound taking over as First Sea Lord. 'Roskill', writes Marder, 'was a Commander in this period and nowhere near the top echelon in the Naval Staff. Certainly he was in no position to know what passed between Churchill and Pound and therefore to have been able to make a perceptive assessment of their relationship.'[40] The first sentence is correct as regards my rank; but many of the officers whose evidence Marder cites in support of his views were of the same rank or only one step higher than me *at that time*;[41] and the desk I took over was the one responsible for all anti-aircraft defence – which I well knew from recent sea experience would prove one of the hottest seats in the Admiralty. As I wrote some years ago, and no one challenged at the time, Pound 'used quite often to summon me to explain some problem . . . or, on several occasions, to act as his emissary on visits to the Home Fleet flagship. I always reported directly to him on return from these visits . . .'* To particularize on the latter I well recall Pound telling me to get to Scapa 'as quickly as possible' and report on the first German air attack on that base on 16 October 1939 – because I chartered a private aircraft in order to avoid the long and very slow rail and ship journey; and I got into trouble when the bill reached the Admiralty! Pound sent me there again early in the Norwegian campaign to collect first-hand information on the German air attacks and the effects (or ineffectiveness) of our A-A gunfire. I was sent up again several times to expedite the construction of an A-A training establishment on the

---

* *Sunday Telegraph*, 18 February 1962. Third of a series of articles entitled 'Churchill and his Admirals'. Since writing the above I have received, quite unexpectedly and unsolicited, a letter from Forbes's former Flag Lieutenant, now Commander Sir Godfrey Style, reminding me how he met me at the flagship's gangway late in 1939 and took me to the C-in-C's cabin. 'I do remember,' writes Style, 'you came up [to Scapa] on some quite specific mission' – which is perfectly true, though the occasion referred to was by no means unique.

Orkney west coast, and to see it at work when it was ready; and I was onboard both the *Hood* and *Prince of Wales* at Scapa as soon as we knew the *Bismarck* was at Bergen in May 1941 in order to check their recently installed main armament radar sets. It is true that I got into the bad books of both Pound and Churchill (the former only temporarily) for opposing the despatch of weapons of which we ourselves were desperately short to help the Finns in their 'Winter War' of 1939–40 against the Russians (because I was sure the Germans would capture them), and for opposing the substitution of Professor Lindemann's abortion known as the Naval Wire Barrage for conventional guns in certain ships. But I regarded all such troubles as part of the day's work, and Pound never allowed himself to show rancour towards me.

When Professor Marder pronounces on my opportunities for informing myself on the exchanges between Pound and Churchill I can only infer that he is speaking *ex cathedra* where appeals to reason or to evidence do not lie. But we are here concerned with history. The relationship between Pound and Churchill was of course a constant subject of discussion among the Staff in 1939–40, as Churchill's exhortations, admonitions and 'prayers' reached us in a never-ending flow; and there is no subject on which I had more correspondence and interviews than this while working on *The War at Sea*. To give only one example Admiral Forbes wrote to me 'I too have thought a lot about what he [Pound] did or did not do as First Sea Lord. I knew him very well [he then recounts how their service often coincided] . . . D. P. was a tired man when he became First Sea Lord. From the time he was a Commander he went from one job straight to another . . . he was very ambitious and had a high sense of duty which led him to work too hard, some of it quite unnecessarily . . . D. P. had no hobbies except shooting and fishing. The trouble is our Service is too competitive. The other trouble is that no naval officer is a match for a Minister politician. Resignation is no answer. It is forgotten in a fortnight.'[42]

I have written elsewhere about Pound's physical disability, namely osteo-arthritis of the left hip, and the probable effects on his sleeping habits and hours of work.[43] For Marder to write that Pound showed no signs of physical deterioration before 1943 is nonsense. Apart from the fact that early in 1939 the Fleet Medical Officer on Pound's staff said to me, perhaps indiscreetly, on the *Warspite*'s quarterdeck in Malta that, if war came, he did not believe the C-in-C fit for the post he then held, Sir Arthur Bryant, quoting from Lord Alanbrooke's diary, remarks how by the autumn of 1941 'The First Sea Lord was growing old and tired', that Brooke found that the COS Committee got through its business far more quickly 'in the chairman's [i.e. Pound's] absence'; and he gives detailed evidence of the same state of affairs in his diary entries for 17 February 1942 and the following day.* And let an officer from my own division of the naval staff describe a meeting quite early in the war which I am sure was not unique. Captain G. H. Roberts, who later ran the Tactical Training School for the Western Approaches Command with outstanding success, was called to a staff meeting held by Pound shortly after Italy entered the war in June 1940 to discuss the supply of our latest type of 6-inch ammunition, of which we were very short, to ships engaged in the campaign against Italian East Africa. Captain A. J. (later Admiral of the Fleet Sir Arthur) Power, the ACNS (Home), was sitting on Pound's right hand. 'After a not very long time', writes Roberts, 'I noticed that Pound was drooling down the stem of his pipe – not just a drop, for I was at least five yards away. He may not have been asleep but he was quite "out for the count". It was noticeable that Power was aware of this, for he continued the meeting as if his Chief was no longer present. I have never said this before, but having read your letter [in the *Daily Telegraph* of 7 March 1970] which I believe is absolutely right I thought you might like to hear of it.'[44] Though my letter in the *Daily Telegraph* produced some strongly expressed contrary views from officers who had been close to Pound in the Admiralty, others wrote fully agreeing with me.† For example Commander R. T. Bower, an MP who was also one of the Naval Liaison Officers at Coastal Command Headquarters in 1940, wrote 'Being often in the Admiralty in the Lower War Room I saw a lot of him [Pound] and the criticisms to which you refer were almost universal, especially among the more junior ranks (Duty Captains etc.). As an MP I was urged to "raise the matter in the House" . . . I felt, however, that as a serving officer this would be undesirable. The matter was, however, seriously discussed . . . When I saw him [Pound] just after the war started he hobbled into the operations room at Coastal Command, and I noticed with horror that he had become a worn out old

* *The Turn of the Tide*, Ed. Arthur Bryant, (Collins, 1957), pp. 275, 285 and 308. 'Am getting more and more worried by old Dudley Pound as First Sea Lord . . . He is asleep 75% of the time he should be working.' Alanbrooke later qualified this diary entry, referring to Pound as 'this very fine sailor who at the time was a very sick man . . .'

† Admiral Lord Ashbourne (20 March 1970), Captain John Litchfield (6 April 1970) and Admiral J. W. A. Waller (28 July 1973) wrote disagreeing with me to a greater or lesser extent. Among those who agreed with me were Admiral J. H. Godfrey (undated received 10 March 1970) and Admiral Sir William James (many letters).

man. His hair was snow-white and wispy, his face seamed and ashen and there was a noticeable distortion of one eye ...'[45]

It is unlikely that the two sides to this controversy will ever be wholly reconciled; but Admiral of the Fleet Sir Algernon Willis, who was Pound's Chief of Staff in the Mediterranean in 1939, probably represents as fair a balance as can be obtained. He wrote to me that 'In those days he [Pound] was sometimes found asleep at his desk at two in the morning. This was due to the bad habit he'd got into of working on papers until a late hour ... I've always thought that for the good of the service and the war effort DP ought to have given up towards the end of 1941 ... Sir Charles Forbes, then C-in-C, Plymouth, was well equipped by experience to be First Sea Lord, but I believe Churchill didn't like him for some reason connected with a signal Forbes made when invasion was considered a possibility' – doubtless a reference to Forbes's 'final appeal' about the disposition of the fleet dealt with above.*[46] What is surely indisputable is that, despite his disabilities, Pound suited Churchill very well as First Sea Lord – because there was never the slightest danger of the sort of crisis provoked by 'Jacky' Fisher in May 1915 arising as long as he was the professional head of the navy. As Anthony Storr has written, Churchill 'demanded total and uncritical acceptance' by his colleagues and associates – a standpoint from which Pound rarely diverged.[47] Indeed the evidence which contradicts Marder's assertion that Churchill 'did *not* dominate his professional advisers',[48] even to the extent of getting rid of those who argued too forcibly with him, is overwhelming; and Churchill's greatness as a war leader would in fact be vitiated were it true.

To return to Marder's book and his remarks about me I can no more accept the evidence of the Private Secretaries and Personal Assistants to Pound, on which he places great reliance than I can accept that of Seal in Churchill's case. But despite this disagreement there are many points on which I am in complete accord with Marder. Pound *was* 'the supreme centralizer' (I recall a late night meeting to which I was summoned to discuss the allocation of Lewis guns to small craft!).[49] Secondly Churchill 'never completely grasped the nature of maritime war',[50] nor, I would add, the complexity and hazards of combined operations. Lastly, though I think Marder exaggerates the skill with which Pound handled Churchill, and some naval disasters might have been avoided had he stood up to him more often and more resolutely,[51] there is surely no doubt that he had a very difficult man to deal with. Moreover his loyalty to Churchill, if sometimes overdone (notably by

* See p. 119.

taking on himself the blame for the loss of the *Prince of Wales* and *Repulse*) is surely to be admired. Pound had none of the arrogance of many of the earlier twentieth-century British admirals, and I here re-assert my view that he was, basically a humble man[52] – as is shown by Lord Alanbrooke's account of the tact and grace with which he handed over to him the chairmanship of the COS Committee on 9 March 1942.[53] But whilst one may respect his humility it is none the less possible to doubt whether he was a big enough man for the job.

Notes and Sources

1 Churchill to Lord Hugh Cecil 24 October 1903. Not actually sent. Randolph S. Churchill, *Winston Churchill* (Heinemann, 1969), II, pp. 70–2. This multi-volume authorized biography is henceforth cited as *Churchill* for vols. I and II, and Gilbert, *Churchill* for the later volumes. His own memoirs of World Wars I and II are cited as Churchill, *World Crisis* and Churchill, *Second World War* respectively.

2 Churchill, *World Crisis*, I, p. 67.

3 ibid., p. 70.

4 Churchill, *My Early Life* (Macmillan, 1930).

5 See N. A. M. Rodger, *The Dark Ages of the Admiralty*, Part I. *The Mariners' Mirror*, vol. 61. no. 4. (November 1975).

6 On Wilson's character and outlook see Churchill, *World Crisis*, I, pp. 79–82 and Arthur J. Marder, *From the Dreadnought to Scapa Flow*, I (Oxford UP, 1961), pp. 255–6. Henceforth cited as *Marder*. Wilson accepted Churchill's offer that he should replace Fisher on the latter's resignation in May 1915, but withdrew when he learnt that Churchill was not to stay on as First Lord.

7 J. S. Sanders, Balfour's private secretary, to Balfour 14 December 1911 and 10 October 1912. See Churchill, *World Crisis*, II, pp. 541–2 and 628–30.

8 See *Marder*, I, pp. 258–9.

9 ibid., pp. 260–1 gives a full account of this row.

10 Richard Hough, *Louis and Victoria* (Hutchinson, 1974) p. 268. Henceforth cited as *Hough*.

11 Fisher to Balfour 5 January 1904. Arthur J. Marder (ed.), *Fear God and Dread Nought. The correspondence of Admiral of the Fleet Lord Fisher of Kilverstone* (3 vols., Cape, 1952–9), I, p. 293. Henceforth cited as Marder, *Fear God*.

12 ibid., II, p. 317.

13 *Hough*, pp. 247 and 255–6. However in my view this biographer has made Battenberg's attitude to promotion from the lower deck appear in too favourable a light. I am indebted to Commander H. Pursey, himself an early promotion from the lower deck, for information about the Fisher-Yexley reforms. See his article in *Brassey's Naval Annual* for 1938; also *Marder*, I, pp. 28–33. A good account of Churchill's efforts to achieve reforms in the field of personnel is in Admiral Sir Peter Gretton's book *Former Naval Person* (Cassell, 1968), ch. 5.

14 Memo. entitled 'Commissioned rank for Warrant Officers' dated 12 March 1912. Broadlands Archive.

15 Hansard, vol. XXXV. The naval estimates were debated on 18, 19 and 20 March 1912. The passage quoted is in col. 1570.

16 ibid., col. 1591.

17 ibid., cols. 1572–3.

17A The reforms initiated by the Brock Committee were summarized in Churchill's statement to Parliament on the Navy Estimates for 1913–14 and are reproduced in *Brassey's Naval Annual* for 1913, pp. 447–56. Punishments such as standing on the upper deck facing the paintwork (the hated no. 10B) were abolished; but the right of Petty Officers to trial by Court Martial as an alternative to summary disrating, for which Yexley had pressed, was not granted.

18 ibid., col. 1950.

19 Command Paper 7118 dated 4 December 1912.

20 *Marder*, I, p. 433. *Hough*, pp. 279–82.

21 Marder, *Fear God*, II, p. 425 and 459.

22 ibid., p. 425, *note*.

23 ibid., I, p. 255 and II, p. 9.

24 Mountbatten to Roskill letter of 4 October 1976.

25 Randolph Churchill is wrong to state (*Churchill*, II, p. 603) that the scheme for lower deck promotion known as the Mate Scheme of 1912 'was an immediate success and continues today in an improved and expanded form'. The Mate Scheme had so many disadvantages that it was dropped in May 1931, and today's scheme bears far more resemblance to the new one then introduced than to the original scheme. See Stephen Roskill, *Naval Policy between the Wars*, II, (Collins, 1976), pp. 31–5 and 342. Henceforth cited as Roskill, *Naval Policy*.

26 See *Marder*, I, pp. 264–71 for a summary of the developments of this period.

27 Churchill to Harcourt 9 September 1912. CO. 418/106. On Australian reaction to this letter see S. D. Webster's unpublished doctoral thesis *Cresswell, The Australian Navalist* (Monash University, 1976), p. 269 (typescript).

28 See S. W. Roskill (ed.) *Documents Relating to the Naval Air Service, 1908–1918* (Navy Records Society, 1969), docs. 15, 16 and 72. Henceforth cited as Roskill, *Naval Air Documents*.

29 Letter to Hankey of 16 December 1911. ibid., doc. 10.

30 Churchill, *World Crisis*, I, p. 313.

31 Roskill, *Naval Air Documents*, nos. 22 and 25. In *Churchill*, II, p. 695 Randolph Churchill wrote of Admiral Wilson's criticisms of airships that many of them 'today appear nonsense', and he quotes the admiral's statement that 'Airships, when out of sight of land very soon lose their reckoning' as an example. But war experience was to prove that the navigation of the German Zeppelins and their reconnaissance reports *were* subject to large errors.

32 Roskill, *Naval Air Documents*, no. 27.

33 ibid., doc. 30.

34 ibid., doc. 64.

35 ibid., doc. 106.

36 ibid., docs. 36, 39 and 42.

37 ibid., doc. 140 *et seq*.

38 See W. J. Wijn's three volumes on the *War of the Spanish Succession* (The Hague, 1956–64). I am indebted to Professor C. R. Boxer for drawing my attention to

this work and to those of other Dutch critics of Churchill's biography of his ancestor.

39 Churchill, *Marlborough*, Book Two (Harrap ed. 1947), p. 84. This edition consists of vols. III and IV of the original work, published in 1936 and 1938 respectively.

40 *Marder*, II, p. 178.

41 ibid., p. 182.

42 Churchill, *World Crisis*, I, pp. 92–3.

43 D. M. Schurman, *The Education of a Navy* (Cassell, 1965), p. 11.

44 ibid., chs. 2 and 3 have a full account of the Colomb brothers' publications, lectures etc.

45 ibid., pp. 7–9.

46 Stephen Roskill, *Hankey: Man of Secrets*, I (Collins, 1970), pp. 51 and 59–60. Henceforth cited as Roskill, *Hankey*.

47 The founding members of the Naval Society were (future ranks) Vice-Admiral Sir Herbert Richmond, Rear-Admiral K. G. B. Dewar, Admiral The Hon. Sir Reginald Plunkett-Ernle-Erle-Drax, Rear-Admiral H. G. Thursfield, Rear-Admiral R. M. Bellairs, Rear-Admiral T. Fisher and Captain E. W. Harding RMA. The first meeting took place in Richmond's house in October 1912. See *The Naval Review*, vol. I, no. 1 (January 1913) and its 50th anniversary number (vol. LI, no. 1) for accounts of the Society's origins, and of its later troubles.

48 Churchill, *World Crisis*, I, p. 78.

49 *Marder*, II, p. 90. Randolph Churchill in *Winston Churchill*, II, p. 550 disagrees with Marder on this point. I incline to accept the view of the latter.

50 By Geoffrey Lowis (Putnam, 1957).

51 An example is Admiral Sir William Pakenham, the 'Paks' to whom the above author devotes a whole chapter.

52 See Churchill, *World Crisis*, I, pp. 55–64 and Roskill, *Hankey*, I, pp. 101–3.

53 Churchill to Lloyd George 14 September 1911. Lloyd George papers.

54 Geoffrey Bennett, *Charlie B.* (Peter Dawnay, 1968), pp. 136–7 and 353–4.

55 *Bennett*, op. cit., pp. 333–7. Marder, *Fear God*, II, p. 193. See Asquith papers, vol. 27, folios 74–84 for Churchill's view of Beresford.

56 Memo. of 8 August 1914. Adm. 1/8333–235.

Chapter 2   pages 32 to 40

1 *Marder*, I, p. 266.

2 See E. W. R. Lumby (ed.), *The Mediterranean 1912–1914* (Navy Records Society, 1970), pp. 135–6 and 146.

3 *Marder*, II.

4 Gilbert, *Churchill*, III, pp. 40–2.

5 *Marder*, I, pp. 368–73 deals fully with the evolution of the blockade strategy and Churchill's opposition to the change.

6 See *Marder*, II, pp. 50–4 for a detailed account.

7 ibid., pp. 55–9.

8 See Churchill, *World Crisis*, I, pp. 323–7.

9 Marder, *Fear God*, I, p. 308 'It's astounding to me . . . how the very best amongst us absolutely fail to realize the vast impending revolution in naval warfare and naval strategy that the submarine will accomplish.' To Balfour 20 April 1904.

10 Churchill, *World Crisis*, I, pp. 380–5.

11 See Basil Liddell Hart, *The Real War* (Faber, 1930) pp. 79–81 for a succinct account of the possibilities inherent in the landings on the Belgian coast.

12 See Churchill, *World Crisis*, I, ch. XV for his defence of his proposals and actions at this time.

13 Marder, *Fear God*, II, p. 84.

14 *Morton and Churchill* (Hodder and Stoughton, 1976), p. 177.

15 *Marder*, II, pp. 85–9 and *Hough*, pp. 300–15 deal fully with the events leading to Battenberg's resignation.

16 Churchill to Mrs Hood 4 January 1913. Hood papers (Churchill College) 6/1.

17 Timed 0340 of 23 October 1914. ibid. 6/2.

18 Signal (no time shown) of 24 October 1914. ibid.

19 Timed 2337 of 27 October 1914. ibid.

20 ibid., 3/20–3/25.

21 Churchill to Hood, 9 April 1915. ibid.

22 Fisher to Hood n.d. ibid.

23 Jellicoe to Hood 1 May 1915: Beatty to Hood 26 April and 15 May 1915. ibid.

24 See *Marder*, IV, pp. 315–16 on Bacon's qualities and failings.

25 The present Lord Hood and his brother The Hon. Alexander Hood are certain that their father's transfer to a major command took place only because Churchill and Fisher had left the Admiralty. Interview August 1976.

26 See Geoffrey Bennett, *Coronel and the Falklands* (Batsford, 1962) p. 50. S. D. Webster in his unpublished thesis *Cresswell: The Australian Navalist* (Monash University, 1976) stresses the frustration felt by Admirals William Cresswell, the First Naval Member of the Australian Board, and George Patey, the commander of the RAN squadron, at this misuse of their forces.

27 Quoted Bennett, op. cit., p. 52.

28 Churchill, *World Crisis*, I, p. 415.

29 Bennett, op. cit., p. 101.

30 It is interesting to find that, once again, the draft of the message to the C-in-C, Devonport (timed 0015 of 10 November), ordering the ships to sail on the 11th, is in Churchill's hand.

Chapter 3　　　pages 41 to 53

1 Recent books on the subject are Arthur J. Marder, *From the Dreadnought to Scapa Flow*, II (Oxford UP, 1965); Alan Moorehead, *Gallipoli* (Hamish Hamilton, 1956); Eric Bush, *Gallipoli* (Allen and Unwin, 1975); George H. Carson, *The French and the Dardanelles* (Allen and Unwin, 1971) and Robert Rhodes James, *Gallipoli* (Batsford, 1965).

2 Evidence to Dardanelles Commission. Cmd. 8490 and 8502 are its first and second reports. Churchill's evidence is in Cab. 19/29 and Fisher's in Cab. 19/33.

3 CID. 92B of 20 December 1906 and meeting of 28 February 1907. See Roskill, *Hankey*, I, p. 85 and Gilbert, *Churchill*, III, p. 294.

4 Gilbert, *Churchill*, III, p. 253.

5 ibid., pp. 269–71.

6 ibid., p. 286.

7 *Marder*, III, pp. 133 and 141–2.

8 Gilbert, *Churchill*, III, pp. 263 and 265. For another example of this habit of Asquith's see Patrick Devlin, *Too Proud to Fight* (Oxford UP, 1974) p. 551.

9 Gilbert, *Churchill*, III, p. 265.

10 *Winston Churchill as I knew Him* (Eyre and Spottiswoode and Collins, 1965) p. 355.

11 Marder, *Fear God*, II, p. 213. Lloyd George, *War Memoirs*, I, p. 395.

12 Quoted Arthur J. Marder, *Portrait of an Admiral* (Cape, 1952), p. 22.

13 ibid., pp. 149–50.

14 ibid., p. 145; Gilbert, *Churchill*, III, pp. 286–7.

15 *World Crisis*, II, pp. 264–72.

16 Dated 16 March 1915. See Roskill, *Hankey*, I, pp. 163–4.

17 Robert Rhodes James, *Gallipoli* (Batsford, 1965), p. 94.

18 Roskill, *Hankey*, I, p. 168.

19 General Sir Ian Hamilton, *Gallipoli Diary* (London, 1920), I, p. 41.

20 Churchill, *World Crisis*, II, p. 233. But Churchill claims (op. cit., p. 234) that he had Oliver's support – which is not borne out by the admiral's evidence to the Dardanelles Commission.

21 ibid., pp. 252–3.

22 See for example Moorehead, op. cit., chs. 13 and 14, and Bush, op. cit., ch. 21.

23 Gilbert, *Churchill*, III, p. 429.

24 ibid.

25 *Great Contemporaries* (Thornton Butterworth, 1939), p. 342.

26 Gilbert, *Churchill*, III, p. 449.

27 ibid., p. 451.

28 *The Prime Minister* (Panther ed.), p. 670.

29 Wilfred Owen, *Mental Cases*.

30 Arthur J. Marder, *From the Dardenelles to Oran* (Oxford UP, 1975), ch. I. Henceforth cited as Marder, *Dardanelles to Oran*.

31 Roskill, *Hankey*, I, pp. 214–15. Hankey's diary entries for 10 September and 6 November 1915.

32 Gilbert, *Churchill*, III, pp. 611–14.

33 ibid., pp. 631–2.

34 ibid., ch. 19.

Chapter 4   pages 54 to 65

1 Gilbert, *Churchill*, III, chs. 20 and 21.

2 ibid., pp. 689–90.

3 ibid., p. 698.

4 Roskill, *Hankey*, I, pp. 254–5.

5 ibid., pp. 699–704.

6 Churchill did not reply to the attacks on the Admiralty's alleged neglect of its responsibility for the defence of London until his speech in Parliament of 17 May 1916. See Gilbert, *Churchill*, III, p. 764.

7 Printed in Gilbert, *Churchill*, III, pp. 710, 712 and 713–14.

8 ibid., p. 715.

9 Roskill, *Hankey*, I, p. 254.

10 Gilbert, *Churchill*, III, ch. 24.

11 ibid., p. 715.

12 Marder, *Fear God*, III, p. 207.

13 To G. Lambert 18 August 1916 and to Lord Cromer 11 October 1916. ibid., pp. 364 and 375.

14 Gilbert, *Churchill*, III, pp. 759–60.

15 Roskill, *Naval Air Documents*, nos. 140 and 143–6.

16 Gilbert, *Churchill*, III, p. 776.

17 Churchill, *World Crisis*, III, p. 112.

18 See Churchill, *World Crisis*, III, p. 141 and CB.0938, *Naval Staff Appreciation*, pp. 84–5 and Diagram 23.

19 See Robin Higham, *Military Intellectuals in Britain 1918–1939* (Rutgers UP, 1966).

20 Stephen Roskill, *Naval Policy between the Wars*, I (Collins, 1968) pp. 559–60. Henceforth cited as Roskill, *Naval Policy*.

21 Churchill to Bridgeman 6 April 1928. Bridgeman papers.

22 Richmond to Bridgeman 1 May 1928. ibid.

23 Marder, *Fear God*, III is the fullest and most up to date of the many accounts of the battle of Jutland. On these errors by Beatty see pp. 51–5, 63–7 and 71–2. It should however be recorded that they can all be attributed in large measure to the chronic inability of Beatty's Flag Lieutenant to translate his expressed intentions into clear and unambiguous signals. See op. cit., II, p. 140 and III, pp. 51–2 and 63–4 regarding this matter.

24 Marder, *Fear God*, III gives the arguments in favour of a 'turn towards' instead of a 'turn away' at this juncture.

25 Churchill, *World Crisis*, III, p. 170.

26 Churchill and Fisher to Asquith, both of 2 June 1916. See Gilbert, *Churchill*, III, pp. 778–9.

27 Sir Ian Hamilton, *Listening for the Drums* (Faber, 1944) pp. 253–4.

28 Roskill, *Hankey*, I, pp. 287–9.

29 Gilbert, *Churchill*, III, pp. 786–8.

30 Roskill, *Hankey*, I, p. 291.

31 ibid., pp. 297–304.

32 Gilbert, *Churchill*, III, pp. 802–8.

33 Roskill, *Hankey*, I, p. 303; Cmd. 8490 (*First Report of Dardanelles Commission*) and Cmd. 8502 (*Supplementary Report* of same); R. R. James, *Gallipoli*, pp. 351–3; Marder, *Fear God*, II, pp. 325–9.

34 Gilbert, *Churchill*, III, ch. 26.

35 ibid., pp. 824–5.

Chapter 5   pages 66 to 71

1 Marder, *Fear God*, II, pp. 83–5 and 91.
2 A. T. Patterson (ed.) *The Jellicoe Papers*, II (Navy Records Society, 1968), Part II. Also the same historian's biography of Jellicoe (Macmillan, 1969) ch. 7.
3 Roskill, *Hankey*, I, pp. 356–7.
4 ibid., pp. 379 and 382.
5 ibid., pp. 366, 373 and 404–5.
6 *Men and Power* (Collins ed.) pp. 152 and 155.
7 Roskill, *Hankey*, I, p. 355.
8 ibid., p. 384.
9 ibid., pp. 472–3.
10 Roskill, article in *Journal of Contemporary History*, I, 4 (October 1966).
11 Churchill, *World Crisis*, IV, chs. XV and *Thoughts and Adventures* (Odhams Press ed. 1947) pp. 129–30.
12 Roskill, *Hankey*, I, p. 380.
13 CID. SAS2 of 25 June 1914. See Roskill, *Naval Air Documents*, I, doc. 46 and esp. p. 152.
14 AWO. 1204/15 of 29 July 1915. ibid., doc. 72.
15 ibid., docs. 147 and 148.
16 ibid., doc. 179.
17 Roskill, *Naval Policy*, I, pp. 235–6.
18 ibid., pp. 237–9.
19 Review article on Gilbert, *Churchill*, IV. *Journal of Royal United Services Institute for Defence Studies*, vol. 120, no. 4 (December 1975).

Chapter 6   pages 72 to 81

1 Roskill, *Hankey*, II, p. 110.
2 ibid., p. 115.
3 Roskill, *Naval Policy*, I, ch. III. A chronology of the principal events in the War of Intervention will be found on pp. 170–7.
4 Cmd. 467.
5 Roskill, *Naval Policy*, I, pp. 390–5. H. Montgomery Hyde, *British Air Policy between the Wars* (Heinemann, 1976) ch. I, esp. pp. 62–8.
6 Paper entitled 'Towards a National Policy' of 17 July 1919. Roskill, *Hankey*, II, pp. 110–12.
7 Four were projected for 1921 and another four in the following year. Roskill, *Naval Policy*, I, pp. 220–1.
8 ibid., pp. 221–5.
9 Roskill, *Hankey*, II, p. 197.
10 Churchill, *Second World War*, I, p. 215 and Gilbert, *Churchill*, IV, ch. 37.
11 Roskill, *Naval Policy*, I, pp. 110–11. Debate of 14 December 1921.
12 ibid., p. 232.

13 Roskill, *Hankey*, II, pp. 154–7 and *Naval Policy*, I, pp. 336–40.

14 *Naval Policy*, I, ch. VIII.

15 ibid., pp. 320–1, and especially with regard to Lloyd George's telegram to Balfour of 9 December 1921 (drafted by Churchill) protesting that the naval members of the British delegation were showing too much independence in seeking terms which accorded with Admiralty policy.

16 Gilbert, *Churchill*, IV, ch. 45.

17 op. cit., V, chs. 2 and 3 for details of these contests.

18 Roskill, *Naval Policy*, I, pp. 351–2 and 412–13.

19 Beatty papers and Bridgeman 'Political Notes' and diary.

20 Roskill, *Naval Policy*, I, pp. 445–52.

21 Hansard, Commons, 5th series, vol. 187, cols. 457–575.

22 Roskill, *Naval Policy*, I, pp. 372–91. See W. J. Reader, *Architect of Air Power: the Life of Lord Weir of Eastwood* (Collins, 1968) and H. Montgomery Hyde, *British Air Policy between the Wars*, pp. 119–20 and 134–40 for the Air side of this controversy.

23 Quoted Gilbert, *Churchill*, V, p. 76. See Roskill, *Naval Policy*, I, chs. XI and XII for a detailed account of these controversies.

24 Roskill, *Naval Policy*, I, pp. 550–1.

25 Roskill, *Hankey*, II, pp. 451–9 and 491–6.

Chapter 7   pages 82 to 91

1 *Churchill, Four Faces and the Man* (Allen Lane, 1969). This work comprises perceptive essays by A. J. P. Taylor, Robert Rhodes James, J. H. Plumb, Basil Liddell Hart and Anthony Storr. Henceforth cited as *Four Faces* preceded by the name of the essayist. The present reference is to Plumb, *Four Faces*, p. 131.

2 Maurice Ashley, *Churchill as Historian* (Secker and Warburg, 1968), p. 18.

3 See Martin Gilbert and Richard Gott, *The Appeasers* (Weidenfeld and Nicolson, 1963) and Martin Gilbert, *The Roots of Appeasement* (Weidenfeld and Nicolson, 1966).

4 For example Hines H. Hall in an article entitled *The Foreign Policy-Making Process in Britain 1934–35* writes of 'the outmoded "Guilty Men" thesis' and 'Thus the dichotomous "Appeasers v Anti-Appeasers" description of internal decision-making does not appear valid, at least with respect to the decision to conduct naval talks with Germany.' *The Historical Journal*, vol. 19, no. 2 (June 1976), pp. 481 *note* and 498.

5 N. H. Gibbs, *History of the Second World War. Grand Strategy*, I, (HMSO, 1976), p. 806.

6 See Roskill, *Hankey*, III, pp. 23–6 for the principal references to the long debate on the India Bill; also K. Middlemas and J. Barnes, *Baldwin* (Weidenfeld and Nicolson, 1969) ch. 26.

7 Liddell Hart, *Four Faces*, pp. 241 and 200 respectively.

8 Correspondence in Cherwell papers (formerly in Nuffield College, Oxford). Also Lord Birkenhead, *The Prof. in Two Worlds* (Collins, 1961), pp. 126–7.

9 Roskill, *Hankey*, I, pp. 380–5.

10 Roskill, *Hankey*, II, pp. 264–6. Churchill, *Second World War*, I, pp. 62–3 has his own account of his association with Lindemann and Morton. Gilbert, *Churchill*, V, *passim* has much interesting material on this subject.

11 Storr, *Four Faces*, p. 241.

12 Roskill, *Hankey*, II, pp. 406–7.

13 *Science and Government* (Oxford UP, 1961), p. 31.

14 Roskill, *Hankey*, III, pp. 143–6 and 233–5. As the detailed source references are given in that work they are not repeated here.

15 Roskill, *Hankey*, III, pp. 145–6.

16 Gibbs, *Grand Strategy*, I, pp. 138–42.

17 Roskill, *Naval Policy*, II, pp. 194–5. —{REPTD. STAFFORD 2016}

18 ibid., pp. 324 and 394.

19 Churchill to Keyes 27 November 1936. Keyes papers KEYS 8/9. Also Keyes's letters to Chatfield of 1 May and 12 August 1937. loc. cit.

20 Mountbatten to Churchill 25 March 1937. Quoted Gilbert, *Churchill*, V, p. 852.

21 Private and Secret memo. A. 0657/39 of 19 January 1940. Adm. 205/31.

22 Roskill, *Hankey*, III, pp. 291–3 and *Naval Policy*, II, ch. XIII.

23 *Naval Policy*, II, pp. 229–30 and Roskill, *The War at Sea 1939–45* (HMSO, 1954), pp. 34, 130 and 355. Henceforth cited as Roskill, *War at Sea*.

24 *Naval Policy*, II, p. 331.

25 See Churchill, *Second World War*, I, pp. 124–7 for his views on the calibre of battleships' main armaments.

26 Hansard, Commons, vol. 304, col. 1554. Also Gibbs, *Grand Strategy*, I, pp. 165–8 and Roskill, *Naval Policy*, II, pp. 302–9.

27 Dated 27 March 1939. Prem. 1/345.

28 Liddell Hart, *Four Faces*, p. 191.

29 ibid., p. 183.

30 ibid.

31 James, *Four Faces*, p. 105 and Gilbert, *Churchill*, V, pp. 869–70.

32 Quoted R. W. Thompson, *The Yankee Marlborough* (Allen and Unwin, 1963) p. 286.

33 Memo. of 27 March 1939. Prem. 1/345.

34 Liddell Hart, *Four Faces*, p. 185.

35 See Gibbs, *Grand Strategy*, I, pp. 774–5 for a judicial summary of this question.

36 Churchill to Keyes 24 September 1935. Quoted Gilbert, *Churchill*, V, p. 663.

37 Roskill, *Naval Policy*, II, ch. XIII.

38 Middlemas and Barnes, *Baldwin* (Weidenfeld and Nicolson, 1969), pp. 916–17 and Roskill, *Hankey*, III, pp. 206–13.

39 Middlemas and Barnes, op. cit., p. 917 and Liddell Hart to John Brophy 7 September 1941, quoted Thompson, *Yankee Marlborough*, p. 286.

40 Hansard, Commons, vol. 333, cols. 656–7.

41 Roskill, *Naval Policy*, II, p. 457.

42 Commander C. P. F. Brown to the author 30 July 1976. Chatfield repeated this anecdote at the party given to celebrate his 90th birthday in 1963.

Chapter 8   pages 93 to 113

1 Churchill, *Second World War*, I, pp. 364–5 and 434–5.
2 Minutes in Adm. 205/4.
3 ibid.
4 Churchill to Cork 29 December 1939. ibid.
5 Cork to Churchill, 5 January 1940. ibid.
6 Pound to Churchill, 10 January 1940. ibid.
7 Office Memo. of 23 January 1940. ibid.
8 Admiral Sir William Davis, who joined the Plans Division in 1940, is certain that this was the cause of Danckwert's removal. Interview August 1976.
9 Arthur J. Marder, *From the Dardanelles to Oran* (Oxford UP, 1974), pp. 122–4 deals fully with the controversy over U-boat sinkings, and he prints Churchill's minute of 25 April 1940 ending 'This conclusion [that 'all the attacks except the 15 of which we have actual remnants' have failed] leads me to think it might be a good thing if Captain Talbot went to sea soon as possible.' Marder describes this proposal as 'crisp and decisive', but to me it demands far harsher condemnation. This source is henceforth cited as Marder, *Dardanelles to Oran*.
10 Minute 55 of 11 December 1939 to First Sea Lord, DCNS and Secretary. Adm. 199/1928.
11 Churchill's Private and Secret paper A. 0657/39 of 19 January 1940. Adm. 205/31.
12 Roskill, *War at Sea*, I, pp. 360–1.
13 For Churchill's account of his part in the events leading to the Norwegian campaign see *Second World War*, I, ch. XXX. T. K. Derry, *The Campaign in Norway* (HMSO, 1952) is the relevant volume of the United Kingdom Military Series of the History of the Second World War (ed. J. R. M. Butler), and Roskill, *War at Sea*, I in the same series deals fully with the naval operations.
14 The first experience of the RAF bombers' ineffectiveness against warship targets had been gained when, on the day after the declaration of war, 14 Wellingtons and 15 Blenheims attacked German warships in Schillig Roads off Wilhelmshaven. They inflicted negligible damage and suffered heavy losses. Roskill, *War at Sea*, I, pp. 65–6.
15 See Reginald Pound, *Evans of the Broke* (Oxford UP, 1963).
16 Churchill, *Second World War*, I, pp. 443–7.
17 Roskill, *War at Sea*, I, pp. 157–9.
18 Derry, op. cit., p. 19.
19 Paper by General Sir Ian Jacob about Churchill's influence on operations and naval appointments in World War II. Copy in author's possession.
20 ibid.
21 Letter Jacob to the author 1 December 1976.
22 Letter Forbes to the author 30 July 1949.
23 Churchill, *Second World War*, II, p. 592.
24 op. cit., I, p. 470.
25 Whitworth to Derry and to Roskill 5 January and 7 August 1950 respectively.
26 Edwards diaries (Churchill College).

27 Keyes to his wife 16 April 1940. Keyes papers. KEYS 2/30.

28 Churchill to Keyes 25 April 1940. KEYS 13/12.

29 Keyes to Pound 26 April and reply by latter of 29 April 1940. ibid.

30 Churchill, *Second World War*, I, pp. 497–500. Roskill, *War at Sea*, I, pp. 186–7. Derry, *Campaign in Norway*, pp. 74–6.

31 Churchill, *Second World War*, I, p. 500.

32 Article by Piers Mackesy entitled *Churchill on Narvik. The Royal United Service Institution Journal*, vol. CXV, no. 670 (December 1970), pp. 28–33.

33 loc. cit., p. 33 c.f. Churchill, *Second World War*, pp. 481–8.

34 See L. E. H. Maund, *Assault from the Sea* (London, 1949), ch. II. Maund was Chief of Staff to Lord Cork at Narvik.

35 See Robert Rhodes James, *Gallipoli* (Batsford, 1965) and Churchill, *World Crisis*, II, pp. 443–8.

36 Churchill, *Second World War*, I, p. 516.

37 Note by Commander E. G. Le Geyt dated 15 May 1968 added to Adm. 199/478 and correspondence with Le Geyt July 1975.

38 Marder, *Dardanelles to Oran*, pp. 166 and 169.

39 Alexander to Churchill 20 May 1940. Prem. 3–475/1.

40 Lindemann to Churchill 5 June 1940 and minute by latter. ibid.

41 Beaverbrook to Churchill 27 June 1940. ibid.

42 Churchill to Ismay 17 July 1940. ibid.

43 Telegram of 22 July 1940. Lord Halifax to F. O. ibid.

44 Ronald Clark, *Tizard* (Methuen, 1965), ch. 11 has a full account of this mission.

45 Churchill to Alexander 22 August 1940 and subsequent exchanges culminating in Pound's protest of 27 December 1940 Adm. 199/1931.

46 Churchill to Alexander, copy to Pound 18 September 1940, reply by latter of same date, minute by Little of 25 September and further minute from Churchill to Alexander of 4 October 1940. ibid.

47 Churchill to Keyes 27 April 1940. Keyes papers. KEYS 13/5.

48 Interview January 1977.

49 Admiral Sir Francis Pridham, unpublished memoirs (Churchill College) pp. 169–70 (typescript).

50 ibid., p. 171 (typescript).

51 ibid., p. 187.

52 See Roskill, *Hankey*, III, *passim* regarding the composition and functions of these two bodies.

53 See R. Stuart Macrae, *Winston Churchill's Toyshop* (Roundwood Press, 1971) for a full account of this organization's work.

54 Quoted Pridham memoirs, pp. 194–5 (typescript).

Chapter 9   pages 116 to 147

1 Pound to Forbes 18 August and reply by latter of 22 August 1939. Forbes papers. Copy in author's possession.

2 Pound to Forbes 25 October 1939. Copy in author's possession.

3 Churchill to Captain G. R. G. Allen, his naval historical assistant 11 August 1953.

4 Record of meeting of 2 June 1942. Adm. 205/23.

5 Forbes to the author letters of 5 and 10 September 1949.

6 Chatfield to Chamberlain 18 and 20 November 1939. Chatfield papers CHT 6/1.

7 Roskill, *War at Sea*, I, pp. 82-8.

8 Quoted ibid., p. 198.

9 Admy. letter M. 010329/40 of 29 May 1940 is the 'General Naval Appreciation of the invasion threat'. The 'General Plan' and dispositions are in Admy. signal timed 1943 of 24 June 1940. Churchill's holograph notes on it emphasize his desire for large numbers of destroyers to be based in the Humber-Portsmouth area. Prem. 3-222/10.

9A Roskill, *War at Sea*, I, pp. 257-9.

10 Cunningham to Roskill 19 October 1960.

11 Churchill to Alexander 17 June 1940. Adm. 199/1930.

12 Churchill to Ismay 18 September 1940 and reply by latter of same day. Adm. 199/1931.

13 Roskill, *Hankey*, III, p. 472-3.

14 Forbes to Sir Godfrey Style, his one-time Flag Lieutenant, 6 February 1947. In author's possession.

15 Pound to Cunningham 20 September 1940. BM. Add. Ms. 52561.

16 Pound to Alexander 8 June 1942, referring to Churchill's minute of 4 June 1942. Adm. 205/14.

17 Tovey to Cunningham 17 October 1940. BM. Add. Ms. 52569.

18 ibid.

19 Churchill, *Second World War*, I, pp. 215-17. Roskill, *Naval Policy*, I, pp. 109-12.

20 Ismay to Churchill 12 July 1940 answering a minute by latter. Prem. 3-361/1.

21 Churchill to Secretary of State for Dominions, minute M. 331 of 22 November 1940. Prem. 3-127/1.

22 See Roskill, *War at Sea*, I, pp. 341-2.

23 Signal of 7 March 1941. Quoted Adm. 199/205.

24 Churchill to COSs (London) 2220Z of 29 December 1941. Copy in Adm. 205/13. All the messages which passed on this subject will be found in Prem. 3-47/1.

25 Admy. to BAD, Personal for First Sea Lord 2159A of 31 December 1941. ibid.

26 COSs to Churchill 1438A of 5 January 1942 and VCNS to First Sea Lord 1813A of same day. ibid.

27 First Sea Lord to VCNS 0510R of 6 January 1942. ibid.

28 Churchill to Ismay for COSs 1040R of 7 January 1942. ibid.

29 Minute of 6 January 1942 on Pound's telegram to Phillips of same day. Adm. 205/13 and Prem. 3-47/1.

30 First Sea Lord to Churchill, minute of 9 January 1942. ibid.

31 Pound to Churchill 29 January and reply by latter of 3 February 1942. ibid.

32 After the war an excessively discreet First Sea Lord's secretary destroyed the original of this letter because of the last sentence of Churchill's minute here quoted. Note by Captain J. R. Allfrey of 8 December 1949. Adm. 205/56. However a copy has survived in Prem. 3-47/1.

33 Tovey to Keyes 23 February and 31 March 1942. Keyes papers KEYS 13/16.

34 Diary entry for 10 June 1942. Alexander papers AVAR 6/1.

35 See Ludovic Kennedy, *Pursuit* (Collins, 1974) for the most recent and impartial account of this famous saga, told from both sides' point of view.

36 First Sea Lord to C-in-C, Home Fleet 1137B of 27 May 1941. See Kennedy, op. cit., p. 225 regarding this signal.

37 Churchill, *Second World War*, III, p. 282.

38 Kennedy, op. cit., p. 226. Lord Tovey dilated at length on this regrettable aftermath to the *Bismarck* chase in several letters to the author. The correspondence about it between Alexander, Pound and Churchill is in Adm. 205/10. After receiving the Admiralty's comments Churchill closed the matter by tersely minuting 'Leave it' on 25 September 1941.

39 The Former Naval Person telegrams are in Prem. 3-462/1 and /3. Originals and prints of them all are in Prem. 3-467 to 473.

40 Roosevelt and Churchill. *Their Secret Wartime Correspondence*. Ed. F. L. Loewenheim and others (Barrie and Jackson, 1976). Henceforth cited as *Loewenheim*.

41 Churchill to Alexander and Pound, minute M.192/1 of 17 February 1941. Adm. 199/1932.

42 Roskill, *Naval Policy*, II, p. 456. The paper is in Prem. 1-345.

43 See Samuel Eliot Morison. *History of United States Naval Operations in World War II* (15 vols. Atlantic, Little, Brown, Boston, 1947–62). III, pp. 389–98 for a full account of the Halsey-Doolittle raid. This source is henceforth cited as *Morison*.

44 Churchill to Halifax 28 April 1941. Adm. 205/10.

45 Churchill to Foreign Office and War Office 29 April 1941. Adm. 199/1933.

46 Churchill to Alexander and Pound 28 May and reply by former of 29 May 1941. ibid.

47 Churchill to Pound 28 June 1941. ibid.

48 Alexander to Churchill 13 April 1942. Prem. 3-57/1.

49 Same to same 28 June and minute by Churchill of 1 July 1941. Adm. 199/1933.

50 Churchill to Alexander 2 September 1941. ibid.

51 Same to same minutes M. 129/1 of 5 February and M. 238/1 of 28 February 1941, and staff minutes in reply to them. Adm. 199/1932.

52 Churchill to Alexander and Pound 10 July and reply by latter of 12 July 1941. Adm. 205/10.

53 Pound to Admiral Kharlamov 2 June 1942. Adm. 205/22A.

54 Roskill, *War at Sea*, II, pp. 278–9 and 287.

55 Adm. 205/13 contains much interesting high-level correspondence about extending and increasing the arctic convoys in 1942. Tovey attended a meeting at which the subject was discussed on 4 June. Three days later he wrote to Pound protesting that the record of the meeting contained 'a gross understatement' of what he had said. Pound replied apologetically on the 10th saying that the record would be amended. Adm. 205/22A.

56 For full accounts of this disaster see David Irving, *The Destruction of Convoy PQ17* (Cassell, 1968); P. Lund and H. Ludlam, *PQ17. Convoy to Hell* (New English Library, 1969); Jack Broome, *Convoy is to Scatter* (Kimber, 1972) and Godfrey Winn, *PQ17. A Story of a Ship* (Hutchinson, 1947).

57 Tovey to Cunningham 23 September 1942. BM. Add. Ms. 52570 (1). On the 'second front in 1942' see Churchill, *Second World War*, III, pp. 339–40, 409–10 and 560.

58 Churchill to Alexander 6 June 1942. Prem. 3–324/17.

59 Minute dated 13 July 1942. Adm. 205/14.

60 The draft reply is in Adm. 205/20, and as Tovey's letter was in fact 'expunged' from the records the reply must surely have been sent to him.

61 Meetings of 17 March and 2 June 1942. Adm. 205/23.

62 Pound to Churchill 7 March 1942. Adm. 205/23. Copy in author's possession.

63 Churchill to Pound 22 January 1942. Prem. 3–191/1.

64 Roskill, *War at Sea*, II, pp. 120–4.

65 Churchill to Pound 13, 16 and 24 March and reply by latter of 15 March 1942 – which did not satisfy Churchill. Adm. 205/13. On Churchill's later attitude towards the Fleet Air Arm see Adm. 205/13, 14, 20, 27 and 56.

66 Churchill to Pound minute M. 475/3 of 16 July 1943. Prem. 3–191/1. On the midget submarine attack on the *Tirpitz* see Roskill, *War at Sea*, III, Part I, pp. 64–8.

67 Patrick Beesley, *Very Special Intelligence* (Hamish Hamilton, 1977) pp. 110–16.

68 C. Webster and N. Frankland, *The Strategic Air Offensive* (4 vols. HMSO, 1961), III, pp. 76–94. This source is henceforth cited as *Webster and Frankland*.

69 John Kennedy, *The Business of War* (Hutchinson, 1957), p. 97.

70 Churchill to Portal 27 August 1941. Prem. 3–8.

71 *Webster and Frankland*, I, pp. 178–80.

72 Review of the above work in *The Listener* of 5 October 1961. The condemnation of 'area bombing' is the more striking because Professor Jones had been a colleague of Lindemann's at Oxford University and has expressed sympathetic views about him to the author.

73 Dated 9 October 1939 and 2 and 15 February 1940. Prem. 1–398. Also letters of 19 May and 1 June 1941 and 26 March 1942. Prem. 3–31.

74 Churchill to Harris 1 June 1941. ibid.

75 *Loewenheim*, pp. 151, 235 and 284.

76 Michael Howard, *Grand Strategy*, IV (HMSO, 1972), pp. 20, 24 and 314. J. R. M. Butler in *Grand Strategy*, III, Part II, p. 314 gives a balanced view of the strength of the Admiralty's case, which is supported by Howard.

77 Apart from the admittedly prejudiced view in C. P. Snow's *Science and Government* and *Postscript to Science and Government* (Oxford UP, 1961 and 1962) this opinion receives strong support from P. M. S. Blackett's *Studies of War* (Oliver and Boyd, 1962), esp. pp. 195–7 and 223–7. Blackett and Tizard both calculated that the Air Staff had exaggerated the number of houses in Germany likely to be destroyed between April 1942 and October 1943 by a factor of 5 to 1. The actual error was we now know 10 to 1. Blackett's analysis of escort vessel requirements and his views on the very great value of air convoy escorts are in AU(43)40 of 5 February 1943. See Prem. 3–414/3.

78 Blackett, op. cit., pp. 226–7.

79 *Loewenheim*, p. 124.

80 See Roskill, *Hankey*, III, pp. 580–1 regarding Churchill's horrified reaction to an

RAF cinema film showing a heavy air raid on a German city.

81 Minute on report by Salter of 22 April 1942. Adm. 205/23.

82 King to Pound 23 April, answering Pound's letter of 20 April 1942. Adm. 205/19.

83 Minute by Pound to Alexander of 22 April 1942. Adm. 205/23.

84 'They [our Asdic methods] certainly are very remarkable in results and enable two destroyers to do the work that could not be done by ten last time.' Churchill to Roosevelt 16 October 1939. *Loewenheim*, p. 91.

85 Churchill to First Lord and First Sea Lord 14 November 1941. Adm. 205/13. On the development of Asdic see Roskill, *Naval Policy*, I, pp. 345–7 and 356, and II, pp. 228–9 and 452–3.

86 Minute of 18 June 1942. Adm. 205/14.

87 The correspondence is in Adm. 205/17. The withdrawn paper was COS(42) 206(o).

88 Minute of 23 July 1942. Adm. 205/24.

89 Minute of 14 July 1942. ibid.

90 Pound to Drax 21 July 1942. Adm. 205/20.

91 Minute by Churchill on Alexander's letter of 13 August 1942. Prem. 3–97/1.

92 Minute of 24 August 1942. Adm. 205/24.

93 Dated 28 August 1942. ibid.

94 Portal to Pound 16 September 1942. ibid.

95 Roskill, *War at Sea*, III, part I, pp. 260–5, esp. table 15.

96 Portal to Pound 11–13 October 1942. Adm. 205/26. The first Lancasters actually entered squadron service at the end of 1941, but the first operation by them did not take place until March 1942. While working on my war history I was told by a former senior officer of the RAF's Coastal Command that Roy Chadwick of A. V. Roe, the brilliant designer of the Lancaster, had offered to design a maritime version of that very successful aircraft for Coastal Command, but that the offer had been turned down by the Air Staff. However Group Captain E. B. Haslam, Head of the Air Historical Branch, writes that no trace of such an offer can be found in the Air Ministry's records. Letter of 6 December 1976.

97 Dated 22 October 1942. Read at COS(42) 297th meeting of same day.

98 Harris to Churchill 5 June with note by latter of 7 June 1942. Adm. 205/14.

99 It became WP(42)374 of 24 August 1942.

100 Minute on above dated 9 September 1942. Prem. 3–7.

101 Minutes by Bruce of 16 June and by Churchill of 3 September 1942. ibid.

102 Churchill to Air Ministry 17 September 1942. ibid.

103 Letter Tovey to Admy. of 11 October and minute by Churchill of 19 October 1942. Prem. 3–7.

104 Roosevelt to Churchill 10 July and reply by latter T. 102/2 of 21 July 1942, Prem. 3–323.

105 Pound to Churchill 20 October 1942. ibid.

106 Leathers's paper DC(5)(42)88 of 5 October and Churchill's minute M. 458/2 of 19 October 1942. Prem. 3–324/19.

107 Churchill to Roosevelt 31 October 1942. *Loewenheim*, pp. 262–4.

108 Churchill to Hopkins no. 202 of 20 November and reply by latter of 2 December 1942. Adm. 205/26.

109 Portal to Pound 10 December 1942. Adm. 205/26.

110 Alexander to Churchill 25 December 1942. Adm. 205/14. But the reference to the 8th meeting of the Anti-U-boat Committee therein must be wrong, as that meeting took place on 24 February 1943 with Sir Stafford Cripps in the chair. Cab. 86/2.

111 Churchill to Alexander 26 December 1942. Adm. 205/14.

112 Interview with Admiral Davis. October 1961.

113 Rear-Admiral K. G. B. Dewar, who was then working in the Admiralty's Historical Section, pressed on Pound the vital importance of extending the convoy system to the South Atlantic and Indian Oceans, where heavy losses were suffered in 1942, but to little or no avail. Dewar to Pound 29 July 1942. Adm. 205/24. In 1957 Dewar made for this author a calculation of the net increase in our escort vessel strength in 1942–3. It came to twenty-four ships – or about one tenth of the increase in U-boat numbers.

114 Whitworth to Cunningham 15 December 1942. BM. Add. Ms. 52570(1).

115 Cripps to Churchill 30 November and Alexander to Churchill 8 December 1942. Adm. 205/14.

116 Lord Cunningham's diary entry for 19 February 1946 has Alexander's account of Churchill's 'fear of the Board of Admiralty' and of his reluctance to appoint Cunningham First Sea Lord.

117 On the prolonged debate on 'area bombing' of the U-boat bases, even at the expense of causing heavy casualties among French civilians, see Prem. 3–72.

118 Churchill to Alexander 5 February and 22 March 1941 about the losses suffered when convoy HX.103 entered one of our own minefields and the culpability of the Convoy Commodore. Also his bitter complaint of 19 February about the loss of the *Siamese Prince* with an exceptionally valuable convoy, which he attributed to destroyers not being sent 'to escort her in'. Adm. 199/1932.

119 Churchill to Alexander and Pound minute M. 330/1 of 21 March 1941 and subsequent exchanges about the battleship *Malaya* being torpedoed when escorting a slow convoy from Sierra Leone. Nothing the Admiralty could say placated Churchill's wrath.

120 Alexander to Churchill 7 January 1941. Adm. 199/1932.

121 Same to same 17 March 1941. ibid.

122 Churchill to Alexander 5 April, reply by latter of 8th and further minute by Churchill of 9 April 1941. Adm. 199/1933.

123 Roskill, *War at Sea*, II, pp. 149–58 and Terence Robertson, *Channel Dash* (Evans, 1958).

124 C-in-C, Home Fleet to Admy. 0130A of 7 February. Churchill to Pound 8 February 1942 and reply by latter of same day. Prem. 3–324/15.

125 Adm. 205/21 has papers on Churchill's desire to have an invasion of Norway (operation 'Jupiter') planned as an alternative to the invasion of France in May 1942.

126 Letter to Cunningham's aunt Helen Browne of 11 June 1942. BM. Add. Ms. 52559.

127 Cunningham to the author 9 September 1961. His autobiography *A Sailor's Odyssey* (Hutchinson, 1951) contains a bowdlerized account of this visit to

Chequers (pp. 462–3). This source is henceforth cited as Cunningham, *Odyssey*.

128 Minute M. 227/2 of 4 June 1942. Adm. 205/14.

129 Pound to Alexander 8 June 1942. ibid.

130 Diary for 10 June 1942. Alexander papers AVAR 6/1.

131 Minute of 9 June 1942. Prem. 3-478/4.

132 On Horton's work as C-in-C, Western Approaches see W. S. Chalmers *Max Horton and the Western Approaches* (Hodder and Stoughton, 1954) Ch. X ff.

133 Cunningham to Godfrey 17 May (?) 1956. In August 1967 Godfrey sent Mountbatten a copy of this letter, and it is now in the Broadlands Archive.

134 Pound to Alexander 16 September 1942. Adm. 205/20.

135 See for example Donald McLachlan *Room 39* (Weidenfeld and Nicolson, 1968) and Patrick Beesly *Very Special Intelligence* (Hamish Hamilton, 1977). McLachlan was one of the brilliant band of outsiders brought into the NID by Godfrey in 1939, while Beesly served in the OIC throughout the war.

136 Churchill to Pound 1 September 1941 enclosing letter of 3 May 1937 to Sir Samuel Hoare, then First Lord. Adm. 205/10.

137 See Roskill, *Naval Policy*, II, pp. 166, 220 and 328–30 regarding the prolonged discussions on battleship design in the 1930s.

138 Hansard, Lords, vol. 122, cols. 116–17.

139 Minute M. 55/2 of 27 February 1942. Prem. 3-324/16. See also Roskill, op. cit., pp. 466–7.

140 Churchill to Chatfield 4 March and reply by latter of 10 March 1942. Prem. 3-324/16.

141 Alexander to Churchill 14 April 1942. Adm. 199/1935.

142 Minute of 16 April 1942. Prem. 3-324/16.

143 Hansard, Lords, vol. 122, col. 657.

144 James, *Four Faces*, p. 112.

145 Roskill, *Hankey*, III, p. 544.

146 Memo. of 4 March by Hankey, sent on by Churchill to Alexander and Pound and answered by latter on 8 March 1942. Adm. 199/1935.

147 WP(42)483 of 24 October 1942.

148 Minute by D of P on above Adm. 205/26.

149 See Churchill, *Second World War*, IV, ch. XVIII on 'Sledgehammer' (invasion of France 1942) and 'Jupiter' (invasion of Norway).

150 Minute by Pound to D of P 27 May 1942. Adm. 205/21.

151 Letter of 15 October 1933. Adm. 205/3.

152 Memo. by Drax of May 1942. Adm. 205/22A.

153 Minute by Pound of 27 May 1942. Adm. 205/21.

154 Churchill to Roosevelt 8 July 1942. *Loewenheim*, p. 222.

155 Churchill, *Second World War*, IV, pp. 430–5.

156 Adm. 205/22A.

157 Churchill to Alexander 24 March and Cab. WP(42)173 of 16 April 1942. Adm. 205/13 and Cab. 66/24.

158 DC(5)(42)88 and Churchill's personal minute M. 458/2 of 19 October 1942. Adm. 203/15.

159 Pound to Alexander 23 December 1942. Adm. 205/20.

Chapter 10   pages 150 to 193

1 *Odyssey*, pp. 230–1.
2 Part 2 of C-in-C, Med. to Admy. timed 2301 of 6 June 1940. Copy in BM. Add. Ms. 52566.
3 First Sea Lord to C-in-C, Med. timed 2300 of 16 June 1940. ibid.
4 Reply to above timed 1905 of 17 June 1940. ibid.
5 C-in-C, Med. to Admy. timed 2159 of 18 June 1940. ibid.
6 Churchill, *Second World War*, II, p. 392.
7 Admy. to Flag Officer, Force H, repeated C-in-C, Med. timed 0435 of 29 June 1940. Copies of all signals relating to the terms to be offered to the French are in Prem. 3–179/1. Most of them are also in Cunningham papers, BM. Add. Ms. 52566.
8 Admy. to C-in-C, Med. timed 1531 of 29 June 1940. ibid.
9 C-in-C, Med. to Admy. repeated Flag Officer, Force H timed 1105 of 30 June 1940.
10 Admy. to C-in-C, Med. timed 2100 of 1 July 1940. ibid.
11 *Odyssey*, p. 246.
12 C-in-C, Med. to Admy. timed 0935 of 3 July 1940. ibid. Full accounts of this meeting are in *Odyssey*, pp. 246–8 and Oliver Warner, *Cunningham of Hyndhope* (Murray, 1967) pp. 97–9.
13 C-in-C, Med. to Admy. timed 1259 of 3 July 1940. ibid.
14 Same to same timed 1429 of same date. ibid.
15 Same to same timed 1727 of same date. ibid.
16 Admy. to C-in-C, Med. timed 1824 of same date. ibid. Received at Alexandria at 2015 (Zone C).
17 *Odyssey*, p. 250. Warner, op. cit., pp. 97–100.
18 C-in-C, Med. to Admy. timed 0049 of 4 July 1940. Prem. 3–179/1 and BM. Add. Ms. 52566.
19 Same to same timed 0827 of same date. ibid.
20 Admy. to C-in-C, Med. timed 1135 of same date. ibid.
21 C-in-C, Med. to Admy. timed 2015 of same date. ibid.
22 Same to same timed 1529 of same date. ibid.
23 Same to same timed 2015 of same date. ibid.
24 Admy. to C-in-C, Med. timed 0034 of 5 July 1940. ibid.
25 Letters to Cunningham's aunt Helen Browne of 18 July 1940 and 10 February 1941. BM. Add. Ms. 52588.
26 Roskill, *War at Sea*, I, pp. 242–3. Marder, *Dardanelles to Oran*, ch. V and Warren Tute, *The Deadly Stroke* (Collins, 1973). Originals of signals are to be found in Prem. 3–179/1 and /4.
27 Godfrey to Cunningham 7 May 1959. BM. Add. Ms. 52575. Marder, op. cit., p. 240; Tute, op. cit., pp. 91–2.
27A Gensoul to French Admiralty 0945 and 1320 of 3 July 1940. Roskill, *War at Sea*, I, p. 243; Marder, op. cit., p. 240; Tute, op. cit., pp. 91–2.

28 Tute, op. cit., pp. 109–10 gives Admiral Gensoul's post-war attempt to explain his action in this matter.

29 See Sir John Colville's introduction to Tute, op. cit., p. 17.

30 What Professor Marder calls, with some exaggeration, the Admiralty's 'icy blast' was sent in reply to North's letter of protest of 4 July, not to his signal of 3 July expressing his opposition to the use of force at Oran. See FOCNA letter X.163/465 of 4 July and Admy. reply M. 013181/40 of 17 July with note on it in Alexander's hand 'Copy sent to PM'. Adm. 1/19178. Alexander papers AVAR 5/4/35(a) and 5/4/42 are also relevant, but Marder, *Dardanelles to Oran*, p. 269 is misleading in this respect.

31 Roskill, *War at Sea*, I, pp. 240 and 245.

32 Pound to Alexander 10 July 1940. Prem. 3–179/4.

33 North to Cunningham 10 May 1940. BM. Add. Ms. 52569.

34 Pound to Alexander 14 July and Alexander to Pound 15 July 1940. Adm. 1/19178. Alexander to Churchill 17 July 1940. AVAR 5/4/43.

35 Marder, *Dardanelles to Oran*, p. 198.

36 Pound to Alexander 16th July 1940. Adm. 1/19178.

37 Alexander to Churchill 17 July 1940. Adm. 1/19177.

38 Churchill to Alexander 20 July 1940. ibid.

39 Marder, *Dardanelles to Oran*, p. 205 and *Operation Menace* (Oxford UP, 1976), [*here 2016*] p. 197.

40 Roskill, *War at Sea*, I, and Marder, *Operation Menace*.

41 Admy. signal timed 2005 of 4 July 1940. The copy in the Cunningham papers has a marginal note (undated) in Lord Cunningham's hand 'I'll be damned if I think this is clear.' BM. Add. Ms. 52575.

42 Admy. signal timed 0012 of 7 July 1940.

43 Keyes to Churchill 22 and 24 August 1940. Prem. 3–276.

44 Hansard, Commons, vol. 365, cols. 298–301 and Churchill, *Second World War*, II, p. 427.

45 Churchill, *Second World War*, II, p. 426.

46 Minute by Carter of 10 October 1940. Adm. 1/19180.

47 Minute by Carter of 12 October 1940. ibid.

48 Admy. letter M. 019598 of 15 October 1940. ibid. See Marder, *Operation Menace*, pp. 203–4 for the text.

49 Minute by Carter of 11 November 1940. Adm. 1/19186.

50 Marder, op. cit., p. 217.

51 FOCNA signal to Admy. timed 0711 of 11 September 1940. Copy in North papers. (Churchill College).

52 Letter of 6 October 1940 to Admy. Adm. 1/19180.

53 Pound to North 3 January 1940. North papers.

54 Same to same 22 September 1940. ibid.

55 Interview with Sir John Lang, Permanent Secretary, Admiralty *c.* 18 March 1953.

56 Marder, *Operation Menace*, p. 231, *note* 9. For the draft message to the Joint Commanders and the decision to authorize them to go ahead with the operation see Prem. 3–276 and WM(40) 250th and 252nd meetings.

57 For examples of Churchill's constant interest in admirals' appointments see Adm. 205/14, 27, 35 and 37.

58 Roskill to Cunningham 30 March 1953. BM. Add. Ms. 52563.

59 Marder, *Operation Menace*, pp. 207-8 gives the main points in North's account of his interviews with Pound and Alexander, which is the only evidence we have regarding what passed at them.

60 Cunningham to Fraser 30 December 1949 and reply by latter of 5 January 1950. BM. Add. Ms. 52575.

61 Cunningham to Roskill 2 June 1957.

62 Same to same 25 March 1953.

63 Marder, *Operation Menace*, ch. 11.

64 Prem. 3-71.

65 Dated 4 October 1940. ibid.

66 Churchill to Alexander minute M. 213 of 19 October 1940. Prem. 3-71.

67 Alexander to Churchill 23 October 1940. Adm. 199/1931.

68 Minute of 23 October 1940. ibid.

69 Pound to Alexander 25 October 1940. ibid.

70 Alexander to Churchill 25 October 1940. ibid., and Prem. 3-71.

71 Minute dated 27 October 1940. ibid.

72 COS(40) 320th meeting.

73 Admiralty narrative of these events. Copy in Prem. 3-276. The signals referred to were *Hotspur*'s 0445 of 11 September 1940 (received by FOCNA 0512) and FOCNA to Admy. 0617 (received 0740) of same day.

74 Churchill to Alexander 16 October 1940, and Admy. signal to C-in-C, Med. of same day. Adm. 199/1931.

75 Admy. to C-in-C, Med. timed 1418 of 9 September 1940 and 0122 of 14 November 1940. BM. Add. Ms. 52563.

76 Somerville to Cunningham referring to Admy. signal timed 2348 of 29 November 1940. BM. Add. Ms. 52563.

77 Churchill to Alexander, holograph note of 19 October 1940 and Pound to Alexander (n.d.) on the same subject. Alexander papers (Churchill College) AVAR 5/4/68(a) and 5/4/72 respectively.

78 Somerville to Cunningham 8 December 1940. BM. Add. Ms. 52563.

79 Churchill to Alexander and Pound 2 December, reply by former of same date and further minute by Churchill of 3 December 1940. Adm. 199/1931.

80 Churchill to Alexander Minute M. 65/1 of 20 January 1941. Prem. 3-390.

81 See for example Paul M. Kennedy, *The Rise and Fall of British Naval Mastery* (Allen Lane, 1976). [2004 en.]

82 Pound to Cunningham 8 February 1941. BM. Add. Ms. 52578.

83 Somerville to Cunningham 7 September 1940. BM. Add. Ms. 52567.

84 Keyes to Churchill 29 October 1940. Keyes papers (Churchill College) KEYS 13/5.

85 Keyes's account of meeting of 19 November 1940. ibid. But the meeting took place in the former Down Street underground railway station, not Dover Street as stated by Keyes.

86 ibid.

87 Signal to C-in-C, Med. timed 2145 of 11 December 1940. BM. Add. Ms. 52567.

88 C-in-C, Med. to Admy. letter no. 829 of about 22 October 1940.

89 Churchill to Alexander and Pound 22 October 1940. Adm. 199/1931.

90 Churchill to Ismay and Hollis 28 December 1940. Copy in KEYS 13/5.

91 Admy. to C-in-C, Med. from Prime Minister timed 2145 of 11 December 1941. BM. Add. Ms. 52567.

92 C-in-C, Med. to Admy. for Prime Minister timed 1615 of 12 December 1941. ibid.

93 Three COS meetings took place on 5 December with Churchill in the chair to discuss 'Workshop'; but 'no minutes were circulated'. They were followed by a Defence Committee meeting on the same subject and it was probably then that Pound made this remark. See Cab. 79/8 for COS meetings and Cab. 69/1 for the Defence Committee meeting DO(40) 48th. The remark by Pound quoted in *War at Sea*, I, p. 304 was given to me by an officer who was present.

94 To Lady Keyes 18 December 1940. KEYS 2/30.

95 COS(40) 35th Meeting of 31 December 1940.

96 Pound to Cunningham 8 February 1941. BM. Add. Ms. 52578.

97 Cunningham to Pound 18 January 1941. BM. Add. Ms. 52567.

98 Keyes to Portal 25 January and reply by latter of 26 January 1941. KEYS 13/5.

99 Paper of 1976 by Admiral Sir William Davis in author's possession.

100 Letter Davis to the author 14 December 1976.

101 Keyes to Eden 12 May 1941. KEYS 13/5.

102 Remarks on 'Exercise Leapfrog' dated 18 August 1941. KEYS 13/7.

103 Keyes to Churchill 4 February 1941. KEYS 13/3.

104 Pound to Cunningham 27 January 1941. BM. Add. Ms. 52578.

105 Admiral Sir William Davis's unpublished memoirs (Churchill College) throw a great deal of light on Keyes and on the planning of operation 'Workshop'.

106 On the plans to occupy the Atlantic Islands see Churchill, *Second World War*, II, pp. 460, 463 and 552, and Roskill, *War at Sea*, I, pp. 272–3 and 379–80.

107 Churchill to Halifax 24 July 1940 and Foreign Office remarks on same. Prem. 3–361/1.

108 Churchill to COSs 22 March and reply by latter of 23 March 1941. ibid.

109 Keyes to Churchill 21 October 1941. KEYS 13/5.

110 See George Millar, *The Bruneval Raid* (Bodley Head, 1974).

111 Churchill to Keyes 5 February 1941. Prem. 3–330/7. The Churchill-Keyes correspondence is in that file and Prem. 3–330/2. Much of it is also in the Keyes papers.

112 In its final form the directive is COS(41)166 of 14 March 1941.

113 Hollis to Keyes 4 and 30 September and Churchill to Keyes 30 September 1941. KEYS 13/1. Also COS(41)589 of 27 September 1941.

114 Churchill to Keyes 4 October 1941. Adm. 199/1933.

115 Same to same 14 October 1941. KEYS 13/3. Although in this letter Mountbatten's title is given as 'Commodore, Combined Operations' he was in fact appointed 'Adviser on Combined Operations (ACO)' and held that appointment until March 1942 when he was appointed 'Chief of Combined Operations (CCO)'. Mountbatten to Roskill 18 May 1977.

116 Pound to Cunningham 25 November 1941. BM. Add. Ms. 52578.

117 Lord Mountbatten to the author. Interview 11 January 1941.

118 Stark to Pound 15 October, Pound to Churchill 29 October and reply by latter of 31 October 1941. Prem. 3–330/2.

119 Churchill, *Second World War*, IV, p. 178.

120 Keyes to Churchill 21 October, to Bracken 22 November, to Eden 4 December and to A. V. Alexander 5 December 1941. KEYS 13/15 and /16.

121 Churchill to Keyes 26 October 1941. KEYS 13/13.

122 Paper of 1966 by General Jacob. Copy in author's possession.

123 Pound to Cunningham 30 March 1940. BM. Add. Ms. 52560.

124 Same to same 1 December 1940. ibid.

125 Churchill to Alexander and Pound 12 July 1940 and reply by latter of same date. Adm. 199/1930.

126 Same to same 15 and 18 July 1940. ibid.

127 Same to same 23 July and 13 August 1940. ibid.

128 Roskill, *War at Sea*, I, pp. 298 and 301–2.

129 ibid., pp. 437–8.

130 Signal of 13 May 1941. Adm. 199/1933.

131 Churchill to Pound 6 January 1941 and reply by latter of same day. Adm. 199/1930.

132 Roskill, *War at Sea*, I, p. 425.

133 Signal of 10 February 1941. Adm. 199/1932.

134 C-in-C, Med. to Admy. timed 1451 of 17 March 1941. ibid.

135 Churchill to Eden 28 February 1941. Prem. 3–124/1.

136 Churchill to Ismay for COSs, minute D.83/1 of 9 March 1941. ibid.

137 Minute of 21 March on C-in-C, Med. signal timed 1451 of 17 March 1941. Adm. 199/1932 and Prem. 3–124/1.

138 Minute to Alexander and Pound of 21 March and reply by former of 25 March 1941. ibid.

139 Prem. 3–314/4 contains interesting exchanges between Lindemann and Churchill about the former's Long Aerial Mines and Naval Wire Barrage.

140 Churchill to Alexander and Pound 26 March, replies by Alexander of 3 April and 2 July and final minute by Churchill of 3 July 1941. Adm. 199/1934.

141 C-in-C, Med. to Admy. timed 2317 of 6 June 1940. BM. Add. Ms. 52566.

142 Quoted R. W. Thompson, *The Yankee Marlborough* (Allen and Unwin, 1963), pp. 311–12.

143 C-in-C, Med. to Admy. timed 1132 of 4 March 1941. BM. Add. Ms. 52567.

144 Diary for 27 January 1946. BM. Add. Ms. 52579.

145 Churchill to Alexander and Pound 14 April, minute by Pound of 15 April, reply by Alexander of 17 April and further minute by Churchill of 22 April 1941. Adm. 199/1933.

146 Admy. to C-in-C, Med. signal timed 0059 of 15 April 1941. BM. Add. Ms. 52567.

147 Personal signal from First Sea Lord timed 1245 of 15 April 1941. ibid.

148 C-in-C, Med. to Admy. timed 2111 of 15 April 1941. ibid.

149 Same to same timed 1144 of 16 April 1941. ibid.

150 The directive is printed in full in Churchill, *Second World War*, III, pp. 186–8.

151 First Sea Lord to C-in-C, Med. Personal timed 1757 of 16 April 1941. BM. Add. Ms. 52567.

152 C-in-C, Med. to Admy. timed 0932 of 16 April 1941 and para. 5 of same to same timed 2115 of 15 April 1941. ibid., also *Odyssey*, p. 344.

153 *Odyssey*, pp. 346–7.

154 Admy. to C-in-C, Med. timed 1215 of 23 April and reply by latter timed 2217 of 25 April 1941. BM. Add. Ms. 52567, also *Odyssey*, pp. 347–8.

155 Churchill to C-in-C, Med. Personal timed 1142 of 26 April 1941. BM. Add. Ms. 52567.

156 Salisbury to Churchill 23 April, minute by latter of 25 April and reply by Alexander of 6 May 1941. Adm. 199/1933.

157 Admy. to C-in-C, Med. timed 2132 of 25 May 1941. BM. Add. Ms. 52567.

158 Churchill to Pound 25 September 1941. Adm. 205/10.

159 Pound to Churchill 25 September 1941. ibid.

160 Churchill to Somerville 3 August 1941. Adm. 199/1934.

161 Cs-in-C, Middle East to COSs timed 2301B of 21 October 1941. BM. Add. Ms. 52567.

162 Same to same 2137B of 27 October 1941. ibid.

163 Admy. to C-in-C, Med. timed 2023A of 28 October 1941. ibid. For details of 'the Plan for and abandonment of operation Whipcord' see Prem. 3–503/1 and /2.

164 First Sea Lord to C-in-C, Med. timed 0012A of 10 December and reply by latter 2022B of 11 December 1941. ibid.

165 Same to same timed 1247A of 23 November 1941. ibid.

166 C-in-C, Med. to Admy. Personal for Prime Minister timed 1026B of 24 November 1941. ibid.

167 First Sea Lord to C-in-C, Med. Personal timed 1740A of 25 November and reply by latter timed 0018 of 24 November 1941. ibid., also *Odyssey*, pp. 423–6.

168 C. Eade (ed.), *The War Speeches of Rt. Hon. Winston S. Churchill*, II, pp. 137–8.

169 Cunningham to Pound 28 December 1941. BM. Add. Ms. 52561.

170 Letter to Cunningham's aunt Helen Browne of 15 February 1942. BM. Add. Ms. 52559.

171 Cunningham to Pound 19 March 1942. BM. Add. Ms. 52561.

172 Minute M. 227/2 by Churchill of 4 June 1942. Adm. 205/14.

173 Pound to Alexander 8 June 1942. ibid.

174 Alexander to Churchill 7 September 1942. Adm. 199/1935.

175 Information from Admiral Sir William Davis who was Naval Secretary to the First Lord 1950–2 August 1976.

176 Signals about the loan of USS *Wasp* are in Adm. 205/13. See also Churchill, *Second World War*, IV, pp. 268–70 and 273.

177 Churchill to Cunningham, Personal and Secret signal timed 1142 of 26 April 1941. BM. Add. Ms. 52563.

178 Churchill to Alexander and Pound 21 July and reply by former of 24 July 1942. Adm. 205/14.

179 Harwood to Pound 12 July and minute by Moore of 18 July 1942. Adm. 205/42.

180 See Roskill, *War at Sea*, II, pp. 302–8. Peter Smith, *Pedestal. The Malta Convoy of August 1942* (Kimber, 1970) tells the story in greater detail.

181 Churchill, *Second World War*, IV. pp. 376–8 and letter by Cunningham of 21 June 1942. BM. Add. Ms. 52559.

182 Churchill's minute to Alexander of 28 August 1942. Adm. 205/14. There is some evidence that the highly efficient German cryptographic organization known as the B-Dienst had obtained warning of the Tobruk raid, but I have been unable to obtain definite confirmation.

183 Churchill to Pound 15 and 16 October and reply by Pound of 15 October 1942. Adm. 205/14.

184 Harwood's memo. of 1 December to Admiral Godfroy and letter to Cunningham of 3 December 1942. BM. Add. Ms. 52570(1).

184A Paper by Captain T. M. Brownrigg dated 8 September 1966 produced for Professor Arthur J. Marder, to whom I am indebted for a copy. Brownrigg had been Master of the Fleet (i.e. Fleet Navigating Officer) during Cunningham's first term in the Mediterranean, accompanied him to Washington and then returned with him to his former station as Staff Officer (Plans).

185 See Churchill, *Second World War*, IV, ch. XXV.

186 This was probably the encounter more discreetly described in *Odyssey*, p. 466.

187 Cunningham to Pound 12 August 1942. BM. Add. Ms. 52561.

187A Brownrigg, loc. cit.

188 Roskill, *War at Sea*, II, ch. XIII.

189 Cunningham to Pound 5 December 1942. BM. Add. Ms. 52561.

190 Ramsay to Cunningham 24 November and 10 December 1942. BM. Add. Ms. 52570(1).

Chapter 11   pages 196 to 210

1 Churchill to Alexander 15 September 1940.

2 Churchill to Roosevelt 15 February 1941. *Loewenheim*, p. 129.

3 Liddell Hart, *Four Faces*, p. 191.

4 *Loewenheim*, p. 163.

5 Churchill, *Second World War*, III, p. 523.

6 op. cit., IV, chs. III and IV give details of the forces rushed to Singapore in late 1941 and early 1942.

7 Churchill to Alexander and Pound 25 August 1941 and reply by latter. Adm. 205/10.

8 Same to same 29 August 1941. ibid.

9 Roskill, *War at Sea*, I, pp. 554–8.

10 Phillips to Pound 17 October 1941 describing meeting of the Defence Committee held that day. Copy in author's possession.

11 Churchill's minutes about the two capital ships being sent to the Far East, the Admiralty's report on the disaster and Churchill's subsequent remarks and questions are in Prem. 3–163/2.

12 C-in-C, China Memo. of 3 September 1941. Adm. 199/1472A.

13 Roskill, *Naval Policy*, II, pp. 186–7 and *passim*.

14 First Sea Lord to C-in-C, Med. signal timed 1759 of 10 October 1941. Adm. 205/10.

15 Quoted F. D. L. Brown to Pound's secretary 12 October 1941. ibid.

16 Signals of 31 October and 5 November 1941. See Roskill, *War at Sea*, I, p. 357.

17 Churchill to Pound 11 November 1941 and reply by latter. Adm. 205/10.

18 Sir John Colville to the author 7 December 1976.

19 Admiral Sir William Davis to the author 26 October 1961. Phillips's account of the Defence Committee meeting of 17 October 1941 (see note 10 above) certainly supports the view that he and Churchill were far from being *en rapport* at that time.

20 Davis to the author 26 October 1961.

21 Lord Cunningham to the author 9 September 1961.

22 Sir John to Sir Andrew Cunningham 30 August 1942. BM. Add. Ms. 52562.

23 Somerville to Cunningham 20 October 1941. BM. Add. Ms. 52563.

24 Churchill to High Commissioner in South Africa for General Smuts 2 November 1941. Adm. 199/1934.

25 Smuts to Churchill 18 November 1941. See Roskill, *War at Sea*, I, p. 558.

26 Pound to Churchill 7 March 1942. Copy in author's possession. I have been unable to relocate this letter in the Prem. 3 or 4 files. Its original reference in the Churchill Operational Papers was File 119.

27 Churchill to Captain G. R. G. Allen 11 August 1953 and reply by latter of 24 August 1953.

28 Somerville to Cunningham 21 December 1941. BM. Add. Ms. 52563.

29 Churchill to Pound 13 March and reply by latter of 18 March 1942. Adm. 205/13. Regarding the attack on the *Tirpitz* of 9 March 1942 see Roskill, *War at Sea*, II, pp. 121–4.

30 This was Freiherr von Tiesenhausen in U.331. See Roskill, op. cit., I, pp. 534 and 555.

31 Alexander to Churchill 10 December 1941 and reply by latter of same day. Prem. 3–324/15.

32 Signals about the naval C-in-C, ABDA Command are in Prem. 3–166/2. It was dissolved on 25 February 1942.

33 Churchill to Pound 22 January 1942. Adm. 205/13.

34 Pound to Churchill 24 January and note by latter of 9 February 1942. ibid.

35 Many such reports are in the Layton papers Adm. 199/1472A.

36 For example the story of the auxiliary vessel *Li Wo* which only came to light after the war and for which her Captain was awarded a posthumous VC. Roskill, *War at Sea*, II, p. 9.

37 Admiral Layton lent me all his papers while I was working on my war history and on completing that work I sent them, as requested by the admiral, to the Admiralty. He later realized this was a mistake, and tried to recover them – but without success. They are now in the PRO under references Adm. 199/1472A– 1477; but his critical report on Singapore, which is probably in Adm. 199/1472B, is 'closed until 1998'. So I have been unable to consult once again papers which were in my hands in the 1950s! Other interesting reports on operations off the

west coast of Malaya, including the fall of Penang, are in Adm. 199/357.

38 Churchill's minute T. 295/2 of 26 February 1942. Prem. 3–153/1.

39 Layton to Pound signal timed 1032Z of 27 February 1942. Copy in ibid.

40 Churchill's minute T. 306/2 of 1 March and Admy. signal to C-in-C, Eastern Fleet timed 0159A of 5 March 1942. Prem. 3–153/1.

41 Layton to Pound 11 March 1942. Adm. 199/1472A.

42 Alexander to Churchill 18 September 1942. Adm. 199/1935.

43 Pound to Alexander 8 November 1942. Adm. 205/20.

44 Churchill to Alexander minute M. 467/2 of 20 October 1942. Adm. 199/1935.

45 On this matter see S. W. Kirby, the official historian of the war against Japan, *Singapore: The Chain of Disaster* (Cassell, 1971), esp. pp. 213 and 255.

46 Pound to Churchill 7 March 1942. See note 26 above.

47 Churchill to Ismay for COSs minute D. 41/2 of 2 March 1942. Prem. 3–119/5.

48 Amery to Churchill and Churchill to Pound 19 and 20 March 1942 respectively. Adm. 205/13.

49 Churchill to Alexander and Pound minute M. 76/2 of 10 March 1942. Prem. 3–324/14. Also DO(42)23, Appendix I.

50 Same to same 10 March 1942 and subsequent exchanges. Prem. 3–324/14.

51 Roskill, *War at Sea*, II, pp. 25–32.

52 Admiral Willis's remarks on draft of above. Willis papers (Churchill College) WLLS 5/5.

53 Roskill, op. cit., p. 28.

54 Churchill to Alexander and Pound minute M. 186/2 of 15 May 1942. Adm. 199/1935.

55 'Notes for PM's speech' of 12th April 1942, and exchange between Churchill and Pound of same date. Adm. 205/13. See Churchill, *Second World War*, IV, pp. 157–62 and Roskill, op. cit., II, pp. 25–9 regarding these events.

56 Quoted in Alexander to Churchill 10 June 1942. Adm. 199/1935.

57 Wavell to COSs 12 April 1942. Quoted Churchill, *Second World War*, IV, p. 165.

58 Willis to Cunningham 10 April 1942. WLLS 5/5.

59 Churchill, *Second World War*, IV, p. 165.

60 Churchill to Alexander and Pound 26 April and reply by latter of 2 May 1942. Prem. 3–163/5. The naval staff's minutes on this exchange are in Adm. 205/20.

61 Exchanges and minutes in Adm. 205/21.

62 Churchill to Alexander and Pound 13 July and 19 December and reply by Alexander of 14 December 1942. Adm. 205/14.

63 Churchill to Pound 16 October 1942. ibid.

64 Churchill's minute M. 267/2 of 4 July 1942 and reply by Pound forwarded by Alexander on 14 July. Adm. 199/1935 and Prem. 3–163.

65 Dill to COSs telegram JSM. 671 of 7 January and minutes on it by naval staff and Pound of 8 January 1943. Adm. 205/32.

66 Churchill to Roosevelt no. 217 of 2 December 1942. Prem. 3–163/1.

67 Same to same T. 1664/2, nos. 226. ibid.

68 Roskill, *War at Sea*, II, pp. 415–16.

69 High Commissioner, South Africa to Dominions Office, telegram of 2 December 1942. Prem. 3–385/1.

70 Churchill to Alexander and Pound minute M. 114/3 of 5 March; Pound to Churchill 9 August; and further minutes by Churchill of 13 and 15 August 1943. ibid.

71 Pound to Churchill 18 August 1943 from Château Frontenac, Quebec. ibid.

72 Telegram Welfare no. 715 of 13 September, Alexander's reply of 15 September, staff proposals of 26 September and Churchill's minute M. 606/3 of 27 September 1943. Prem. 3–163/7. The exchanges and staff remarks are in Adm. 205/27.

Chapter 12   pages 211 to 227

1 Minute of approx. 7 January on a signal from General Eisenhower 'Can't the Navy do anything with submarines?'; reply by Pound of 12 January and further minute by Churchill of 12 January 1943. 'Good. But what about surface action?' Adm. 205/27.

2 Pound to Alexander of 4 January 1943. Adm. 205/32.

3 Memo. for Churchill, unsigned but presumably by Pound, dated 6 February 1943. Adm. 205/27.

4 Pound to Harwood 13 February 1943. Adm. 205/56.

5 Harwood to Pound 12 March 1943. ibid.

6 Churchill to Casey 11 February 1943. Prem. 3–179/5. That file and Prem. 3–179/6 contain all the messages and letters about the protracted efforts to force Admiral Godfroy off the fence on which he had been sitting since July 1940. He finally did so on 17 May 1943 by deciding 'to join the French navy in North Africa'. These exchanges suggest that Harwood's description of Churchill's 'venom' against the Frenchman was not an exaggeration.

7 Sir Andrew Cunningham to Pound 15 March and reply by latter of 25 April 1943. BM. Add. Ms. 52561. Pound told Cunningham that after the row about the opening of Tripoli harbour Harwood's blood pressure was 255; so he was certainly not a fit man at the time of his relief. Cunningham to Roskill 12 November 1956 gives his account of what he called his 'tiff' with Pound about the sacking of Harwood.

8 Roskill, *War at Sea*, II, pp. 435–8.

9 Lord Cunningham's private correspondence (BM. Add. Ms. 52558–61) contains many criticisms of General Alexander on this score.

10 Churchill to Cunningham 11 June 1943. Adm. 199/1936.

11 Note by Pound dated 10 February 1943 on draft of Churchill's speech. Adm. 205/27.

12 Hansard, Commons, vol. 386, cols. 1168–1488. Also printed in C. Eade (ed.) *The War Speeches of Winston S. Churchill*, II, pp. 407–23.

13 Pound to Ismay 9 March 1943. Adm. 205/27.

14 Same to same 12 March 1943. ibid.

15 Sir John to Sir Andrew Cunningham 23 March 1943. BM. Add. Ms. 52562.

16 Shakespeare, *King Henry IV*, part II, V, ii, 48.

17 Letter to the author of 15 December 1976 and Admiral Sir Manley Power's unpublished memoirs.

18 Cunningham to Pound 28 April 1943. BM. Add. Ms. 52561.

19 Admiral Power to Lord Cunningham 10 and 23 September 1949. BM. Add. Ms. 52575. Power was at the time advising Cunningham on the handling of these events in his autobiography.

20 James, *Four Faces*, p. 71.

21 Quoted *Odyssey*, p. 546.

22 Letter to Cunningham's aunt Helen Browne of 6 June 1943. BM. Add. Ms. 52559.

23 See *Loewenheim*, pp. 310–13.

24 Churchill to COSs minute D. 1503 of 2 August 1943. Prem. 3–3.

25 Cs-in-C, Middle East to COSs 31 August 1943. ibid.

26 Signal timed 0345Z of 9 September 1943. See also Churchill, *Second World War*, V, p. 182.

27 Roosevelt to Churchill 7 October 1943. *Loewenheim*, pp. 370–2.

28 Admiral of the Fleet Sir Algernon Willis stresses this point in his unpublished memoirs (WLLS/12) and in his letters to the author.

29 See Lord Tedder, *With Prejudice* (Cassell, 1966), pp. 469–87 and Lord Douglas, *Years of Command* (Collins, 1966), pp. 208–14.

30 Churchill to Sir Andrew Cunningham (First Sea Lord from 15 October 1943) of 16 October and to Alexander of 19 October 1943. Adm. 205/27.

31 Churchill, *Second World War*, V, ch. XII, significantly entitled 'Island Prizes Lost', and *Loewenheim*, pp. 370–1.

32 Churchill to Cunningham 11 October 1943. Adm. 199/1936. Compare Churchill's description of Leros as 'a fortress' with his application of the same description to Singapore early in 1942 (see p. 203). In neither case did it bear any resemblance to reality.

33 See Marder, *Dreadnought to Scapa Flow*, II, pp. 245–8.

34 Cs-in-C, Middle East telegram of 17 November 1943. Prem. 3–3.

35 See pp. 171–4.

36 Churchill to Roosevelt 23 October 1943. *Loewenheim*, p. 389. Churchill was obviously referring to Matthew, XV, 27 'And she (the woman of Canaan) said, Truth, Lord: yet the dogs eat of the crumbs which fall from their masters' table.'

37 For a full account of the Aegean operations of 1943 (apart from Churchill's and this author's) see Admiral Willis's despatch (Supplement to the London Gazette of 8 October 1948). However that despatch was heavily censored before publication in order to eliminate all references to the fact that British warships had made frequent use of Turkish territorial waters in order to prolong their patrols off the islands without returning to Alexandria to refuel. In his memoirs Admiral Willis deals fully with this matter. WLLS/12.

38 Willis memoirs WLLS/12.

39 Churchill, *Second World War*, IV, pp. 381–7.

40 Admiral Power's unpublished memoirs pp. 65–6 (typescript).

41 Quoted Churchill, *Second World War*, IV, pp. 383–4.

42 Admiral Power, loc. cit.

43 Churchill, *Second World War*, V, p. 432.

44 Sir John to Sir Andrew Cunningham 25 September 1944. BM. Add. Ms. 52562.

45 Churchill, op. cit., pp. 431–2.

46 Lord Cunningham's diary for 1 December 1944. BM. Add. Ms. 52577.
47 *Loewenheim*, pp. 542-6 has the most important telegrams which passed between Churchill and Roosevelt on this issue. For complete texts see Prem. 3-467 to 473.
48 Churchill to Ismay for COSs minute D. 28/4 of 2 February, reply by COSs of 8 February, and further minute by Churchill D. 128/4 of 22 April 1944. Prem. 3-271/1. Also COS(44) 39th meeting of 8 February 1944.
49 *Loewenheim*, pp. 628 and 634-6 has most of the telegrams which passed between Churchill and Roosevelt on the Greek imbroglio of October-December 1944. Complete texts are in Prem. 3-467 to 473.
50 Churchill, *Second World War*, VI, pp. 97-100 and ch. XVIII.

Chapter 13   pages 228 to 247

1 Churchill to Eden, Alexander and Pound 9 January 1943. Adm. 205/27.
2 Pound to Churchill 18 January 1943. ibid.
3 Same to same 3 March 1943. ibid.
4 Cherwell to Churchill 28 March 1943, copies to Alexander and Pound. ibid.
5 Edelsten to Pound 1 March 1943. Adm. 205/32.
6 On a motion by Lord Strabolgi. Hansard, Lords, vol. 126, cols. 863-904. See also Prem. 4-59/2.
7 Pound to Churchill 10 April and Portal to same 23 April 1943. Adm. 205/32.
8 Portal to Churchill 18 April 1943. ibid.
9 Pound to Churchill 20 April 1943. ibid.
10 Churchill to Roosevelt 4 and 24 March 1943. *Loewenheim*, pp. 320 and 322.
11 Admiral Sir Charles Lambe, interview, 1958.
12 Roskill, *War at Sea*, II, ch. XIV.
13 Churchill's minute of 2 May 1943. Adm. 205/27.
14 Pound to Alexander 3 May 1943 and message to same from Churchill. Adm. 205/27. Also in Adm. 199/1936.
15 Pound to naval staff 18 July 1943. Adm. 205/27.
16 Cherwell to Churchill and Churchill to Alexander and Pound 24 July 1943. ibid.
17 Churchill to Pound 13 July and reply by latter of 14 July 1943. ibid.
18 Adm. 205/30.
19 See P. M. S. Blackett, *Studies of War* (Oliver and Boyd, 1962), part II, ch. 3.
20 Alexander to Churchill 8 July 1942. Adm. 205/14. On Admiral Dreyer's earlier record see Roskill, *Naval Policy*, II, *passim*.
21 Dreyer to Pound 10 March 1943. Adm. 205/12. Dreyer's letters to Pound in this file strongly suggest instability of mind.
22 Churchill to Alexander, Pound and Ismay, minute M. 237/3 of 4 April 1943. ibid.
23 Pound to Dreyer 8 April. ibid.
24 Same to same 14 April. ibid.
25 Churchill to Alexander 23 July 1943 and minutes by naval staff and Fifth Sea Lord. Adm. 205/56 and 205/43.
26 John Connell, *Wavell: Scholar and Soldier* (Collins, 1964) p. 265.
27 Minutes and draft reply to Churchill (not sent) in Adm. 205/43.

28 Minute by Fifth Sea Lord of 6 November 1943. Adm. 205/41.

29 See Roskill, *Naval Air Documents*, p. xvii and part v.

30 WP.(43)295 and 296 contain Churchill's proposals for a heavy cut in naval man power. Discussed by War Cabinet 9 July 1943. WM(43) 96th meeting.

31 WM(43) 100th meeting of 16 July 1943.

32 WP(43)319.

33 Alexander to Churchill 18 July 1943. Adm. 205/27.

34 Churchill to Alexander 23 March 1943. Adm. 205/29 and Prem. 3-322/5.

35 Churchill's minute of 28 March 1943 on Alexander's proposals of 25 March regarding the naval building programme for 1944. ibid.

36 First Interim Report of the Future Building Committee. Copy in Adm. 205/29 is undated but the report was rendered in December *1942*. Admiral Kennedy-Purvis, the chairman of the committee had been appointed Deputy First Sea Lord in July 1942 with the object of reducing the load on Pound – especially in the technical and scientific field. For an appreciation of his character and services see article by 'G.F.' (Captain Godfrey French) in *The Naval Review*, vol. 64, no. 2 (April 1976).

37 Cunningham diary for 27 November 1944. BM. Add. Ms. 52577.

38 Alexander-Churchill exchanges of 3, 10 and 24 October and 11 and 20 November 1943. Adm. 205/27.

39 Alexander-Churchill exchanges of 1 November 1943 and 2 January 1944. Adm. 205/27 and /32.

40 Churchill to Alexander, minute of 27 May 1944. Adm. 205/35.

41 Churchill to Tovey 23 March 1943. Adm. 199/1936.

42 Pound to Churchill 23 August 1943. Adm. 205/27.

43 Churchill to Pound, Portal and Ismay 24 August 1943. Adm. 205/37.

44 Pound to Churchill 23 August 1943. ibid.

45 Summary by First Sea Lord's secretary of 28 September 1943, presumably made for Sir Andrew Cunningham who was about to take over as First Sea Lord. ibid.

46 Admiralty letter to Admiral Little of 12 October 1943, signed J. S. Barnes. ibid.

47 Little to Cunningham 7 October 1943. ibid.

48 Churchill to Alexander and Cunningham 20 February, reply by latter of 22 February and minute by Churchill of 25 February 1944. Adm. 205/35.

49 See W. S. Chalmers, *Full Cycle. The Biography of Admiral Sir Bertram Ramsay* (Hodder and Stoughton, 1959) p. 206.

50 Churchill, *Second World War*, V, pp. 145-6.

51 ibid., p. 145.

52 On Fraser's reaction to Churchill's offer of the post of First Sea Lord see ibid.

53 Cunningham diary for 19 February 1946. BM. Add. Ms. 52577.

54 See *Odyssey*, pp. 573-4.

55 See Roskill, *War at Sea*, III, part I, pp. 273-9 for a full account of this operation. The signals which passed between Cunningham and the C-in-C, Home Fleet start with the former's 1732 of 3 April and end with Admiral Moore's 0825 of 25 April abandoning the operation. Although by this date the Royal Navy had adopted the US Navy's system of recording Times of Origin of signals, by which the two quoted above were shown as 031732 April and 250825 April respectively,

I have thought it less confusing to adhere to the earlier British system in this work.

56 *The Ballad of East and West.*

57 Churchill to Cunningham 20 February and reply by latter of 24 February 1944. Adm. 205/35.

58 Minute by Churchill of 11 March and reply by Cunningham of 18 March 1944. ibid.

59 J. R. M. Butler, *Grand Strategy*, III, part II (HMSO, 1964) p. 570. COS(42) 78th meeting, minute 6, Confidential Annex.

60 COSSAC(43)32 (Final) of 27 July 1943. Also Prem. 3–342 and 343.

61 See Churchill, *Second World War*, V, pp. 66–8.

62 COS(Q)21 of 13 August 1943.

63 Letter to the author 11 February 1977.

64 See Roskill, *War at Sea*, III, part II, chs. XIV and XV for a full account of the naval side of operation 'Overlord'. On the deception plan (operation 'Fortitude') see Sir John Masterman, *The Double Cross System* (Yale, UP, 1972).

65 Quoted in Churchill to Roosevelt of 12 June 1944. *Loewenheim*, p. 530.

66 Churchill to Alexander and Cunningham 22 June and reply by latter of same date. Adm. 205/35.

67 Cunningham diary for 22 June 1944. BM. Add. Ms. 52577.

68 Churchill to Alexander and Cunningham 5 July 1944, reply by former of 8 July and further minute by Churchill of 11 July 1944. Adm. 205/35.

69 Exchanges of 12, 14, 20 and 26 July 1944 between Churchill and Admiralty. ibid.

70 Churchill to Cunningham 10 July, reply by latter of 11 July and further minute by Churchill of 13 July 1944. ibid.

71 Roskill, *War at Sea*, III, part II, pp. 54–9 and 67–9.

72 Churchill to Cunningham 4 August and reply by latter of 7 August 1944. Adm. 205/35.

73 Cunningham to Churchill 28 August and minute by latter of 1 September 1944. ibid.

74 Churchill to Ismay for COSs. Minute D(O) of 9 September 1944. Prem. 3–149/8.

75 Reply by COSs of same date.

76 *Loewenheim*, pp. 544–8 and Churchill, *Second World War*, V and VI, *passim.*

77 Cunningham diary for 6 July, 1, 8 and 9 September and 30 October 1944. BM. Add. Ms. 52577.

78 The interdepartmental exchanges are in Adm. 205/35. See also Churchill to Roosevelt 21 January 1944. *Loewenheim*, p. 416.

79 Churchill to Roosevelt, 1 February 1944. op. cit., p. 423.

80 Churchill to Eden 2 March 1944. Copy in Adm. 205/35.

81 Churchill to Alexander and Cunningham 28 May 1944. ibid.

82 Churchill to Sir Alexander Cadogan (Permanent Secretary, Foreign Office) 18 April 1944. Copy in ibid.

83 Cunningham diary 4 October 1944. BM. Add. Ms. 52577.

84 ibid., entry for 2 November 1944.

85 Churchill to Cunningham 2 September and reply by latter of 4 September 1944. Adm. 205/35.

86 Cunningham diary 7 September, 4 and 6 October 1944. BM. Add. Ms. 52577.

87 ibid.
88 Alexander and Churchill exchanges of 5, 6, 7 and 9 January 1945. Adm. 205/43. Also Cunningham diary for 6, 7 and 8 January 1945. BM. Add. Ms. 52577.

Chapter 14   pages 248 to 262

1 See John Ehrman, *Grand Strategy*, V (HMSO, 1956), pp. 139 and 144.
2 Drafts by Ismay in Prem. 3–53/3.
3 Telegram no. 320 of 19 June 1943. ibid.
4 Telegram no. 293 of 25 June 1943. ibid.
5 Minute by Ismay of 26 June and telegram Churchill to Roosevelt of 28 June 1943. ibid.
6 Minutes by Portal and Churchill of 25 and 26 June 1943. ibid.
7 Telegram Dill to COSs of 28 June 1943. ibid.
8 Roosevelt to Churchill, telegram no. 298 of 30 June 1943. ibid.
9 Minute D. 128/3 to COSs of 13 July 1943. Prem. 3–53/3.
10 Telegram Roosevelt to Churchill T. 997/3. ibid.
11 COSs to Churchill 21 July 1943. ibid.
12 Minute to COSs of 24 July 1943. ibid.
13 Churchill to Attlee 7 August 1943. Prem. 3–53/4.
14 Attlee to Churchill and Churchill to Attlee 11 August 1943. ibid.
15 Churchill, *Second World War*, V, p. 109.
16 Churchill to Attlee and Eden 15 August 1943. Prem. 3–53/4.
17 Mountbatten to Churchill. Holograph from Château Frontenac, Quebec, 28 August 1943. ibid.
18 Churchill to Somerville 1 September 1943. ibid.
19 [Pound to Churchill 31 August 1943. ibid. This must have been one of Pound's last actions as First Sea Lord, since early in September he suffered the stroke which ed to his resignation. See Churchill, *Second World War*, V, p. 118.
20 Message timed 1430Z of 2 September 1943. Prem. 3–53/4.
21 COS(43) 145th meeting of 2 July 1943.
22 Somerville to Pound 27 August 1943. This letter came on to Cunningham, presumably because of Pound's resignation. BM. Add. Ms. 52561.
23 Admiral Sir Kaye Edden, who was Staff Officer (Plans) to Somerville at the time, to the author 20 January 1977.
24 Mountbatten to Somerville 2 September 1943. Somerville papers (Churchill College) SMVL 8/3.
25 Quoted in full in Donald Macintyre, *Fighting Admiral* (Evans, 1961) pp. 231–4.
26 The directive is WP(43)414 of 22 September 1943. For a summary see Roskill, *War at Sea*, III, part I, pp. 213–15.
27 Somerville to Cunningham 27 October 1943. BM. Add. Ms. 52563.
28 Director of Plans to First Sea Lord 9 November 1943. Adm. 205/27.
29 Cunningham to Churchill 10 November 1943. ibid.
30 Alexander to Churchill 14 November 1943. ibid. Also Ismay to Churchill of same date. Prem. 3–53/7.

31 Churchill to Cunningham and Ismay 17 November 1943. Adm. 205/27 and Prem. 3–53/7.

32 Cunningham to Churchill 20 November 1943. Unsigned copy in Adm. 205/27.

33 Churchill to Cunningham and Ismay 21 November 1943. ibid.

34 Cunningham to Churchill 24 November 1943 and to Somerville. Adm. 205/27 and Prem. 3–53/7.

35 Somerville to Cunningham 27 October and 4 December 1943. BM. Add. Ms. 52563.

36 Same to same 3 January 1944. ibid.

37 Cunningham to Somerville 19 December 1943. SMVL 8/2.

38 Correspondence in BM. Add. Ms. 52563.

39 Cunningham to Somerville 10 March 1944. SMVL 8/2.

40 Mountbatten to Cunningham 28 March 1944. Copy in author's possession.

41 Somerville to Cunningham 12 June 1944. SMVL 8/2.

42 Admy. to C-in-C, Eastern Fleet timed 1635A of 12 (?) February 1944. Copy in SMVL 8/3 (month indecipherable).

43 Alexander to Churchill 28 March and reply by latter of 29 March 1944; further minute by Churchill of 15 April 1944. Adm. 205/35.

44 Prem. 3–164/1 and COS(44)202(0) of 28 February 1944.

45 Cunningham to Churchill 18 March and reply by latter of 1 April 1944. Adm. 205/35.

46 See Churchill, *Second World War*, V, ch. XXI.

47 Churchill to Alexander and Cunningham 19 April and reply by Alexander of 20 April 1944. Adm. 205/35.

48 Diary entries for 19 and 20 April 1944. BM. Add. Ms. 52577.

48A COS(44)129(0) of 20 April 1944. Cab. 79/89.

49 Churchill to Alexander and Cunningham 29 April 1944. Adm. 205/35.

50 Macintyre, *Fighting Admiral*, p. 245 quoting from Somerville's diary.

51 Alexander to Churchill 3 May 1944. Adm. 205/35.

52 Churchill to Ismay for COSs 6 December 1943. Prem. 3–147/7.

53 Telegram timed 1730Z of 10 January 1944. ibid.

54 Churchill to Alexander and Cunningham 14 February, reply by former of 20 February and further minute by Churchill of 23 February 1944. Adm. 205/35.

55 Roskill, *War at Sea*, III, part I, pp. 344–6.

56 Churchill, *Second World War*, V, p. 78.

57 JP(Q)12 of 12 August 1943. Prem. 3–147/3.

58 Dated 17 August 1943. ibid. (Written at Quebec).

59 COS(Q)38 of 20 August 1943. ibid. (Written at Quebec).

60 Diary for 2 April 1944. BM. Add. Ms. 52577.

61 See Churchill, *Second World War*, pp. 78–80 and 505–6 regarding his advocacy of 'Culverin'. On Roosevelt's opposition to it see *Loewenheim* p. 454, telegram to Churchill of 24 February 1944. The editors of this work consider that this telegram, in common with many others sent by Roosevelt, was drafted by Admiral W. D. Leahy USN, the President's personal Chief of Staff. op. cit., p. 678, *note*.

62 Diary for 14 July 1944. BM. Add. Ms. 52577.

63 See Roskill, op. cit., III, part I, pp. 356–7.

64 The *Tirpitz* was finally sunk in Trömso by RAF bombers on 12 November 1944. See Roskill, op. cit., III, part II, pp. 168–9.

65 Churchill to Alexander and Cunningham 21 May and reply by former of 24 May 1944. Adm. 205/35.

66 Minute by Churchill of 27 May 1944. ibid.

67 Layton to Cunningham 7 February 1944. BM. Add. Ms. 52571.

68 BM. Add. Ms. 52577. Also Somerville to Cunningham letter of 12 June 1944. BM. Add. Ms. 52563.

69 Admiral Sir Charles Lambe to the author 27 August 1957. See Roskill, *War at Sea*, III, part I, pp. 215–18.

70 Macintyre, *Fighting Admiral*, p. 253.

71 Letters to the author of 26 February (Cunningham), 15 March (Alanbrooke) and 13 March 1954 (Portal).

72 Mountbatten to Ismay 26 June 1944. Copy in Broadlands Archive, and interview with Lord Mountbatten in amplification of this controversy 11 January 1977.

73 Pownall to Roskill, undated but commenting on Mountbatten to same of 11 February 1959. On Pownall's visit to England in May–June 1944 and his intervention with Churchill and the COSs regarding the Somerville-Mountbatten fracas see *Chief of Staff; The Diaries of Lieutenant-General Sir Henry Pownall*. ed. Brian Bond, vol. II, pp. 168 and 175–6. (Leo Cooper, 1974).

74 Churchill to Ismay for COSs 24 July 1944. Prem. 3–148/9.

75 Alexander to Churchill 25 October and minute by latter of 28 October 1944. Prem. 3–164/3.

76 Churchill to Alexander 29 October and reply by latter of 31 October 1944. Adm. 205/35 and Prem. 3–164/3.

77 Diary for 30 October 1944. BM. Add. Ms. 52577.

78 Minute of 4 November 1944. Adm. 205/35.

79 Interview with Admiral of the Fleet Sir Arthur Power 1956.

80 Diary entry for 11 October 1944. BM. Add. Ms. 52577.

81 Same for 18 November 1944. ibid.

82 See for example Churchill to Cunningham 3 February 1944 and reply by latter of same day. Adm. 205/35.

83 Fraser to Cunningham 14 November 1944 and Cunningham diary for 20 November 1944. BM. Add. Ms. 52571 and 52577 respectively.

84 Fraser to Cunningham 14 and 21 March 1945 and other letters in file. BM. Add. Ms. 52572.

85 COS(44) 61st meeting of 25 December 1944 and COS(44) 63rd meeting of 25 February 1945. Cab. 79/89.

Chapter 15   pages 263 to 273

1 See Roskill, *War at Sea*, III, part II, pp. 141–2, 285–6 and appendix X regarding the new Type XXI and XXIII U-boats, which represented a very real threat to the Anglo-American superiority won in May 1943 and kept ever since.

2 BM. Add. Ms. 52578.

3 Diary for 18 May 1945. ibid.
4 See W. S. Chalmers, *Max Horton and the Western Approaches*, ch. XV.
5 op. cit., pp. 237–8.
6 Diary for 18 May 1945. BM. Add. Ms. 52578.
7 Same for 20 April.
8 For Lord Tedder's account of this fracas see his autobiography *With Prejudice* (Cassell, 1966) pp. 661–4.
9 Diary for 13 March 1945. BM. Add. Ms. 52578.
10 Same for 1 June 1945.
11 For example Sir John to Sir Andrew Cunningham 30 August 1941. 'Operational control is not nearly half the battle because you cannot possibly expect operational efficiency from unsuitable training. We *must train* and *operate* our own auxiliaries . . .' BM. Add. Ms. 52562. Sir John had been Fifth Sea Lord with responsibility for the Fleet Air Arm when control of it was returned to the Admiralty in 1938. See Roskill, *Naval Policy*, II, ch. XIII.
12 Alexander to Churchill 10 April and reply by latter of 12 April 1945. Adm. 205/43.
13 See Churchill, *Second World War*, VI, pp. 515–16 for the text of this letter.
14 BM. Add. Ms. 52578.
15 ibid.
16 Diary for 26 May 1945. loc. cit.
17 Same for 29 May 1945.
18 Same for 31 May 1945.
19 Same for 23 July 1945.
20 Churchill, *Second World War*, VI, pp. 582–4.
21 Diary for 26 July 1945. loc. cit.
22 See John Colville, *Footprints in Time* (Collins, 1976) p. 198.
23 See Churchill, *Second World War*, IV, p. 740.
24 See *The Autobiography of D. N. Pritt*, 3 vols. (Lawrence and Wishart, 1965–6), I, p. 287 and II, pp. 86–7.
25 The story of Pritt's lectures to the forces is in Prem. 4–14/13. Grigg remained implacably hostile to him and to Wigg. On the Servicemen's vote in 1945 see Ronald Lewin, *Slim the Standard Bearer*, p. 246. On returning home temporarily in June 1945 Slim told Churchill 'Well, Prime Minister, I know one thing. My army won't be voting for you.'
26 Churchill to Cunningham 8 August 1945. BM. Add. Ms. 52578.
27 Diary for 30 November 1945. ibid.
28 Cunningham to Alexander 'Personal and Private' 4 December 1945.
29 Prem. 3–149/8 contains papers about operations 'Dracula' and 'Capital' – respectively the capture of Rangoon and the advance across the Chindwin river into north Burma, Churchill had originally been opposed to the latter. See p. 259.
30 SEACOS signal 292, para. 2.
31 Churchill to Cunningham 11 January, reply by latter of 12 January, further minutes by Churchill of 14 January and by Cunningham of 27 January 1945. Adm. 205/43.
32 Diary for 26 January 1945. loc. cit.
33 Minutes by staff of 17 January, Cunningham to Churchill of same day, and

minute by latter of 18 January 1945. Adm. 205/43.

34 Diary for 6 March 1945. loc. cit.

35 Same for 7 March 1945.

36 Letter of 4 October 1976.

37 Interview with Pownall *c.* 1958.

38 Diary for 8 March 1945.

39 Same for 3 April 1945.

40 Same for 23 April 1945.

41 Churchill to Alexander and Cunningham 10 January and reply by former of 21 January 1944. Adm. 205/35.

42 Macintyre, *Fighting Admiral*, p. 257.

43 See S. W. Kirby and others, *The War Against Japan*, V (HMSO, 1969) pp. 4–9 regarding the Phuket Island and 'Zipper' plans, and the transfer of the 11th Aircraft Carrier Squadron to the BPF.

44 Mountbatten to COSs signal timed 1529Z of 4 May 1945. Prem. 3–149/10.

45 Same to same 1145Z of 18 May 1945. ibid.

46 Discussions with Lord Mountbatten, January 1977.

47 Kirby, op. cit., V, chs. VII, VIII and XV; also Lewin, op. cit., p. 252.

Conclusion   pages 274 to 282

1 Gilbert Murray to George Bernard Shaw, quoted *British Museum Quarterly*, vol. XXIV, nos. 1–2, p. 17 (1961).

2 R. W. Thompson, *The Yankee Marlborough*, p. 296.

3 Churchill to First Sea Lord and Controller, minute M. 112 of 21 September 1940; also minute M. 593/2 to First Lord of 7 December 1942. Prem. 3–46/2.

4 John Colville, *Footprints in Time*, p. 188.

5 *Loewenheim*, p. 30.

6 J. McGregor Burns, *Roosevelt: Soldier of Freedom* (New York, 1970) p. 552.

7 Hankey diary for 31st August 1942. See Roskill, *Hankey*, III, p. 563.

7A Marder, *Dardanelles to Oran*, pp. 107–8.

8 Churchill, *Second World War*, VI, pp. 13 and 360–5.

9 See Lionel Dawson, *Sound of the Guns* (Pen-in-Hand, Oxford, 1949).

10 Churchill to Sinclair 2 June 1941. Prem. 3–9. The dispute was over who should be given the secondary appointment of command of the Atlantic Ferry Service.

11 See Lord Fraser's contribution to *Winston Spencer Churchill. A Tribute* (Cassell, 1954) p. 88.

12 Prem. 3–322/1 and 322/5.

13 Admiral of the Fleet Lord Fraser to the author 15 July 1961.

14 James, *Four Faces*, p. 112.

15 ibid.

16 Dewar to Roskill, 1957 (undated).

17 Mountbatten to the author 4 October 1976.

18 Review of Gilbert, *Churchill*, V in RUSI Journal, vol. 120, no. 4 (December 1975).

19 Churchill, *Second World War*, II, p. 24. Speech in House of Commons, 13 May 1940.

Appendix   pages 283 to 299

1 Letter Lang to Roskill 27 August 1975.

2 *Dardanelles to Oran*, pp. 109 and 137. No indication is given in this book of the corrections and insertions made after the article in the EHR was published.

3 ibid., p. 105, *note* (1).

4 Taylor, *Four Faces*, p. 35.

5 Churchill, *World Crisis*, I, p. 240.

6 Marder, *Fear God*, II, p. 39.

7 Churchill, *Second World War*, I, p. 343.

8 Taylor, *Four Faces*, p. 35.

9 Michael Howard, *Grand Strategy*, IV (HMSO, 1972), p. XIV.

10 See Marder, *Fear God*, II and III, *passim* but esp. II, ch. XII.

11 Hansard, series 5, vol. 126, cols. 105–6.

12 See Iain Hamilton, *Sir James Graham; The Baltic Campaign and War-Planning at the Admiralty in 1854. The Historical Journal*, vol. 19, no. 1 (March 1976).

13 E. W. R. Lumby (ed.), *Policy and Operations in the Mediterranean 1912–1914* (Navy Records Society, 1970), pp. 135–6 and 146.

14 Pound to Forbes 20 January 1940. Forbes papers. BM. Add. Ms. 52565.

15 Marder, *Dardanelles to Oran*, p. 137.

16 Churchill's minute M. 265–53 of 11 August and Captain Allen's reply of 24 August 1953.

17 Marder, *Dardanelles to Oran*, p. 171.

18 Article in RUSI Journal, vol. 117, no. 4 (December 1972).

19 Pitcairn-Jones to Roskill, 4 April 1950.

20 Marder, op. cit., p. 164 and *note* 120. The PRO file in question is Adm. 199/1929. All signals here quoted are, except where otherwise stated, to be found in that file.

21 First Lord to FO Narvik timed 2332 of 17 April 1940.

22 FO Narvik to Admy. for First Lord timed 1317 of 18 April 1940.

23 Personal and Private First Lord to Lord Cork timed 1926 of 19 April 1940.

24 Admy. to FO Narvik timed 0055 of 21 April 1940. Sent from First Lord's Private Office, presumably by Seal.

25 Personal First Lord to FOIC Narvik for Lord Cork timed 1429 of 22 April 1940.

26 First Lord to Lord Cork timed 0148 of 28 April 1940. The approving officer on this signal is shown as 'First Lord'.

27 Personal First Lord to Lord Cork timed 0013 of 3rd May 1940. The approving officer is shown as 'for First Lord'.

28 Same to same with identical prefix timed 0038 of 4 May 1940.

29 Signal timed 1406 of 7 May 1940.

30 Personal and Private First Lord to Lord Cork timed 1926 of 19 April 1940.

30A The message in question was drafted by Churchill and approved by Admirals Fisher and Oliver. It was sent to Admiral Carden, then in command at the Dardanelles, on 11 March 1915. The critic quoted by Professor Marder was Captain A. C. Dewar, brother of Admiral K. G. B. Dewar, mentioned above. See *Marder*, II, p. 243.

31 Roskill, *War at Sea*, I, p. 197.

32 Forbes to Roskill 30 March 1949.

33 FO Narvik to Admiralty timed 1415 of 9 May 1940.

34 Private from Prime Minister to Lord Cork timed 1729 of 14 May 1940.

35 Admy. to FO Narvik. Personal from First Lord timed 1730 of 14 May 1940. Prem. 3–328/4.

36 Lord Cork to Prime Minister. Personal timed 0815 of 18 May 1940. ibid.

37 Same to same timed 1506 of 21 May 1940. ibid.

38 Same to same timed 2204 of 4 June 1940. ibid. Also in Adm. 199/1929.

39 Roskill, *War at Sea*, II, pp. 145–6 and III, part II, pp. 405–6.

40 Marder, *Dardanelles to Oran*, pp. 173–4.

41 ibid., p. 105. Of 21 senior officers cited by Marder 9 were Commanders and 8 Captains in 1939.

42 Forbes to Roskill 1 December 1949.

43 *Sunday Telegraph* 18 February 1962 and Roskill, *Naval Policy*, II, p. 463.

44 Roberts to the author 7 March 1970.

45 Bower to the author 8 March 1970.

46 Willis to the author 7 March 1970.

47 Storr, *Four Faces*, p. 242.

48 Marder, *Dardanelles to Oran*, p. 109.

49 ibid., p. 137.

50 ibid., p. 121.

51 Lord Mountbatten expressed agreement with this view. Interview January 1977.

52 *Sunday Telegraph*, 18 February 1962.

53 See Arthur Bryant, *The Turn of the Tide* (Collins, 1957), p. 318.

Index

Ranks and titles are as they most commonly occur in the text